Retooling Social Security for the 21st Century

C. EUGENE STEUERLE
AND JON M. BAKIJA

Retooling Social Security for the 21st Century

Right and Wrong Approaches to Reform

WITHDRAWN

THE URBAN INSTITUTE PRESS
Washington, D.C.

THE URBAN INSTITUTE PRESS
2100 M Street, N.W.
Washington, D.C. 20037

Library of Congress Cataloging in Publication Data

Steuerle, C. Eugene, 1946–
   Retooling Social Security for the 21st century : right and wrong approaches to reform / C. Eugene Steuerle and Jon M. Bakija.

ISBN 0-87766-601-6 (casebound : acid-free paper)
ISBN 0-87766-602-4 (paperback : acid-free paper)

   1. Social security—Government policy—United States. I. Bakija, Jon M. II. Title.

HD7125.S747   1994   93-41038
368.4'3'00973—dc20   CIP

Urban Institute books are printed on acid-free paper whenever possible.

Printed in the United States of America.

Distributed by National Book Network
4720 Boston Way   3 Henrietta Street
Lanham, MD 20706   London WC2E 8LU ENGLAND

THE URBAN INSTITUTE is a nonprofit policy research and educational organization established in Washington, D.C., in 1968. Its staff investigates the social and economic problems confronting the nation and public and private means to alleviate them. The Institute disseminates significant findings of its research through the publications program of its Press. The goals of the Institute are to sharpen thinking about societal problems and efforts to solve them, improve government decisions and performance, and increase citizen awareness of important policy choices.

Through work that ranges from broad conceptual studies to administrative and technical assistance, Institute researchers contribute to the stock of knowledge available to guide decision making in the public interest.

Conclusions or opinions expressed in Institute publications are those of the authors and do not necessarily reflect the views of staff members, officers or trustees of the Institute, advisory groups, or any organizations that provide financial support to the Institute.

To Norman and Helen Lang, Domagoj and Anita Bakija, and to the dedicated officials, past and present, within the Social Security Administration's Office of the Actuary and Office of Research and Statistics.

ACKNOWLEDGMENTS

A large number of individuals, many of whom are among the nation's leading experts on Social Security, devoted countless hours to help improve our manuscripts. Robert Ball (former Commissioner of Social Security), Stephen Goss (SSA Office of the Actuary), Robert Myers (former Chief Actuary of SSA), Stanford Ross (former Commissioner of Social Security), Stephen Sandell (Health and Human Services, then at the Urban Institute), Lawrence Thompson (now Deputy Commissioner of Social Security), and Carolyn Weaver (Director of the American Enterprise Institute's Social Security and Pension Project) read much or all of the manuscript, offered numerous pages of comments each, and corrected many errors and omissions.

Many valuable suggestions and insights were offered as well by Joseph Applebaum (Chief Actuary, Pensions, Welfare Benefits Administration, Department of Labor), Neil Howe (author of *Generations* and a forthcoming book on entitlements), George Kopits (International Monetary Fund), Virginia Reno (Social Security Administration and National Academy of Social Insurance), and Paul Van De Water (Assistant Director, Congressional Budget Office).

We received immeasurable assistance from the SSA Office of the Actuary—particularly Harry Ballantyne (Chief Actuary), Felicitie Bell, Stephen Goss, William Kelley, Steve McKay, Orlo Nichols (whose own research often led the way to our own), and Alice Wade—and from the Health Care Financing Administration Office of the Actuary— including Roland E. King (Chief Actuary) and Sol Mussey.

Invaluable discussions were held with the AARP Public Policy staff, including Laurel Beedon, Lee Cohen, and John Gist, and with current and former Urban Institute staff, including Bret Birdsong, who helped get the project and modelling started, Michael Stohl, who interned with us briefly, Rudy Penner (now National Director of Economic Studies at KPMG Peat Marwick) and Isabel V. Sawhill (now Program Associate Director for Human Resources at the Office of Management and Budget).

Molly Ruzicka performed an outstanding job in editing this complex text, while Felicity Skidmore edited two crucial chapters. Both helped clarify some rather complicated material. Ann Guillot typed and organized numerous drafts and kept several projects running smoothly at the same time, while Deborah Chien assisted in the final stages of the project. Christina Dietrich and Scott Forrey performed the herculean job of keeping the publication process orderly and timely.

The early development of our empirical models was financed by the John D. and Catherine T. MacArthur Foundation, while completion of this manuscript was made possible by The Lynde & Harry Bradley Foundation.

CONTENTS

Tables

Figures

One of the fundamental challenges of policy research, which the Urban Institute takes extremely seriously, is to anticipate important problems before they become crises. *Retooling Social Security for the 21st Century* follows in this tradition of thinking ahead.

This book addresses primarily the part of Social Security that sends monthly checks to elderly and disabled Americans—Old Age, Survivors, and Disability Insurance (OASDI). This is the program most people mean when they refer to Social Security. The OASDI trust fund out of which Social Security cash benefits are paid is in surplus, a surplus that will continue to increase over the next two decades. If nothing else changes, the program will then start paying out more than it takes in, running dry about four decades from now.

Since Congress is required to keep the Trust Fund solvent, change is, in fact, inevitable. So the question is not whether the program will be reformed but *how*.

The authors argue for a comprehensive strategy, starting while there is still time to make wise decisions. If we do this right, we can use the long-term fiscal problems of Social Security as an opportunity—not only to resolve the fiscal problem (which can be done in any number of ways), but *to improve the system's responsiveness to our changing economic needs at the same time, without breaking the bank.* Major demographic and societal changes since Social Security was designed and enacted—longer life expectancies, changing health needs, and more two-earner families are the most obvious— have led some groups to need more help than before and some to need less. Reform, if thought about correctly, can improve the matching of benefits to needs, without destroying the link between contributions and benefits. But how can we think about it correctly, given the high political profile of the program?

One of the contributions this book makes is to draw up a set of equity and efficiency principles to serve as a benchmark against which reform proposals should be measured. The authors derive these principles from the theory of public finance as it has developed over the past two hundred years. They illustrate how these principles guided the original formulation of the Social Security program, and how they can guide the reform process in the future. The authors also highlight reform alternatives according to how well they score, emphasizing that, although some proposals are unambiguously good or bad, many will be judged differently by different observers, depending on how heavily they weight each principle in relation to the others.

The authors do not propose these principles as a replacement for the tradeoffs and compromises that mark the political process. They simply argue that these tradeoffs and compromises can be made more effectively, for the greater good of greater numbers of people, if the process can benefit from the information provided by the benchmark exercise.

It is my hope that this book will inform the continuing debate on Social Security reform, and help shed light on the changes that should be made if Social Security is to be as responsive to today's and tomorrow's needs as it was to the needs as perceived by its founders nearly 60 years ago.

William Gorham
President

AIME   Average Indexed Monthly Earnings
COLA   Cost of Living Adjustment
DI   Disability Insurance
DRC   Delayed Retirement Credit
GDP   Gross Domestic Product
GNP   Gross National Product
HCFA   Health Care Financing Administration
HI   Hospital Insurance (Medicare Part A)
OASI   Old Age and Survivors Insurance
OASDI   Old Age, Survivors, and Disability Insurance
OASDHI   Old Age, Survivors, Disability, and Hospital Insurance
PIA   Primary Insurance Amount
SMI   Supplementary Medical Insurance (Medicare Part B)
SSA   Social Security Administration
SSI   Supplemental Security Income

Part One

GUIDING PRINCIPLES FOR SOCIAL
SECURITY AND ITS REFORM

Chapter One

A BLUEPRINT FOR REFORM

The United States Social Security system is the largest and one of the most successful federal social policies. It provides cash and health insurance to the elderly and disabled, removes millions from poverty, and gives the elderly the means to live their last years with dignity. Despite these tremendous achievements, the system is ripe for reform—so ripe that we can state unequivocally that it *will* be reformed. Indeed, the issue facing the nation is not whether, but how and when. It is to these latter questions that this book is mainly addressed.

That future reform is inevitable, and not simply a political intention, is crucial for policymakers and the American public to comprehend. If intention were the issue, most politicians would probably just as soon leave Social Security alone. There is a reluctance, after all, to "tamper" with the system and change people's expectations. But this course cannot be maintained for long.

Why is reform inevitable? One important reason is that a major long-run fiscal imbalance is projected under all but the most optimistic assumptions.[1] Promised benefits significantly exceed promised tax revenues for the future even though current Social Security taxes temporarily are sufficient to cover current benefits. For several years now, the trustees of the Social Security system, both Democratic and Republican, have warned of impending financial problems. Old-Age, Survivors, and Disability Insurance (OASDI)—the program that sends monthly Social Security checks to elderly and disabled Americans— is expected to begin paying out more in benefits than it collects in taxes in a little more than two decades. OASDI is currently accumulating a moderate amount of reserves in "trust funds" to prepare partially for the financial demands it will face during the next century. Spending down accumulated reserves or "running deficits" in these trust funds, however, is a questionable policy from the standpoint of federal budgets and deficits. Even if allowed, this spend-down would provide only a limited reprieve for about another 20 years and probably could be achieved only if taxes were raised in other parts of the budget. Medicare, the Social Security program that serves as the main source of health care benefits for the elderly and disabled, faces even more severe and immediate financial distress. In their 1993 report, the Social Security Trustees projected that the trust fund for the Hospital Insurance portion of Medicare (HI, or Part A) would go bankrupt before the turn of the century unless prompt action were taken. Actions taken in a 1993 budget agreement[2] will help forestall bankruptcy in HI only for a little while; the major long-run problems remain. Even significant cost control as a result of a broader health policy for the nation would not eliminate the large increase in medical costs that will derive from an aging population. Finally, Supplementary Medical Insurance (SMI, or Part B), the portion of Medicare that pays doctors' bills, remains solvent only because it is heavily subsidized by general funds of the federal government.

Because of the likely inadequacy of the Social Security trust funds, legislators will be required by law to make changes within these programs. Every year of delay in resolving these issues will make the required changes harder and harder to bear. Expected liabilities are accumulating quickly relative to assets and anticipated revenues. The longer that reform is delayed, the greater the adjustment required of beneficiaries and taxpayers.

Even if the trust funds were adequate, fundamental economic and demographic changes require the Social Security system to adapt to current conditions. Married couples have become more likely to put two earners, instead of one, in the labor force. People live longer. Health needs are different today than they were 50 years ago, and they will be very different again 50 years from now. Interstate migration and the decline in the extended family have helped to place more elderly in nursing homes and have increased the financial strain on both individuals and Medicaid programs. Evolving societal patterns, in turn, are accompanied by changing perceptions of how any governmental system might be designed most fairly and efficiently to meet today's and tomorrow's most pressing needs. Inertia, of course, may continue for awhile, protecting those who favor the current tax and benefits structure and allowing politicians to avoid creating "losers" in the process of paying for a new policy. The cost of inertia, however, is greater inequity and inefficiency, as well as a program that becomes more out of tune with the society it is meant to serve.

Finally, the nation's large fiscal deficit puts constant pressure on all governmental programs. According to a recent General Accounting Office (GAO) study, if current policies continue unchanged, expenditure programs already in place will force federal government outlays to rise from about 23 percent of gross national product (GNP) today to more than 42 percent of GNP by the year 2020, while taxes would increase only slightly—leading to impossible deficits on the order of 20 percent of GNP.[3] Social Security taxes have now become the second largest source of federal revenues, whereas spending on the elderly currently comprises about one-half of all federal domestic spending other than interest on the debt (U.S. Congress, House Committee on Ways and Means 1992: 1579). This spending is expected to continue growing steadily as a share of the budget into the indefinite future. It should not be surprising, therefore, that these taxes and benefits are likely to be affected by inevitable future deficit reduction efforts. In a modest budget agreement reached in 1990, for instance, attempts were made to further limit Medicare expenditures, while also enacting a small increase in the HI portion of Social Security taxes. Similarly, deficit-reduction efforts in 1993 involve further spending cuts and revenue increases for Medicare, as well as increased income taxation of Social Security benefits.

This study provides some detail on the financial status of Social Security, while examining how different demographic and economic patterns affect the demands placed upon the system and determine who pays to meet those demands. In some cases, the demands on Social Security will require an increase in taxes or a reduction in benefits to bring the system back into balance. In other cases the pressure derives less from a concern with financial balances than with reorienting existing resources to deal with evolving societal patterns—for instance, the increase in the number of elderly making use of long-term care, the expansion of the number of two-earner couples in the labor market, and the improving well-being of the near-elderly and the younger-elderly.

Both the calculations of financial imbalance and the economic and demographic facts presented in this volume speak for themselves. They are neither Republican nor Democratic, liberal nor conservative, right nor left. They are offered neither as a defense of, nor an attack on, the idea of Social Security. They are simply the circumstances under which the system must operate and with which citizens and policymakers must deal.

The requirement to restore balance is neither partisan nor new. In 1983 a Democratic Congress and a Republican president agreed to a bipartisan set of amendments that included both tax increases and benefit reductions. The goal then, as now, was to move the system closer to ensuring adequate future revenues to pay for promised benefits.

Facts by themselves are not enough to guide action. They do not make obvious the paths toward achieving reform or bringing the system back into a balance so that future taxes match future expenditures. A wide variety of changes can achieve the narrow goal of reducing the long-term imbalance in the system. Yet not all changes are equal: they vary widely in both quality and form.

We are concerned especially with policymakers' tendency to ignore problems for a long time and let them fester, and then act suddenly to try to amputate them. This bold and rash approach to policymaking often serves the public poorly by precluding careful consideration of alternatives. The opportunity for gradual implementation of solutions is foregone when problems are allowed to grow until they become crises that require immediate action.

Take two Social Security proposals that recently came close to enactment: one involving benefit reductions and the other tax increases. First, in several recent deficit-reducing efforts, it has become commonplace for some policymakers to suggest that a cutback in the cost-of-living adjustments be applied to the benefits of Social Security retirees.[4] In the second case, Senator Daniel Patrick Moynihan (D.-N.Y.) proposed that OASDI be put on a pay-as-you-go basis[5] that would impose substantial tax increases in the future to cover expected benefit payments for the retiring baby boom— although tax reductions would be provided during the next couple of decades while the elderly population remained stable.

Neither proposal was badly intentioned. Both, after all, were aimed at dealing with legitimate problems: huge fiscal deficits and an increasingly regressive tax burden on low- and moderate-income workers. One of us has testified before Congress on both these concerns. But neither proposal came up in the context of a fuller examination of alternatives to deal with these same issues. Had the problems been viewed from a more comprehensive perspective, we believe that a consistent and logical adherence to the principles underlying Social Security would have shown that a cutback in cost-of-living adjustments to beneficiaries is an inferior means of reducing benefits, and that allowing future tax rates to increase significantly is an inferior method of financing the system. We attempt to establish both cases in the course of this study.

After watching debates on such proposals unfold, we became convinced more than ever that future consideration of reform of Social

Security should start not with proposals but with principles against which different proposals and approaches can be judged. This study, therefore, first puts forward a set of principles that we believe are consistent with the broader theory of public finance as well as with the core or fundamental rationales that underlay the creation and need for a Social Security system. Only after these principles are established and the economic and demographic facts surrounding Social Security are delineated in greater detail will it be possible to make distinctions among a variety of proposed reforms to the system.

This study could have taken a very different, but common, tack. With respect to the issue of an imbalanced system, dividing lines are often drawn between those who favor benefit cuts and those who favor tax increases. This hasty taking of sides often precludes a more thorough examination of issues, especially when one side tends to favor any tax increase over any benefit reduction, and the other side lobbies for the opposite result. Even when the two compromise, as often they must, different tax options tend to become treated either as equally meritorious or as equally unworthy. The same holds true for the benefit options. A goal of this volume is to convince policy-makers, when they finally decide to tackle the overcommitted or underfinanced Social Security system, to avoid simply jumping immediately into one of the two camps, but, instead, to give attention to the importance of choosing among and ranking independently both tax alternatives and benefit alternatives. Another goal is to encourage policymakers to look mainly at the long term, rather than focusing on the next year or even the next few years.

In sum, this study aims to provide a blueprint for future reform. We focus primarily on the largest of the programs serving the elderly—the system of Old-Age and Survivors Insurance—although we deal to a lesser extent with Medicare and point to a few important relationships with other programs such as Medicaid, Social Security Disability Insurance, and the private pension system.[6] Like many architectural blueprints, it is relatively easy to make modest adjustments in scale or size so long as basic design principles are followed. Both the value and cost of any structure are related not simply to size but to the way that structure, in all its components, helps to meet the purposes for which it was intended.

Having conducted an extensive review of the literature on Social Security, it is clear to us that no one will agree to all of our conclusions—or anyone else's, for that matter. Perhaps this is to be expected: no two persons are likely to agree on every detail of how a welfare system, a tax system, a health system for the nonelderly, or any other large social system ought to be designed. We will consider this effort successful if we can establish the case that Social Security reform must be based upon principles and that both tax and benefit options should be considered, and sometimes ranked, on the basis of such principles.

Notes

1. These estimates are derived from intermediate projections in the 1993 Social Security Trustees reports (U.S. Board of Trustees of the Federal Old-Age, and Survivors Insurance, and Disability Insurance (OASDI) Trust Funds [henceforth, Board of Trustees, OASDI]. Annual Report, 1993. U.S. Board of Trustees of the Federal Hospital Insurance (HI) Trust Fund. Annual Report, 1993. Washington, D.C.: Superintendent of Documents). Long-run fiscal imbalance in OASDI is avoided only under the Trustees' optimistic projections, which assume that *all* economic and demographic variables turn out considerably better than the best-estimate projections. Medicare faces a significant imbalance even under the optimistic assumptions. Although it is certainly probable that some variables will perform better and some worse than expected, the assumption that everything turns out much better than the intermediate assumptions is, in our judgment, highly unlikely, and would be a poor basis for making policy. These issues are discussed more thoroughly in chapter 3.

2. Omnibus Budget Reconciliation Act of 1993.

3. Gross national product (GNP) and gross domestic product (GDP) are two alternative measures of the total value of goods and services produced by a nation in a given year. The two measures are virtually identical: in 1990, GDP was $5,513 billion, whereas GNP was $5,524 billion (*Economic Report of the President* 1993: 320). The only difference is that GDP includes interest, dividends, and profits earned in the United States by foreign residents and corporations, while excluding the same kinds of income earned in other countries by American residents and corporations. GNP excludes the former and includes the latter.

In 1992, the U.S. federal government switched from GNP to GDP as its main measure of the size of the national economy. GDP is regarded as the superior statistic for most purposes, and was already the primary measure used in most other industrialized nations. As a result, we use GDP, rather than GNP, wherever possible in our analysis. GNP, however, will still be used occasionally when referring to other studies that based their analysis on this measure.

4. For instance, in May 1993 Senators Boren and Danforth recommended COLA reductions in their Bipartisan Alternative Budget Proposal. See Wessel, David. 1993. "Politics and Policy: Entitlements-Cap Proposals Resurface Ahead of Vote on Deficit Reduction." *The Wall Street Journal*, May 24, A12.

5. Moynihan first presented this proposal in January 1990. See Elving, Ronald D. 1990. "Lawmaker's Agenda for Year Begins and Ends with Cuts." *Congressional Quarterly*, 48, 4 (January 27): 221–225.

6. See Bakija and Steuerle (1993) for a closely related study of Disability Insurance (DI). In every study of Social Security we have examined, the issue of how far to extend the coverage has been a difficult one. To ignore programs that are intended to affect the well-being of the elderly and disabled is to be incomplete and often

misleading—among other reasons because all programs compete for scarce budgetary resources. On the other hand, DI requires an understanding of disability determination rules, health insurance requires a grasp of the nation's broader health policies, and so forth—issues that go beyond the scope of this book. A middle ground was chosen here.

Chapter Two

SOCIAL SECURITY PRINCIPLES AND RATIONALES

The structure of the Social Security program is based on principles (equity, efficiency, etc.) as mediated by politics.[1] This mixture of principle and politics characterizes the design and evolution of most public programs and, indeed, is fundamental to policymaking in a democratic society. A crucial issue is how and when those principles are allowed to influence the political process. In our judgment, developing a set of principles, though not a sufficient requirement, is the *first* requirement for the future reform of Social Security to be effective. The political process can only judge proposals as "better" or "worse" when it has a common benchmark against which to compare them. It is our purpose in this chapter to lay out a set of principles to serve as that benchmark.

The set of principles we present is derived from the theory of public finance as it has developed over the past two hundred years.[2] The original designers of Social Security appealed to these principles in crafting the system and in selling it to the public. They also made compromises, often tried to blur distinctions among different principles, and on occasion—for political and other reasons—made decisions that were inconsistent with all the principles. Even so, we believe it valuable to determine the extent to which principles did guide the original program design.

Some of the architects of the system, as well as some of its most intelligent critics, have reviewed our manuscript. The architects seem more comfortable tracing through the original rationales of the system, the critics with noting the inconsistencies. Our intent, of course, is to do both.

In theory, it probably does not matter for the reform debate what was intended in the 1930s, as long as there is agreement on the principles to be applied in the future. But in practice the question of how and why the system evolved does matter, in part because agreement about future reform is facilitated by recognizing the basic objectives of the past. A brief review of the history of social security, indeed, shows that some reform options currently on the table can be regarded as a return to the basic principles that guided the original program design. We are not rigid "back to basics" people. But we believe that it can be helpful to look for the fundamental goals of the initial program and ask how and whether they can be related to modern circumstances.

In addition to presenting the principles themselves, therefore, we use this chapter to examine the role these principles played in the original design, justification, and promotion of Social Security. We look, in particular, at the extent to which Social Security's founders and most ardent defenders publicly recognized these principles as both goals and justifications for the program, even when they did not use the same terms as we do to refer to those principles.

We draw especially on the reports of the two committees that drew up its initial blueprints: the Committee on Economic Security of 1935, and the Advisory Council on Social Security of 1937–38.[3] The former produced the detailed social insurance plan that led to the original 1935 Social Security Act. It set up a contributory retirement system that began collecting taxes in 1937 and was scheduled to start paying out monthly benefits in 1942.[4] The latter commission made recommendations that resulted in extensive amendments to the program, among which were bringing the starting date for monthly benefit payments forward to 1940. These 1939 amendments form the basis for the Social Security Old-Age and Survivors Insurance system as we know it today.[5] Discussion of Social Security's goals and principles can also be found in a variety of other sources, such as speeches by President Franklin Roosevelt, debates in Congress, and the reports of the various Advisory Councils on Social Security.[6]

PRINCIPLES FOR JUDGING REFORM

The principles underlying the theory of public finance can be captured in four categories that, together, provide a useful framework for thinking about, and evaluating, Social Security and other public programs:

□ Progressivity (sometimes referred to as "vertical equity") holds that government ought to undertake at least some redistribution from the better-off to the worse-off—to those with lower incomes, greater health problems, and so forth. The goal of this type of redistribution is to reduce inequality in the society or to assure that people are able to meet certain basic needs. Progressive goals can be met through patterns of public expenditures as well as through adjusting tax burdens according to ability to pay.

☐ *Individual equity* holds that the taxes an individual pays to the government ought to be related to the benefits that individual receives, and vice versa. In the context of social insurance, it means that insurance protection should be related to premiums paid.

☐ *Horizontal equity* holds that people in equal circumstances ought to be treated equally. People with equal levels of economic well-being, according to this principle, should pay equal amounts of taxes.

☐ *Economic efficiency* holds that an economy ought to operate so that individuals can achieve the maximum well-being possible with their limited resources. Market signals and freedom of choice are often important in attaining this goal.[7]

These four principles sometimes overlap and sometimes conflict. When we get to the point of discussing these conflicts in more depth, the economic concept of "opportunity cost" also becomes useful. This analytic tool simply recognizes that efforts to achieve one goal inevitably reduce opportunities to do other things, and that the alternatives have to be measured in the same coinage if informed choices—political or otherwise—are to be made. We also discuss how the founders used the concept of "social insurance" to try to resolve the conflict, in particular, between individual equity and progressivity.

Redistribution from the Better-Off to the Less Well-Off (Progressivity)

We do not have to examine the statements of the founders of the system to know that one motivation dominated all others: the needs of the elderly. If in the 1930s the elderly had no needs that were not shared by the rest of the population, there would have been no Social Security program—at least none that bore any resemblance to the program we know. Social Security was meant to redistribute resources to the elderly from the rest of the population because the elderly as a group were considered less well-off. In other words, it was meant to be progressive. Two main features were adopted to achieve this goal.

First, a new tax system collected from the better-off (workers) to finance benefits for the less well-off (retirees). Benefits were to be paid only to those who had contributed at least some amount to the system during their working years. But most participants who retired during the first several decades of the program, even up to today, received benefits which greatly exceeded their lifetime tax contributions. The immediate effect of this process was to redistribute income from later generations that, on average, were better-off to earlier generations that, on average, were worse-off. Because "retirement" was a rather rough measure of "need," of course, some of this redistribution ended up benefiting individuals who were not particularly needy. This is a crucial issue that we will examine in later chapters. The important points here are that a large amount of intergenerational redistribution occurred, and that a primary justification for this policy was the belief that the older generations were, generally speaking, needier than those that would follow them.

The second progressive feature of the original program was a rate structure in the benefit formula that provided a higher rate of return on the contributions of workers with low wages than for those with high wages. The formula in effect during the 1940s, for example, paid a basic monthly benefit equal to 40 percent of the first $50 of a worker's average monthly wages covered by Social Security taxation, plus 10 percent of the next $200.[8] Under this formula, someone who had paid Social Security taxes on wages averaging $50 per month would receive a basic monthly benefit of $20. Someone who had contributed twice as much would receive only $5 more in monthly benefits. Only when the system had matured and people had contributed over their entire careers would the system in fact redistribute from richer to poorer *within* generations. But the system was designed from the beginning with this redistributional aim in mind.

The Committee on Economic Security of 1935 made clear these needs-based progressivity goals by stressing that poverty among the elderly was the primary problem to be addressed.

> [I]t should not be overlooked that old-age annuities are designed to *prevent destitution and dependency.* (Report of the Committee on Economic Security: 33) [Italics here and in subsequent quotations are added.]

The Committee noted that a large portion of the elderly were forced to depend on the uncertain goodwill of relatives, charitable and community organizations, and state and local governments—and that this often degrading dependency led to intergenerational conflict and tension.[9] As a growing portion of the population survived to old age, moreover, these traditional means of support would be increasingly strained. In the context of the Great Depression—which robbed people of not only their jobs but their life savings—these problems were particularly immediate.

> At least one-third of all our people, upon reaching old age, are
> *dependent* upon others for support . . . For those now old, insecurity is
> doubly tragic, because they are *beyond the productive period*. Old age
> . . . is a misfortune only if there is insufficient income to provide for the
> remaining years of life. With a rapidly increasing number and
> percentage of the aged, and the impairment and loss of savings, this
> country faces, in the next decades, an even greater old-age security
> problem than that with which it is already confronted. (Report of the
> Committee on Economic Security: 2)

Social Security's founders also argued that America's evolution from an agrarian society of small, close-knit communities to a modern, industrialized, and highly mobile society had made it more likely that elderly persons would become destitute. Workers in increasingly strenuous industrial jobs would have great physical difficulty working past a certain age, while at the same time traditional means of support were becoming less reliable. President Franklin Roosevelt expressed these sentiments on numerous occasions. We quote two:

> Security was attained in the earlier days through the interdependence
> of members of families upon each other and of the families within a
> small community upon each other. The complexities of great
> communities and of organized industry make less real these simple
> means of security. Therefore, we are compelled to employ the active
> interest of the Nation as a whole through government in order to
> encourage a greater security for each individual who composes it.
> (Franklin D. Roosevelt, Message to Congress, June 8, 1934)

> The civilization of the past hundred years, *with its startling industrial
> changes, has tended more and more to make life insecure.* Young
> people have come to wonder what would be their lot when they came
> to old age. (Franklin D. Roosevelt, Presidential Statement Signing the
> Social Security Act, August 14, 1935)

In response to these perceived needs, the architects of the Social Security system sought to provide participants with retirement benefits adequate to secure a basic subsistence standard of living. "Social adequacy" (in other words, a minimum standard of living), however, could not be financed entirely by the contributions of low-income individuals. Nor would anyone retiring during the first few decades of the program have contributed for enough years to the system to finance even a modest pension. Therefore, the system was crafted not only to give a higher return on the contributions of low-income workers, but also to transfer large amounts to the first generations of retirees who had, by definition, contributed little.

In a radio address to the nation discussing the purposes of the Social Security Act, President Roosevelt made the goal of a guaranteed minimum living standard clear:

> This act does not offer anyone, either individually or collectively, an easy life—nor was it ever intended so to do. None of the sums of money paid out to individuals in assistance or insurance will spell anything approaching abundance. But they will furnish that *minimum* necessary to keep a foothold; and that is the kind of protection Americans want. (Franklin D. Roosevelt, Radio Address on the Third Anniversary of the Social Security Act, August 15, 1938)

The recommendations of the 1937–38 Advisory Council—responsible for many program features that remain today—are typical of the many statements emphasizing need as a reason for program benefits:

> [T]he council has become increasingly impressed by the need to revise the existing old-age insurance program in the direction of fitting the structure of benefits more closely to the *basic needs* of our people, now and in the future. . . . Since it is the purpose of old-age insurance to prevent dependency in old age, the benefits payable under the program should, as soon as possible, be sufficient in amount to afford the aged recipient at least *a minimum subsistence income*. (Final Report of the 1937–38 Advisory Council on Social Security: 12–13)

Ensuring a Fair Return on Contributions (Individual Equity)

If the architects of Social Security had only a single goal—to alleviate poverty and dependency among the elderly—they could have stopped with the creation of a welfare program of Old Age Assistance and targeted benefits only at the poor elderly. Instead, the United States followed the lead of several European nations and created a mandatory public annuity program designed eventually to cover the vast majority of workers. All participants who contributed to the system for a modest number of years and reached retirement would receive benefits.

The original architects likened the system to private pensions and annuities, under which benefits bear a clear relationship to contributions.[10] This analogy implies adherence to the principle of individual equity, which is related closely to the philosophical concept of "commutative justice." Individual equity means that parties to any exchange should each receive a fair return from the transaction, in other words "get their money's worth." The private market achieves this goal through voluntary transactions. Individuals engage in private transactions when they believe it is worth their while to do so. An exchange is deemed "unfair" or "unjust" when one party ends up losing because the other does not honor the terms of a contract, presents misleading information, or uses coercion.

In an annuity or pension system—which is basically a system that insures against the economic risks of old age—individual equity is measured by whether individuals receive an "actuarially fair" return on their contributions. Actuarial fairness requires roughly that, when each year of contributions and benefits is weighted by the probability that someone will be alive during that year and adjusted for accumulated interest, total expected lifetime benefits will equal total expected contributions.[11] Individuals should be paid retirement benefits that, on average, equal their contributions plus a fair interest rate. Because an insurance system pools the risks of large numbers of people into an average risk, those who die young will receive less than an equal share of benefits, and those who live longer than average will receive more.

Applying the individual equity principle to government tax and expenditure policy is somewhat more controversial and complicated than its application to private programs, but is has a long tradition, dating back at least to Adam Smith.[12] In public finance theory, this concept is related closely to the "benefit principle." Taxes and fees may be regarded as the price society pays for publicly provided goods and services. The benefit principle holds that the price government charges each individual for public goods should correspond to the amount of these goods he or she consumes; in other words, people should be taxed according to the benefits they receive from the government.

This formulation involves some obvious complications. First, how can one determine how much of a government-provided good or service each individual consumes, or how to value it in the absence of a price system? Fees for parkland use present an easy case. National defense, the criminal justice system, and environmental protection, in contrast, are all examples of public programs or goods that benefit the public at large for which exact values cannot be allocated easily to individuals. The problem is somewhat reduced in the case of Social Security, since one can at least measure the cash benefits going to each participant.

A second problem, which is extremely relevant to Social Security, is that a strict application of the benefit principle precludes any redistribution by government to reduce inequality or ameliorate need. Some public finance theorists have dealt with this issue by dividing government functions into separate "distributive" and "allocative" branches. The distributive branch takes care of redistributing income and wealth in order to achieve whatever degree of "distributive justice" (i.e., fairness) is desired by a given society. Once this function is performed, the satisfaction of public desires not met by the private market acting alone is left to the allocative branch. To the extent possible the allocative branch should be guided by the benefit principle and allow private choices to help determine which goods and services should be consumed and produced (Musgrave 1959).

The architects of Social Security combined the allocative and distributive functions of government into a single program. To satisfy a perceived public demand for a safe, secure, and universally available retirement savings vehicle, the government established a mandatory annuity program that would pay benefits related to contributions (more precisely, to earnings on which taxes have been paid). This annuity was woven together with the redistributive element already mentioned into a single benefit formula designed specifically as a compromise between progressivity and individual equity.

Another obvious difference between Social Security and the private insurance and pension model is that the program was designed to pay out benefits before adequate "contributions" had been built up. Essentially, benefits of current retirees were to be paid for partially, and sometimes wholly, out of the contributions of current workers ("pay-as-you-go"). Although a partial reserve was set up by investing surplus Social Security taxes into government bonds, these reserves were far from sufficient to cover accrued liabilities. Since the reserves were in government bonds, moreover, they often amounted to little more than IOUs that would have to be redeemed by future taxpayers. When these workers eventually retired, their benefits, in turn, would depend on the ability and willingness of the next generations of workers to pay Social Security and other taxes.[13]

This was a clear divergence from the private annuity model, but it did not by itself preclude the system from meeting individual equity standards. In theory, so long as each successive generation of workers paid enough taxes, participants could receive fair returns on their contributions. One must also remember that in the 1930s many private pensions were not backed up by funds or savings either.[14]

The founders of the Social Security system repeatedly emphasized the contributory and annuity aspects of the program, at least for the employee's share of the taxes. For example:

> Contributions by the employees represent a self-respecting method through which workers *make their own provision* for old age. (Report of the Committee on Economic Security 1935: 33)

Social Security's founders also envisioned a strong individual equity component to the program, which, under certain calculations, would ensure that people would "get their money's worth" out of the program:

> [M]embers shall not receive less than the actuarial equivalent of their own contribution. (Report of the Committee on Economic Security of 1935: 31)

> [W]orkers who enter the system after the maximum contribution rate has become effective will receive annuities which have been paid for entirely by their own contributions and the matching contributions of their employers. (Report of the Committee on Economic Security of 1935: 31)

Given the redistributive elements of the plan, of course, this was a promise that could not be kept for everyone. The conflict between the two principles was sidestepped during Social Security's first few decades through intergenerational redistribution and through further legislated increases in benefits that were not tied to past contributions. As it turned out, the system went well beyond providing a fair return on the contributions of the first few generations of participants. No participants—not even the highest earners—were required during Social Security's youth and adolescence to make contributions that came close to covering the value of benefits received.

But this situation could not persist forever. As we discuss in more detail later, the proportion of the population receiving benefits would grow dramatically, and those who had contributed to the system throughout their careers would finally begin to retire. As a result, the system would have to impose ever-increasing taxes (a) to provide everyone with an actuarially fair return on individual contributions, and (b) to supplement the benefits of low-income persons. Eventually these tax rates would reach a political limit and some tradeoff between progressivity and individual equity would have to occur within each generation. This, indeed, is exactly what is starting to happen now.

The conflict between progressivity and individual equity was recognized to a degree by the 1935 and 1937–38 Councils. At times they argued in individual equity terms only with respect to the employee contribution, leaving the employer contribution available for redistributive purposes (an argument not satisfactory to economists, since the employer contribution is widely recognized as being paid by employees through lower cash wages).

At other times they recognized the conflict by proposing to support the system in the future with contributions or interest payments from general government revenues. This idea would have preserved the letter but not the spirit of an actuarially fair return on contributions. It would have allowed later working populations to pay lower Social Security payroll tax rates, which in turn would provide them an actuarially fair return on their Social Security payroll taxes—but *not on all the taxes they would have to pay to support the system.* In the end, the President and Congress decided to forgo general government financing and rely exclusively on payroll taxes.

Equal Treatment of Equals (Horizontal Equity)

The principle of equal treatment of equals is pervasive throughout government policy, though it is so intuitively obvious that is often left implicit. If you and I commit equal crimes and are equal in all other circumstances, then we should face the same penalty. If you and I have equal income and are equal in all other respects, then we should pay the same income tax. If our homes in the same community are of the same value, and if there are no other economic differences between us, we should pay the same amount of property tax. To the extent that there is redistribution toward the needy, those with equal needs and in equal circumstances ought to be provided with equal assistance. And so forth.

Anyone who would deny the importance of this principle should be reminded that the stimulus for many reforms in tax and expenditure policy, civil rights, and other areas has been the outcry when horizontal equity is violated—the sense that equals were not being treated equally under the law.

One beauty of the horizontal equity principle is its lack of conflict with other principles. It is the only one, for example, that never conflicts with progressivity. You and I may disagree on how progressive we would like government to be, but we can still agree that, whatever the level of progressivity, two persons in equal circumstances should be treated equally under the law.

Another beauty is that horizontal equity has the side benefit of promoting economic efficiency (the next principle discussed immediately below). A tax policy that tends to favor one type of income or expenditure over another, for example, not only causes people with equal economic resources to pay different amounts of tax. It also creates an incentive to engage more in the favored activity and less in the taxed activity than economic efficiency would dictate.

Horizontal equity is applied in the Social Security system through such features as equal assessment of payroll taxes on those with equal earnings (up to the earnings maximum), and payment of equal benefits to those born in the same year, with equal earnings histories, and of the same family type—admittedly narrow definitions of equals.

Achieving Maximum Benefit to Society from Available Resources (Economic Efficiency)

Economic efficiency in its purest version requires that society should not be left in a situation where someone could have been made "better off" without anyone else being made "worse off." More generally, it means society ought to get the most out of its limited resources. One of the most fundamental precepts of economic theory is that if consumers and firms are left to pursue their own self-interest and make exchanges as they choose, the operation of price and incentive systems in a free market will tend to lead towards an economically efficient outcome.

In some cases, however, the decisions of individuals acting separately in the private market do not achieve outcomes that are as efficient as those that could be obtained if these same individuals act together as a society. In such cases, government intervention may be appropriate. Government may also intervene in the market to achieve other socially desirable goals such as progressive redistribution to those in need. When the government undertakes such an effort, it is important to minimize any losses of efficiency that might arise unintentionally. For example, very high marginal tax rates should be avoided when possible. Moreover, programs that offer recipients choices are often more efficient than those that provide benefits in-kind. We pursue this issue with respect to Medicare health benefits in chapter 10.

"Efficiency" concerns can be found in the early Social Security literature with respect to incentives to work. The effect of both tax rates and Social Security benefits on the efficiency of labor markets was emphasized mainly through arguments that tax rates should be kept low to prevent detrimental effects on the economy. The tying of benefits to covered earnings was also regarded as a way to preserve economic incentives—by offsetting the disincentive of additional payroll taxes with the prospect of additional benefits.

> The council believes that such a method of encouragement of self-help and self-reliance in securing protection in old age is essentially in harmony with *individual incentive* within a democratic society. . . It is only through the encouragement of individual incentive, through the principle of paying benefits in relation to past wages and employment, that a sound and lasting basis for security can be afforded. (Advisory Council on Social Security of 1937–38: 11)

As the system evolved, other aspects of labor market efficiency were occasionally addressed. The financial penalties of working past normal retirement age, for instance, have been gradually reduced, partly because of their adverse effect on the labor supply of older workers.

Opportunity Cost

The concept of "opportunity cost," a favorite of economists, is a useful way of comparing alternative uses of resources. For every dollar the government spends on providing public annuities to the elderly, for example, there is one less dollar to be spent on other goals or left in the taxpayer's pocket. If government is to be progressive (in the sense of aiming help where the need is greatest), and efficient (in the sense of spending each dollar where it will produce the best result), it must be able to measure and make tradeoffs among competing programs and priorities. And these tradeoffs must be made on a continuing basis if programs are to adapt to inevitable demographic and societal changes.

Social Security's founders recognized the concept of opportunity costs when they cautioned that aid to the elderly, though important, should not use up so many resources as to lead to the neglect of other societal needs.

> The council is also aware of the great financial costs, particularly in the

future, involved in an insurance program. The pattern cannot be larger than the cloth; the degree of security afforded must be limited by the national income and the proportion of that income properly available for any specific purpose. Old-age insurance is only one element in the whole structure of governmental social services. *The protection of the aged must not be at the expense of adequate protection of dependent children, the sick, the disabled, or the unemployed; or at the cost of impairing such essential services as education and public health or of lowering of the standard of living of the working population. . . .* (Final Report of the 1937–38 Advisory Council on Social Security: 11–12)

The need to weigh aid to the elderly against other social goals, in fact, played a role in the decision to finance Social Security through a separate, earmarked payroll tax:

The council believes that the contributory insurance method safeguards not only the wage earner but the public as well. By this method benefits have a reasonable relation to wages previously earned, and *costs may be kept in control* relative to tax collections. Through careful planning, the continued payment of benefits can be assured without undue diversion of funds needed for other governmental services. (Final Report of the 1937–38 Advisory Council on Social Security: 11)

The founders also clearly intended to leave future generations with some choice over what share of national income they would devote to Social Security as opposed to other needs.

No benefits should be promised or implied which cannot be safely financed not only in the early years of the program but when workers now young will be old. (Final Report of the 1937–1938 Advisory Council on Social Security: 26)

THE OVERARCHING CONCEPT OF SOCIAL INSURANCE

As the designers and advocates of the Social Security system struggled with compromises among a number of conflicting principles—particularly between progressive redistribution on the one hand, and individual equity and economic efficiency on the other—they sometimes tried to justify the entire system through a broader conception of individual equity and efficiency known as "social insurance." This concept also enabled them to move beyond a welfare-like system and to downplay explicit discussion of redistribution.

The "social insurance" argument is at the same time ambiguous and revealing. Insurance by its very nature involves some after-the-fact redistribution among the insured from those who do not experience the insured event to those who do. Fire insurance is a straightforward example. In an analogous way, redistributive government policies could and did come to be defined as "insurance" against a wide variety of risks. If the insured event is "an impoverished old age" or "loss of earnings," society's transfers to the poor or retired elderly become forms of "insurance" payments. Since any individual's level of lifetime income is subject to some uncertainty and risk, redistribution can be regarded as insurance against doing poorly in the lifetime-income distribution sweepstakes.[15]

People who were completely ignorant of the economic circumstances they would face over a lifetime would probably view the "risk reduction" provided by social insurance as a valuable commodity indeed.[16] In a private market for insurance, however, premiums must be sufficient to cover the risks for which insurance payments are made. Often people are more informed than insurers about conditions that make their risk different from the average risk. If the insurer assesses premiums according to average risk, those knowing their risks are low may well decide not to buy insurance. If only high-risk persons are left in the insurance pool, premiums must be raised to pay for the protection. This is the problem of adverse selection, which bedevils the current health insurance market when the healthy opt out of insurance coverage or band together to buy cheaper plans.

Now let's take the case of future impoverishment. Normally, by the time people have enough money to pay for such insurance, they already have a pretty good idea what some of their social risks are. Those who consider poverty an unlikely fate will not purchase insurance against it. For society as a whole to provide all its members insurance against that risk, government must do the job.

Franklin Roosevelt, in particular, used this social insurance emphasis to sell the program, framing the problems and needs of the elderly as "hazards" against which prudent citizens should be insured. This was a particularly persuasive argument in the wake of the Great Depression.

People want . . . *some safeguard against misfortunes* which cannot be wholly eliminated in this man-made world of ours. (Franklin D. Roosevelt, Message to Congress, June 8, 1934)

We can never *insure* one hundred percent of the population against one hundred percent of the hazards and vicissitudes of life, but we have tried to frame a law which will give some measure of *protection* to the average citizen and to his family against the loss of a job and *against poverty-ridden old age*. (Franklin D. Roosevelt, Presidential Statement Signing the Social Security Act, August 14, 1935)

There is one big difficulty with the social insurance argument, as developed so far, when applied to the Social Security program. It only justifies benefits to those who have had bad luck. Why should social insurance include annuity payments to all retired participants, regardless of need?

RATIONALES FOR A BROAD PUBLIC ANNUITY PROGRAM

Even those who advocate abolition of the existing Social Security system typically agree that the government should provide some assistance to elderly persons who are truly needy.[17] Their criticism focuses on the mandatory public annuity aspect of Social Security. Such critics argue that the system requires all workers to devote a specific portion of their income to the purchase of a government-sponsored annuity and denies them the choice of consuming with that money or investing it privately—thus limiting the range of individual choice and reducing economic efficiency. If individual equity is the goal, why doesn't the government simply provide assistance targeted at the needy elderly, and leave pensions and annuities for the rest of the population to private markets?

It is undeniable that Social Security sacrifices consumer choice and individual freedom; any government program does. The real question is whether there are persuasive reasons for such a tradeoff. Building an annuity element into the original program design has three possible justifications: the desire to stimulate popular support, the need to ensure government efficiency in the presence of private market failure, and the requirement to avoid the efficiency and equity problems inherent in a program targeted on the poor. Once a pay-as-you-go program is in full operation there is a fourth justification. It is impossible to change from a public annuity program to private insurance without running into major equity problems.

Need for Popular Support

Although the fundamental purpose of Social Security was to prevent destitution among the elderly, its architects also wanted the program to receive enthusiastic and sustained popular support. They believed that a universal annuity component was necessary to gain public support for the redistributive efforts.[18] By making it easier to think of Social Security as "insurance" rather than a "handout"—social insurance rather than welfare—they made the redistributional component of the program more palatable to the American public.[19]

These rationales are expressed clearly in the words of Wilbur J. Cohen, a former Secretary of Health, Education, and Welfare who played an important role in the evolution of the Social Security system for almost five decades:

> . . . I am convinced that, in the United States, a program that deals only with the poor will end up being a poor program. There is every evidence that this is true. Ever since the Elizabethan Poor Law of 1601, programs only for the poor have been lousy, no good, poor programs. And *a program that is only for the poor—one that has nothing in it for the middle income and the upper income—is, in the long run, a program the American public won't support.* This is why I think one must try to find a way to link the interests of all classes in these programs. (Cohen and Friedman 1972: 55)

The contributory annuity aspect of the program was also intended to help ensure its long-term political survival by giving participants a sense of "entitlement" to their promised benefits. Some benefit would be available to all workers as an "earned right" that was related to working and to paying Social Security taxes. Franklin Roosevelt, in an oft-quoted response to a close advisor, summarized the argument:

> . . . I guess you're right on the economics, but those taxes were never a problem of economics. They are *politics all the way through.* We put those payroll contributions there so as to give the contributors a legal, moral, and political right to collect their pensions. . . With those taxes in there, no damn politician can ever scrap my Social Security program. (Schlesinger 1958: 308–309)

Many of Social Security's advocates also felt very strongly that a contributory annuity approach was necessary to preserve the "dignity" and "self-respect" of recipients.[20]

A final political rationale behind the annuity concept was that it attracted the support of those taxpayers who would have to pay for the transfers required in the early years of the program. As we have noted, because large numbers of elderly in the 1930s had standards of living below what society deemed acceptable even at that time, one important goal was to pay at least subsistence-level benefits to those retiring in the near future. Such benefits required substantial subsidies from younger generations of workers through their tax contributions.[21] Promising a quid pro quo in the form of universal annuities for all taxpayers made these transfers much easier to achieve politically. As it would turn out, almost everyone of voting age at time of enactment received more than a fair return—benefits in excess of what their taxes could possibly cover.

Program opponents, not surprisingly, have denounced this strategy as fooling the community into voting for a program they would have been against had they known the full redistributive truth.[22] Whatever one may think of the ethics of the strategy, it certainly worked. According to public opinion polls, Social Security remains immensely popular among all age groups.[23] This popularity, of course, is about to be tested in a period when many will pay in more than they receive.

Correcting for Market Failure

A second rationale for a universal public annuity program was the idea that the private market was failing to accommodate the needs not only of the poor but also of the middle class. Thus, government provision of annuities might be regarded as an efficient response to a private market failure.[24] Put another way, insurance is often desirable to deal with a variety of risks, not just those related to poverty. Where private insurance markets are believed to provide inadequate protection, as in the case of insurance of bank deposits, government insurance may step in on a more universal basis.[25] This is the argument we put forward in our discussion of the efficiency principle a few pages back.

Prior to the Great Depression of 1929, a fairly large and robust life insurance market had developed in the United States, and private retirement annuities were available though not common (Weaver 1983).[26] Some companies were also beginning to institute employer-sponsored pension plans. By 1930, about 15 percent of all workers were covered by such plans. Such plans that did exist, however, were not very safe or reliable. In particular, employees often lost benefit eligibility when they changed jobs and, since funds were rarely set aside separately for the plans, declining profits—not to mention bankruptcy—left many employees with no pensions and no recourse.[27]

Even so the American public was reluctant to follow the lead of other industrial countries in backing a government-sponsored social security system. This mood changed, of course, when bank failures and widespread loss of private savings accompanying the Great

Depression made people throughout the income distribution feel economically insecure. Providing a universal public annuity system that would be secure and resistant to economic fluctuations thus became a powerful rationale for a government-guaranteed (and mandated) method of "saving" for retirement.

Another argument held that individuals might want to commit themselves to saving for retirement to avoid irrational but tempting behavior. To the extent that people believe that they would fail to save sufficiently for retirement on their own, they may feel that a government-forced saving program is in their own best interests. "Ulysses paternalism" is the inspired name Alan Blinder applies to this rationale, named after "the ancient mariner of mythology who tied himself to the mast so as not to be lured by the Sirens' song."[28] Ulysses was in a somewhat different circumstance, though. Being tied to the mast was his own choice.

Yet another argument is that the majority of the public seem to want a social security system more because of what it does for their parents than for what it does for themselves. No private system can help most of us provide to our parents transfers that we consider sufficient without incurring some risks associated with our own financial and employment situations. The government can. It can also adjust our premiums according to how much we earn, and at the same time mute intergenerational resentment between dependents and providers within a family.

Once individuals value Social Security as a system for dealing with the needs of their parents, however, the individual equity case for providing a quid pro quo for the contributions of current workers is weakened. The problem is that a quid pro quo has already been obtained. Paying premiums that are used fully to insure your parents hardly allows you to decide that those premiums also entitle you to insurance. That is double counting. Your children are free to decide in their own way how much to provide to you, just as you were for your parents.

Avoiding the Inequities and Inefficiencies Associated with "Means Testing"

We have talked so far as if benefit programs can be designed for the poor alone without running into equity and incentive problems for those higher up in the income distribution. In practice, this is impossible. Of all the arguments for social insurance, it is here that we find the case for a more universal program most potent.

Suppose that a person saves for retirement and that these savings are invested in a way that earns them a positive return. The earnings on this saving are already subject to normal income taxation. In a means-tested system, such earnings would also cause a reduction in Social Security benefits. Together the various benefit reductions and taxes may add up to a significant reduction in the net earnings obtained from saving. The only way to reduce this disincentive to save is to pare benefits for the truly poor or cut back the rate at which benefits are reduced as earnings increase under the means test. The latter extends benefits to higher income groups and by definition makes the program more universal. Social Security was, in fact, designed originally so that retirement benefits would be unaffected by savings.[29]

The disincentive to save is not the only problem with means testing. The other is the temptation for those earning above the benefit cut-off point to change their behavior to end up qualifying for benefits. When contributions are made over a lifetime, but assessment of need is made at retirement, this gaming of the system is especially easy. As middle- or high-income earners approach retirement, they can simply spend all their wealth or give it to their children (as the elderly often do today to become eligible for means-tested Medicaid nursing home benefits).

The horizontal equity violations in a poor-only program are, thus, severe. Suppose taxpayers A, B, and C have equal lifetime incomes, but only A and B save for retirement, and B gives his saving to his children. Taxpayer A is rewarded for her prudent behavior by being forced to transfer money to both B and C. This is patently unfair. Efficiency violations are severe also. By saving more, the taxpayer decreases the transfer that she will receive at retirement; by working more, she pays more taxes to support others but not to provide for her own retirement.

If, in contrast, everyone at all income levels is made to contribute in their pre-retirement years, all will have borne part of the cost of their own retirement. Analogous arguments are often made in favor of requiring every car driver to buy automobile insurance or everyone to get health insurance. The case here is one of horizontal equity and efficiency, not progressivity. By reducing the number who could have paid for their own retirement but did not (economists call them, quite descriptively, free riders), mandated insurance at all income levels can effectively *reduce* the net amount of redistribution and the amount of net taxes (in excess of benefits) needed for redistribution.[30] Surprisingly, then, universality sometimes brings a system closer to the efficiency goal than can means-testing, even though means-testing results in a smaller program.

The Problem of Dissolving a Pay-as-you-go System

The final rationale for a universal system deals with changing a program that is already firmly established and covers most of the population. Once a mandatory government annuity system is set up on a pay-as-you go basis, privatizing the annuity component is virtually impossible without violating some of the principles we have discussed.[31] Recall, in particular, that the Social Security system paid large transfers to the first generations of retirees. Given this payout, if promises of individual equity were to be honored, later generations would have to transfer income to the generation that paid for the early transfers—and the process would have to continue forever.[32]

As the system now stands, several trillion dollars worth of liabilities to current and future retirees have been incurred for which funds have not been set aside. Past contributions have already been spent; promises based on those contributions can be met only by taxing current and future workers. Since current retirees' benefits are paid for by current workers, converting contributions into private investment alternatives would require either withdrawing benefit promises already made to current retirees (and for which contributions had already been made) or requiring the current generation of workers to pay twice for only one benefit—that is, to pay for both themselves and previous generations of workers whose benefits were not funded. Either option would violate same notions of both horizontal and individual equity.

Other Rationales

In addition to the rationales that we have discussed, all of which have some merit, there were a few that were either based on economic propositions that were plain wrong or that are less relevant today than they were in the 1930s.

The most conspicuous incorrect proposition was that there were only so many jobs in the economy. Encouraging the retirement of older (or "superannuated") individuals was believed, commonly and incorrectly, to be a means of opening up jobs to younger individuals.

For example, Senator Robert Wagner, in the debates surrounding the bills that would become the original Social Security Act of 1935, argued that "The incentive to the retirement of superannuated workers will improve efficiency standards, will make new places for the strong and eager, and will increase the productivity of the young by removing from their shoulders the uneven burden of caring for the old."[33] Although not everyone involved in the design of the Social Security system necessarily held this view, they did establish a rather strict "earnings test" which provided a strong financial incentive to retire.[34] Inadequate recognition was given to the simple economic proposition that an older worker both earns income and produces output. The spending of that income creates demand for additional output to be produced by other workers. When older workers produce output, they also provide a bigger economic pie to be shared.

One concern that is less relevant today is the need to design a Social Security system to deal with increasing insecurities created by industrial changes and the inability of older workers to perform strenuous physical labor. We earlier cited Franklin Roosevelt's use of this argument. The economy has since moved from an industrial age to a post-industrial technological and information age; in the process, many manufacturing jobs for men have been replaced by less strenuous service sector jobs for both men and women. If President Roosevelt's argument justified earlier retirement in the 1930s, it justifies later retirement today.

IMPLICATIONS FOR SOCIAL SECURITY REFORM

As the next chapters make clear, reform of the Social Security system is inevitable, both because the system is financially imbalanced and because, as a contributory system based partly on need, it must adjust to the evolving resources and needs of the population as we move into the 21st century.

This chapter has sketched the principles of public finance that can be applied to the Social Security system. As we have stressed repeatedly, the principles sometimes overlap and sometimes conflict. In addition, the rationales used by Social Security's founders vary in their persuasiveness, as well as in the accuracy and consistency with which they were applied.

Even so, we believe that the four major principles of progressivity, individual equity, horizontal equity, and economic efficiency, are valuable in sorting through and ranking proposals for reform. We can also learn valuable lessons from the way these principles were applied and compromises made along the way. Using these principles as a lens allows us to sort reform proposals into three major categories. "Right" ways increase program consistency with principles balanced or weighted in coherent ways. "Wrong" ways reduce the consistency of the program with at least one principle without increasing consistency with any of the others. A middle group cannot be unambiguously categorized as better or worse than the current system in terms of the principles we have laid out.

Even within "right" ways individuals will still rank proposals differently depending upon the weights they give different principles—in particular, the value they place on overall progressivity. This does not mean that there is no meeting ground. No reform that both makes the system regressive and fails to provide any return on contributions, for instance, can be viewed as a legitimate compromise between progressivity and individual equity. Similarly, while in practice the equal treatment of equals requires some judgment as to whether equals are measured by current income, lifetime income, wealth, or a combination, a system that does not adhere to horizontal equity under any measure has little merit. As an exaggerated example, to determine benefits simply on the basis of race is "wrong" because it violates the principle of horizontal equity and cannot be justified as consistent with any other principle. As we see in later chapters, there are features of both the current system and proposals to change it that fail to meet these criteria in similar ways.

Notes

1. See Derthick (1979) for a detailed discussion of the political dimensions of Social Security's development.

2. See for example, chapter 11 in Musgrave and Musgrave (1984). In point of fact, these principles usually have been applied more rigorously in tax policy than in expenditure policy analysis. Because taxes and expenditures are integrated so closely within Social Security, we apply the principles consistently across both tax and expenditure functions.

3. These two reports, as well as the speeches by President Roosevelt quoted here, were compiled recently in a single volume, *The Report of the Committee on Economic Security of 1935 and Other Basic Documents Relating to the Development of the Social Security Act—50th Anniversary Edition.* (1985). When referring to these reports and speeches in the text, however, we will cite the original sources and page numbers, which are preserved in the 50th Anniversary publication.

4. Some lump sum benefits were paid out as early as 1937.

5. Robert M. Ball, who served as Commissioner of Social Security from 1962 to 1973, has noted that "In a very real sense, the 1939 Act more than the old-age benefit provisions of 1935 formed the Social Security structure we know today." *(Report of the Committee on Economic Security of 1935 . . . , 1985, p. 162)*

6. Seminal discussions of the development of and fundamental goals and rationales for the Social Security system are included in Ball (1978), Myers (1993), Altmeyer (1966), Cohen (1983), and the reports of various Advisory Councils on Social Security (for example: 1939, 1949, and 1964).

7. For a detailed discussion of equity and efficiency principles in government policy, see Musgrave (1959 and 1990), Musgrave and Musgrave (1984), and Head (1992). Literature on the Social Security system has often focused on the tradeoff among basic principles. In particular, it has focused on the compromise between "individual equity" and "social adequacy." See, for example, chapter 2 of Myers (1993) and chapter 10 of Derthick (1979). In our discussion, we retain the commonly used "individual equity" terminology, but treat "social adequacy" as a subset of the broader principle of "progressivity."

8. U.S. Social Security Administration (1990: 4). A credit of 1 additional percent for every year with at least $200 in wages also applied. A more detailed discussion of the relationship between contributions and benefits, and exactly how the social security benefit formula works, is offered in chapter 4.

9. For discussions of the problems associated with old age dependency prior to the establishment of the social security system, see Achenbaum (1978) and Fischer (1977).

10. Benefits were actually based upon earnings subject to tax, not the amount of tax paid. This usually resulted in a de facto positive relationship between taxes and benefits within each cohort. Between cohorts, however, using the wage base allowed greater net transfers to be made over time to the earlier generations of retirees. Those who contributed to the system at a 3 percent tax rate, for instance, would be treated the same as those who later contributed at a 6 percent tax rate. The effect on net benefits and net taxes paid is discussed in chapter 5.

11. Adjustments must be made for profits, costs of administration, and marketing, although this may be reflected in the interest rate. Interest relates the value of money over time and represents the "opportunity cost" of forgoing consumption today. When someone buys insurance, moreover, their decision is based on the gains they achieve because of the protection from risk, as well as the expected monetary value of the insurance. Thus, private insurance is often purchased when the expected monetary value of benefits is less than the cost. Otherwise the wages and profits of the insurance company could never be earned. A more detailed explanation of "actuarial fairness" is presented in chapter 4.

12. See Musgrave (1959), chapter 4, and Head (1992) for detailed discussions of the benefit principle and its intellectual origins.

13. As noted by Robert J. Myers (1988), "for about the first 20 years after its inception in 1935, OASI was financed on a partial reserve system, although moving toward a current cost (or pay-as-you-go) basis."

14. It wasn't until the Employee Retirement Income Security Act of 1974 (ERISA) that many of today's current funding standards were established for defined benefit plans. Private annuities purchased through insurance companies, however, met stricter insurance standards. Even today, many private defined benefit plans are not adequately funded, partly because of exceptions to ERISA standards. In the Depression, of course, many private pensions failed for the very reason that future pension liabilities were not funded.

15. A formal economic argument along these lines has been made by Varian (1980).

16. See Rawls (1971), chapter 4, for a related discussion of the "veil of ignorance" construct in theories of justice. In this type of philosophical inquiry, the citizen is asked what distribution of income might be chosen if he or she were ignorant of his or her economic circumstances.

17. These include Milton Friedman (1962) and Peter Ferrara (1980).

18. For a detailed discussion of the role of political factors in the development of Social Security, see Derthick (1979).

19. Robert Ball, Commissioner of Social Security for three presidents, expresses great concern for this difference in attitude toward welfare and social insurance. He notes the "negative attitude toward welfare . . . growing out of the punitive and paternalistic poor-law tradition (Ball, 1978: 339)" . . . "Public assistance is not paid because of an economic service, as wages and social insurance are (p. 342)" . . . "Programs designed solely for the poor do not get the same sustained interest and support as programs that serve us all. Whenever the budget is tight, it is the programs for the poor that are likely to suffer (p. 347)."

20. For evidence of this, see Derthick (1979). An additional rationale, cited commonly in Europe but less frequently in the United States, was the desire to build "solidarity" among people of different income classes in order to foster social cohesion.

21. Waiting a long period of time before paying out significant funds would also have created large budget surpluses at a time when some believed that a deficit stimulus was necessary to help the depressed economy.

22. Milton Friedman has written "in essence what this argument says is that the community can be fooled into voting for a measure that it opposes by presenting the measure in a false guise (Friedman, 1962: 185)."

23. See, for example, Yankelovich, Skelly, and White, Inc. (1985) for polling data on the popularity of the system.

24. For related discussions of "market failure" rationales behind social insurance, see Musgrave and Musgrave (1984), Meyer (1987), and Blinder (1988).

25. Social Security also works as countercyclical policy in the sense that payments continue even when taxes temporarily go down because of a recession. The 1949 Advisory Council seems to have given some attention to this issue. The same could be true, of course, for a well-funded and insured system of private pensions.

26. Weaver (1983) further discusses the relationship between this private sector development and the lack of a political consensus for Social Security, even among labor unions with higher priorities, before the Depression.

27. See Achenbaum (1986: 15).

28. See Blinder (1988: 29). Also see Elster (1979) for origins of the idea of "Ulysses Paternalism."

29. In 1983 Congress first inserted legislation to subject benefits of high-income retirees to income taxation. Because income from savings is included in the test of whether benefits are taxable or not, one's level of private savings now has a modest effect on one's net after-tax level of benefits.

30. In effect, the net tax rate—the tax rate less the benefits derived from those taxes—can also be reduced.

31. For a more detailed discussion of the problems associated with privatization and other radical reform proposals, see Meyer (1987).

32. Note that the start-up of a private pension plan can also involve transfers among generations and increase the amount of consumption of older persons relative to younger persons.

33. U.S. Congress, Senate, *Congressional Record*, 74th Cong., 1st sess., 1935, 79, pt. 9, p. 9286. Quoted in Graebner (1980: 185).

34. Graebner (1980) makes a strong case that the retiring of older workers was commonly seen as a means of opening up jobs for younger workers, and that this played an important role in political support for Social Security. Robert Ball and Robert Myers, who have been instrumental in the development of the Social Security system through much of its history, contend that this idea did not play a major role in the adoption or maintenance of Social Security or the earnings test. Indeed, many of Social Security's founders and advocates were opposed to this argument, and cited other rationales for maintaining the earnings test. Nonetheless, it is clear that many people, including Congressmen, business and labor leaders, and some members of the Council on Economic Security, did subscribe to this argument. Their political support was important to the passage of the Social Security Act.

Part Two

AN EXAMINATION OF THE SOCIAL SECURITY SYSTEM

Chapter Three

THE INEVITABLE REFORM OF AN IMBALANCED SYSTEM

Change and reform are bound to occur periodically in a public program as massive and important as Social Security. A nation's social and economic circumstances tend to undergo dramatic transformation over long time periods; it is only natural that governmental programs and institutions should adapt to these evolving conditions. Even the most ardent defenders and advocates of the Social Security system agree that no such system can remain static forever. For example, Wilbur J. Cohen, a leader in the development of the Social Security system, once stated:

> Historical background, economic and political institutions and beliefs, attitudes toward incentives, thrift, work, leisure, health, retirement, life expectancy, children, parents, family and the future—all of these factors play a part in determining what kind of a Social Security program a nation wants or accepts. . . . I do not believe, therefore, that our present Social Security system is the last word, nor do I believe it should be immune to change. On the contrary, I believe it can, it should, and it will change and that each generation should be free to remake and remold it to its needs and liking. (Cohen and Friedman 1972: 1–2)

Social Security, indeed, has been transformed considerably over the course of its history. Most of this change has been in the direction of greater generosity and expansion to meet the needs of the elderly. In recent years, however, it has become apparent that America faces increasingly difficult choices regarding its policies for the elderly. A variety of factors, including demographic trends and rising health care costs, can be expected to put strenuous demands on Social Security and the federal government. Despite recent efforts to put Social Security and Medicare on sound financial footing, promised spending greatly exceeds expected tax revenues even under relatively optimistic assumptions. Reforms that increase tax revenues and/or reduce growth in outlays have been enacted, and more will eventually be required. In a climate of fiscal constraint, moreover, efforts to meet additional pressing needs, to adapt to changing societal conditions, or to alleviate inequities will require that explicit trade-offs be made. The natural tendency is to try to avoid such difficult choices, but they are ultimately inescapable. This chapter examines the causes and extent of Social Security's long-run financial trouble, and its relationship to the broader fiscal posture of the nation.

DEMOGRAPHIC TRENDS

The fiscal balance within Social Security is affected strongly by demographic trends in the population. Longer life spans and changing birthrates, in particular, have dramatically affected who retires, how many years of retirement are supported, and how many persons in the work force provide the funds necessary to support the retirement system. Like most projections, those based on demographics are subject to error and are less reliable the further into the future that one proceeds. Barring dramatic changes in immigration, however, it is possible to make reasonably reliable projections of the size of the elderly population and, to a lesser extent, of the working-age population, for many decades to come. The number of persons born before the current year—the principal determinant of the number who will become elderly for the next several decades—is already known.

Living Longer and Retiring Earlier

Retirement has become a much more common phenomenon in America than it was at the advent of the Social Security system. A larger proportion of the population survives to old age and people are more likely to stop working at an earlier age. For most Americans, years in retirement can no longer be considered the last few years of life. Today the average person can count in decades, not just years, the amount of time likely to be spent in retirement. Many experts believe that these trends will continue unabated well into the future.

Largely because of improvements in health care and standards of living, the portion of the population that survives its adult years and reaches old age has increased dramatically since Social Security was

Table 3.1 HISTORICAL AND PROJECTED IMPROVEMENTS IN
LIFE EXPECTANCY

Year Cohort Turns 65	Percentage of population surviving from age 21 to age 65		Average remaining life expctancy for those surviving to age 65	
	Male	Female	Male	Female
1940	53.9	60.6	12.7	14.7
1950	56.2	65.5	13.1	16.2
1960	60.1	71.3	13.2	17.4
1970	63.7	76.9	13.8	18.6
1980	67.8	80.9	14.6	19.1
1990	72.3	83.6	15.3	19.6
2000	76.0	85.5	15.8	20.1
2010	78.4	87.1	16.3	20.5
2020	79.3	88.1	16.8	21.0
2030	80.4	88.8	17.2	21.5
2040	81.8	89.5	17.6	22.0
2050	82.7	90.0	18.0	22.4

Sources: Mortality data underlying the 1992 Social Security Board of Trustees reports, from U.S. Social Security Administration, Office of the Actuary (1992a and unpublished tables; henceforth, SSA, Office of the Actuary).

Note: Figures are specific to each cohort (i.e., a group of people born in the same year)

first adopted (see table 3.1). Only about 54 percent of men and about 61 percent of women born in 1875 would survive from age 21 to age 65 in 1940, the first year in which Social Security benefits were available. By contrast, approximately 72 percent of men and about 84 percent of women who were born in 1925 and survived to age 21 lived to see age 65 in 1990. According to estimates by the U.S. Social Security Administration (SSA), these figures will increase to 80 percent for males and 89 percent for females among those born in 1965 (turning 65 in 2030).[1] As a result, a larger proportion of those who contribute to the Social Security system will actually live long enough to receive benefits.

Those who do survive to age 65 can now expect to have many

more years ahead of them than was once the case. Among those turning 65 in 1940, the average remaining life expectancy was 12.7 years for males and 14.7 years for females (see table 3.1). By 1990, the life expectancy at age 65 had jumped by 2.6 years for males and 4.9 years for females, to 15.3 years and 19.6 years, respectively. Mostly because of advances in medical science, life expectancy will almost surely increase in the future. The SSA estimates that life expectancy at age 65 for both males and females will increase by about 2 additional years over the next four decades.

Some recent research has indicated that expected life spans might be extended beyond those projected by the SSA. The SSA's projections are based on the reasonable assumption that in the future, mortality rates at advanced ages will continue to decline at about the average rate experienced during this century. Some demographers, on the other hand, point out that death rates at age 65 and over declined nearly 2 percent per year between 1968 and 1982, as opposed to the average for this century of only about 0.5 percent. They suggest that sustained declines of 2 percent per year might occur in the future as well. James Vaupel of Duke University (in Kolata 1992) has suggested that by 2080 the U.S. population aged 85 or over could be about four times larger than the current projections of the Social Security Administration indicate.[2] The latest projections of the U.S. Bureau of the Census (1992a) also predict a slightly faster improvement in life expectancy than does the SSA. On the other hand, the Census Bureau also predicts higher birth and immigration rates, which would tend to offset the impact on retiree-to-worker ratios. Although there is plenty of room for debate on this question, most experts agree that the average human life span can be expected to increase by at least a few years during the next century, and there is some possibility of even more impressive improvements.

In the meantime, as indicated, retirement has become much more common, and people have been retiring at earlier and earlier ages (see table 3.2). Between 1950 and 1991, the civilian labor force participation rate for males aged 65 and over fell from 45.8 percent to only 15.8 percent. For men aged 55 to 64, it dropped from 86.9 percent to 66.9 percent. During this same period, the rate for females 65 and over declined from an already-low 9.7 percent to just 8.6 percent, despite large increases in labor force participation among younger women.[3]

The average age at first receipt of Social Security retirement benefits for male workers remained above 68 until the late 1950s. It has dropped precipitously since then, to 63.7 in 1991 (in part because

Table 3.2 TREND TOWARD EARLIER RETIREMENT

Year	Civilian labor force participation rate of people aged 65 or over		Average age at which workers begin receiving OASI retirement benefits	
	Male	Female	Male	Female
1940	*	*	68.8	68.1
1950	45.8	9.7	68.7	68.0
1960	33.1	10.8	66.8	65.2
1970	26.8	9.7	64.4	63.9
1980	19.0	8.1	63.9	63.5
1991	15.8	8.6	63.7	63.5

Sources: SSA, Office of the Actuary (1993: 247) and U.S. Bureau of Labor Statistics (1989 and 1992).

Note: Asterisks denote data not available.

an early retirement option for men was made available in Social Security beginning in 1962). The trend for female workers was similar; their average age at first receipt fell from 68.1 in 1940 to 63.5 in 1991.[4] Currently, about half of all new retired-worker benefits are awarded at age 62, and more than two-thirds are awarded before age 65.[5]

As a result of longer life expectancies and earlier retirements, the average number of years a retired worker will collect Old-Age and Survivors Insurance (OASI) benefits is now approaching two decades (it is already in excess of two decades for females). The average duration of an OASI benefit going to a couple is even longer. Consider a worker retiring at age 62 with a spouse of the same age. Social Security provides annuity payments that will last until both spouses are deceased. Payments can be expected to last an average of 25 years, or one-quarter of a century.[6] If the spouses are of different ages, as is usually the case, the duration of receipt of annuity payments is likely to be longer still.[7]

Although declining mortality rates are widely recognized to increase Social Security costs, some may argue that early retirements do not really impose much of a cost on the system. Those who retire early receive an "actuarial reduction" in their OASI benefit level so that the expected value of their benefits over the entire retirement span does not change much. For example, a worker who fully retires today at age 62 will receive a monthly benefit for the rest of his or her life that is only 80 percent as large as the monthly benefit payable if he or she waited until age 65 to retire. Early retirements do, however, impose costs on Social Security and the economy. First of all, they reduce the national economic output and shrink Social Security and other tax revenues. Second, to the extent that socially adequate benefit levels are sought for those who choose to retire early, they require basic Social Security benefit levels to be higher.[8] If people worked longer, they not only would have more private resources to support themselves in retirement, but Social Security would be able to provide better support at older ages, at less total cost.

Longer life spans and earlier retirement ages have been among the most important factors contributing to the growing costs of the Social Security system. Had retirement ages in Social Security been "indexed" for life expectancy—for instance, if the average number of years of support in retirement had been kept constant since first enactment—then the cost of old-age insurance benefits could be significantly smaller than it is today without any decline in real annual benefit levels provided to those receiving payments.[9]

In 1983, Social Security legislation acknowledged for the first time some of the problems associated with providing more and more years of retirement assistance. It scheduled an increase in the Normal Retirement Age (the age at which unreduced OASI benefits are first available) from age 65 to age 67, to be phased in gradually for workers turning 65 between 2003 and 2025.[10] The two-year increase was roughly equal to the growth in average life expectancy at age 65 projected to occur over the four decades between enactment of the bill (in 1983) and when full implementation is achieved. No adjustment, however, was made for past growth in number of retirement years nor for future growth beyond 2025. The earliest age at which one can receive reduced OASI benefits, moreover, was scheduled to remain constant at 62, while the age at which all persons become eligible for Medicare was left at 65.

The Social Security Administration projects that this increase in the Normal Retirement Age will have only a modest impact on decisions as to age of retirement, although future trends in this area are difficult to predict. Many people are expected to accept reduced benefit levels rather than delay retirement. Thus, the tendency of the system to support more and more years in retirement is likely to continue. For those retiring at age 62 in the year 2027, for instance, a Social Security pension can be expected to last on average about

Figure 3.1 TOTAL FERTILITY RATES, 1920–2020

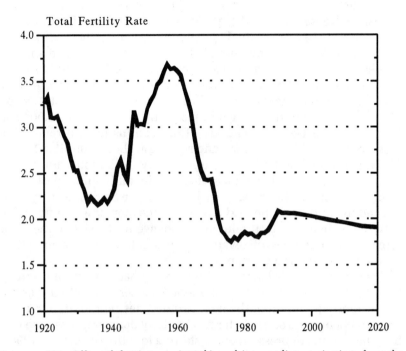

Sources: SSA, Office of the Actuary (1992b), and intermediate projections from the Board of Trustees, OASDI (1993).

19 years for a male, 23 years for a female, and 27 years for a couple (that is, until both are deceased).[11]

The consequences of longer lives and earlier retirement are clear: there are many more retired people than there used to be, and they spend a much longer time out of the labor force. These trends can be expected to continue for many decades into the future.

Baby Bust, Baby Boom, Baby Bust

The birthrate is a second major demographic factor that strongly affects both benefits and taxes within Social Security. Demographers usually illustrate changing birthrate patterns by reference to the "total fertility rate," which is a measure of the average number of children that would be born to a woman in her lifetime if she were to experience the birthrates prevailing in a selected year.[12]

Figure 3.1 illustrates how fertility rates have changed over time.

Following a period of high fertility rates in the 1920s, there was a "baby bust": the fertility rate dropped to relatively low levels during the Great Depression of the 1930s and World War II, reaching a minimum of 2.17 in 1939. This was followed by the well-known post–World War II "baby boom." The fertility rate jumped sharply immediately after the war and stayed above 3.00 from 1947 to 1964, reaching a peak of 3.68 in 1959. During the mid- to late-1960s, fertility began to decline dramatically, shrinking to a low of just 1.74 by 1976.[13] Since then, it has edged up slightly, to just above 2.00. The SSA's 1993 best-estimate actuarial projections have it remaining close to this level in the future, and settling at about 1.90 after 2020.[14] There is a significant degree of uncertainty in the long-run projections, since the rates have fluctuated considerably in the past. Later years of projection, however, have little effect on Social Security until beyond the middle of the next century, since there is a significant lag between a change in birthrates and a change in the size of the labor force, as well as a lag of several decades before there is any effect on the size of the retired population.

The simple story is baby bust followed by baby boom followed by baby bust. Despite frequently expressed concerns about an increasingly elderly population, the next two decades represent, in reality, the quiet before the storm in terms of elderly demographics. The first baby bust of the depression era is starting to retire during the 1990s, making for a relatively small elderly cohort. The large postwar baby boom, moreover, has swelled the size of the labor force and increased Social Security tax collections. Beginning about 2010, however, the leading edge of the postwar baby boom will start to retire. After that, the retirement population is expected to increase dramatically, while the size of the working-age population will have become rather stagnant because of low birthrates since the mid-1960s. In sum, the current cash-flow situation of Social Security is misleading, since a small baby bust population of retirees can depend upon an exceptionally large baby boom working population; in the not too distant future, those baby boomers will retire and be dependent upon a succeeding baby bust population.

The impact of these birthrate patterns may be softened to some extent by two factors. First, low-to-moderate birthrates mean there will be fewer children per worker. This can be expected to slow the growth in an overall dependency ratio, a measure of the number of dependent nonworkers per worker. There is considerable danger, however, in taking this comparison too far. Except for educational expenses, children are supported more out of private funds, the elderly out of public funds. Thus, the pressures on the public sector are not eased significantly. Spending on children also may be more likely to result in future productivity increases. Finally, even if the demands of children on society decrease, there is no inherent reason why any savings or surplus generated should be predetermined to be spent on the elderly. Other needs of society may cry out for greater attention, as well.

A second factor that may help mitigate the decline in the number of workers per retiree is immigration. Although the SSA projects an increase in the net immigration rate in the future, some experts contend that these projections are on the conservative side. A larger-than-expected influx of immigrants over the next few decades might improve the demographic picture for Social Security slightly, since most immigrants are relatively young. Even significant increases in the immigration rate, however, have only a modest impact on the financial balance in Social Security.[15] Despite these possibilities, there remains little doubt that the growth in the retired population will significantly increase burdens on workers during the next century, especially when the baby boom retires.

Working Women Save the Day—But Only for Awhile

One modern trend has taken some pressure off the Social Security system: the growth in labor force participation in recent decades (see table 3.3). The overall civilian labor force participation rate rose from 59.2 percent in 1950 to 66.3 percent in 1992. Partly because of the increasing popularity of earlier retirement, labor force participation rates among males actually declined significantly over that time span, from 86.4 percent to 75.6 percent. Growth in overall participation, therefore, was due entirely to a rapid increase among women. Between 1950 and 1992, female labor force participation jumped dramatically, from 33.9 percent to 57.8 percent.[16]

Over these past decades, increased female participation has meant that many more workers have been available to contribute to the financial support of the elderly. Higher female labor force participation has been particularly fortuitous for Social Security financing because it raised payroll tax revenues far more than it increased benefit outlays. As these women entered the labor force, they contributed immediately to Social Security. Only years later would these women retire and become eligible for benefit payouts. Even when they finally do retire, secondary workers in households often receive

Table 3.3 CIVILIAN LABOR FORCE PARTICIPATION
RATE OF TOTAL POPULATION AGED 16
OR OVER

Year	Total	Male	Female
1950	59.2	86.4	33.9
1960	59.4	83.3	37.7
1970	60.4	79.7	43.3
1980	63.8	77.4	51.5
1992	66.3	75.6	57.8
2005	69.0	75.4	63.0

Sources: U.S. Bureau of Labor Statistics (1989 and 1993);
projection for 2005 is from Fullerton (1991).

Social Security benefits that are the same or only slightly higher than what they would have received in spousal and survivors benefits.[17]

Although greater labor force participation among women historically has offset some costs of a growing retiree population with increasingly long life spans, the trend cannot be expected to continue forever. Starting from a much higher level of participation, eventually a limit must be reached. Some believe that female participation rates will increase only moderately, if at all, during the next century, while the overall participation rate is likely to stagnate.[18]

The evolving work force has implications not only for the overall burden of the Social Security system, but also for how it should be structured. A system designed mainly for a worker with a stay-at-home spouse must now adapt to a working population where the norm has moved toward work by both spouses. At the same time, one spouse frequently takes off for intervals or works part-time to deal with child care. The rising rate of divorce has made the model of an intact, two-spouse couple more inadequate. Substantial pressure has been exerted on the Social Security system to react to these changes, but accommodating new needs has been made difficult by the political calculus: either taxes must be raised to support additional expenditures or, at a given level of expenditures, benefits must be redistributed in a way that would create some losers.

More Retirees per Worker

One consequence of the demographic trends is that the number of Social Security beneficiaries has grown much faster than the working

Table 3.4 GROWTH IN ELDERLY POPULATION AND ITS
IMPACT ON SOCIAL SECURITY SYSTEM

Year	Persons aged 65 or over as a percentage of the total population	OASI beneficiaries as a percentage of the total population	OASI beneficiaries per 100 covered workers
1950	8.0	1.8	6.1
1970	9.7	10.5	24.3
1990	12.3	13.6	26.6
2010	12.9	14.5	28.2
2030	19.9	20.5	42.7
2050	20.8	21.5	45.4

Sources: Board of Trustees, OASDI (1993), historical data and
intermediate projections.

population that supports them. When the post–World War II baby
boom generation begins to retire early next century, the problem
will begin to intensify considerably. By 2030, about one-fifth of the
population is expected to be receiving Old-Age and Survivors Insurance benefits.

In 1950, OASI beneficiaries represented just 1.8 percent of the total
U.S. population (see table 3.4). Only 8.0 percent of the population
was aged 65 or over, many people worked beyond age 65, and only
a fraction of the elderly had contributed to OASI long enough to be
eligible for benefits. The share of the population receiving OASI
benefits jumped to 10.5 percent by 1970, and then to 13.6 percent
by 1990. After remaining fairly stable for the next two decades, this
figure is expected to skyrocket, reaching 20.5 percent by 2030. Thereafter, the proportion is projected to continue growing, albeit at a
reduced pace.[19]

A summary measure of the effect of demographic trends on the
burden of the Social Security system is the ratio of OASI beneficiaries to workers in employment covered by Social Security. In
1990, the ratio stood at 27 beneficiaries for every 100 workers. By
2030, it is expected to rise to 43 beneficiaries for every 100 workers.
In other words, the number of OASI beneficiaries per taxpayer
is expected to increase by about 60 percent over the next four
decades.[20]

FISCAL IMBALANCE

The potential for fiscal imbalance in Social Security is easy to under-stand given the demographic trends just noted. In the Old-Age, Survivors, and Disability Insurance (OASDI) programs, benefit levels are designed to increase at the same rate as average wages for each successive cohort of beneficiaries (see chapter 4 for a more detailed explanation). As a result, under some simplifying assumptions, OASDI benefit outlays would grow at roughly the same rate as the national economy if the ratio of beneficiaries to workers were to remain constant.[21] Health care spending, on the other hand, has tended to grow at a much faster rate than the economy.[22] As a result, Medicare could be expected to consume an ever-larger portion of gross domestic product (GDP) even if the elderly remained a constant share of the population. When programs already structured to grow with wage levels and health costs are applied to an elderly population that will grow dramatically as a share of the total population, outlays can be expected to increase tremendously as a percentage of GDP. Unless taxes increase so that they, too, absorb a greater share of the national economy, large deficits will result under this benefit structure.

Social Security Deficits and the Trust Funds

Recent reforms of the Social Security system—in particular, the Social Security Amendments of 1983 and, to a lesser extent, those of 1977—have been designed to deal with some of the fiscal imbalance that otherwise could be caused by these longer-term demographic trends. A traditional focus of Social Security reform efforts, when they have occurred, has been to put the Social Security trust funds in an actuarial balance for 75 years—the maximum number of years for which benefit and cost estimates are prepared by the Social Security actuaries.[23] Such an "actuarial balance" is not the same as one that would be imposed in the private sector, where assets sufficient to meet accrued liabilities would be required. Within Social Security, the notion is simply that over the next 75 years, taxes, plus interest accumulated on taxes saved rather than spent, must be sufficient under the SSA's best-estimate projections to pay out scheduled benefits. Note that although such long-term constraints have served as a guide for Social Security's cash benefit programs, they have not traditionally had much affect on Medicare policy.

One part of the solution adopted in 1977 and reinforced in 1983 was to move to a combined tax rate for the OASDI programs that would be constant for 1990 and thereafter and would be sufficient to cover the 75-year cost of the system. Because of the irregular effect of the baby bust, baby boom, baby bust cycle, the system would move beyond what is often called a pay-as-you-go system—one that collects just enough taxes each year to pay out benefits that year (and keep a small reserve). The combined employer and employee tax rate for the OASDI portion of Social Security was set at a level rate of 12.4 percent for 1990 and thereafter. Temporary surpluses were to be deposited in the "trust funds" and "saved" until the baby boom retires. Eventually, rising costs would force the Social Security system to use the accumulated principal and interest to help finance benefit payments.

Projections now show the reforms of 1977 and 1983 to be inadequate, even though Social Security does accumulate funds temporarily. Figure 3.2 illustrates historical figures and the Social Security Administration's best-estimate projections for spending and revenues in the OASDI portions of Social Security, under law scheduled as of the beginning of 1993. The combined OASDI programs have been running surpluses since 1984. By 1992, revenues from payroll taxes and taxation of benefits exceeded spending by 1.09 percent of taxable payroll, or about $25 billion. In other words, the combined employer and employee OASDI tax rate, which stood at 12.4 percent, could have been reduced by 1.09 percentage points and still could have raised enough funds to support current benefits and administrative expenses. OASDI tax revenues are expected to continue to exceed outlays until about 2015.[24]

Since the enactment of the 1977 and 1983 reforms, projections of the long-run financial situation of the system have worsened, partly because assumptions for the future have been revised in a less optimistic direction. As apparent in figure 3.2, OASDI is expected to start running deficits around 2015, and spending will exceed income by an ever-increasing margin thereafter. OASDI deficits are projected to reach about 3.1 percent of taxable payroll by 2030, and 3.7 percent by 2050. The cumulated reserves and interest within the trust funds are expected to be sufficient to cover these deficits until about 2036, a little over four decades from now.[25] This date of exhaustion has moved considerably closer since the 1983 projections, when it was predicted to occur after 2057, or more than 75 years away.[26] If actual economic and demographic trends turn out less favorably than the SSA's best predictions, complete depletion of the OASDI trust funds could occur less than three decades from now.

Figure 3.2 OASDI TAX REVENUES AND SPENDING AS PERCENTAGE OF
TAXABLE PAYROLL

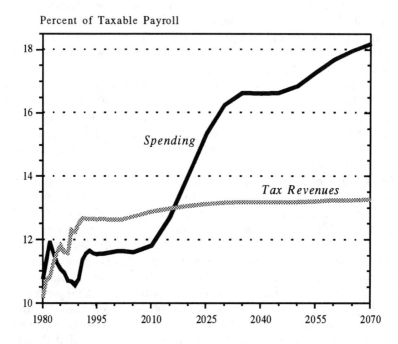

Percent of Taxable Payroll

Source: Board of Trustees, OASDI (1993), intermediate projections.

Note: Tax revenues include payroll tax and income taxation of benefits.

Under current law and best-estimate assumptions as of 1993,
OASDI faced a 75-year actuarial deficit equal to 1.46 percent of taxable payroll.[27] This represents the amount by which the payroll tax
rate would have to be increased immediately to establish actuarial
balance in the OASDI portion of the system for the next 75 years.
Balance could, of course, be restored through benefit reductions as
well.

No increases in the 12.4 percent OASDI tax rate are scheduled
under current law. A reallocation of tax rates between the Old-Age
and Disability portions within OASDI, however, is likely to be
enacted in 1993 or 1994. Under the 1983 Social Security Amendments, the Disability Insurance (DI) tax rate was already scheduled
to rise from 1.2 percent to 1.42 percent starting in 2000, in exchange
for an equal decrease in the OASI tax rate from 11.2 percent to 10.98
percent. The DI trust fund, however, faced very serious financing

problems under this tax schedule. It had already started running deficits by 1992, and its trust fund reserves were expected to run out as soon as 1995. As a result, legislators began considering an acceleration and an increase in the reallocation. The most commonly discussed proposal would permanently raise the DI tax rate to 1.75 percent and reduce the OASI rate to 10.65 percent. This accounting change temporarily allows legislators to dodge dealing with longer-term problems affecting the combined programs. It also shifts nearly all of the long-run OASDI imbalance to the Old-Age and Survivors Insurance portion of the program. Under such a tax schedule, the 75-year actuarial deficit rises from 0.97 percent to 1.32 percent of taxable payroll in OASI, and falls from 0.49 percent to 0.14 percent of taxable payroll in DI. Either way, however, the government eventually will be required to take action that will raise the combined tax rate above 12.4 percent, cut benefits, or both.

The longer the delay in dealing with OASI's financial imbalance, the more dramatic will be the changes that must be achieved. Benefit cuts or tax increases required in 20 years will appear much sharper and more significant relative to a gradually implemented change over that 20-year period. If money from a tax increase or benefit cut enacted today is truly saved, and not spent in other parts of the budget, the amount of federal borrowing from the public would be reduced, hence easing burdens on future generations. Enacting reforms in a timely fashion, moreover, allows an adequate phase-in period and enables people to adjust and prepare for the changes.

Restoring a 75-year actuarial balance to Old-Age and Survivors Insurance, unfortunately, could still be inadequate for a number of reasons. First, some reforms that merely restore long-run actuarial balance would leave a problem for the longer run. Second, the much larger Medicare imbalance would remain. Finally, more fundamental problems exist in the fiscal situation of the federal government; Social Security cannot be separated from this broader fiscal issue.

The first problem is reflected in the OASDI Board of Trustees' annual reports. Benefit outlays are expected to continue to exceed tax revenues by a widening margin beyond the 75-year horizon (see figure 3.2). Thus, as each year passes, a past year of surplus drops out of the 75-year projection and a new year of deficit is added on. As a result, every year the extent of the long-run actuarial deficit deepens.

Suppose the OASI system were brought back into exact 75-year actuarial balance with an increase in tax rates today. As soon as one more year passed, the trustees would issue a report stating that the system was out of balance once again. Although projections so far in the future are always very tentative, the gap remains too substantial to ignore. Thus, something must eventually be done to bring long-run revenues and expenditures closer together.

Of more importance for the nearer term, Medicare is in horrible financial shape. The Hospital Insurance (HI) portion of Medicare is financed primarily by a payroll tax, set at a combined employer and employee rate of 2.9 percent as of 1993. As with OASI, no increases in this tax rate are currently scheduled. HI tax revenues, however, were already less than expenditures by 1992.[28] The Health Care Financing Administration's (HCFA's) best-estimate projections, published in the Trustees' 1993 reports, suggested that spending would continue to exceed tax receipts by a growing margin, and that the HI trust fund would be fully exhausted before the turn of the century.[29] Legislators made a small dent in this problem in the 1993 deficit reduction act. The $135,000 cap on earnings subject to the HI tax was removed, which would increase payroll tax revenues by about 6 percent of their current annual total.[30] Congress also enacted some spending cuts in both the HI and Supplementary Medical Insurance (SMI) portions of Medicare, mainly through a freeze in prices paid to hospitals and doctors. In addition, revenues from increased taxation of OASDI benefits may be credited to the HI trust fund.

Although the 1993 deficit reduction efforts may provide a temporary reprieve for Medicare, the program still faces enormous problems over the long run. Longer-term projections of health care spending are subject to a wide margin of error, but the projections of the HCFA should still be cause for serious concern. Under the HCFA's best-estimate projections at the beginning of 1993, the annual HI deficit was projected to balloon to 6.4 percent of taxable payroll by 2030 and to 8.3 percent in 2050.[31] The 75-year actuarial deficit for HI was estimated at 5.1 percent of taxable payroll.[32] Changes enacted in the 1993 deficit reduction act can be expected to have only a marginal impact over the long run, improving the actuarial balance by a fraction of 1 percent at best. Even the near-term impact may be minimal; similar cuts totaling $42.5 billion over five years were enacted in the 1990 budget act, yet Medicare spending did not end up deviating significantly from baseline projections made before the act, and long-run projections of imbalance actually grew worse.[33]

Although these figures reflect an almost impossible scenario, they do not even include the effects of large increases in the SMI portion of Medicare. Calculations of SMI actuarial deficits are not performed because general government funds, not Social Security taxes, already pay for nearly all costs beyond what enrollees contribute in premiums. Almost three-quarters of SMI funding currently comes from general federal tax revenues and deficit financing, and this ratio will rise in the future unless further legislative action is taken.[34] Unless national health care reform successfully constrains cost growth, SMI is expected to grow to be about as large as HI during the next century—implying that taxpayers will be required indirectly to shoulder additional taxes equivalent to several more percentage points of their wages.

Finally, neither the HI nor the SMI calculations take into account the health costs being incurred under Medicaid. About one-third of Medicaid spending currently supports health care, particularly long-term nursing home care, for the elderly. Barring any change, growth in these costs will also be substantial. Long-term care would also be expanded under many national health proposals, including President Clinton's in 1993.

Social Security and the Federal Budget

Measures of actuarial deficits within Social Security trust funds do not capture the full impact of Social Security on the broader federal budget. Social Security's surplus tax revenues are currently invested in government bonds, which provide a positive cash flow to the federal government. This cash flow helps ease other fiscal pressures. In the absence of these surplus revenues, the government would have three options: increase other taxes, cut spending, or borrow more money from the public, which would only increase the federal budget deficit and decrease national saving further. What government would do without the surpluses is open to speculation; the most likely scenario is some combination of the three.[35] The important point here is that while the government is currently having great difficulty trying to raise taxes and cut spending in response to the budget deficit, it would have to do even more to achieve the same overall deficit if the Social Security surpluses were not available.

When the time comes next century to draw down the trust funds to pay out benefits, the cash flow will be reversed and the federal government will face a much more difficult fiscal situation. First of all, it will no longer have access to Social Security surpluses as a means of relieving fiscal pressures outside of Social Security. If Social Security is to pay out the benefits it has promised to the baby boom generation, moreover, the federal government will have to find money to repay what it borrowed from the trust funds, with interest. The

Table 3.5 OASDI AND MEDICARE SPENDING AS PERCENTAGE
OF GDP

Year	OASDI (SSA 1993 best estimate)	Assuming Medicare grows according to HCFA 1993 best estimate		Assuming Medicare cost per enrollee grows at the same rate as per capita GDP after 1995	
		Medicare	OASDI & Medicare	Medicare	OASDI & Medicare
1950	0.3	0.0	0.3	0.0	0.3
1970	3.1	0.6	3.7	0.6	3.7
1993	4.8	2.1	6.9	2.1	6.9
2010	4.6	4.3	8.9	2.6	7.2
2030	6.0	7.0	13.0	3.8	9.8
2050	6.0	7.7	13.7	4.0	10.0

Sources: Authors' calculations based on OMB (1993a, b) and intermediate
projections from Board of Trustees, OASDI, HI, and SMI (1993), adjusted
for estimated impact of 1993 enactments.

Notes: Income taxes on benefits and SMI premiums are counted as expenditure reductions. Table assumes SMI premiums remain at 25 percent of
program costs indefinitely. Years 1950 through 1993 are fiscal years; 2010
through 2050 are calendar years.

only way it will be able to make up for the lost surpluses and repay
the trust funds is to increase other taxes, cut other spending, and/or
increase the deficit still further.

One way to illustrate the full impact of Social Security's growth
on the federal government's fiscal posture is to show how total Social
Security and Medicare spending is expected to change as a percentage
of the national economy, or GDP. To give a rough impression of
the magnitude of future fiscal problems, we have included some
projections based on the 1993 best estimates of the SSA and the
HCFA, as well as some very conservative estimates that assume that
growth in health costs is brought under control almost immediately
(see table 3.5). Our estimates of spending levels include outlays for
Old-Age, Survivors, and Disability Insurance and Medicare, but sub-
tract out offsetting receipts paid by beneficiaries, such as SMI premiums and income taxes on Social Security benefits.[36] SMI premiums
are assumed to remain at 25 percent of program costs permanently,
although this would require further legislative action. Finally, we
adjust our projections for the estimated impact of 1993 enactments

such as Medicare cuts and increased taxation of OASDI benefits. These adjustments all improve the long-run picture moderately, but challenging problems remain. Projections into the distant future, of course, should be taken with a grain of salt. It should be noted, however, that a broad array of economic and demographic variables would have to be considerably more favorable than expected over a long period of time for the general picture in OASDI to improve significantly.

By themselves, OASDI outlays (less income taxes on benefits) are expected to rise from 4.8 percent of GDP in 1993 to about 6 percent of GDP in 2030 (table 3.5). This amounts approximately to a 25 percent increase over today's spending levels, relative to GDP. Under these projections, OASDI would force the federal government to raise taxes, reduce other spending, and/or increase the deficit relative to 1993 levels by roughly 1.2 percent of GDP in 2030. This is equivalent to around $75 billion at 1993 levels of economic activity.[37] If, for example, this amount were to be raised through increased individual income taxes, tax rates would have to be set about 14 percent higher than their present levels.[38]

The potential fiscal impact of OASDI is significant, but would probably be manageable by itself, especially if benefit and tax changes are phased in over time. Potential problems arising from growth in Medicare costs, however, are much larger still. Although projections here are highly speculative, the 1993 best estimates of the HCFA actuaries suggest that total net Medicare spending will soar from about 2.1 percent of GDP in 1993 to about 7 percent in 2030 (table 3.5), even after we conservatively adjust this spending downward to account for 1993 enactments and assuming SMI premiums remain at 25 percent of program costs. If we add these numbers to those for OASDI, we can see that in 2030, additional resources equal to roughly 6.1 percent of GDP would have to be diverted from other uses to provide the OASDI and Medicare benefits promised under current law. To use the earlier analogy, to pay for these costs through taxes would require changes equivalent to a 71 percent increase in individual income taxes.[39] Alternatively, spending in the federal budget besides Social Security and Medicare would have to be cut by more than a third relative to its current share of GDP.[40]

Projections of Medicare spending are considerably less reliable than those for OASDI. Because OASDI benefits are determined by a known formula that is designed to keep pace with economic growth, it is possible to predict the share of GDP consumed by OASDI with a reasonable degree of accuracy (more about this later). Health care costs, on the other hand, depend on a wide variety of difficult-to-predict factors. The dramatic HCFA projections noted previously actually assume that in the future, the real rate of growth in Medicare spending per enrollee will be considerably *lower* than the average over the past two decades.[41] Nonetheless, even this situation is unsustainable. The government would almost certainly adopt measures to slow the escalation in health care costs before the situation got as bad as projected by the HCFA. Even under very optimistic assumptions, however, Medicare could still be expected to grow significantly as a percentage of GDP (see table 3.5). If, for example, strict cost-control measures were to limit growth in Medicare spending per enrollee to the rate of growth in per capita GDP (which would be well below the historical pace) after 1995, net Medicare spending would still rise to roughly 3.8 percent of GDP in 2030 simply because of demographic changes.

Figure 3.3 provides a hypothetical illustration of the bind that government will find itself in when projected growth in Social Security and Medicare is combined with already-potent deficit pressures. Under the best-estimate SSA and HCFA projections, OASDI and Medicare (less premiums and taxes on benefits) would increase from 6.9 percent of GDP today to 13.0 percent of GDP by 2030. On the one hand, if tax rates were to remain constant at 1998 levels (after full implementation of the Clinton administration's tax increases), spending on all other federal government functions—defense, federal aid to education, environment, assistance to children, interest on the debt, and so forth—would have to be squeezed from 16.8 percent of GDP in 1993 to 6.3 percent of GDP in 2030 to produce a balanced budget. On the other hand, if all government spending other than OASDI and Medicare were to be held constant as a percentage of GDP, total federal taxes would have to be further increased above 1998 levels by 8.9 percent of GDP to balance the budget. Even under the more optimistic assumption that Medicare spending per enrollee could be held to the rate of growth of per capita GDP, tax increases or expenditure cuts of close to 6 percent of GDP would be required to balance the budget in 2030.

These figures may even give an optimistic impression of the problem, since many other categories of government spending, such as Medicaid and interest on the federal debt, can also be expected to grow rapidly relative to the national economy unless major reforms occur. The U.S. General Accounting Office estimated in a recent report that if current law were to remain unchanged, federal government spending would rise from about 23 percent of gross national

Figure 3.3 FUTURE GROWTH IN SOCIAL SECURITY AND MEDICARE MEANS
HIGHER TAXES, LARGER DEFICITS, OR LOWER SPENDING ON
EVERYTHING ELSE

Percentage of GDP

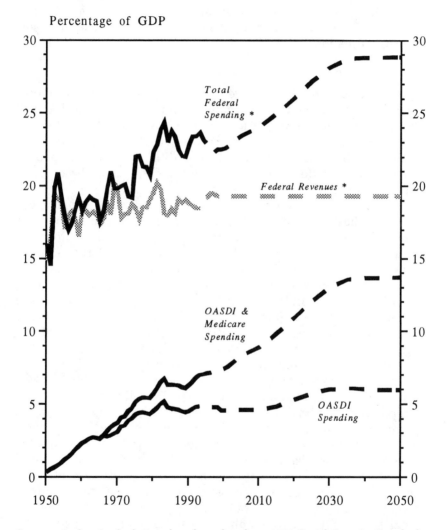

Sources: Authors' calculations based on data from 1993 Social Security Board of
Trustees reports' intermediate projections, and OMB (1993a, b), adjusted for estimated
impact of 1993 enactments.

Notes: SMI premiums and income taxes on benefits are counted as expenditure reductions. Assumes SMI premiums remain at 25 percent of program costs indefinitely.

*Projections assume spending—besides OASDI and Medicare—and taxes remain con-
stant as percentage of GDP after 1998.

product (GNP) today to 42 percent of GNP in 2020, while federal tax revenues would only rise from 20 percent to 22 percent of GNP over that same period (GAO 1992: 6). The report noted that spending on the elderly, health, and interest on the debt account for the vast majority of this expected rise in spending. This is obviously an unsustainable situation.

SHARING THE GOVERNMENT PIE

The share of the federal budget devoted to the elderly has grown enormously over the past four decades and is expected to grow still more. Spending on the elderly now accounts for nearly one-third of the federal budget, and more than one-half of all federal domestic spending other than interest.[42] If expenditures on other important government functions are being "crowded out," then it becomes all the more likely that some reform will have to occur.

Figure 3.4 shows how the composition of federal government spending has changed over the postwar period.[43] The bottom four categories in the chart are mainly pension and health programs, which devote a large share of their budgets to the elderly and near-elderly. These include OASDI, Medicare, other retirement and disability programs (such as Supplemental Security Income and pensions for federal employees, veterans, and military personnel), and other health programs (mainly Medicaid and health benefits for civil servants and veterans).[44] We estimate that about three-fourths of aggregate outlays in these programs go to those who are elderly and/or retired.[45] Expenditures on these items grew from around 11 percent of the total federal budget in 1950 to about 45 percent in 1993. Under projections incorporating President Bill Clinton's 1993 budget proposals (including significant Medicare cuts), these outlays are expected to rise to approximately 52 percent by 1998 and perhaps more under health reform; a virtually identical increase was expected under Bush administration proposals. OASDI accounted for most of this growth between 1950 and the mid-1970s. Since then, this program has stabilized as a percentage of the budget, with future growth to occur again after the turn of the century. In the meantime, federal health care expenditures, about two-thirds of which go to the elderly,[46] have continued to grow rapidly.

The fifth category in figure 3.4, which has also been consuming an increasing portion of the budget, is net interest on the public debt. Altogether, spending on the elderly and disabled, health care, and net interest are expected to account for slightly more than two-thirds of the federal budget by 1998.

Figure 3.4 CHANGE IN COMPOSITION OF FEDERAL BUDGET, 1950–98

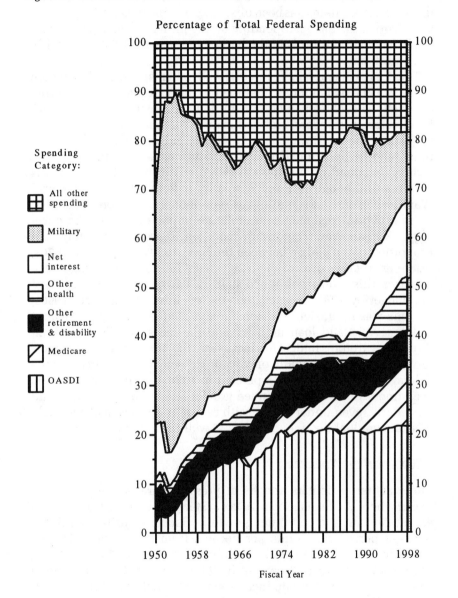

Sources: Authors' calculations based on OMB historical tables and President Clinton's FY 1994 budget proposal (OMB 1993a, c).

As is apparent in figure 3.4, much of the postwar growth in expenditures on these items has been offset by a decline in defense spending as a share of the budget. Spending on the military[47] decreased steadily, from over two-thirds of the budget in the early 1950s to roughly one-fifth today.

The final category in figure 3.4, "all other spending," is where pressure is being felt today. Included in this category are a vast array of functions such as welfare, unemployment insurance, investment in infrastructure, federal aid to education, foreign aid, administration of justice, the environment, agriculture, aid to the cities, disaster relief, and insurance of financial institutions, among many others. Aggregate spending on these assorted government functions was dominant (although in a much smaller federal sector) until World War II, when defense spending rose enormously. As figure 3.4 shows, these functions resumed some relative importance until the onset of the Korean War. They again managed to grow moderately as a proportion of the budget between the early 1950s and the late 1970s, reaching a relative peak of about 29 percent in 1980. During the 1980s, however, this category dropped sharply, falling below 18 percent of the budget by 1987. A small rebound occurred in the early 1990s, but this was a transient phenomenon caused largely by the bailout of the savings and loan industry and the recession. Projections in President Clinton's budget for fiscal year 1994 indicated that expenditures in this category would once again decline from 21 percent of the federal budget in 1992 to 18 percent in 1998, despite new domestic spending initiatives.[48] Continued growth in spending on health and the elderly, even under most health reform proposals, make it likely that this gradual decline may persist well into the next century.

TAXATION OF WORKERS

These actuarial deficits and fiscal pressures are taking place in a world where the Social Security tax system has already matured. An era of constant and continual growth in Social Security payroll tax rates—3 percentage points per decade, from 3 percent of taxable wages in 1950 to 6 percent in 1960, to 9.6 percent in 1970, to 12.26 percent in 1980, to 15.3 percent in 1990—appears to have come to an end. As yet, no tax rate increase is scheduled after 1990.

Social Security tax rates, in fact, have finally reached such a level that serious proposals are emerging to reduce the rates. Most notable among these is one by Senator Daniel Patrick Moynihan (D.-N.Y.), which would have reduced the current Social Security tax rate from

15.3 percent to about 13.1 percent, returning the system to a pay-as-you-go basis. This and other proposals have been motivated by concerns that payroll taxes are regressive and are being improperly used to finance general government spending. The relative merits and problems associated with a Moynihan-type proposal are discussed in fuller detail in chapter 7 in this volume. The important point here is that such a proposal was seriously considered and gained widespread public attention, suggesting, at a minimum, that future increases in payroll tax rates may be more controversial and difficult to achieve than in the past.

Social Security and Economic Growth

Stronger economic growth always makes it easier to deal with budgetary pressures, whether they arise in Social Security, from the deficit itself, or from any other pressure on government. Likewise, slower economic growth tends to exacerbate fiscal problems. Many economists have noted that strong, sustained economic growth is crucial to our ability to meet the future demands of an aging population, and have suggested a variety of measures, including deficit reduction and greater public investment, as means for achieving that goal.[49] It is indeed true that America's ability to provide for its elderly in the next century will depend heavily on the productivity of its economy at that time.

Although economic growth is almost always advantageous, one should not be misled regarding what it would achieve. Even very high rates of economic growth would not automatically solve the problems of imbalance in the Social Security system. Initially, higher-than-expected economic growth rates would increase Social Security tax receipts (which are based on wages) but not payments to those already retired (which are adjusted only for price changes). Benefit levels for each new generation of retirees, however, are tied to wage levels. As a result, benefit increases would gradually work their way into the system and would eventually force payouts from the trust funds that offset much of the gain in tax revenues. There would be some net improvement in the financial balance of the Social Security system, but not much. Actuarial analyses performed by the SSA have demonstrated that even major improvements in rates of real wage growth, all else being equal, would have only a marginal effect on the long-run fiscal balance of the system.[50] The system would still be imbalanced, taxes would still be insufficient to cover promised expenditures, and reform would still be required.[51]

Better-than-expected economic growth could also improve the financial situation for Medicare somewhat. The demand for and cost of health care, however, has often risen more than proportionately with income. Hence, economic growth might simply allow greater dollar amounts of health care to be consumed, without necessarily improving Medicare's financial status or reducing its pressure on the budget.[52]

The estimates reported here already presume healthy rates of economic growth over the long-term future. Average wages are projected to grow at a rate of 1.06 percent per year in real (inflation-adjusted) terms.[53] This appears reasonable in relation to the average rate between 1951 and 1990, which was 1.04 percent. This wage growth, however, has been much slower over the past two decades than in the 1950s and 1960s. It averaged only 0.05 percent annually between 1970 and 1990, and 0.58 percent per year between 1980 and 1990. Part of the slowdown during the 1970s may be attributed to a decline in the percentage of total compensation provided in the form of wages; employee benefits consumed a growing share of compensation. A real decline in productivity, however, was a more important factor.[54]

Predicting economic growth rates into the distant future is necessarily a very uncertain affair, and it is hard to say which historical period serves as the best guide. The performance of the fifties and early sixties may have been a historical aberration, resulting from unprecedented improvements in productivity and technology following a long period of pent-up demand.[55] Recent experience could simply represent a return to more normal rates of economic growth. On the other hand, the last 20 years may have been part of a temporary cyclical downturn, implying that growth rates will rebound to a somewhat higher average level over the long-run future. The SSA's projections take the latter view. If real wage and productivity growth in the future were to more closely resemble that of the past 20 years, however, all of the future fiscal problems we have just discussed would be exacerbated.

Finally, healthy long-term economic growth doesn't just "happen." It is achieved partly through saving and investment. Greater saving and investment mean less consumption today—a temporary cost that all segments of American society, including Social Security recipients and taxpayers, may be called upon to share. If deficit reduction or investment in education are among the measures used to try to promote long-term growth, for instance, then such efforts will create additional pressures to reduce other expenditures or to increase taxes.

CONCLUSION

The Social Security system is out of balance. When regarded as a self-contained program, Social Security suffers from long-run actuarial deficits that will eventually require either tax increases or benefit reductions. When examined in the broader context of the overall federal budget, the situation appears even more challenging. It is also clear, given these fiscal constraints, that any efforts to meet additional needs of the elderly or to improve the equity and efficiency of the system will require difficult, explicit trade-offs to be made. Since reform is inevitable, it is important now to begin to distinguish between appropriate and inappropriate options.

Reform of the OASI retirement benefit system, by itself, is a manageable task, if dealt with in a timely and responsible fashion. The tremendous growth expected in Medicare and other health programs, however, creates much more difficult fiscal pressures. This growth will force difficult choices not only within our health care programs but in all government programs, including Old Age and Survivors Insurance.

One reason for acting soon is that individuals make plans on the basis of expectations. Expectations of Social Security benefits strongly affect decisions about age of retirement, private saving patterns, and consumption levels before and after retirement. In addition, reforms in Social Security could require other institutional changes, such as alteration in the design of private pension plans, that could themselves take years to be put in place. For these reasons it is very difficult at any given time to change significantly the benefits of current or near-future retirees. Delay in reform, however, puts increasing pressure on policymakers to implement changes that will affect recipients immediately, without any time delay that would allow people to adjust their plans. It could also increase the extent to which benefits would have to be cut, taxes raised, or both.

We know that expectations formed around existing tax rates and existing benefit formulas cannot be entirely accurate—as already noted, the two are incompatible. Fortunately, taxes are currently sufficient to support benefits for the near future, implying that changes can gradually be phased in if they are enacted relatively soon.

The next few years should be viewed as a crucial period of opportunity during which the nation should be readying itself for the demands of the future. We should not be lulled into inaction by the relative stability of retiree-to-worker ratios in the near term, while a potent demographic challenge looms right around the corner. Rather than responding later to a crisis that could have been avoided, policymakers should prudently prepare for the inevitable—so that Social Security recipients and taxpayers can in turn prepare prudently for their own futures.

Notes

1. Authors' calculations based on SSA cohort life tables (U.S. Social Security Administration, Office of the Actuary 1992a, and unpublished tables). These same probabilities were used for the intermediate assumptions in the 1992 OASDI Trustees annual report (Board of Trustees, OASDI 1992).

2. Source: Gina Kolata, "New Views on Life Spans Alter Forecasts on Elderly," *The New York Times.* Nov. 16, 1992, p. 1, and comments by Steven Goss of the Social Security Administration's Office of the Actuary. Among recent research cited is a study of Swedish population records dating back to 1750. These records indicated that "the mortality rate among those over age 85 remained steady until about 1950 but has steadily dropped since then at a rate of about 2 percent per year." Data from 27 other countries also indicated a "steady, sustained" increase since 1950 in life expectancies of those over age 85. Other research examining the longevity of human twins and insects provided evidence that appears to contradict the hypothesis of a genetically programmed maximum lifespan.

A separate study by Lee and Carter (1992) also predicted greater improvement in life expectancy over the next century than does the SSA. Lee and Carter extrapolated future improvements in mortality rates based purely on historical trends since 1900, using standard statistical time-series methods. They predicted a period life expectancy at birth of 86.05 by 2065, in contrast to the 80.45 intermediate estimate of the SSA (Lee and Carter 1992: 668).

3. U.S. Bureau of Labor Statistics (1989: 25–27, and 1992), and Fullerton (1991: 36). The civilian labor force participation rate is defined as the percentage of the noninstitutionalized population aged 16 or above, excluding resident armed forces, that is working or actively looking for work.

4. U.S. Social Security Administration, Office of the Actuary (1993: 247). Note that this figure represents the average age at which Social Security OASI benefits are awarded, which is lower than the average age at which people stop working. An act passed in 1956 allowed OASI benefit payments to women between ages 62 and 64; another act in 1961 extended this option to men.

5. U.S. Social Security Administration (1993: 247). In 1991, 46.8 percent of male and 56.1 percent of female retired-worker awards were made at age 62. 65.8 percent of male retired-worker awards and 72.7 percent of female retired-worker awards occurred at ages 62 through 64.

6. The average remaining life expectancy for people turning 62 in 1992 is estimated at 17.0 for males, 21.6 for females, and 25.2 for the longest-living member of a couple (Source: see note 1 above). Life expectancy for the longest-living member of a couple is greater than that of either individual member because the probability that any one member of a two-person group will survive through a given year is greater than the

probability that one specific member of the group will survive through that year. For example, suppose two people each have a 50 percent chance of dying in a given year. The probability that *both* will be dead at the end of the year is only 25 percent (0.5 × 0.5 = 0.25). Note that these calculations do not take into account differences in survival probabilities between single persons and married persons (married persons tend to live longer).

7. Where spouses are younger than the worker receiving benefits, the spouse benefit itself is delayed until age 62, thus lowering the value of initial benefits paid to the couple. In later years, however, there is a greater probability that a spouse will receive survivors benefits, which are paid at a rate even higher than spousal benefits.

8. Part of the ongoing debate over benefit levels, for instance, centers on the incomes of the elderly, including income derived from current Social Security benefits. Those who retire early receive reduced annual benefits, and over their remaining lives help to depress the measure of the average annual income of the elderly.

9. The exact saving would depend on a wide variety of variables, including options for early retirement, how the benefit formula would have counted the additional years of work, and, at any point in time, the age distribution of Social Security beneficiaries. Since younger Social Security beneficiaries have higher levels of benefits than the older beneficiaries, the saving would likely be more than proportional to the decline in number of beneficiaries.

10. The new rules apply to those turning 65 in those years.

11. Source: See note 6 above.

12. Technically, the "total fertility rate" is "the average number of children who would be born to a woman in her lifetime if she were to experience the birth rates by age observed in, or assumed for, the selected year, and if she were to survive the entire child-bearing period" (Board of Trustees, OASDI 1993: 66).

13. U.S. Social Security Administration, Office of the Actuary (1992b: 3).

14. Board of Trustees, OASDI (1992: 66).

15. The SSA's 1993 intermediate projections assume that total net immigration (legal and nonlegal immigration less emigration) will ultimately rise to 850,000 per year. During the 1980s, it is estimated that the total net immigration rate hovered around 650,000 per year. A sensitivity analysis conducted by the SSA suggests that OASDI's 75-year actuarial balance would improve by 0.05 percent of taxable payroll for each 100,000 increase in the net immigration assumption. A larger-than-expected increase in immigration would thus improve Social Security's financial situation, but the increase would have to be extremely large to have a very significant impact (Board of Trustees, OASDI 1993: 64, 141–42). Thomas Espenshade of Princeton University has unpublished estimates that demonstrate that immigration would need to increase by millions per year to have a significant impact on worker-to-retiree ratios.

16. U.S. Bureau of Labor Statistics (1989: 25–27, and 1993: 74), and Fullerton (1991: 36).

17. More-detailed discussions of this issue are offered in chapters 4, 5, and 9.

18. One study, for instance has suggested that female labor force participation rates are likely to level off after the year 2000 (Johnston and Packer 1987: chap. 3). Among the reasons cited are an already-stagnant participation rate among women aged 55–64, and polls indicating that the majority of working mothers want to work less than they do now. The Bureau of Labor Statistics has also predicted that growth rates in female and overall participation will be significantly slower between 1990 and 2005 than they were between 1975 and 1990 (Fullerton 1991: 33–34).

19. Authors' calculations based on data from Board of Trustees, OASDI (1993: 129, 152).

20. "OASI beneficiaries" includes some "nonelderly" people, such as young dependents and survivors. Our purpose in table 3.4 is not to compare the number of beneficiaries with the size of the population over age 65, but to show that the two move hand-in-hand.

21. This simple statement ignores some complicating factors. As previously noted, most people are expected to respond to the scheduled increases in the Normal Retirement Age by accepting reduced benefits rather than delying retirement. Since a greater portion of benefits will be subject to early retirement penalties, average benefits will grow somewhat more slowly than wages in the long run. In addition, income taxation of OASDI benefits is expected to increase over time, and this may be regarded as a reduction in net benefit outlays (see chapter 8). Finally, cash wages have been declining as a share of employee compensation. So long as this trend persists, cash wages subject to Social Security tax will not grow as fast as the economy, and benefits based on those wages will also be reduced. These factors help explain why the ratio of OASDI beneficiaries to covered workers is projected to increase by about 60 percent between now and 2030, while the ratio of OASDI benefits (less income taxes on benefits) to gross domestic product (GDP) is projected to increase by only about 25 percent over that period.

22. Total health expenditures in the United States grew from 5.3 percent of GDP in 1960 to 12.1 percent of GDP in 1990. (Economic Report of the President 1993; Levit et al. 1991). Over the same period the percentage of the population aged 65 or over grew from 9.1 percent to 12.3 percent. See Newhouse (1992) for a discussion of the sources of growth in health care spending.

23. Note that a number of different actuarial tests and benchmarks are often used in the evaluation of Social Security financing. For instance, a short-range actuarial test, based on projections over the next 10 years, plays an important role in Social Security policymaking. For a trust fund to meet the short-term adequacy test, its reserves must remain at or above 100 percent of annual outlays over each of the next 10 years. In the event that the trust fund is already below 100 percent of outlays, it should be projected to rise to 100 percent within 5 years and then remain at or above 100 percent for the remaining years. Failure to meet the short-term test of adequacy has traditionally been much more likely to prompt legislative action than has long-term inadequacy.

24. Board of Trustees, OASDI (1993: 117).

25. Board of Trustees, OASDI (1993: 29, 117).

26. Board of Trustees, OASDI (1992 and 1983).

27. Board of Trustees, OASDI (1993: 119).

28. HI benefit expenditures were 3.01 percent of taxable payroll in calendar year 1992, while the payroll tax rate was 2.9 percent (Board of Trustees, HI 1993: 19).

29. In the 1993 HI Trustees report, the intermediate projections estimate trust fund exhaustion in 1999 (Board of Trustees, HI 1993: 3).

30. Increased revenues from removing the HI tax cap are estimated at $6 billion in fiscal year (FY) 1995 (Office of Management and Budget 1993b: 12; henceforth, OMB). This represents slightly more than 6 percent of the $94.7 billion in HI payroll tax revenues already projected for FY 1995 (Board of Trustees, HI 1993: 8).

31. Ibid., p. 20.

32. Ibid., p. 22.

33. The Omnibus Budget Reconciliation Act of 1990 included $42.5 billion dollars in Medicare premium increases and spending cuts for fiscal years 1991 through 1995. Total Medicare spending (minus premiums) during those years was projected to be $678.3 billion before enactment of those cuts (OMB 1990: D-7). Three years later, however, the OMB estimated that Medicare spending over this five-year span would total $674.2 billion, or only $4.1 billion lower than the projected baseline before the

cuts (OMB 1993b: 165). Thus, increases in Medicare costs appear to have offset almost all of the 1990 cuts. This has occurred despite a significantly lower rate of general inflation than was predicted in 1990. The HCFA's best estimate of the 75-year actuarial deficit in HI, meanwhile, worsened from 3.62 percent of taxable payroll in 1990 to 5.11 percent in 1993 (Board of Trustees, HI 1990: 7 and 1993: 22).

34. In calendar year 1992, contributions from the general funds of the federal government accounted for 72.3 percent of all SMI income, while interest payments from the federal government accounted for an additional 3.1 percent (Board of Trustees, HI 1992: 1). Initially Medicare recipients were required to pay 50 percent of SMI costs. Later, annual increases in SMI premiums were required by law to be no greater than the cost-of-living adjustments (COLAs) applied to OASDI benefits. Since SMI program costs grew much faster than the rate of inflation, premiums gradually decreased to slightly less than a quarter of total program costs. In recent years, ad hoc legislation has suspended the COLA-only adjustment and maintained premium cost at roughly one-quarter of program costs (U.S. Congress, House Committee on Ways and Means 1992: 188). The Omnibus Budget Reconciliation Act of 1993 extends the 25 percent premium guideline through 1998.

35. For a more detailed discussion of the implications of Social Security surpluses, particularly their impact on national saving and future productivity, see Weaver (1990) and Aaron, Bosworth, and Burtless (1989).

36. SMI premiums and income taxes on OASDI benefits are treated here as reductions in net spending because we are interested primarily in the total amount of economic resources that will have to be transferred from the working generation to the retired generation at any one point in time. Offsetting contributions by retirees effectively reduce these transfers.

Data for years 1950 to 1998 are on a fiscal year basis and are derived from OMB historical tables and President Clinton's FY 1994 budget estimates (OMB 1993a, b). Data for years after 1999 are on a calendar-year basis and come from Board of Trustees, OASDI, HI, and SMI (1993), intermediate projections. We adjust all projections for the estimated impact of increased benefit taxation and Medicare cuts enacted in 1993.

37. Gross domestic product in calendar year 1993 is estimated at $6.254 trillion (OMB 1993b: 6); 1.2 percent of this is about $75 billion.

38. Federal individual income tax receipts in FY 1994 are estimated at $560 billion, or 8.6 percent of GDP (OMB 1993b: 11). Income taxes would have to be increased by 20.3 percent to raise revenues equivalent to 1.2 percent of GDP $(1.2 \div 8.6 = .14)$.

The federal individual income tax base in 1988 (the latest year for which data are available) was approximately 49.7 percent of personal income (Bakija and Steuerle 1991: 461). Personal income was approximately 83.2 percent of GDP in 1988 (U.S. Bureau of Economic Analysis 1992b). Thus, the income tax base was about 41.6 percent of GDP $(.497 \times .832 = .414)$. Increasing individual income taxes by 1.2 percent of GDP would therefore require that all marginal rates be raised by about 2.9 percentage points $(1.2 \div .414 = 2.9)$.

39. In 1993 individual income tax receipts equaled 8.6 percent of GDP; raising another 6.1 percent of GDP would thus require receipts to rise by 7.1 percent relative to 1993 levels.

40. In FY 1993, total federal expenditures—excluding OASDI and Medicare and counting SMI premiums and taxes on OASI benefits as offsetting receipts—were 16.8 percent of GDP. If those expenditures were cut by 6.1 percent of GDP, the reduction would be about 36 percent.

41. Between 1970 and 1990, total Medicare outlays per enrollee increased from $1,388 to $3,717 in constant 1993 dollars. This amounted to a real annual growth rate of 5.05 percent. According to our calculations, the average Medicare outlay per enrollee

would increase to $13,212 in constant 1993 dollars by 2030 under the HCFA's intermediate projections. This represents a real average annual growth rate of 3.22 percent.

42. According to an analysis by the Congressional Budget Office, spending on the elderly accounted for roughly 28.3 percent of total federal outlays in FY 1990, and is expected to grow to 33.9 percent by FY 1995. As a percentage of federal noninterest domestic spending, this amounted to 46.1 percent in 1990 and will grow to 61.7 percent in 1995 (U.S. Congress, House Committee on Ways and Means 1992: 1579). For a fuller discussion of the growth of spending on the elderly relative to other federal government functions, see Penner (1991 and 1993).

43. The historical data and projections in figure 3.2 are derived from OMB (1993a, b). These projections include the estimated effects of presidential proposals contained in Clinton's FY 1994 budget.

44. More specifically, "other retirement and disability" includes Supplemental Security Income (SSI), railroad retirement, pensions for government employees, military pensions, pensions for disabled and elderly veterans, and benefits for disabled coal miners. "Other health" includes federal grants for Medicaid, veterans' health benefits, federal civilian employee health benefits, health research, education and training of the health work force, consumer and occupational health and safety, and a small amount of miscellaneous health expenditures.

Some additional spending on health and the elderly falls into the other categories in figure 3.4. Health benefits for military personnel could not be separated out and are included in the "military" category. In addition, some federal spending goes to the elderly through programs such as Food Stamps and housing assistance; this falls into the "all other spending" category. For a more detailed discussion of what is included in the various spending categories, see OMB (1988: sec. 5).

45. In FY 1990, we estimate that 69.4 percent of spending in these bottom four categories (see figure 3.4) (except veteran's health benefits, for which estimates are not available) went to individuals aged 65 or over (based on U.S. Congress, House Committee on Ways and Means 1992: 1579). An additional several percent went to "near-elderly" retirees and pensioners, such as OASI recipients aged 62 to 64, military and civil service pension recipients younger than 65, people who go on Disability Insurance in their early sixties, and so forth.

46. In FY 1990, about 87 percent of Medicare went to those over age 65. In addition, Medicaid support for persons aged 65 and over, mainly for indigent elderly in nursing homes, accounted for approximately 33 percent of federal outlays for that program. As a result, those aged 65 or older absorbed roughly 65 percent of total federal civilian health spending (U.S. Congress, House Committee on Ways and Means 1992: 1597, 1663; OMB 1993a).

47. The "military" category in figure 3.4 includes spending on national defense and the portion of veterans spending not directly related to pensions or health care.

48. Note that the FY 1993 budget of the Bush administration had projected this category would decline to 14 percent of the budget by 1997.

49. See, for example, Aaron et al. (1989); see also Weaver (1990) for further discussion of the issue.

50. The long-run average real wage growth assumption underlying the SSA's intermediate projections is 1.06 percent per year. If average real wages were to grow instead at 1.63 percent per year, the 75-year actuarial deficit of the OASDI system would be reduced by 0.62 percent of taxable payroll. Much of the improvement is due to the fact that contributions increase before benefits do, enabling the trust funds to earn additional interest income in the meantime. Nonetheless, an actuarial deficit of 0.84 percent of taxable payroll would remain. If real wages were to grow at a lower average annual rate of 0.58 percent, OASDI's 75-year actuarial deficit would be increased by 0.54 percent of taxable payroll (Board of Trustees, OASDI 1993: 143).

The changes in actuarial balance may appear significant, but are actually quite modest when one considers that these different wage–growth assumptions imply vastly different levels of economic performance over the long run. The more optimistic assumption implies a national economy, as well as payroll tax revenues, one-and-a-half times as large in real terms 75 years from now than does the intermediate assumption. Thus, a huge increase in the standard of living and in the real value of tax revenues yields only a marginal improvement in Social Security's fiscal balance.

51. Reform might be easier to obtain, of course, if the economic growth were used to reduce the non-Social Security deficit.

52. For a discussion of the demand for medical care, see Newhouse (1992).

53. The average wage measure used here is the same one used to index the Social Security benefit formulas. It is currently derived by dividing the total amount of wages and salaries reported on W-2 forms by the total number of full- and part-time employees. For the historical series and an explanation of the methodology behind this wage measure, see SSA, Office of the Actuary (1993: 22). The historical real wage growth figures were calculated by deflating nominal wages by the consumer price index for all urban consumers.

The best-estimate projections in the 1993 Social Security Trustees report assume that in the long-run future, the nominal average wage will grow at 5.1 percent annually, while inflation is assumed to be 4.0 percent per year. "Real wage growth" is thus approximately 1.06 percent $(1.051 \div 1.04 = 1.0106)$. This differs slightly from the "real wage differential," a measure referred to frequently in the Social Security Trustees reports, which is simply nominal wage growth minus inflation, or 1.1 percent in this case (see Board of Trustees, OASDI 1992: 57).

54. Total compensation per employee, as measured by the U.S. Bureau of Economic Analysis, grew at an average real annual rate of only 0.28 percent between 1970 and 1990 (deflated here by the CPI-U, for consistency's sake). Authors' calculations in this paragraph are based on data from the U.S. Bureau of Economic Analysis (various years).

55. According to a recent study (Baumol, Blackman, and Wolff 1989), productivity growth in the United States has exhibited much cyclical variation since 1908, but has not shown significant evidence of a long-term secular decline. Baumol and colleagues did note, however, that the two decades immediately after World War II represented an anomalous period of very high productivity growth following a long period of pent-up demand. They consider the growth pattern since 1965 to be a return to the normal historical trend in productivity growth.

A panel of technical experts from the fields of actuarial science and economics recently reviewed the assumptions underlying the SSA's projections. Based on an analysis that takes into account all wage growth experience since 1951, but weights recent experience most heavily, they recommended a real wage growth rate assumption of about 1.0 percent (see Social Security Technical Panel 1990: 17–18).

Chapter Four

BASIC FEATURES OF THE SOCIAL SECURITY SYSTEM

This chapter provides a brief overview of the Social Security system's basic features, focusing mainly on those components specifically directed at the elderly—the central emphasis of this book—while also touching upon other relevant federal programs.[1]

SOCIAL SECURITY PAYROLL TAX

The Social Security payroll tax is a flat-rate tax paid on all employment earnings up to a specified limit. The limit is increased every year to keep pace with wage growth. In 1993, all cash earnings up to $57,600 were subject to a tax of 15.3 percent, split evenly between employer and employee. At the beginning of 1993, 11.2 percentage points of the tax were devoted to Old-Age and Survivors Insurance (OASI), 1.2 percentage points were for Disability Insurance (DI), and 2.9 percentage points were set aside for Medicare Hospital Insurance (HI). Legislators were considering changing this mix soon; the most commonly discussed proposal would raise the DI rate to 1.75 percent in exchange for a reduction in the OASI rate to 10.65 percent.[2] Since 1991, the cap on earnings subject to the HI portion of the tax has been higher than that for Old-Age, Survivors, and Disability Insurance (OASDI). Deficit reduction legislation enacted in 1993 eliminated the HI cap entirely, so that all earnings are now subject to the 2.9 percent HI tax.

Table 4.1 illustrates how the payroll tax has changed over time. A rough rule of thumb traces the growth in tax rates between 1950 and 1990; *three percentage points per decade*. The rate of tax paid by employers and employees together equaled 3 percent in 1950, 6 percent in 1960, 9.6 percent in 1970, 12.26 percent in 1980, and 15.3 percent in 1990. The maximum amount of taxable earnings, or

Table 4.1 PAYROLL TAX RATES AND EARNINGS BASE, 1940–94

Year	Tax Rates (Combined employer and employee)				Earnings Base (Nominal dollars)	
	Total	OASI	DI	HI	OASDI	HI
1940	2.00	2.00	--	--	3,000	--
1950	3.00	3.00	--	--	3,000	--
1960	6.00	5.50	0.50	--	4,800	--
1970	9.60	7.30	1.10	1.20	7,800	7,800
1980	12.26	9.04	1.12	2.10	25,900	25,900
1990	15.30	11.20	1.20	2.90	51,300	51,300
1993 *	15.30	11.20	1.20	2.90	57,600	135,000
1994 **	15.30	10.65	1.75	2.90	59,700	No limit

Sources: SSA, Office of the Actuary (1990) and Board of Trustees, OASDI (1993)
Note: "Earnings Base" is the maximum earnings level subject to the payroll tax. Dashes
(—) denote program did not yet exist.
*Before tax rate reallocation between OASI and DI.
**Estimated, after enactment of 1993 deficit reduction act and tax rate reallocation
between OASI and DI.

"earnings base," has also been increased over time in real terms. By
1990, about 87 percent of all earnings in covered employment was
subject to OASDI taxation.[3]

Most economists agree that practically all of the burden of the
"employer" portion of the Social Security tax falls on the worker, who
effectively pays through reduced wages.[4] In a competitive market,
an employer will pay a worker total compensation—cash wages,
contributions to social insurance, employee benefits—commensurate
with the value of output produced by the worker. If the amount of
total compensation is fixed, an increase in the employer portion of
the payroll tax necessarily implies an equal decrease in some other
form of compensation, such as cash wages. Although this might not
occur in the short run if cash wages are inflexible, in the long run
firms can reduce the rate of wage growth and thus gradually shift
the burden to employees. Whereas there may be some small effect
on profits and other income of capital owners, few economists believe
that payroll taxes have a significant impact on this income.[5] Even if

some of the tax burden is passed on to the consumer through higher prices, the distribution of the burden would be similar, since a tax on consumption reduces the real value of wages and also tends to be regressive (Musgrave and Musgrave 1984: 497).

In any event, the full amount of the employer tax should be attributed to the worker when measuring the lifetime "individual equity" or "annuity value" of the system. Social Security taxes paid by an employer are analogous to contributions made to a private annuity or defined-contribution pension plan on a worker's behalf.[6]

When viewed by itself, the Social Security tax is regressive. Consider, for example, two workers in 1994, one making $20,000 and the other earning $200,000. The lower-income worker pays Social Security taxes (including the employer tax) equal to 15.3 percent of his or her wages. Because only a small portion of the higher-income worker's salary falls below the OASDI payroll tax limit, he or she pays Social Security taxes equal to just 6.6 percent of earnings. When measured as a percentage of total income, the payroll tax is even more regressive, since high-income persons are far more likely to receive large amounts of nonwage income, such as capital gains and dividends.[7] Thus, any progressivity within Social Security must derive from the way benefits are distributed in relation to taxes.

HOW OASI BENEFITS ARE RELATED TO PAST EARNINGS

Benefits have never been based directly on one's payroll tax contributions but, rather, on earnings upon which the taxes were paid. The process by which benefit payments are related to past earnings has changed frequently over the course of Social Security's history, but the basic idea has remained roughly the same. First, some measure of a worker's average monthly earnings subject to Social Security taxes over a number of years is calculated. Then a progressive benefit formula is applied to this earnings measure to determine the basic monthly benefit amount.

The current benefit calculation process has been in place since the 1977 amendments to the Social Security Act, and is summarized briefly here. It differs from previous practice mainly in that automatic indexing for wage and price growth plays a much larger role. Prior to the 1970s, adjustments in benefit levels and calculation procedures were made from time to time on an ad hoc basis. Automatic indexing was eventually enacted in 1972, and was then reformed and expanded in 1977 legislation, to prevent the rather arbitrary fluctuations in real benefit levels that had often occurred under the old method.[8]

Average Indexed Monthly Earnings (AIME)

The first step in the current benefit calculation process is the determination of average indexed monthly earnings (AIME). All earnings upon which a worker paid Social Security taxes from 1951 to the year he or she turned 60 are "wage indexed" to compensate for past inflation and real wage growth. To accomplish this, each year's wage is multiplied by an "indexing factor," which equals the ratio of the average national wage in the year the worker turns 60 to the average national wage in the year to be indexed.[9] For administrative convenience, wages earned at age 60 or later are left at their nominal values in the indexing process. From this set of earnings, the best 35 years[10] are selected, added together, and divided by 420 (the number of months in 35 years). The result is the AIME.

To illustrate how the AIME is calculated, table 4.2 displays earnings histories for some hypothetical workers turning 65 in 1995. We assume the "average"-wage worker has earnings equal to the SSA's measure of the average national wage, or wage index, in each year from age 21 to the year before OASI Normal Retirement Age (currently 65) is reached. The "low"-wage worker is assumed to earn 45 percent of the average wage, while the "high"-wage worker earns the maximum wage subject to OASDI taxation in each year. (We use workers with hypothetical earnings histories of this sort for illustrative purposes throughout this book.)

Consider the high-wage worker as an example. Since the AIME calculation only includes the best 35 years, we can drop the 9 lowest years of indexed earnings from 1951 to 1994,[11] which turn out to be 1953–54, 1957–58, and 1961–65. Adding up earnings in the remaining years and dividing by 420 yields an AIME of $3,224. Performing the same process on the wages of average- and low-wage workers yields AIMEs of $1,772 and $797, respectively (see table 4.2).

Primary Insurance Amount (PIA)

Next, the primary insurance amount (PIA) is calculated. The PIA is the basic monthly benefit paid to someone who has stopped working and then begins to collect benefits at the normal retirement age. To

Table 4.2 EARNINGS OF HYPOTHETICAL WORKERS TURNING 65 IN 1995

Year	Nominal Earnings			Indexing	Indexed Earnings		
	Low	Average	High	Factor	Low	Average	High
1951	1,260	2,799	3,600	7.5122	9,463	21,028	27,044
1952	1,338	2,973	3,600	7.0722	9,463	21,028	25,460
1953	1,413	3,139	3,600	6.6980	9,463	21,028	24,113
1954	1,420	3,156	3,600	6.6636	9,463	21,028	23,989
1955	1,486	3,301	4,200	6.3693	9,463	21,028	26,751
1956	1,590	3,532	4,200	5.9530	9,463	21,028	25,002
1957	1,639	3,642	4,200	5.7742	9,463	21,028	24,252
1958	1,653	3,674	4,200	5.7238	9,463	21,028	24,040
1959	1,735	3,856	4,800	5.4536	9,463	21,028	26,177
1960	1,803	4,007	4,800	5.2477	9,463	21,028	25,189
1961	1,839	4,087	4,800	5.1454	9,463	21,028	24,698
1962	1,931	4,291	4,800	4.9000	9,463	21,028	23,520
1963	1,978	4,397	4,800	4.7827	9,463	21,028	22,957
1964	2,059	4,576	4,800	4.5950	9,463	21,028	22,056
1965	2,096	4,659	4,800	4.5137	9,463	21,028	21,666
1966	2,222	4,938	6,600	4.2581	9,463	21,028	28,103
1967	2,346	5,213	6,600	4.0334	9,463	21,028	26,621
1968	2,507	5,572	7,800	3.7740	9,463	21,028	29,437
1969	2,652	5,894	7,800	3.5678	9,463	21,028	27,829
1970	2,784	6,186	7,800	3.3992	9,463	21,028	26,513
1971	2,924	6,497	7,800	3.2365	9,463	21,028	25,245
1972	3,210	7,134	9,000	2.9477	9,463	21,028	26,529
1973	3,411	7,580	10,800	2.7741	9,463	21,028	29,960
1974	3,614	8,031	13,200	2.6184	9,463	21,028	34,563
1975	3,884	8,631	14,100	2.4364	9,463	21,028	34,353
1976	4,152	9,226	15,300	2.2791	9,463	21,028	34,870
1977	4,401	9,779	16,500	2.1502	9,463	21,028	35,479
1978	4,750	10,556	17,700	1.9920	9,463	21,028	35,259
1979	5,166	11,479	22,900	1.8318	9,463	21,028	41,948
1980	5,631	12,513	25,900	1.6804	9,463	21,028	43,523
1981	6,198	13,773	29,700	1.5267	9,463	21,028	45,344
1982	6,539	14,531	32,400	1.4471	9,463	21,028	46,885
1983	6,858	15,239	35,700	1.3799	9,463	21,028	49,261
1984	7,261	16,135	37,800	1.3032	9,463	21,028	49,263
1985	7,570	16,823	39,600	1.2500	9,463	21,028	49,500
1986	7,795	17,322	42,000	1.2140	9,463	21,028	50,986
1987	8,292	18,427	43,800	1.1412	9,463	21,028	49,984
1988	8,700	19,334	45,000	1.0876	9,463	21,028	48,943
1989	9,045	20,100	48,000	1.0462	9,463	21,028	50,217
1990	9,463	21,028	51,300	1.0000	9,463	21,028	51,300
1991	9,841	21,812	53,400	1.0000	9,841	21,812	53,400
1992	10,184 *	22,631 *	55,500	1.0000	10,184 *	22,631 *	55,500
1993	10,544 *	23,432 *	57,600	1.0000	10,544 *	23,432 *	57,600
1994	11,000 *	24,444 *	60,000 *	1.0000	11,000 *	24,444 *	60,000 *
Average Indexed Annual Earnings					9,569	21,262	38,687
Average Indexed Monthly Earnings					797	1,772	3,224

Source: U.S. Congress, House Committee on Ways and Means (1992: 11).
Notes: "Average" wage is equal to the SSA average wage index; "High" wage is equal to the maximum wage subject to OASDI taxation; "Low" wage is equal to 45 percent of the average wage.
*Intermediate projection from Board of Trustees, OASDI (1993).

determine this PIA, a progressive benefit formula is applied to the worker's AIME. This formula works something like a progressive income tax schedule, but in reverse. There are three brackets with successively decreasing rates, and benefits are a higher percentage of one's AIME the lower one's AIME is. For workers turning 65 in 1995 (born in 1930),[12] the formula for determining the PIA is: 90 percent of AIME below $387, plus 32 percent of AIME between $387 and $2,333, plus 15 percent of AIME above $2,333.

For our hypothetical workers, the formula results in tentative PIAs (before any cost-of-living adjustments) of $1,105 for the high-wage worker, $792 for the average-wage worker, and $480 for the low-wage worker. These PIAs replace approximately 34 percent, 45 percent, and 60 percent of AIME for the high-, average-, and low-wage workers, respectively.

Beginning at age 62, the PIA is subject to a cost-of-living adjustment (COLA) every year.[13] This has the effect of keeping the PIA constant in real (inflation-adjusted) terms after age 62. From then on, the real value of the PIA will increase only if the worker has earnings at age 62 or later that are high enough to displace earlier years in the AIME calculation. After the application of COLAs from ages 62 to 64, for example, our hypothetical average-wage worker would be eligible for a PIA of approximately $866 upon retirement at age 65 in 1995.[14]

The PIA formula also has its own brand of "wage indexing." The dividing points between the different brackets in the formula ($387 and $2,333, in our example) are known as "bend points." These bend points are determined for each cohort (i.e., group of people born in the same year) when they reach age 62, and remain fixed thereafter.[15] Bend points are increased for each successive cohort to keep pace with average wage growth in the economy. For example, because average wages grew by about 3.7 percent between 1990 and 1991, the bend points in the PIA formula for those turning 62 in 1993 are 3.7 percent higher than for those turning 62 in 1992, rising to $401 and $2,420. Meanwhile, the percentage rates in the PIA formula (i.e., 90 percent, 32 percent, and 15 percent) remain unchanged. If the bend points in the PIA formula were unindexed, or indexed only for inflation, each successive cohort of retirees would find that its earnings grew faster than the bend points and that a larger portion of its AIME fell into the upper brackets of the formula. As a result, PIAs would gradually decline as a percentage of AIME for each new generation. Eventually, almost all new retirees would find most of their AIME falling into the 15 percent bracket. Wage indexing of bend points, by contrast, tends to keep the ratio between PIA and AIME constant for people with similar relative earnings histories but different birth years, and keeps average benefit levels for each successive cohort growing at roughly the same rate as average wages in the economy.

A "special minimum PIA" guarantee is available to workers who paid Social Security taxes for many years and earned wages that were very low, but not so low as to lack Social Security coverage. Since the guarantee is rather small, however, it affects the benefit levels of less than 1 percent of OASDI recipients.[16]

Those who contributed to the system for only a few years or earned extremely low wages are generally ineligible for benefits. To qualify for OASI, workers turning 65 in 1995 must have earned at least 40 "quarters of coverage" in employment covered by Social Security. In 1993, a worker received 1 quarter of coverage for each $590 in covered earnings, up to a maximum of 4 quarters per year; this base amount is indexed to keep pace with wages. A worker who meets these requirements is "fully insured."

OTHER IMPORTANT ADJUSTMENTS TO BENEFITS

Once the PIA is calculated, a variety of adjustments may be made that can have a major impact on the net benefit amount paid to a worker and his or her dependents. Among the most significant are adjustments for early or delayed retirement, spousal and survivors benefits, and income taxation of benefits. Many of these adjustments have only a tenuous relationship to one's lifetime tax contributions or earnings history.

Adjustments for Early or Delayed Retirement

When workers retire earlier or later than the normal retirement age, their benefits typically are reduced or supplemented to some degree. If our hypothetical workers were to fully retire at age 62, for example, they would receive a monthly benefit equal to 80 percent of their PIA for the rest of their lives; if they delayed retirement until age 67, their monthly benefits would be 109 percent of PIA. In addition, an "earnings test" reduces or eliminates the benefits of those between ages 62 and 70 who have substantial employment earnings, although this reduction is at least partially compensated with higher benefits later. Although the Normal Retirement Age for OASI has remained 65 since the program's inception, legislation enacted in 1983 will cause it to rise gradually to 67 for those retiring during the next century. These features are discussed in greater detail in chapters 8 and 9.

Spousal and Survivors Benefits

Additional benefits are available for dependents and survivors of an insured worker. The rules governing these benefits apply equally to men and women, but the vast majority of these supplementary benefits currently go to retired wives and widows. A husband (or wife) of any insured worker is eligible, upon reaching age 65, to receive a "spousal benefit" equal to 50 percent of the worker's PIA. If the insured worker dies, a widowed spouse aged 65 or older may receive a "survivors benefit," which equals 100 percent of the worker's PIA. Spouses and survivors who retire before age 65 are eligible to receive a reduced benefit.

A spouse is often entitled to a benefit based on his own earnings record, as well as for being the spouse or survivor of an insured worker. The spouse then receives an amount equal to the larger of the two available benefits. A beneficiary is labeled as "dually entitled" if she earned enough to qualify for her own benefit, but receives a spouse's benefit based on her higher-earning spouse's record instead. That is, a dually entitled beneficiary has her own personal benefit "supplemented" until it reaches the level of the spousal or survivors benefit available to her.

Spousal and survivors provisions have at least some effect on the benefits of most women over the course of their retirements. Many women do not earn enough to qualify for their own benefits, while many more only qualify for worker's benefits that are less than 50 percent of their husband's PIA. Even many women who initially receive a benefit based solely on their own earnings eventually receive a survivors benefit based on their husband's earnings record.

In 1991, 24 percent of female beneficiaries aged 62 or over were considered dually entitled (i.e., the benefits based on their own earnings were less than the spousal or survivors benefits available because of their husbands). About 37 percent were receiving benefits that were based entirely on their own earnings histories. These women may have also been eligible for a spousal benefit, but the benefit based on their own earnings was higher. The remaining 39 percent were listed as receiving benefits based solely on their husband's earnings record. This category includes a large number of women who had not earned enough to qualify for any benefits on their own. It also includes some women (perhaps one-sixth of the total) who may have been eligible for benefits on their own, but became widowed before age 62 and thus received survivors benefits immediately upon retirement.[17] The percentage of women falling into the first two categories can be expected to increase significantly during the next century as a result of higher female labor force participation.

Several other kinds of supplementary benefits are also available in some circumstances. For example, surviving dependent children aged 18 or under are generally eligible for benefits equal to 75 percent of a deceased parent's PIA. A widowed spouse of any age may receive a survivors benefit equal to 75 percent of the PIA if caring for an eligible child under age 16. If the surviving spouse has employment earnings, his or her benefits are subject to an earnings test. In the event of remarriage before age 60, the spouse's survivors benefit will usually be terminated. In both cases, surviving children generally will still be eligible for full benefits. A divorced spouse who was married for at least 10 years is also eligible for full spousal and survivors benefits during retirement, in the same way as a nondivorced spouse.

A "maximum family benefit" restriction is placed on the total amount of benefits that can be paid in any month to a worker and to his or her dependents or survivors based on that worker's earnings record. Maximum benefits are limited to between 150 percent and approximately 187.5 percent of a worker's PIA, depending on the size of the PIA.[18] Note that this limit is applied separately to each worker's benefit within a family. For example, each spouse in a two-earner couple can receive a full worker's benefit based on his or her own PIA without any reduction.

Taxation of Benefits

Throughout most of Social Security's history, benefits were completely exempt from federal income taxation. As a result of 1983 Social Security Amendments, however, up to one-half of benefits could be included in the taxable income of certain households with higher incomes. Deficit reduction legislation enacted in 1993 then raised the maximum portion of benefits that can be subject to taxation from 50 percent to 85 percent.

The rules governing taxation of benefits are complicated. If the sum of a retiree's adjusted gross income (AGI),[19] tax-free interest income, and one-half of OASDI benefits exceeds an initial threshold amount ($25,000 for a single taxpayer or $32,000 for a joint return), then some portion of OASDI benefits will be subject to taxation. Above this threshold, taxability is phased in gradually; for every dollar by which this sum exceeds the threshold, 50 cents' worth of OASDI benefits become included in taxable income. Legislation enacted in 1993 introduced a second set of thresholds: $34,000 for a single taxpayer and $44,000 for a joint return. For every dollar that the sum of AGI, tax-free interest, and one-half of OASDI benefits exceeds these secondary thresholds, 85 cents' worth of OASDI benefits become taxable. The maximum proportion of OASDI benefits that can be included in taxable income will be limited to 85 percent.

As an example, suppose an elderly married couple has an AGI of $37,000, no tax-exempt interest income, and an OASI benefit of $18,000 in 1995. AGI plus one-half of the OASI benefit is $46,000. The amount of OASI benefits subject to tax will equal 50 percent of the amount between the first and second thresholds, plus 85 percent of the amount above the second threshold (but no more than 85 percent of benefits). Performing the calculation

$$0.5 \times (\$44,000 - \$32,000) \qquad (4.1)$$
$$+ \ 0.85 \times (\$46,000 - \$44,000) = \$7,700.$$

Thus, we find that $7,700, or about 43 percent of OASI benefits, will be included in the couple's taxable income. Since this couple is in the 15-percent federal income tax bracket, they would pay a tax of $1,155 on their benefits. This tax burden amounts to about 6.4 percent of their OASI benefit.

Around 22 percent of all OASDI beneficiaries currently are above the first set of thresholds, and thus pay at least some income tax on their benefits.[20] Most of these payments are small; tax payments amounted to only about 2 percent of total benefit payments in recent years.[21] Because the thresholds are not indexed for inflation, more and more people's benefits will gradually become subject to taxation in the future. Even so, the future impact will still be modest. Under the old tax law, the SSA's best-estimate projections suggested that by 2030 income taxation of benefits would have recaptured 4.3 percent of total benefit outlays.[22] Raising the maximum taxable amount to 85 percent will probably increase this by around 3 percent of benefit outlays. It will modestly increase the tax burden on most people who would already be subject to benefit taxation anyway, without having much impact on the number of people affected. When combined with the 1993 increase in top income tax rates, a very small number of retirees with extremely high incomes could lose about a third of their benefits to taxation.[23] Most people with high lifetime earnings, however, will be in low tax-rate brackets during retirement. Much of their income in retirement is not subject to tax, as it represents capital income that can be sheltered in the form of equity in one's home or capital gains assets for which income is never recognized or recognized only sporadically.

MEDICARE

Medicare, an extremely important and rapidly growing component of the Social Security system, was established in 1965. It consists of two parts: Part A, or Hospital Insurance (HI); and Part B, or Supplementary Medical Insurance (SMI). The Hospital Insurance program is financed by the 2.9 percent HI portion of the Social Security payroll tax. About one-quarter of SMI costs are covered by monthly premiums that are deducted directly from the Social Security checks of program recipients. The SMI premium is set at $41.10 per month for 1993. The remaining three-quarters of SMI program costs are paid for out of general revenues of the federal government. Everyone who reaches age 65 becomes covered by HI automatically, provided they made at least a minimal amount of contributions through the HI payroll tax. Those who did not contribute enough during their career to be automatically eligible may obtain HI coverage by paying a special monthly premium. SMI technically is voluntary and available to anyone aged 65 or over who pays the premium; the subsidies are so large, however, that nearly all elderly people choose to enroll. Both programs also cover a few other categories of people, such as those receiving Social Security disability benefits (after a two-year waiting period) and people with severe kidney disease. Nearly 90 percent of Medicare spending goes to people aged 65 or over.

Among the expenses covered by Medicare Hospital Insurance are: "reasonable" expenses for the first 60 days of an inpatient hospital stay above a single deductible amount ($676 in 1993); an additional 30 days of hospital stay, subject to a per-day coinsurance payment ($169 in 1993); and, for stays longer than 90 days, a "lifetime reserve" of 60 days, although this is subject to a large coinsurance payment ($338 per day in 1993).[24] Supplementary Medical Insurance, on the other hand, generally pays 80 percent of "recognized" fees for doctors' services and a variety of medical procedures, subject to an annual deductible of $100. Continual attempts to reform health and reduce government Medicare expenditures imply that significant changes may be forthcoming in the ways in which these benefits are provided.

Medicare is considered a "secondary payer" for people who are covered as active employees by private employer health insurance. In other words, Medicare will only pay for health care costs not covered by one's employer-provided health policy. Firms with 20 or more employees are required to offer workers aged 65 or over the same health benefits they offer everyone else, although an elderly worker may choose to forgo the private coverage and be covered only by Medicare.

Neither HI nor SMI covers long-term care in a nursing home or one's own home. Many elderly persons who require such services have to pay for it themselves or, when they have depleted enough of their resources, must rely on Medicaid, another government program discussed in the next section.

OTHER RELEVANT PROGRAMS

Disability Insurance

Social Security's Disability Insurance (DI) program provides earnings-related disability pensions to disabled workers who are younger than the Normal Retirement Age, as well as to their dependents. This book focuses mainly on policies for the elderly; nonetheless, DI's relationship to other parts of the Social Security system is important to the policy choices in OASI and Medicare.[25]

The DI program is similar in many ways to the Old-Age and Survivors portion of Social Security. Disability benefits are related to covered earnings in the same way as OASI benefits, except that a smaller number of years is included in the AIME calculation.[26] Workers who are younger than the Normal Retirement Age and meet certain minimum requirements for time spent in covered employment may apply for disability benefits. Eligibility for benefits is then determined through an administrative evaluation process, which may involve multiple appeals. To qualify for benefits, the worker must be found incapable of performing "substantial gainful activity," which is currently defined as the ability to earn at least $500 per month from employment (less impairment-related work expenses). Workers may qualify due to a broad range of impairments. The most common currently are mental disorders (24 percent of beneficiaries in 1991), musculoskeletal disorders (19.4 percent), and circulatory diseases (16.1 percent).[27]

If found eligible, a worker receives benefits equal to 100 percent of PIA, following a five-month waiting period from the onset of disability. If the worker has any dependent children under age 16, this benefit will generally be raised to 150 percent of PIA, the maximum allowable family benefit for disabled workers. Disability Insurance benefits may be terminated for three reasons: death, recovery, and attainment of the Normal Retirement Age. When disabled workers reach the Normal Retirement Age or die, they and their dependents or survivors switch over to OASI benefits.[28]

About 2.4 percent of men and 1.4 percent of women aged 16 through 64 were disabled-worker DI beneficiaries in 1991. A fairly large proportion of workers become eligible for DI benefits during their fifties and sixties. In 1991, about 10.5 percent of men aged 60–64, and 7.2 percent of men aged 55–59, were DI disabled-worker beneficiaries.[29] The percentage of the population receiving DI benefits has been increasing in recent years, and is expected to grow significantly in the future, especially as the baby boom population born after World War II begins to age. The number of disabled-worker beneficiaries per 100 covered workers, which stood at about 2.3 in 1990, is projected to more than double to 4.8 by 2010 under the SSA's 1993 intermediate assumptions.

The Disability Insurance trust fund was facing some serious financial difficulties as of the beginning of 1993. Expenditures were already exceeding revenues, and the small DI trust fund was projected to go bankrupt as early as 1995. As a result, a portion of the Social Security payroll tax was proposed for reallocation from OASI to DI. This action will shore up the DI trust fund, but it will obviously worsen the condition of the OASI trust fund by an equal amount.

Supplemental Security Income (SSI)

Supplemental Security Income (SSI) is a federal program, separate from the Social Security system,[30] that provides means-tested benefits to people who are disabled, blind, or aged 65 or over, and have very low incomes and assets.[31] Although this study does not provide a detailed examination of SSI, it is important to emphasize that SSI acts as another important safety net for the elderly, particularly those with little or no Social Security benefits. In 1991, about 5.1 million persons were receiving SSI benefits. Approximately 1.5 million of the elderly, or about 4.5 percent of the total population aged 65 or over, were recipients.

SSI program rules are rather complex; we offer only a brief sketch here. The maximum monthly federal SSI benefit was $422 for an individual and $633 for a couple in 1992, and is indexed every year to keep pace with inflation. Many states provide modest supplements to these benefit levels. Individuals and couples with "countable income" of less than these basic benefit amounts may be eligible for benefits.[32] Many recipients receive only partial benefits, since benefit levels are reduced by one dollar for each dollar of countable income. A strict asset test is also applied.[33]

SSI benefits effectively provide a floor of income for the elderly, blind, and severely disabled. This floor is not very high; the maximum federal SSI benefit amounted to about 78 percent of the official poverty line for single elderly persons, and 89 percent for elderly couples in 1991. State SSI supplements, Food Stamps, and disregarded Social Security benefits and earnings can bring this floor up to or above the poverty line for some recipients. Participation rates in the SSI program have traditionally been low. In 1990, only about 56 percent of elderly people with incomes below the poverty line participated in SSI; a much larger percentage was probably eligible.[34] Surveys conducted in the 1980s found that typically only 5 or 6 out of every 10 eligible elderly persons participated in SSI.[35]

Medicaid

Medicaid is a means-tested health program for the poor that is run jointly by the federal government and individual state governments. Eligibility is usually tied to participation in other means-tested welfare programs such as Aid to Families with Dependent Children and Supplemental Security Income; eligibility rules vary from state to state. Importantly, elderly persons who have very low incomes and few resources may become eligible for Medicaid. As a result, Medicaid sometimes pays for needs of the elderly that are not covered by Medicare, particularly long-term care in nursing homes. Many elderly people, when faced with difficult expenses such as long-term care, end up spending all of their assets and eventually qualify for Medicaid. In fiscal year 1990, about 3.2 million people aged 65 and over were Medicaid recipients. This amounted to about 10 percent of all people aged 65 or over, and 13 percent of all Medicaid recipients.

Expenditures on these elderly people were relatively large, accounting for approximately 33 percent of total Medicaid spending.[36]

Medicaid has been one of the fastest growing government programs in recent years, and its costs are expected to continue to rise dramatically. Federal spending on Medicaid is expected to be about $81 billion in fiscal year 1993, while state governments are expected to spend in the vicinity of $60 billion.[37] Federal Medicaid expenditures rose from 2.1 percent of total federal outlays in 1975 to an expected 5.5 percent in 1993. Medicaid is projected to account for 8.4 percent of the federal budget by 1998. Currently pending health care reform efforts would try to both control costs and simultaneously increase other subsidies to low-income individuals. Spending on Medicaid consumes an even larger share of most state budgets. A number of factors are responsible for this growth, including the rising cost of health care, rapidly growing enrollment, and some modest expansion of services.

Notes

1. For a more comprehensive discussion of current and historical features of the Social Security system, the definitive source is Myers (1993). See also U.S. Congress, House Committee on Ways and Means (1992, Sec. 1) or SSA, Office of the Actuary (1990).

2. H.R. 2264, which was passed by the U.S. House of Representatives in 1993, would have made this exchange of OASI and DI tax rates.

3. SSA, Office of the Actuary (1992b: 134).

4. See Pechman (1983: 215), Musgrave and Musgrave (1984: 497), or Pechman, Aaron, and Taussig (1968: 175–78) for a fuller discussion of the incidence of employer payroll taxes.

5. The after-corporate-tax income of capital owners (real retained earnings plus dividends plus net interest income) has remained fairly steady over the past five decades, hovering around 5 percent of net national product between 1940 and 1990. This has occurred despite a dramatic increase in payroll taxes over this period (see Steuerle 1992: 28).

6. Some private pension plans, particularly those with defined benefits, involve a number of rather arbitrary redistributions that may result in an employee receiving more or less than the fair annuity value of employer contributions made on his or her behalf. Nonetheless, the annuity value of employer and employee contributions remains the only standard against which the individual equity of such a system can be measured.

7. The Social Security payroll tax may also consume only a small percentage of the total income of very poor people whose income comes from nonwage sources such as Food Stamps, Aid to Families with Dependent Children (AFDC), and so forth.

8. The automatic indexing provisions first adopted in 1972 became effective in June 1974. The 1977 provisions became effective for those becoming eligible (for OASI, attaining age 62) in 1979.

9. The "average national wage" measure used by the SSA is essentially the total amount of wages reported on W-2 forms in the United States divided by the total number of workers, both full- and part-time. All wages, including those above the Social Security tax cap, are included. This measure is affected to some extent by the changing composition of the work force and the increasing prevalence of part-time and temporary work. As a result, it has grown somewhat more slowly than would a measure of wages for full-time equivalent workers. See Sandell (forthcoming) for a discussions of these issues.

10. The number of years included in average monthly earnings calculations has changed frequently throughout the history of the program. Under current law, workers turning 62 in 1992 or later will have 35 years of earnings included in their average indexed monthly earnings (AIME) calculation. This rule was phased in gradually, increasing from 23 years for those turning 62 in 1979. The number of years may be reduced if the worker was disabled for some period of time.

11. Note here that actual earnings after age 60 are used as indexed earnings in the calculation.

12. Technically, those born on January 1st of a given year are treated as part of the cohort born in the previous year. For example, the PIA formula for those turning 62 in 1992 would apply to those born on any day between January 2, 1930, and January 1, 1931, inclusive.

13. The Social Security COLA goes into effect every December. It is based on the increase in the Department of Labor's consumer price index for all urban wage earners and clerical workers between the third quarter of the current year and the third quarter of the preceding year. In the event that average wage growth is lower than CPI growth *and* trust fund balances are low (which is not now the case), the COLA is limited to the rate of growth in average wages (Myers 1985: 96).

14. This calculation is based on an actual December 1992 COLA of 3 percent and estimated COLAs of 3 percent for December 1993 and 3.1 percent for December 1994.

15. In the event of disability or death before age 62, the PIA formula is determined in the year in which death or disability occurs, although it is not necessarily fixed permanently.

16. In 1990, approximately 0.5 percent of OASDI beneficiaries had benefits based on the special minimum guarantee. The rules for calculating the guarantee are quite complex. Every year in which a worker earns wages subject to Social Security tax that exceed a threshold ($6,435 in 1992) is counted as a "creditable year." The number of creditable years above 10, but less than 30, is then multiplied by a specified amount ($24.60 for December 1992 through November 1993, adjusted each year according to the COLA) to determine the minimum PIA for that worker. Assuming COLAs of 3.4 percent in December 1993 and 3.6 percent in 1994, the low-income worker in our example (see text) would be eligible for a "special minimum PIA" guarantee of $527 at age 65. His benefit level would be unaffected, however, since the guaranteed minimum is less than the normally calculated PIA of $529 at age 65 (after application of COLAs). See Myers (1993b: 87) and SSA, Office of the Actuary (1992b, tables 2.A8 and 5.A8) for details.

17. SSA, Office of the Actuary (1993, Table 5.A14). Steven Sandell (forthcoming) estimates that about 1.25 million widows, or about 16 percent of women entitled as an auxiliary only, are actually eligible for benefits but had husbands who died before age 62.

18. The maximum family benefit for those who die or become eligible for OASDI in 1993 is: 150 percent of the first $513 of PIA, plus 272 percent of PIA between $513

and $740, plus 134 percent of PIA between $740 and $966, plus 175 percent of PIA above $966. As a result, the maximum can range between 150 percent and 187.5 percent of PIA (Myers 1993b: 92). The maximum family benefit for disabled workers is always 150 percent of PIA.

19. Adjusted gross income, as used for income tax purposes, includes such items as wages and salaries, taxable interest, dividends, capital gains, and most pension income.

20. The Congressional Budget Office has estimated that approximately 21.5 percent of all OASDI recipients paid at least some income tax on their benefits in 1993 (U.S. Congress, House Committee on Ways and Means 1992: 30). The new law will have little effect on this proportion, since it does not change the portion of benefits included in the test to see whether someone is subject to tax or not.

21. U.S. Congress, House Committee on Ways and Means (1992: 28–30)

22. Board of Trustees, OASDI (1993: 127, 181, and 185). In 2030, income taxation of benefits was projected to raise revenues equal to 0.70 percent of taxable payroll. Since taxable payroll in 2030 is projected at $19,535 billion, this amounts to $137 billion. Total OASDI outlays are projected at $3,174 billion. Hence, taxation of benefits is equal to 4.3 percent of total outlays (137 ÷ 3174 = .043).

23. The new effective top income tax rate (including the 10 percent surcharge and 1.2 percent itemized deduction phase-out) is 40.8 percent for people with taxable incomes above $250,000. Including 85 percent of benefits in taxable income will thus cost such a taxpayer 34.68 percent of benefits.

24. In 1993 HI also covered up to 100 days in a skilled nursing facility, subject to a coinsurance payment of $84.50 per day after the first 20 days. It also pays for a limited amount of home health services, and up to six months of hospice care for the terminally ill.

25. We address some issues in the DI program in an Urban Institute research report, "Social Security Disability Insurance: Fiscal Imbalance and Lifetime Value" (1993).

26. Currently, the number of years included in AIME for a disabled worker equals the number of years from age 22 to the age of disablement (or age 61, whichever is later) inclusive, minus between zero and five dropout years. The number of dropout years depends on one's age at disablement.

27. U.S. Social Security Administration (1993: 204).

28. The DI program interacts with OASI in an important way through the "disability freeze" provision. The number of years used in the AIME calculation for OASI benefits is reduced by one for every year spent on the DI rolls. As a result, being disabled for a few years may reduce one's OASI tax contributions without having much effect on the benefit level.

29. Authors' calculations based on data in U.S. Social Security Administration (1993).

30. Some of SSI's claims administration is performed by the Social Security Administration, although the programs are legally separate.

31. See U.S. Congress, House Committee on Ways and Means (1992: 777–827) for a detailed explanation of the SSI program, and Zedlewski and Meyer (1989) for a discussion of major issues relating to the program and options for reform.

32. "Countable income" excludes or disregards $20 of monthly non–means-tested benefits, such as Social Security, and $65 of monthly earned income plus one-half of remaining earnings.

33. Individuals must have less than $2,000 in "resources," and couples less than $3,000 in resources, to qualify for benefits. Resources are defined to exclude one's home, car, household items, and a modest life insurance policy. Benefits may also be reduced for a number of other reasons, such as living in another person's home and receiving substantial support from that person.

34. U.S. Congress, House Committee on Ways and Means (1992: 807).

35. Zedlewski and Meyer (1989: 31).

36. Source: U.S. Congress, House Committee on Ways and Means (1992: 1640–72).

37. Source: OMB, *Budget of the United States Government, Fiscal Year 1994* (1993a: A-26). State expenditures are estimated assuming states will continue to account for about 43 percent of total Medicaid spending, as they did in 1991 (U.S. Congress, House Committee on Ways and Means 1992: 1652).

Chapter Five

HOW SOCIAL SECURITY REDISTRIBUTES INCOME

Social Security is the largest transfer program in the United States, each year redistributing hundreds of billions of dollars between generations. It also reallocates the shares of income enjoyed by different income groups within each generation. Yet the nature of this redistribution remains a mystery to the vast majority of the American public. Although it is widely recognized that the Social Security payroll tax by itself is mildly regressive—it tends to take a larger percentage of income from low- and moderate-wage workers than it does from those with high incomes—less well understood are the progressive features of the benefit formula. Very few Americans know the exact ways in which their retirement benefits are related to the value of their lifetime contributions or whether the program as a whole is progressive or regressive on a lifetime basis.[1]

Although in theory the relationship between benefit payments and taxes within Social Security might be viewed as a compromise between the two principles of progressivity (or redistribution according to need) and individual equity (or fair returns on all contributions), in practice the system's development has not been so precise. The relationship has varied over time in ways not always consistent with either of these principles. Historically, a large amount of the redistribution caused by Social Security has been arbitrary or even regressive in nature. In the future, on the other hand, redistributive patterns will change in ways that may have a profound effect on the equity and political popularity of the system. A clear understanding of how benefits, taxes, and net redistribution change over time, therefore, is essential if one is to make an informed judgment about options for long-run reform.

ANNUAL BENEFITS

Real Value of Benefits

Annual Social Security benefits have risen dramatically in real (inflation-adjusted) terms since the inception of the program. During Social Security's early decades, increases in real benefit levels resulted from a combination of wage growth and a variety of ad hoc legislative actions. As recently as 1972, for example, all benefits were increased across-the-board by 20 percent. Since 1974, annual benefit amounts for retirees have been automatically indexed to keep pace with inflation. Since the late 1970s, moreover, the benefit formula has been indexed in a way that keeps average real benefit levels growing for each successive cohort of retirees at roughly the same rate as economy-wide wages. Thus, so long as there is real wage growth, real benefit levels continue to increase for every new generation of recipients.

To illustrate how benefit levels change in value over time, figure 5.1 displays the real (inflation-adjusted) Old-Age and Survivors Insurance (OASI) benefit paid in the first year of retirement for a set of hypothetical workers and their spouses (more detail is offered in Appendix table A.1). Our hypothetical "low-," "average-," and "high-" wage workers are again assumed to have earnings histories like those displayed earlier in table 4.2. Note that for a "two-earner" couple, a high-wage husband is assumed to have an average-wage wife, while average- and low-wage men are both assumed to be married to women with low-wage earning histories.

Substantial increases in the real value of annual benefits can usually be seen for each successive cohort of retirees at each income level and marital status. Consider, for example, the OASI benefits going to single workers retiring at age 65 in 1990. Annual benefits for high-, average-, and low-wage workers are worth about $13,600, $9,700, and $5,900, respectively, in constant 1993 dollars. In real terms, these amounts are 2.7 to 3.1 times as large as the annual benefits received by these workers' counterparts in 1940. Benefits for married couples, of course, are much larger than for single individuals.

The path of benefit growth has not always been smooth. Early in the program's history, real benefit levels were often eroded by inflation during the years between legislative acts. The year 1950 represents a low point for the real value of benefits because no action had been taken to offset the effects of inflation during the 1940s; a large benefit

Figure 5.1 OASI BENEFIT IN FIRST YEAR OF RETIREMENT (IN THOUSANDS OF CONSTANT 1993 DOLLARS)

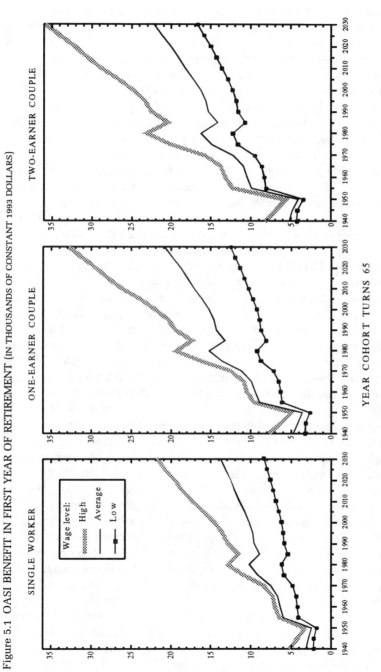

Notes: Figure depicts OASI benefit in first 12 months of retirement, assuming retirement at OASI Normal Retirement Age. Couples are assumed to be the same age. Data cover cohorts born every five years beginning in 1875.

increase implemented for all recipients in 1952 compensated for this. More recently, benefit values have sometimes declined slightly from one group of retirees to the next during recessions or periods of transition to a new benefit calculation procedure.[2] The general trend in benefit levels, nonetheless, exhibits a steep upward slope. Recall that for most people retiring after the introduction of automatic index-ing in the early 1970s, the basic benefit level remains constant in real value after the first year of retirement. Those retiring in earlier years often benefited from rising real postretirement benefits despite years of inflationary decline between legislative enactments.

Reasonable projections suggest that the real value of Social Security benefits will continue to climb steadily for future retirees if current law remains intact. Under the best-estimate economic assumptions of the Social Security Administration, for example, we calculate that an average-wage worker retiring at age 67 in 2032 can be expected to receive a basic annual benefit, excluding spousal and other bene-fits, of about $13,900 in constant 1993 dollars. Thus, as a result of growth in real wages, the purchasing power of his or her benefit would be approximately 42 percent greater than that of a similar worker who retired in 1995. For a high-wage worker, the increase is expected to be almost 61 percent in real terms.[3] If this high-wage worker were married to someone earning the average wage, he or she could expect to receive combined benefits equal to about $35,700 (in constant 1993 dollars) upon retiring in 2032. This would be about 53 percent higher than the $23,300 going to such a couple retiring in 1995.

Income taxation of Social Security benefits can be expected to offset some portion of the benefit growth, as the unindexed taxation thresholds decline in real value over time. Budget legislation in 1993, which increased the maximum portion of benefits that can be included in taxable income to 85 percent and also raised the top income tax rate, will also offset some of this growth. The average tax rate on Social Security benefits can be expected to rise gradually from around 2 percent in 1993 to perhaps 7 percent or 8 percent by 2030.[4] The reduction for a very few individuals at the very highest income levels could rise to about a third of benefits,[5] but most recipi-ents will continue to face only modest burdens, if any, from benefit taxation.[6]

A second factor that could offset some real growth in OASI benefits is a rise in the cost of SMI premiums, which are subtracted directly out of Social Security checks. In 1993, SMI premiums reduced the annual OASI benefit going to each recipient by about $493, which amounted to about 5 percent of the benefit paid to a newly retired average-wage worker. If SMI premiums were to be maintained at 25 percent of program costs, they would rise by 2030 to more than $1,700 annually (in constant 1993 dollars) under the HCFA's intermediate projections.[7] This would amount to about 12 percent of an average-wage worker's cash OASI benefit.

When increased taxation of benefits and higher SMI premiums are taken into account, the SSA's best-estimate projections still suggest that Social Security benefits will normally provide a more comfortable standard of living during the next century than they do today. For example, the real after-tax, after-premium value of OASI benefits for newly retired average-wage workers rises by 22 percent between 1995 and 2030 if we assume the average tax rate on benefits, and that SMI premiums grow as just described.[8]

Although these projections predict a fairly healthy growth in the value of Social Security benefits, a recent poll indicated that almost a third of nonretired Americans considered it "very likely" that Social Security payments would no longer be available *at all* when they retire (Yankelovich, Skelly, and White, Inc. 1985). Although fears that the nation will not be able to afford any Social Security benefits are unfounded, there are valid reasons to be skeptical of the benefit projections reported here. First of all, the system's imbalance makes it likely that Congress will reduce the rate of future benefit growth. Second, long-term economic projections of real wage growth—the source of real benefit growth under Social Security formulas—are always uncertain. Despite these caveats, even with pessimistic assumptions about future wage growth and congressional action, the real value of cash benefits for most future retirees is still likely to be higher than today's benefit levels. The real value of health benefits, moreover, is expected to grow also.

Replacement Rates

The "replacement rate" is a measure of the percentage of a worker's previous annual wage that is replaced by Social Security benefits. Most commonly, replacement rates are expressed as a percentage of wages in the last year preceding retirement, or as a share of the average wage in the three highest-earning years. Maintaining "adequate" and stable replacement rates over time for workers at all earnings levels has been a primary goal of policymakers throughout much of Social Security's history.[9]

Figure 5.2 illustrates how replacement rates for hypothetical workers have evolved over time and are expected to change in the future (see also Appendix table A.2). The figure shows OASI benefits paid in the first full year of retirement as a percentage of earnings in the year prior to retirement, after adjusting for inflation.[10] Replacement rates for low- and average-wage workers retiring today and in the future are somewhat higher than the historical norm. Rates for high-wage workers, in turn, are higher than at the inception of the program, but slightly lower than typical of the 1950–80 period.[11]

According to Robert J. Myers, former chief actuary of the Social Security Administration, the 1939 Social Security formula was set so that a worker earning the average wage and retiring at age 65 *today* would receive—in the absence of changes in wage and price levels— a replacement rate of approximately 40 percent.[12] This is almost exactly the same percentage as determined under the newer formulas. Thus, replacement rates have, in a sense, been kept more stable throughout time than is indicated by figure 5.2.

Various indexing provisions in the current benefit formula are designed to keep this particular replacement rate fairly constant for workers retiring at the Normal Retirement Age in the future—at about 53 percent for a single low-wage worker, 40 percent for an average-wage worker, and 26 percent for a high-wage worker. Rates for workers with spouses or dependent beneficiaries, of course, are much higher.

This traditional replacement rate measure provides a useful illustration of the value of Social Security benefits relative to wages prevailing near the time of retirement. It helps us see how a standard of living can be maintained over time. It should, however, be interpreted with caution. First of all, the traditional measure does not take into account that people typically face much lower taxes after retirement than before. OASI replacement rates would look significantly higher if expressed as a percentage of after-tax earnings. Second, a number of other burdens, such as child-care, work expenses, rent, and mortgage payments, also tend to have less effect on the disposable incomes of the elderly than the nonelderly. Adjusting for these factors would make Social Security replacement rates look even better.[13] Third, replacement rates are much higher for those receiving spousal benefits. Fourth, pensions and property income often add substantially to the well-being of middle- and higher-income workers when they retire, thus adding to their "replacement" income. Fifth, the traditional replacement rate compares benefits to income in one of a worker's highest-earning years.[14] Replacement rates would be much

Figure 5.2 OASI REPLACEMENT RATES

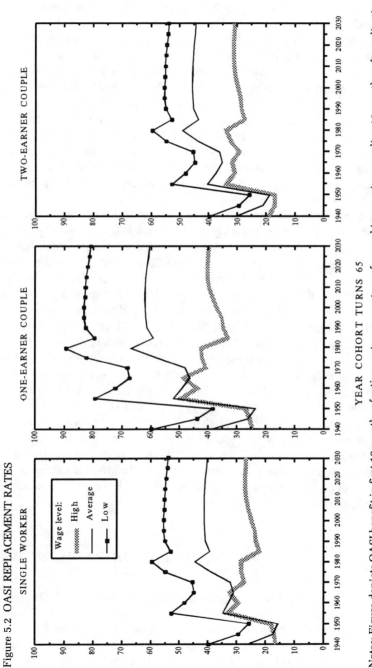

Notes: Figure depicts OASI benefit in first 12 months of retirement as percentage of earned income in preceding 12 months, after adjusting for inflation. Assumes retirement at OASI Normal Retirement Age. Couples are assumed to be the same age. Data cover cohorts born every five years beginning in 1875.

higher if expressed as a percentage of a person's normal preretirement standard of living.

It is also important to remember that constant replacement rates often mean that the real purchasing power of benefits is growing substantially from one cohort of retirees to the next. This is particularly important in a budgetary context. Our current budget process treats any growth in most programs as an "increase," even if it only offsets inflation, because nominal expenditures have risen. At the same time, any change that reduces Social Security replacement rates is considered a "cut," even though the program may be growing significantly in real terms. A government budgetary process needs to focus, instead, on how real expenditures and real growth in *all* programs should be allocated.

The use of the replacement rate as a criterion for setting policy is problematic, moreover, because it does not follow logically from basic principles. A replacement rate is a nice target, perhaps, but it is not a principle.[15] As noted in chapter 2, benefits for middle- and upper-income individuals are justified primarily on the grounds of "individual equity" (i.e., those who contributed to the system should get back a fair return on their investment). Redistribution to lower-income workers, in turn, is justified on grounds of "progressivity" (i.e., by the presumed neediness of some recipients relative to others in society). The replacement rate criterion, however, goes well beyond the simple requirements of both individual equity and progressivity. It suggests that participants at all income levels should receive an "adequate" percentage replacement of past income that is not necessarily related to what they contributed to the system or to their need. Thus, when Social Security policy is set by simple reference to "replacement" rates, middle- and high-income persons can be granted large redistributions beyond what they contribute, as well as beyond their need. Indeed, as we shall see, this is exactly what happened.

MOVING TO A LIFETIME PERSPECTIVE

How does the Social Security system redistribute income? The preceding discussion of benefit levels and replacement rates reveals something about how Social Security outlays are distributed among retirees in any given year, but not the complete picture. A more thorough understanding of Social Security's redistributive nature requires moving to a *lifetime* perspective, that is, examining how Social Security benefits actually compare in value with tax contributions over a lifetime for people of different generations, income levels, and family types. A number of researchers have tackled this question using a wide variety of techniques.[16] Our approach builds on methodologies developed by Nichols and Schreitmueller (1978), Pellechio and Goodfellow (1983), Myers and Schobel (1983 and 1993), Hurd and Shoven (1985), and Boskin et al. (1987), among others. Essentially, it involves using standard actuarial procedures to compare the value of the annuity provided by Old-Age and Survivors Insurance with the value of a private annuity or pension that could be purchased with a worker's lifetime OASI contributions.

Assumptions and Methods

Our approach calculates the *annuity value* (also known as the "actuarial present value") of all OASI contributions made by a worker *and* his or her employer over a lifetime,[17] given certain assumptions about wage level, family type, probability of death, and year of birth. The employer's portion of the payroll tax is included here, since it is analogous to contributions made to a pension or annuity plan on a worker's behalf. We can then compare these contributions with the full annuity value of the OASI benefits that a worker and his or her dependents or survivors may receive over a lifetime. If the system were to meet the "individual equity" standard perfectly, these two amounts would be identical: an "actuarially fair" annuity would have been purchased through one's contributions. To the extent that the system is progressive on a lifetime basis, one would expect the value of benefits to exceed that of contributions for low-wage workers and to fall short of contributions for higher-wage workers.

To measure and compare contributions and benefit payments occurring at many different points in time, an annuity calculation must adjust all possible payments for the effects of inflation, interest, and probability of occurrence. We compensate for inflation by converting all amounts into their real value in constant 1993 dollars, using the consumer price index.[18] Next, to account for interest, all benefits and taxes are converted to their equivalent *present value* at age 65. Essentially, this means taking the value of lifetime tax contributions and adding the interest that these contributions would have accumulated by age 65. Likewise, all benefit payments after age 65 are converted to the amount that would have to be invested at age 65 to yield the benefit stream realized.[19] Our analysis calculates present values at the same age for every cohort, so that fair comparisons may be made among different generations. We use a real (after-inflation) interest rate of 2 percent[20] for all past and future years, which seems reasonable when compared to average real interest rates over time for safe investments.[21] Social Security is an extremely safe investment that is uniquely resistant to economic fluctuations and inflation and receives favorable tax treatment.

Finally, an annuity calculation must adjust values according to their probability of occurrence, which in this case depends on the likelihood of survival. We make two types of calculations here. The first examines the actuarial present value of lifetime benefits and taxes *assuming survival to age 65*. In this fairly common type of calculation, the tax number is simply the total value of lifetime OASI tax contributions, plus interest, for someone in this group who exhibits a particular pattern of lifetime earnings. The benefit number is determined by multiplying the present value of each possible benefit payment by the probability that someone will be alive to receive that payment, given that he or she has already survived to age 65. For example, a woman who was alive at age 65 in 1970 had about an 80 percent chance of surviving to age 75, so the value of a benefit at age 75 is multiplied by 0.8. Dependents and survivors benefits are similarly weighted according to probability of occurrence. All possible benefit payments through age 110 are adjusted in this manner and then summed together. This procedure expresses the value of Social Security benefits in terms of a "lump sum" of money that someone would have to pay to purchase a similar annuity from a private insurance company at age 65. Calculations of this sort are very useful for examining the obligations that Social Security incurs and its responsiveness to the needs of those who do survive to retirement.

Our second calculation takes into account the chance of death in all years after age 21. Some people may contribute to the system for many years, but receive no retirement benefits because they die before reaching retirement age. Their survivors, on the other hand, may be eligible for benefits that partially offset this loss. Taking these factors into account is useful when trying to compare the insurance protection provided by Social Security with the value of contributions *over an entire lifetime*.[22] This approach has the advantage of measuring how the system treats *all* adult members of a cohort, not just those fortunate enough to survive to old age.

In this second calculation, we continue to adjust for inflation and interest as before, but weight each year's benefit or tax payment according to the probability that someone will be alive in that year, assuming only that they were alive *at age* 21 (in effect, that they were old enough to join the system in the first place).[23] For example, a male born in 1920 had, on average, an 89 percent chance of surviving from age 21 to age 50, so the expected value of a tax paid at age 50 is multiplied by 0.89. Likewise, since his chance of surviving from 21 to age 70 is about 67 percent, the expected value of the benefit received at age 70 is multiplied by 0.67.

Our model also performs the elaborate calculations necessary to determine the benefit that would be paid to a worker's survivors if the worker died in any year after age 21, and weights each possible benefit stream according to the probability of occurrence. This includes the value of benefits not only for retired widows but also for young surviving children and their widowed parents.[24] Thus, our calculations include the full actuarial value of all Old-Age and Survivors Insurance benefits. For our purposes here, Disability Insurance benefits and taxes, and the chance of disability, are excluded from the analysis.[25]

A unique set of survival probabilities is used for each sex and cohort, based on mortality tables published by the Social Security Administration.[26] These take into account the longer life expectancies of women, as well as improvements in life expectancy for each new generation. Unfortunately, mortality tables that differentiate among people with different lifetime income levels are not available. Since there is evidence that income level has a significant effect on life expectancy, we present a sensitivity analysis later to provide appropriate qualifications to our general conclusions.

We continue to focus here on hypothetical workers and families with "low," "average," and "high" earnings histories. Although these workers may be unrealistic in some respects (e.g., uninterrupted employment between age 21 and retirement), the simplifying assumptions will not significantly affect most of our conclusions.[27] Calculations are performed for cohorts born every five years between 1875 and 1985 (reaching age 65 between 1940 and 2050).

To see how the system treats people of different family types, we examine four types of households: single male and female workers, one-earner couples, and two-earner couples. Again, among two-earner couples, a high-wage man is assumed to be married to an average-wage woman, while average- and low-wage men are assumed to be married to low-wage women. Widowed spouses are assumed not to remarry, and divorce is not taken into account.[28] Couples are assumed to be the same age and to have two children, born when the parents are 25 and 30, who may be eligible for survivors benefits in the event that the worker dies at an early age.[29]

A number of results can be foreseen. Women will fare better than men with identical earnings histories,[30] since their life expectancies are considerably longer. The single worker naturally does worse than couples, since the survivors and dependents insurance portions of OASI will have zero value for such a worker. Although workers who remain single over their entire lives will tend to fare relatively badly under such a system, they represent a very small portion of the population. The one-earner couple category is a best-case scenario because the couple is eligible to receive full spousal and survivors benefits even though the wife in this example pays no Social Security taxes. This family type can be expected to become increasingly rare in the future. Falling between these two extremes is the two-earner couple, probably the most representative for cohorts of current workers. In this family type, survivor benefits have at least some value, since they typically supplement the benefits earned by a widow in her own right, and also provide benefits to surviving children.

All projections are based on currently scheduled law (assuming a 10.65 percent OASI tax rate after 1992) and the best-estimate economic assumptions in the 1993 Social Security trustees reports (Board of Trustees, OASDI 1993). OASI faces a 75-year imbalance of about 1.32 percent of taxable payroll under these assumptions. As a result, our projections represent what current law requires, not what it can produce. Eventually, there would have to be some change in tax rates, benefit levels, or both. These projections, nonetheless, accurately portray the baseline from which reform efforts will have to begin, and show the direction in which the current unamended program is heading.

Annuity Value of Benefits and Taxes: An Example

To illustrate the results of these actuarial calculations, we start with the cohort of individuals who turn 65 in 1995. As demonstrated in figure 5.1, the OASI benefit in the first year of retirement ranges from about $5,900 for a low-wage single person to $23,300 for a two-earner couple with high and average wages. In the top half of table 5.1, we add up the expected value of these payments over the remaining lives of the beneficiaries, assuming they have already survived to age 65. Because remaining life expectancy at age 65 is substantial, the annuity value of benefits—the amount that would have to be paid to an insurance company at age 65 to provide the same level of

Table 5.1 LIFETIME OASI BENEFITS AND TAXES FOR COHORT TURNING 65 IN 1995 (IN THOUSANDS OF CONSTANT 1993 DOLLARS)

	Single Male			Single Female			One-earner Couple			Two-earner Couple		
	Low wage	Avg. wage	High wage	Low wage	Avg. wage	High wage	Low wage	Avg. wage	High wage	Low & Low	Avg. & Low	High & Avg
Assuming survival to age 65												
(A) Total OASI benefits	**78.1**	**128.8**	**179.8**	**95.1**	**157.0**	**219.1**	**143.6**	**237.1**	**330.9**	**173.2**	**244.3**	**357.3**
Worker's benefit	78.1	128.8	179.8	95.1	157.0	219.1	78.1	128.8	179.8	173.2	224.0	336.8
Spousal and survivors benefits	0.0	0.0	0.0	0.0	0.0	0.0	65.6	108.2	151.1	0.0	20.4	20.5
(B) OASI taxes	**49.5**	**110.0**	**190.2**	**49.5**	**110.0**	**190.2**	**49.5**	**110.0**	**190.2**	**99.0**	**159.6**	**300.2**
(C) Net transfer (A - B)	**28.5**	**18.8**	**-10.4**	**45.6**	**47.0**	**29.0**	**94.1**	**127.0**	**140.7**	**74.2**	**84.8**	**57.1**
Adjusting for the chance of death in all years after age 21												
(D) Total OASI benefits	**58.0**	**95.7**	**133.6**	**80.6**	**132.9**	**185.5**	**134.9**	**223.4**	**305.4**	**155.2**	**226.6**	**312.6**
Worker's benefit	58.0	95.7	133.6	80.6	132.9	185.5	58.0	95.7	133.6	138.5	176.2	266.5
Spousal and survivors benefits	0.0	0.0	0.0	0.0	0.0	0.0	76.9	127.7	171.8	16.6	50.4	46.1
(E) OASI taxes	**45.4**	**100.8**	**170.7**	**47.2**	**104.8**	**179.0**	**45.4**	**100.8**	**170.7**	**92.5**	**148.0**	**275.5**
(F) Net Transfer (D - E)	**12.6**	**-5.1**	**-37.1**	**33.4**	**28.1**	**6.5**	**89.5**	**122.5**	**134.7**	**62.6**	**78.6**	**37.1**

Notes: All amounts are discounted to present value at age 65 using a 2 percent real interest rate. Includes actuarial value of all OASI workers, spousal, and survivors benefits payable over a lifetime. Includes both employer and employee portions of OASI payroll tax. Couples are assumed to be the same age and to have two children born when parents are aged 25 and 30. Assumes retirement at OASI Normal Retirement Age. Projections are based on intermediate assumptions from the 1993 OASDI Board of Trustees report. OASI tax rate is assumed to be set at 10.65 percent beginning after 1992.

benefits—ranges from $78,100 for the low-wage single male to $357,300 for the high-income two-earner couple. The taxes these two types of households would have paid over their lifetimes would have been $49,500 and $300,200, respectively. As a result, they receive positive subsidies, or *net transfers*, of $28,500 and $57,100, respectively, beyond what they contributed.

Next, in the bottom half of table 5.1, we adjust for the chance of death in all years after age 21. This reduces the value of both benefits and taxes. After all, some members of this cohort simply will not survive long enough either to collect old-age benefits or to pay taxes in all years up to age 65. A male in this cohort has about a 74 percent chance of surviving from age 21 to age 65; thus, adjusting for the chance of death in all adult years reduces the value of benefits for a "typical" male member of this cohort to about three-quarters of what it would be if he were guaranteed to survive to age 65. Taxes are reduced by a smaller amount, since workers who die before age 65 are likely to have contributed to the system for many years, with the average age at death being closer to 65 than to 21. Therefore, the net transfer for a single worker decreases significantly under this adjustment. Among couples, however, the reduction in a worker's benefits is offset to some extent by benefits for surviving spouses and children. In the one-earner couple examples, the compensating survivors benefits are so large that there is almost no reduction in the net transfer when we move to a calculation accounting for the chance of death in all adult years.

Calculations similar to table 5.1 are made for 23 different cohorts who turn 65 between 1940 and 2050. They are shown in summary form for a few cohorts in table 5.3, and in fuller detail for all these cohorts in Appendix tables A.3–A.9. The subsections following demonstrate some significant trends and draw some important conclusions about the distributional impact of Social Security.

Growth in Lifetime Benefits

In the Social Security program to date, lifetime benefits have increased in value even more dramatically than have annual benefits. Table 5.2 provides a simple example to illustrate the nature of this growth. Consider one-earner couples where the worker earns average wages. For such a couple retiring in 1960, the annual benefit was about $9,400 at age 65. For a couple retiring in 1995, the annual benefit is approximately $14,600, an increase of about 56 percent. Now consider the value of these benefits over the entire retirement

Table 5.2 OASI BENEFITS FOR AVERAGE-WAGE,
ONE-EARNER COUPLES (IN THOUSANDS OF
CONSTANT 1993 DOLLARS)

Year cohort turns 65	Benefit in first year of retirement	Lifetime benefits	
		Assuming survival to age 65	Adjusting for the chance of death in all years after age 21
Amount			
1960	9.4	143.7	98.9
1995	14.6	237.1	223.4
2030	20.8	323.6	312.8
% Increase			
1960 - 1995	56%	65%	126%
1995 - 2030	42%	37%	40%

Notes: All amounts are discounted to present value at age 65 using a 2 percent real interest rate. Couples are assumed to be the same age and to have two children born when parents are aged 25 and 30. Assumes retirement at the OASI Normal Retirement Age. Projections are based on the intermediate assumptions from the 1993 OASDI Board of Trustees report.

span, assuming survival to age 65. Total retirement benefits for the couple turning 65 in 1995 are worth $237,100, or about 65 percent more than the $143,700 annuity their counterparts received 35 years earlier. The faster rate of growth in the value of lifetime benefits mainly reflects improvements in life expectancy.

When one adjusts for the chance of death in all adult years (not just post-65), the historical growth in benefit payments is yet more dramatic. The annuity value of lifetime benefits for an average-wage one-earner couple grows from $98,900 in 1960 to $223,400 in 1995, a 126 percent increase. Because this calculation takes into account the fact that people are now far more likely to survive their adult years and to reach retirement, it reflects the full growth in the value of retirement insurance protection provided to a typical family. These numbers also reflect considerable growth in the value of survivors insurance, partly because of longer periods of coverage as the system matured.[31] Both of these factors help explain how the cost of the

Social Security system could rise so much in its early decades, even when annual benefit levels rose at a more moderate rate.

Between 1995 and 2030, the value of lifetime benefits is projected to grow at a rate much closer to that of annual benefit levels. A statutory increase in the Normal Retirement Age tends to offset the effects of improving life expectancy. The expected growth in the lifetime value of OASI benefits is nonetheless still quite large. After adjusting for the chance of death in all adult years, OASI benefits are expected to be worth about $312,800 to an average-wage one-earner couple in the cohort turning 65 in 2030, which is 40 percent more than the value of benefits going to their counterparts born 35 years earlier (see table 5.2).

Growth in Lifetime Tax Contributions

Continuously increasing tax rates have been required throughout Social Security's history to pay for longer retirement spans, more retirees relative to workers, and higher benefit levels. Each successive cohort has contributed to Social Security at higher tax rates for longer time periods. Those who retired at the beginning of 1960, for example, paid Old-Age and Survivors Insurance (OASI) taxes for 23 years at most, and never paid at a combined employer-employee rate higher than 4.5 percent. Steady workers retiring in the recent past have typically been subject to the payroll tax for 40 years or more, but also paid at relatively low rates for most of those years. Those retiring after 2030, by contrast, will have paid OASI taxes at combined employer-employee rates exceeding 10 percent over their entire adult lives.

The magnitude of growth in lifetime Social Security tax contributions is apparent in table 5.3. For an average-wage male worker in the cohort turning 65 in 1960, the annuity value of lifetime OASI contributions was only about $9,000 (excluding those who died before age 65, the amount is still only $12,000). This figure increased more than elevenfold in constant dollars, to $100,800, for the cohort turning 65 in 1995. Even without any further increases in payroll tax rates after 1995, the actuarial value of taxes for average-wage males in the cohort turning 65 in 2030 is expected to nearly double in real terms, to $195,800.

Net Transfers

The *net transfer* provides perhaps the best summary measure of how the system redistributes income within and across generations. A

Table 5.3 LIFETIME OASI BENEFITS, TAXES, AND TRANSFERS (IN THOUSANDS OF CONSTANT 1993 DOLLARS)

Year cohort turns 65		Single Male			Single Female			One-earner Couple			Two-earner Couple		
		Low wage	Avg. wage	High wage	Low wage	Avg. wage	High wage	Low wage	Avg. wage	High wage	Low & Low	Avg. & Low	High & Avg
1960	Benefits	30.1	45.5	50.6	45.7	69.0	76.7	66.3	98.9	111.0	76.8	102.0	122.1
	Taxes	4.0	9.0	13.8	4.3	9.6	14.6	4.0	9.0	13.8	8.4	13.3	23.4
	Net Transfer	26.1	36.5	36.8	41.4	59.4	62.1	62.3	89.9	97.2	68.4	88.7	98.7
1980	Benefits	54.3	90.2	114.6	80.8	134.3	170.5	129.3	209.9	264.3	146.9	208.4	273.2
	Taxes	22.9	51.0	71.9	24.2	53.9	76.1	22.9	51.0	71.9	47.2	75.2	125.7
	Net Transfer	31.4	39.3	42.7	56.6	80.5	94.4	106.4	158.9	192.4	99.7	133.3	147.5
1995	Benefits	58.0	95.7	133.6	80.6	132.9	185.5	134.9	223.4	305.4	155.2	226.6	312.6
	Taxes	45.4	100.8	170.7	47.2	104.8	179.0	45.4	100.8	170.7	92.5	148.0	275.5
	Net Transfer	12.6	-5.1	-37.1	33.4	28.1	6.5	89.5	122.5	134.7	62.6	78.6	37.1
2010	Benefits	69.0	115.2	175.9	93.6	156.1	238.4	154.6	258.8	388.6	178.9	261.7	394.2
	Taxes	68.2	151.5	310.8	70.4	156.5	322.4	68.2	151.5	310.8	138.6	221.9	467.3
	Net Transfer	0.9	-36.3	-135.0	23.2	-0.4	-84.1	86.5	107.3	77.7	40.3	39.8	-73.1
2030	Benefits	84.0	139.6	220.3	113.7	189.0	298.1	187.4	312.8	493.0	215.9	316.5	498.1
	Taxes	88.1	195.8	468.8	91.3	202.8	485.4	88.1	195.8	468.8	179.4	287.1	671.6
	Net Transfer	-4.1	-56.2	-248.5	22.5	-13.8	-187.3	99.3	117.0	24.2	36.5	29.4	-173.5

Notes: All amounts are discounted to present value at age 65 using a 2 percent real interest rate. Adjusts for chance of death in all years after age 21. Includes actuarial value of all OASI workers, spousal, and survivors benefits payable over a lifetime. Includes both employer and employee portions of OASI payroll tax. Couples are assumed to be the same age and to have two children born when parents are aged 25 and 30. Assumes retirement at the OASI Normal Retirement Age. Projections are based on the intermediate assumptions from the 1993 OASDI Board of Trustees report. OASI tax rate is assumed to be set at 10.65 percent after 1992.

positive net-transfer—the difference between lifetime benefits and taxes—means that an individual or family receives a subsidy above and beyond the fair annuity value of contributions, whereas a negative net transfer indicates that benefits are worth less than contributions. Those with positive net transfers have lifetime income redistributed *toward* them, while those with negative net transfers have lifetime income redistributed *away* from them. Changes in net transfers over time, adjusting for the chance of death in all years after age 21, are illustrated in table 5.3 and figure 5.3. An examination of these transfers yields a number of interesting results, summarized in the paragraphs following.

First, almost all individuals who have retired in any year between 1940 and today—no matter what their income level or family type—have received large positive transfers from Social Security beyond the sum of their contributions to the system and a reasonable rate of return on those contributions.

This phenomenon—large positive transfers to virtually all past and current retirees—is largely a function of the way in which Social Security has evolved over the years. For the first generations of retirees, almost no taxes were paid into the system. Benefit payments represented mainly transfers from the working generation. As Social Security matured, this early phenomenon continued. Although lifetime benefits and taxes were both growing rapidly for each successive cohort of retirees, benefits for new retirees over most of this period grew by a larger amount than the taxes they had paid during their working lives. As a result, the gap between benefits and taxes—the net transfer—actually increased. Even people who earned well above the maximum wage subject to Social Security taxation throughout their careers have historically received very large net transfers from the system.[32]

Second, for most of Social Security's history, the system has been **regressive within generations.** *That is, within a given cohort of retirees, net transfers have been inversely related to need: people with the highest lifetime incomes have tended to receive the largest absolute transfers above and beyond what they contributed.*

This result may appear surprising given the "progressive" nature of the benefit formula. An example can illustrate how within-generation regressivity could occur even though the benefit formula is intended

Figure 5.3 NET LIFETIME OASI TRANSFER (IN THOUSANDS OF CONSTANT 1993 DOLLARS)

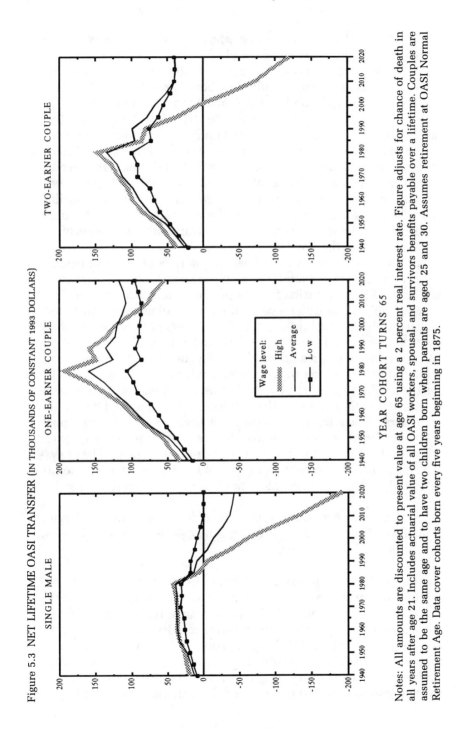

Notes: All amounts are discounted to present value at age 65 using a 2 percent real interest rate. Figure adjusts for chance of death in all years after age 21. Includes actuarial value of all OASI workers, spousal, and survivors benefits payable over a lifetime. Couples are assumed to be the same age and to have two children born when parents are aged 25 and 30. Assumes retirement at OASI Normal Retirement Age. Data cover cohorts born every five years beginning in 1875.

to provide a higher rate of return on the contributions of low-income workers. Consider one-earner couple families from the cohort that turned 65 in 1980. The annuity value of lifetime OASI contributions for a low-wage one-earner family was about $22,900 in constant 1993 dollars. This family's lifetime OASI benefits are worth more than 5.6 times as much, or $129,300, for a net transfer of $106,400 (see table 5.3). A high-wage one-earner family's contributions, in turn, amounted to about $71,900. Their benefits are worth about 3.7 times that amount, or $264,300, for a net transfer of $192,400. As one would expect from the way the benefit formula is structured, the lower-income family receives a much higher rate of return on its contributions. More importantly, however, the absolute amount of money transferred to the high-income family is nearly double the size of the transfer going to the low-income family.

This example shows why comparisons of rates of return or benefit-to-tax ratios are incomplete if one wants to know how different people fare under Social Security. Simply put, these measures do not show how to "weight" for differences in the amount of money contributed. If you receive a subsidized return of 25 percent on $100 worth of contributions and I receive a subsidized return of 20 percent on $1,000, I am being treated much more generously than you, even though your "rate of return" is higher. Moving beyond Social Security for the aged, imagine that the government created a welfare system for the population in which the rich received back tens of thousands of dollars for paying a few dollars of taxes, while the very poor received a grant of a few hundred dollars without paying any taxes. One could hardly claim this to be a progressive or need-related system, even though the poor had a rate of return (and a benefit-to-tax ratio and perhaps a replacement rate) that was infinitely higher.[33]

Third, for the first century of retirees in the system, the largest amount of net transfers go to high-income individuals who turn 65 around the year 1980.

Suppose we want to ask which group in the population received the best treatment from the system. Given the small contributions made by those retiring early in the system's history, we might be suspicious that they were the grand winners. Because of the progressive benefit formula and the way benefits are scheduled to grow over time, on the other hand, we might also suspect that those low-income individuals retiring many years hence would fare the best. In actuality, however, for the first century of retirees in the system, the largest amount of net transfers go to high-income individuals who turned 65 around the year 1980.[34] Net transfers going to high-income families in this cohort amount to $147,500 for two-earner couples and $192,400 for one-earner couples (see table 5.3). No low-income workers, past, present, or in the foreseeable future, will ever receive treatment this generous.[35] Within each income group, the historical peak in net transfers also occurs around 1980. Thus, among average-income workers, those retiring in 1980 receive much more favorable treatment than those retiring in 1960 or those retiring in 2030.

Fourth, net transfers will decline for most people among future generations of retirees, and the distribution of net transfers will become increasingly progressive within generations.

Although Old-Age and Survivor's Insurance has been essentially regressive within generations for most past and current retirees, the system is becoming more progressive. This is not because low- and moderate-income people will be faring better under the system, but mainly because high-income people will be faring worse. Using current law and best-estimate economic and demographic assumptions of the Social Security Administration, we find that net transfers will decline slightly for most low- and average-wage persons retiring in the next century, but will still generally remain positive. Meanwhile, net OASI subsidies will gradually be phased out for many high-income persons. Lifetime contributions begin to exceed lifetime benefits for high-wage single males retiring in the 1980s. Positive net transfers are eliminated for high-/average-wage two-earner couples retiring after the turn of the century. Figure 5.3 demonstrates that high-wage single workers and two-earner couples retiring in the 2020s and later will face very large *negative* transfers (or positive net lifetime taxes) from the system. For example, a high-/average-wage two-earner couple turning 65 in 2030 faces net taxes or negative transfers of approximately $173,500 (see table 5.3); their benefits will be worth about 74 percent of their contributions.

The changing income tax treatment of Social Security, which is not included in these calculations, can also be expected to increase the progressivity of the system over time. Employer OASI contributions (as well as accumulated "interest" on contributions) have always been excluded from income taxation. This represents preferential tax treatment relative to other forms of income and savings, and is most valuable to higher-income people. A growing proportion of this tax preference will be offset in the future, however, by income taxation of benefits, which will also have its largest impact on those with high incomes.[36]

The decline in net transfers during the next century occurs not because of any slowdown in benefit growth, but because lifetime contributions are growing faster than benefits. Since the system is set up mainly on a "pay-as-you-go" basis, benefit payments to retirees are dependent on the tax revenues raised from the working population. The growth in transfers going to those who have retired since 1940 could be financed only by rapidly accelerating payroll tax rates on the working population. In effect, the system has been able to keep tax rates rising fast enough to provide more than a generous quid pro quo for almost all workers who have reached retirement age up to now. Those retiring in the future, however, will have contributed vast amounts over their lifetimes to support the transfers going to those who retired before them. Meanwhile, the ratio of retirees to workers will increase dramatically. As a result of these two factors, payroll tax rates would have to rise astronomically if they were to continue to finance net subsidies for all participants, including high-income persons.

So long as there is some transfer to low-income recipients remaining in the system—a natural consequence of a benefit schedule that pays higher rates on initial dollars of earnings—high-income recipients inevitably have to start paying more in present-value terms than they take out. The transition to this type of system, although only partial and incomplete, began only recently.

Fifth, under current law, many middle- and upper-income households will continue to receive generous positive transfers from Social Security far into the future.

Although the largest of positive transfers have been granted to those who retired in the past (particularly those who are now in their late seventies and early eighties), many current and future retirees will still receive significant subsidies from the OASI system despite being quite well-off economically.

The one-earner couple provides perhaps the major future exception to the increasing within-cohort progressivity of the system. Households of this type continue receiving positive net transfers well into the next century, regardless of income level. High-wage one-earner couples retiring in the near future receive very large transfers, often exceeding $100,000 (see table 5.3). Indeed, high-income one-earner couples retiring before the turn of the century continue to receive *larger* net transfers than anyone else. Under our projections, positive subsidies continue to flow to high-wage one-earner couples retiring as late as 2050. As we move into the next century, moreover, average-wage one-earner couples will continue to receive larger transfers than low-wage couples.[37] Of course, many fewer couples will fit the one-earner profile in the future. Nevertheless, it remains clear that even in the distant future, not all the subsidies provided by Social Security system will be targeted in a fair or efficient manner or one that follows a logical set of principles.

Net Transfers as Percentage of Lifetime Income

To put the amount of redistribution caused by Social Security in perspective, figure 5.4 shows net transfers as a percentage of lifetime earned income.[38] Lifetime earned income here excludes any income above the maximum wage subject to Social Security taxation, and includes wages earned before the system began. Transfers going to cohorts retiring in the recent past are quite large relative to lifetime earnings. As an extreme example, consider one-earner couples turning 65 in 1980. Net lifetime OASI transfers represented 21.2 percent of lifetime income for a low-wage worker with a non–wage-earning wife and two children. In other words, this worker not only receives insurance protection equal to the full value of his lifetime OASI contributions but also receives a redistribution of income from Social Security that is equivalent to a lifetime *negative* tax on earnings of 21.2 percent. The corresponding figures for average- and high-wage workers in this year are 14.2 percent and 11.3 percent, respectively. Not only do these middle- and high-income workers receive back their OASI tax contributions with interest; for many, the redistributions even offset much or all of lifetime federal income tax payments.

On the other hand, consider a high-/average-wage two-earner couple turning 65 in 2030. As stated earlier, this couple faces a lifetime actuarial loss from the OASI system of about $173,500 (table 5.3). While the amount may appear quite large, it represents only a small portion of this couple's lifetime income—approximately 2.77 percent. In other words, if this couple faces a statutory OASI tax rate of 10.65 percent over most of their careers, approximately 7.88 percentage points could be considered provision for their own retirement, while only 2.77 percentage points represent a transfer to the less fortunate. If the high-wage worker in this family were to earn more than the maximum wage subject to OASI taxation, moreover, the

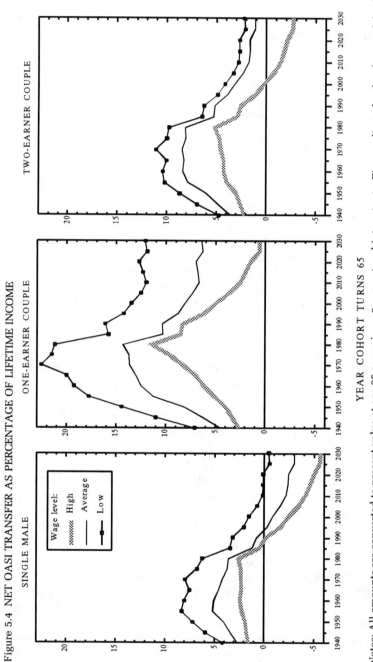

Figure 5.4 NET OASI TRANSFER AS PERCENTAGE OF LIFETIME INCOME

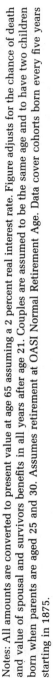

Notes: All amounts are converted to present value at age 65 assuming a 2 percent real interest rate. Figure adjusts for the chance of death and value of spousal and survivors benefits in all years after age 21. Couples are assumed to be the same age and to have two children born when parents are aged 25 and 30. Assumes retirement at OASI Normal Retirement Age. Data cover cohorts born every five years starting in 1875.

negative transfer would represent an even smaller portion of lifetime income.

Even in a worst case—a single male worker retiring many years hence—the net tax is significantly smaller than the gross rate of tax. For a high-wage single male worker retiring in 2030, the net tax equals about 5.67 percent of lifetime earnings subject to Social Security.

ADJUSTING FOR SURVIVAL DIFFERENCES AMONG INCOME GROUPS

One difficulty with the preceding calculations is that they assume identical mortality probabilities for all people of the same gender and birth cohort, regardless of income level or other characteristics. As indicated earlier, lower income and shorter life expectancies are related. Among the factors that may cause lower-income people to experience higher mortality rates are limited access to health care, poor diet, stress, dangerous jobs, and exposure to violent crime. As a result, their likelihood of receiving Social Security retirement benefits is probably lower than for high-income people. Many analysts have argued that Social Security's progressivity may be reduced significantly by differential mortality rates. Indeed, both Duggan, Gillingham, and Greenlees (1993a, b) and Henry Aaron (1977) have demonstrated that differential mortality rates may have a significant impact on the distributional nature of the Social Security system.

Substantial evidence has existed for some time that there is a strong correlation between race and longevity. In 1989, for example, white men and women had life expectancies at age 21 that were about 15 percent and 9 percent longer, respectively, than those of their black counterparts.[39] Much of this difference is probably attributable to the lower average incomes, educational levels, and living standards of blacks relative to whites. A number of recent studies have also found a strong relationship between income and mortality that is independent of race.[40] Rogot, Sorlie, and Johnson (1992) examined a U.S. Bureau of the Census sample of over 800,000 white persons between 1979 and 1985, and constructed estimated life expectancies by income level based on the observed mortality rates in the sample. As table 5.4 demonstrates, males and females in the highest category of family income were found to have life expectancies at age 25 that were 7.2 percent and 1.8 percent longer than average, respectively. Men and women in the lowest income category, by contrast, had life

Table 5.4 ESTIMATED REMAINING LIFE EXPECTANCY
FOR WHITE MALES AND FEMALES AT AGE
25, BY FAMILY INCOME

Family income in 1980 dollars	Remaining life expectancy at age 25, in years		Percentage difference from overall average life expectancy	
	Male	Female	Male	Female
Less than $ 5,000	43.6	53.7	- 12.8 %	- 5.8 %
$ 5,000 - 9,999	46.1	56.0	- 7.8 %	- 1.8 %
$ 10,000 - 14,999	48.7	56.6	- 2.6 %	- 0.7 %
$ 15,000 - 19,999	50.8	56.9	+ 1.6 %	- 0.2 %
$ 20,000 - 24,999	51.5	57.9	+ 3.0 %	+ 1.6 %
$ 25,000 - 49,999	52.4	57.8	+ 4.8 %	+ 1.4 %
$ 50,000 or more	53.6	58.0	+ 7.2 %	+ 1.8 %
Overall average	50.0	57.0	0.0 %	0.0 %

Source: Rogot, Sorlie, and Johnson (1992).
Note: Data are based on the National Longitudinal Mortality
Study 1979–85 follow-up, which itself is based upon sam-
ples drawn from Current Population Surveys (CPS) of the
U.S. Bureau of the Census.

expectancies of 12.8 percent and 5.8 percent lower than average.
Another study by Duggan and colleagues (1993b) analyzed a sample
of 38,000 workers who were born between 1900 and 1923, and examined their subsequent mortality patterns between 1937 and 1988.
They found a strong correlation between wages earned at ages 41 to
45 and remaining life expectancy after age 45. According to the
relationship they estimated,[41] a male with twice-average income
would live about 10.2 percent longer than average, while a male with
only 45 percent of average income would face a life expectancy 5.6
percent shorter than average. The corresponding figures for women
were plus 8.1 percent and minus 4.5 percent, respectively.

Adjusting our own results precisely for differential mortality rates
by income is impossible, since the necessary information is not available in sufficient detail. We can, however, use these previous studies
to make some reasonable assumptions about differential mortality
rates and see what effect they have on our calculations. Let us assume

that men and women in our low-income households have life expectancies at age 21 that are 7 percent and 4 percent shorter than average, respectively. Men and women in high-income households, by contrast, can be assumed to have life expectancies at age 21 that are 7 percent and 4 percent longer than average, respectively. We further assume that the impact of income on mortality rates at different ages shows a pattern similar to the impact of race on mortality at each age. The ratio of black-to-white mortality rates is fairly high at young ages, peaks during the forties, and then declines gradually; at very advanced ages, there is only a small difference in mortality rates between blacks and whites.[42] The upshot is that the income-mortality relationship probably causes many more low-income people to die *before* reaching retirement, but has only a modest effect after retirement.

Table 5.5 displays the estimated value of lifetime OASI benefits, taxes, and transfers for two selected cohorts, under the revised mortality assumptions just described. Although our differential mortality rate assumptions do cause a modest reduction in the apparent progressivity of the system, the impact is not large enough to change significantly any of the major conclusions we drew in the last section. The lifetime net transfer for low-income male workers retiring in 1995, for instance, is reduced only by about $7,500 under these assumptions, whereas the lifetime transfer going to high-wage male workers increases by $16,300.

Among couples, the impact of our revised mortality assumptions is even smaller, because changes in the value of a worker's benefits are offset partially by changes in survivors benefits. For one-earner couples retiring in 1995, the net transfer falls by about $3,500 for those with low wages and rises by about $9,900 for those with high wages. The impact is slightly larger for two-earner couples. In any case, the net change is only a small percentage of the total value of benefits and net transfers for these families.

When one examines the cohort turning 65 in 2030, the impact of differential mortality rates is larger than in 1995 only when the absolute value of transfers is compared. Relative to total benefits, differential mortality rates are even less important in the future. Although progressivity is again reduced slightly, the basic pattern of redistribution remains close to that in our earlier analysis. Single high-wage workers and high-/average-wage two-earner couples still face very large negative transfers, while others continue to receive positive subsidies.

These tables, of course, do not take into account some other possi-

Table 5.5 LIFETIME OASI BENEFITS, TAXES, AND TRANSFERS, ASSUMING INCOME HAS A STRONG EFFECT ON MORTALITY
(IN THOUSANDS OF CONSTANT 1993 DOLLARS)

Year cohort turns 65	Single Male			Single Female			One-earner Couple			Two-earner Couple		
	Low wage	Avg. wage	High wage	Low wage	Avg. wage	High wage	Low wage	Avg. wage	High wage	Low & Low	Avg. & Low	High & Avg
1995 Benefits	48.4	95.7	158.0	73.3	132.9	203.2	129.3	223.4	323.5	142.6	226.6	338.9
Taxes	43.3	100.8	178.9	46.2	104.8	182.8	43.3	100.8	178.9	89.5	148.0	285.5
Net Transfer	**5.1**	**-5.1**	**-20.8**	**27.0**	**28.1**	**20.4**	**86.0**	**122.5**	**144.6**	**53.1**	**78.6**	**53.5**
Net effect of income-related mortality	**-7.5**	**0.0**	**+16.3**	**-6.4**	**0.0**	**+13.9**	**-3.5**	**0.0**	**+9.9**	**-9.5**	**0.0**	**+16.4**
2030 Benefits	70.9	139.6	259.4	102.9	189.0	328.3	178.9	312.8	520.0	204.6	316.5	534.1
Taxes	84.7	195.8	483.8	89.9	202.8	491.2	84.7	195.8	483.8	174.6	287.1	689.0
Net Transfer	**-13.8**	**-56.2**	**-224.3**	**13.0**	**-13.8**	**-162.9**	**94.2**	**117.0**	**36.2**	**30.0**	**29.4**	**-154.9**
Net effect of income-related mortality	**-9.7**	**0.0**	**+24.2**	**-9.5**	**0.0**	**+24.4**	**-5.1**	**0.0**	**+12.0**	**-6.5**	**0.0**	**+18.6**

Notes: Amounts are discounted to present value at age 65 using a 2 percent real interest rate. Table adjusts for the chance of death in all years after age 21. In high-income households, men and women are assumed to have life expectancies at age 21 that are 7 percent and 4 percent longer than average. In low-income households, men and women are assumed to have life expectancies at age 21 which are .7 percent and 4 percent shorter than average, respectively. Includes actuarial value of all OASI workers', spousal, and survivors benefits payable over a lifetime. Includes both employer and employee portions of the OASI payroll tax. Couples are assumed to be the same age and to have two children born when the parents are aged 25 and 30. Assumes retirement at the OASI Normal Retirement Age. Projections are based on the intermediate assumptions from the 1993 OASDI Board of Trustees report. OASI tax rate is assumed to be set at 10.65 percent after 1992.

ble differences between income classes. For example, the tendency of those with lower incomes to enter the labor force at an earlier age could reduce the progressivity of the Social Security system a bit further. Suppose that a high-wage male completes some graduate school and delays entry into the labor force until age 24, while a low-wage male begins working at age 18. Among past and current retirees, this differential working pattern would have little effect on net transfers. Tax rates were so low when they were young that paying a few more years didn't matter much. In the cohort turning 65 in 1995, for instance, entering the labor force three years later only improves a high-wage male's lifetime net transfer by about $1,700. Entering the labor force three years earlier reduces the transfer for a low-wage male in this cohort by less than $500. Among cohorts retiring in the future, however, the impact would be more substantial. In the cohort turning 65 in 2030, delaying work until age 24 would improve a high-wage worker's net transfer by about $17,300. Entering the labor force at age 18 reduces the net transfer by about $3,000 for a low-wage male in this cohort. On the other hand, these changes may be offset to some extent by the greater likelihood that a low-wage worker will become unemployed or disabled. Indeed, if entry and exit from the work force is more probable among lower-income workers, then the system is even more progressive.

In sum, certain characteristics that are closely related to one's income level, such as mortality rates and age when one begins working, probably do weaken the progressivity of Social Security.[43] Even under strong assumptions, however, it appears that the impact is not very large. The basic story remains largely unchanged: within-generation redistribution in the Social Security system remains regressive for most past and current retirees, but turns strongly progressive for most people retiring in the distant future.

MEDICARE BENEFITS

The Medicare system adds significantly to the total amount of benefits and net transfers provided to retirees. Table 5.6 offers a rough estimate of the lifetime value of Medicare benefits, including both Hospital Insurance (HI) and Supplementary Medical Insurance (SMI), for selected cohorts of individuals who survive to age 65.

For these calculations, we make the simple assumption that the insurance value of Medicare for each enrollee in any given year is

Table 5.6 ANNUAL AND LIFETIME MEDICARE BENEFITS
(IN THOUSANDS OF CONSTANT 1993 DOLLARS)

Year cohort turns 65	Avg. annual Medicare benefit per enrollee (at age 65)	Average annual real percentage increase since previous listed year	Actuarial present value at age 65 of lifetime Medicare benefits	
			Male	Female
1970	1.4		27.3	39.0
1980	2.3	5.3%	48.2	66.6
1990	3.7	4.8%	79.8	106.3
1995	4.8	5.3%	100.9	130.7
2000	6.4	5.7%	123.1	155.5
2010	9.9	4.5%	159.0	196.7
2020	11.5	1.5%	191.6	236.4
2030	13.2	1.4%	223.5	273.6

Notes: Data are discounted to present value at age 65 using a 2 percent real interest rate. Table assumes survival to age 65. Each recipient is assumed to receive Medicare insurance benefits, in every year after age 65, which equal the average Medicare outlay per enrollee in that year. Projections are based on the intermediate assumptions of the 1993 Social Security Board of Trustees reports, adjusted by the authors for the estimated impact of 1993 enactments. Subtracting out Medicare premiums paid by retirees would reduce these figures slightly; they offset about 10 percent of total Medicare costs in 1990.

equal to total Medicare expenditures divided by the total number of enrollees. Future Medicare benefit levels are much more difficult to predict than OASI benefits. We rely here on the 1993 best-estimate projections of the Health Care Financing Administration (HCFA), adjusted for the estimated impact of 1993 enactments. These projections assume that Medicare spending per enrollee will rise a bit faster than the historical trend over the next 10 to 15 years, and then drop sharply to a rate well below that trend (see the second column of table 5.6). Given the uncertainty behind Medicare cost projections and the likelihood of many changes to the nation's health care system over the next couple of decades, the results shown here should again be treated only as suggestive.

As is apparent from table 5.6, Medicare benefits are quite large and have been rising dramatically in value over time. The average

Medicare benefit per enrollee is expected to be about $4,800 in 1995. Because the HCFA projects Medicare spending to continue rising at a rapid pace, the total expected value of Medicare benefits for a couple retiring at age 65 in 1995 is over $230,000. These same projections imply that Medicare benefits will be worth almost half-a-million dollars (in constant 1993 dollars) to a couple turning 65 in 2030. Even if we were to assume a rate of growth well below the historical pace, these numbers would still be very large.

These Medicare calculations suggest that the Social Security system as a whole is rapidly moving toward a system where larger shares of benefits are paid in kind—that is, in the form of designated goods and services—rather than in cash. This is especially true for workers with low lifetime earnings.

If we consider Medicare and OASI benefits together, it is clear that the total amount of resources society is devoting to the typical elderly household is large and growing. An average-income couple alive at age 65 in 1970 would receive retirement and health benefits worth around $250,000 over the course of their retirements. The expected value for an average-wage couple is close to $500,000 for those surviving to age 65 in 1995, and roughly $800,000 for those reaching 65 in 2030. For a high-wage couple turning 65 in 2030, the figure is about 1 million dollars.

Table 5.7 provides rough estimates of the redistribution of lifetime income caused by Medicare (see Appendix table A.10 for more detail). Since we are interested here in measuring redistribution over an entire lifetime, we adjust for the chance of death in all years after age 21. Calculating net transfers in the Medicare system is a bit more complicated than for OASI. Unlike OASI, a significant portion of Medicare funding comes from general revenues of the federal government. As a result, it is more difficult to determine how much each individual contributes to support the Medicare system over his or her lifetime. Projections of payroll tax rates are also far less reliable for Medicare than for OASI. Although the HI payroll tax rate is not currently scheduled to rise above 2.9 percent, the imbalance eventually runs to several percentage points of taxable payroll. Failing to take these factors into account would cause us to grossly understate the amount a worker pays to support the Medicare system. To fully account for the costs of the system, therefore, we move beyond current law and assume that HI payroll taxes are set at rates necessary to keep the system solvent on a pay-as-you-go basis after 1995. In accordance with 1993 legislation, we also assume that the cap on earnings subject to the HI tax is removed. Under this sce-

Table 5.7 LIFETIME MEDICARE BENEFITS, TAXES, PREMIUMS, AND TRANSFERS (IN THOUSANDS OF CONSTANT 1993 DOLLARS)

Year cohort turns 65		Single Male			Single Female			One-earner Couple			Two-earner couple		
		Low wage	Avg. wage	High wage	Low wage	Avg. wage	High wage	Low wage	Avg. wage	High wage	Low & low	Avg. & low	High & avg.
1980	Benefits	32.7	32.7	32.7	53.8	53.8	53.8	86.5	86.5	86.5	86.5	86.5	86.5
	Taxes & premiums	7.6	10.5	13.2	13.0	16.1	19.2	18.2	21.1	23.8	20.7	23.5	29.5
	Net Transfer	**25.1**	**22.2**	**19.5**	**40.9**	**37.7**	**34.6**	**68.4**	**65.5**	**62.7**	**65.9**	**63.0**	**57.0**
1995	Benefits	75.0	75.0	75.0	110.7	110.7	110.7	185.7	185.7	185.7	185.7	185.7	185.7
	Taxes & premiums	23.3	34.7	57.6	33.5	45.6	70.2	47.5	59.0	81.7	57.1	68.5	104.6
	Net Transfer	**51.7**	**40.3**	**17.3**	**77.2**	**65.1**	**40.5**	**138.1**	**126.7**	**104.0**	**128.6**	**117.2**	**81.1**
2010	Benefits	124.7	124.7	124.7	171.4	171.4	171.4	296.1	296.1	296.1	296.1	296.1	296.1
	Taxes & premiums	47.3	78.1	154.7	61.0	93.3	173.8	83.0	113.8	187.6	108.4	139.4	252.1
	Net Transfer	**77.4**	**46.6**	**-30.0**	**110.3**	**78.1**	**-2.5**	**213.1**	**182.3**	**108.5**	**187.7**	**156.7**	**44.0**
2030	Benefits	179.8	179.8	179.8	242.9	242.9	242.9	422.7	422.7	422.7	422.7	422.7	422.7
	Taxes & premiums	87.2	160.8	383.0	106.6	183.7	416.6	131.4	204.6	414.8	197.0	276.2	599.8
	Net Transfer	**92.6**	**19.0**	**-203.3**	**136.3**	**59.2**	**-173.7**	**291.3**	**218.1**	**7.9**	**225.7**	**146.5**	**-177.1**

Notes: All amounts are discounted to present value at age 65 using a 2 percent real interest rate. Adjusts for chance of death in all years after age 21. "Taxes and premiums" include the actuarial value of all employer and employee HI payroll taxes, all SMI premiums, and estimated portion of federal income tax burden devoted to financing SMI. Projections are based on HCFA 1993 intermediate assumptions, adjusted by the authors for the estimated impact of 1993 enactments. Assumes HI payroll taxes are set at rates necessary to keep the system solvent on a pay-as-you-go basis after 1995. SMI premiums are assumed to remain tied to 25 percent of program costs after 1995. Recipients are assumed to receive Medicare insurance protection, in each year after age 65, which equals in value the average Medicare outlay per enrollee in that year.

nario, the HI tax rate would rise from 2.9 percent today to 5.10 percent in 2010 and 8.78 percent in 2030. In addition, we assume that SMI premiums remain tied to 25 percent of program costs permanently. Finally, we assume that the general revenue financing of SMI is borne through the income tax, and estimate the portion of a worker's income tax burden that would be devoted to financing SMI.

Most current and near-future retirees receive very large net transfers from the Medicare system, even when HI payroll taxes, SMI premiums, and income tax payments for supporting SMI are all taken into account. For example, a high-/average-wage two-earner couple retiring in 1995 is expected to receive a net transfer of about $81,100 (table 5.7). A high-wage one-earner couple receives an even larger transfer. Most high-income people retiring as late as 2010 are also projected to receive large positive transfers from Medicare. In all of these cases, the transfers going to average- and low-wage families are even greater. By 2030, the distribution of Medicare transfers begins to look more like that for OASI; high-/average-wage two-earner couples and upper-income singles face large negative transfers from the system, whereas everyone else continues to receive positive subsidies.

All of these figures will be changed significantly by inevitable health-care reforms over the coming years, but it would be difficult to change the basic picture much. Current and near-future retirees at all income levels would continue to receive large positive transfers even under sharply curtailed benefit growth, because of their low levels of lifetime contributions into the system. High-wage individuals, moreover, will eventually have to pay in more than they receive under almost any possible scenario.

Table 5.8 shows what happens when we add together net transfers from Medicare and the OASI system. The redistributional pattern for the combined programs, for the most part, is similar to the one we identified earlier for OASI, only more pronounced. Total net transfers going to current and near-future retired couples are very large indeed. For one-earner couples retiring in 1995, the lifetime net transfer ranges between $227,600 and $249,200. A high-/average-wage two-earner couple receives a net transfer of $118,200, while an average-/low-wage two-earner couple receives a transfer of $195,800. On the other hand, when we look a few decades into the next century, those who face negative transfers under the OASI system fare even worse when we take Medicare into account. A high-/average-wage two-earner couple turning 65 in 2030 pays about $350,600 more in taxes

Table 5.8 LIFETIME COMBINED OASI AND MEDICARE NET TRANSFERS (IN THOUSANDS OF CONSTANT 1993 DOLLARS)

Year cohort turns 65	Single Male			Single Female			One-earner Couple			Two-earner Couple		
	Low wage	Avg. wage	High wage	Low wage	Avg. wage	High wage	Low wage	Avg. wage	High wage	Low & Low	Avg. & Low	High & Avg
1980	56.5	61.5	62.2	97.5	118.2	129.0	174.8	224.4	255.1	165.6	196.3	204.5
1995	64.3	35.2	-19.8	110.6	93.2	47.0	227.6	249.2	238.7	191.2	195.8	118.2
2010	78.3	10.3	-165.0	133.5	77.7	-86.6	299.6	289.6	186.2	228.0	196.5	-29.1
2030	88.5	-37.2	-351.8	158.8	45.4	-361.0	390.6	335.1	32.1	262.2	175.9	-350.6

Notes: Amounts are discounted to present value at age 65 using a 2 percent real interest rate. Adjusts for chance of death in all years after age 21. Includes actuarial value of all OASI and Medicare workers', spousal, and survivors benefits payable over a lifetime. Includes both employer and employee portions of the OASI and HI payroll taxes, SMI premiums, and the estimated portion of the federal income tax burden devoted to financing SMI. Assumes HI payroll taxes are set at rates necessary to keep the system solvent on a pay-as-you-go basis after 1995. SMI premiums are assumed to remain tied to 25 percent of program costs indefinitely. Recipients are assumed to receive Medicare insurance protection, in each year after age 65, which equals in value the average Medicare outlay per enrollee in that year. Couples are assumed to be the same age and to have two children born when the parents are aged 25 and 30. Assumes retirement at OASI Normal Retirement Age. Projections are based on the intermediate assumptions from the 1993 OASDI, HI, and SMI Board of Trustees reports, adjusted by the authors for the estimated impact of 1993 enactments. OASI payroll tax rate is assumed to be set at 10.65 percent after 1992.

and premiums to support OASI and Medicare over a lifetime than the benefits are worth to them. OASI and Medicare together redistribute about 5.6 percent of this couple's lifetime income to other people.

CONCLUSION

This chapter has helped to illuminate not only the historical growth in Social Security benefits and taxes but also ways in which a blurring of principles can affect the eventual outcomes of a program. Some of the redistribution caused by Social Security is *not* consistent with the principles of individual equity and progressivity, nor with any compromise among them. Individual equity would suggest that participants receive benefits equal to the annuity value of their taxes. Progressivity would suggest that to the extent there is any redistribution at all, it should be directed from those with the greatest resources to those with the greatest need. In practice, however, policymakers were concerned not only with these two principles but also with strengthening the earnings-related image of the program and with setting replacement rates and then maintaining a substantial differential between the benefits of low- and high-income participants. As one consequence, large subsidies have gone to people who were economically very well-off, and the largest of these subsidies have gone to those with the highest lifetime incomes. Many higher-income families, especially one-earner couples, will continue to be subsidized for some time to come.

Positive net transfers to retirees at all income levels, however, could not be sustained forever by constantly increasing tax rates on workers. Among those already scheduled to bear a net lifetime Social Security tax—that is, lifetime taxes in excess of lifetime benefits— are future retirees with high incomes who are single or live in two-earner families. Although they will begin to bear some of the cost of the redistribution achieved by Social Security, their net tax rate, on average, will still remain significantly below their gross rate of tax. That is, they will still receive back a substantial portion of what they put into the system.

If one moves beyond individual equity issues and instead focuses on how well Social Security meets the needs of the elderly over time, the numbers are even more striking. A middle-income couple retiring today can expect OASI and Medicare benefits with an annuity value approaching one-half million dollars. Despite the fact that a higher-income couple may not get back as much as they put in, such a couple turning 65 in 2030 is scheduled to receive approximately $1 million worth of benefits. These numbers suggest that inadequacies in our programs for the elderly may not be due to a shortage of money being spent on each elderly family, but rather to the way that money is spent.

Notes

1. For example, a recent article in the *New York Times* noted: "No one knows for sure whether the Social Security system, on balance, is progressive or regressive—whether, in other words, the taxes and benefits tilt in favor of the rich or the poor" (Rosenbaum 1991). This is not to argue that there is no research on the subject. On the contrary, a large number of studies have examined this issue in a variety of ways, although not all come to the same conclusions (see note 16 below). We merely mean to suggest that an issue that is complex even among experts may be considerably more murky to the public.

2. Perhaps the most notable recent exception to the smooth growth path came about with the retirement of the so-called notch babies, a group born between January 2, 1917, and January 1, 1922, who reached age 65 between 1982 and 1986. The 1977 overhaul of the Social Security benefit formula took away from these notch babies some of the unintended benefits accruing to those who were born just a few years beforehand. The 1972 amendments to the Social Security Act contained a technical error that resulted in an overindexing of benefits—that is, benefit levels for most retirees were rising at a much faster rate than Congress had intended (see figure 5.1 for an illustration of this growth). This rapid growth was seriously threatening the financial health of the Social Security system, and the overindexing could not be maintained. It took legislators until 1977, however, to correct for this overindexing. Notch babies were those who retired during the transition correction period when benefits were brought back down to the growth path that was originally intended. For a more detailed explanation, see U.S. General Accounting Office (1988) and National Academy of Social Insurance (1988). From numbers presented here, it can also be seen that notch babies were still among the big winners in the Social Security system in terms of net transfers received.

3. Benefits for future high-wage workers increase faster than those of low- and average-wage workers because the maximum wage subject to Social Security taxation was increased significantly in real value during the late 1970s and early 1980s.

4. Under the old 50 percent maximum, the SSA intermediate projections indicated a 4.3 percent average tax rate on benefits for 2030. Estimates by the Joint Committee on Taxation (1993) and the Office of Management and Budget (OMB 1993a: 12) on the near-term impact of the new law suggest an ultimate increase in revenues of between 60 percent and 80 percent relative to the old law.

5. The final rate of reduction of benefits depends upon the statutory rate at which the last dollars of tax are paid, as well as the Social Security benefit inclusion rate. If a top-bracket taxpayer were paying a tax rate of 40 percent on 85 percent of benefits, for instance, then net benefits would be reduced by 34 percent.

6. In the 15 percent tax bracket, for instance, taxation of 50 percent of benefits implies

a marginal reduction of only 7.5 percent under current law. Taxation of 85 percent of benefits increases that rate to 12.9 percent. Most benefits, however, would not even fall in the 15 percent bracket. Although inflation will erode the base levels of income at which Social Security taxation begins to apply, personal exemptions, standard deductions, and other special provisions for the elderly are still likely to keep a significant amount of Social Security income nontaxable.

7. Authors' estimate based on the intermediate projections in the Board of Trustees, SMI (1993), adjusted for the estimated impact of 1993 enactments.

8. Assume a retired average-wage worker faces an average tax rate on benefits of 2 percent in 1995 and 8 percent in 2030, and the annual SMI premium rises from $493 in 1993 to $1,729 in 2030 in constant 1993 dollars. An average-wage worker's after-tax, after-premium OASI benefit still rises from $9,056 to $11,088 in constant 1993 dollars, a 22 percent increase.

9. See, for example, Derthick (1979).

10. These figures differ slightly from those usually published by the SSA, since their replacement rate calculations generally do not adjust for inflation in this last year.

11. For high-income individuals, the cycle in replacement rates (see figure 5.2) is due largely to fluctuations in the maximum wage subject to Social Security taxation. The maximum declined in real value relative to the average wage until the mid-1960s, then was increased again through later legislative enactments.

12. Replacement rates were so low at the beginning of Social Security because workers had only participated in the program for a few years before retiring. Barring changes in wage and price levels, longer spans of participation would have eventually caused the original formula to produce replacement rates similar to those we have today. See Robert Ball in *The Report of the Committee on Economic Security of 1935: 50th Anniversary Edition* (1985: 167) and Myers (1993a: 361–65).

13. See Myers (1993a: 205–11) for estimates of net replacement rates after taxes and work expenses.

14. Replacement rate measures used here and by the SSA express benefits as a percentage of earnings in the last year or few years before retirement. Because these calculations are based on hypothetical workers whose wages grow in each year at the same rate as average wage growth in the economy, earnings in the last years before retirement are higher in real value than earnings in earlier years of work.

15. The logic of replacement rates derives from a notion that one will be happier if expenditures out of one's lifetime income are balanced over the life cycle. For instance, adequate food at all points in life is probably better than an abundance at one time and an absence at another. At best, then, the replacement rate can be a means of measuring whether or not a program is responding to one particular pattern of needs of individuals (for balanced spending). If the basic concern is need, however, then one must return to the more fundamental progressivity principle—which requires a comparison with other needs in society—in trying to determine whether replacing one person's income (say, that of a millionaire who has contributed little to the system) is more important than meeting some other need. As we will see, consideration of the replacement rate as a principle has historically led to large net transfers to high-income individuals even when there were many greater needs in society.

16. Meyer and Wolff (1987) offer a good survey of this literature. Some studies that have examined various aspects of this question include: Aaron (1977), Boskin, Arvin, and Cone (1983), Boskin et al. (1987), Bulkhauser and Warlick (1981), Cohen and Male (1992), Feldstein and Pellechio (1979), Goss and Nichols (1993), Hurd and Shoven (1985), Kollman (1992), Myers and Schobel (1983, 1993), Nichols and Schreit-mueller (1978), Pellechio and Goodfellow (1983), and U.S. Congress, House Committee on Ways and Means (1992: 1258–69). Most of these studies, however, show only

selective or limited results (such as benefit to contribution ratios only for a selected cohort), so that comparisons with our results are limited.

The technique employed by Boskin et al. (1987) is one of the closest to ours. They show distributional patterns that are generally similar to those shown here. Our study, however, shows somewhat higher internal rates of return and better net transfers. A number of factors may account for these differences. They use a 3 percent real interest rate to calculate present values, whereas we assume 2 percent (this only affects the net transfer calculations, not the internal rates of return). Our calculations are on a before-income-tax basis, whereas they make a rough estimate of the impact of income taxation of benefits. We also assume that the OASI tax rate is reduced to 10.65 percent after 1992, in accordance with currently pending legislation. Our calculations include the value of survivors benefits for young children and widow(er)s of deceased workers, whereas theirs do not. Their calculations are based on the assumptions in the 1983 Trustees reports, while ours are based on the 1993 reports (Board of Trustees, OASI, 1983, 1993) (except for mortality rates, which we base on 1992 assumptions). Our more recent mortality rate assumptions result in significantly longer life expectancies than theirs, although this is offset to some extent by our lower real wage growth assumptions. Finally, the earnings levels of their "low-" and "middle-"income workers are considerably higher than ours, and they use different assumptions for wage growth over the life cycle.

Myers and Schobel (1993) perform calculations of benefit-to-tax ratios for single workers that are also comparable to ours, using similar assumptions for wage growth, mortality, and interest rates. After adjusting for the fact that they consider only the employee portion of the OASI tax, and assume survival to retirement, we found that our results are consistent with theirs. Goss and Nichols, of the SSA Office of the Actuary (1993), also perform actuarial calculations of OASDI benefit-to-tax ratios for hypothetical workers, using approaches and assumptions that are not far from ours. Our results also appear roughly consistent with those in this latter study, after adjusting for differing assumptions.

17. Calculations in this chapter assume that the combined employer-employee OASI tax rate is set at 10.65 percent in all years after 1992, in accordance with currently pending bills that would reallocate tax rates between OASI and DI. Under this tax rate and the SSA's 1993 intermediate assumptions, OASI suffers a 75-year actuarial imbalance of approximately 1.32 percent of taxable payroll. Appendix table A.12 illustrates what table 5.3 would look like under the tax rates scheduled before this reallocation. Net transfers are a bit worse for future retirees under this assumption, but the basic pattern is the same.

18. The consumer price index for all urban consumers (CPI-U) is used here. As with all other economic variables, we use the SSA's 1993 intermediate assumptions to project future growth in the CPI. A number of different inflation indices are sometimes used by economists, but the CPI-U is the most common. Cost-of-living adjustments in Social Security, by contrast, are based on the CPI for urban wage and clerical workers (CPI-W). The CPI-U is regarded as superior to the CPI-W for most purposes, since it covers a wider spectrum of consumers. The difference between the two indices is negligible; average annual inflation between 1968 and 1988 was 6.3 percent when measured by CPI-U and 6.2 percent under the CPI-W.

19. In precise terms, the present value of a benefit or tax in any given year is determined by multiplying its real value by $(1+r)^x$, where r is the real interest rate and x is 65 minus the worker's age during the year in question. This, of course, means that any taxes or benefits paid before age 65 are *increased* by conversion to present value, while taxes or benefits after age 65 are *reduced*. Present value calculations thus adjust for the *time value of money*: a dollar today is worth more than a dollar, say, 10 years from now, since a dollar today could be invested and accumulate a large amount of interest over those 10 years.

20. The nominal interest rate in any given year is 1.02 times the inflation rate; that is, if inflation were 4 percent, the nominal interest rate would be 6.08 percent (1.04 × 1.02 = 1.0608). We believe that a constant real interest rate over time is the fairest way to make comparisons among different generations. This prevents our results from being affected by arbitrary fluctuations in rates over time, and provides a uniform standard of individual equity for all generations.

21. It might be argued that higher-income individuals should be granted a higher rate of return because they make "better" investments. As a matter of policy, of course, it would be highly questionable to argue that the rich should get better treatment for each tax dollar contributed. In addition, high-income investors can still offset Social Security contributions by borrowing at the prevailing interest rate, and then make high-yield investments with the borrowed money. The appropriate discount rate, therefore, would be the interest rate on the borrowing, which is lower than the average yield on their investments.

22. Technically, an annuity calculation that assumes survival to age 65 slightly over-states the return one receives on lifetime contributions. Like any other insurance scheme, a private annuity system pools risks. The contributions of those who do not survive to retirement, therefore, can be used to supplement the benefits of those who do. In an actuarially fair annuity system where workers contribute over their entire careers, the expected value of benefits for someone who survives to age 65 would exceed the value of his or her contributions plus interest. This effect may be offset to some extent by survivors benefits for the families of workers who die before retire-ment. Our calculations, which adjust for the chance of death in all years after age 21, fully account for both of these effects, and thus provide a comparison of the value of contributions and benefits in a broader annuity framework.

23. We adjust for the chance of death in all years after age 21 for *all* cohorts, even those who turned 21 before the system was established. This effectively provides a comparison of how the system treated typical members of different cohorts.

24. Once again, we adjust for the probability of death each year for each of these beneficiaries. Children's chance of death is taken into account at all ages after birth. The SSA's 1992 intermediate cohort- and gender-specific mortality rates are used for all children born in 1990 or earlier, assuming the elder child is male and the younger child is female. For children born later than 1990, we had to use the 1990-cohort gender-specific mortality tables, since they are the last cohort for which the SSA produced such tables. This has an insignificant impact on the total value of benefits.

Surviving children are assumed to be eligible for survivors benefits until the maxi-mum possible age for a nondisabled child; for instance, the calculations include benefits for surviving full-time students aged 18–21 during the years when that provi-sion was in effect. Our calculations include the value of benefits for surviving mothers and fathers with eligible children, adjusted according to the earnings test when appro-priate.

Widowed members of two-earner couples may adopt a "switching" strategy that will unambiguously increase the lifetime value of their benefits. They can begin to receive either their own benefit or a survivors benefit before the Normal Retirement Age (NRA), and then switch to the other kind of benefit upon attainment of the NRA, without suffering any actuarial reduction on the second benefits. Our calculations assume that they take advantage of this provision, but continue to work until the NRA. All earnings test reductions, actuarial adjustments, and historical rule changes are accounted for when appropriate. A widowed member of a low-wage two-earner couple is assumed to begin receiving survivors benefits as early as age 60, and then to switch to his or her own benefits at the NRA. A low-wage widow of an average-wage husband is assumed to begin collecting her own benefits as early as age 62, and then to switch to survivors benefits at the NRA. An average-wage widow of a high-wage husband is assumed to begin collecting her benefits a year before the NRA, and then to switch to survivors benefits at the NRA (the earnings test makes this her optimal strategy). Average- and high-wage men in our examples cannot take advantage of the switching provision because the earnings test wipes out their survivors benefits. In our tables in the text and Appendix, we count all extra benefits arising from the switching provision as survivors benefits, regardless of their official designation.

25. These factors are omitted because of the scarcity of data on these topics and the vast uncertainty surrounding future projections. Adding in DI benefits and accounting for the chance of disability would probably improve net transfers from the Social Security system slightly for most workers. In a separate study (Bakija and Steuerle 1993), we estimate the impact of Disability Insurance on the value of Social Security for hypothetical workers born in 1965. The distributional impact of DI in this cohort is similar to that of OASI, but on a much smaller scale.

A related issue is the interaction between DI and OASI programs. A so-called disability freeze provision improves net transfers for workers at all income levels. The disability freeze allows years spent receiving DI payments to be excluded from the AIME calculation. As a result, the chance of disability reduces the actuarial value of lifetime tax contributions without affecting benefit levels significantly. The net result of adjusting for DI taxes and benefits and the disability freeze adjustment would be a small improvement in net transfers for most workers. For the purposes of this book, the value of the disability freeze provision—mainly the lower taxes required to support later old-age benefits—is treated as a disability benefit even though there is no technical or formal reimbursement from the DI to the OASI trust funds for this purpose.

26. These mortality tables published by the SSA are the same as those used to construct the intermediate or "best-estimate" projections in the 1992 Social Security Trustees reports (SSA, Office of the Actuary 1992a). Data for a few additional cohorts not covered in this publication were furnished to the authors by the SSA. Mortality assumptions in the 1992 Trustees report are virtually identical to those used in 1993.

27. The assumption of continuous work between age 21 and the Normal Retirement Age is somewhat unrealistic, particularly in the case of working women. Because of drop-out years in the average indexed monthly earnings (AIME) calculation, a few years spent out of the labor force would tend to reduce lifetime tax contributions somewhat without significantly reducing benefits.

For simplicity's sake, low- and average-wage workers' earnings are assumed to grow at the same rate as the average national wage in each year. A worker's income, however, typically starts lower and rises faster over the life cycle. If we were to examine workers with the same level of aggregate lifetime earnings, but with more realistic life-cycle earnings patterns, we would also find that their benefit payments were slightly higher relative to taxes paid. This occurs because most years of lower earnings would be dropped out of the benefit calculation, while years that are included in the calculation would be somewhat higher. There would, however, be some offset for many cohorts whose higher-earning years were at the higher tax rates later in life. For high-wage workers, fluctuations in income above the base limit do not affect the calculations, but few probably began to earn such high wages immediately at age 21. This probably causes us to overstate their tax payments slightly, without affecting benefit levels.

28. The assumption that widows remain single has only a small impact on our analysis. Survivors benefits going to those who are widowed at an early age, when remarriage is at least somewhat likely, represent an extremely small portion of the total value of benefits in our analysis.

29. We also assume a larger number of children would have little impact on the results, since annual benefits for a surviving parent and two children are already above the maximum family benefit level. Additional children, however, would likely add to the number of years that the maximum benefit was made available.

30. No adjustment is made here for the fact that women have lower earnings than

men on average. This does not, however, affect the validity of our results for the benefits and taxes for women at the hypothetical earnings levels. One simply needs to remember that women have been more likely than men to fall into the "low-" and "average-", rather than "high-", wage categories.

31. The cohort retiring in 1995 was covered by survivors insurance for a much longer time than was a cohort retiring in 1960, since the system only started up in 1937. For the earlier cohort there were no Social Security benefits for survivors of workers who died before age 44.

32. As noted in chapter 2, OASI benefits may alternatively be viewed as replacing transfers that workers would have made otherwise to their retired parents. Workers retiring during the first few decades of the system often had parents who had not been covered by Social Security. Some of these workers may have made significant private transfers to help support their retired parents. When these workers retired, however, Social Security made private transfers from their children less necessary. The smaller lifetime private transfers these workers receive from their children might be viewed as an offset to large public transfers given to them (Goss and Nichols 1993).

Trying to trace the net transfers under such a scenario would not be easy, and there would still be many large winners and losers, both within and between generations. Among the issues raised are the following. First, it is impossible to measure private transfers; later generations may be just as generous to their parents as previous ones, since they have greater economic resources. Second, earlier generations of workers were far less likely to have parents survive to retirement than today's workers. Third, those who retired during the 1970s and 1980s received the largest public transfers of all, yet had parents who were usually covered by Social Security themselves. Finally, treating OASI contributions as gifts to one's parents weakens the whole individual equity argument for tying benefits to past contributions. Although contributions to a pension plan clearly entitle one to commensurate retirement benefits, the fact that someone makes a generous gift to his parents does not necessarily entitle him to an equally generous gift from his children.

33. Internal rates of return, of course, do serve other purposes. They can provide a way to check on the sensitivity of present-value calculations to interest rate assumptions. They also permit a comparison of Social Security and market rates of return. For comparisons of the redistribution achieved among people with different amounts of contributions, however, they are inadequate. Benefit-to-tax ratios and internal rates of return for each cohort are presented in the Appendix tables A.8 and A.9, respectively.

34. These results are only moderately sensitive to discount rate and similar assumptions, given the low tax rates and increasing benefits in the first few decades of the program.

35. If one performed calculations going out into the 22nd century, low-income couples retiring then might be found to receive the same level of real transfers as high-income individuals in the late 1970s and early 1980s, although even this appears unlikely under our projections.

36. Since OASI benefits were completely exempt from taxation for many years, but employer contributions and accumulated interest received favorable tax treatment, taking these factors into account would improve the value of OASI slightly for most past retirees. The introduction of taxation of benefits, and its recent expansion, will offset some or all of the value of the tax exclusion for employer contributions for most future retirees. The exact portion that is offset depends on a variety of factors, and the calculations would be quite complicated. Recent calculations by the SSA Office of the Actuary (Goss 1993) suggest that taxation of 85 percent of OASI benefits is consistent with the current practice of taxing pension benefits, even for most future retirees. This implies that OASI, on a lifetime basis, receives income tax treatment at least as favorable as tax-preferred private pensions, and more favorable than most other private savings.

37. Note that these results are affected to some extent by our assumption that the wife never works for wages; if the wife worked for at least a few years, the family's net transfer would be reduced. Many couples will fall somewhere between our one-earner and two-earner couple examples. In general, the less a wife works for wages, the better will be the family's net transfer from the system.

38. Lifetime earned income, like benefits and taxes, is discounted to age 65 using a 2 percent real interest rate and adjusting for the chance of death in all years after age 21. All lifetime wages since age 21 are used in these calculations even if those wages were earned before the inception of the Social Security program. Wage histories before 1935 are constructed by assuming that all workers experienced real wage growth every year equal to the real growth in average wages for all U.S. employees, based on an estimated historical series published by the U.S. Bureau of the Census (1975: ser. D 722-727 and D 735-738).

39. The average life expectancy at age 21 was 53.0 years for white males, but only 46.2 years for black males. Among females, the figures were 59.2 years for whites and 54.4 years for blacks (U.S. Bureau of the Census 1992a: 76). Note that this is a "period" life expectancy, which is typically lower than the cohort-specific life expectancies used throughout the text. A period life expectancy is constructed based on mortality rates at each age in a given year, while a cohort life expectancy is constructed using mortality rates at each age for a given cohort.

40. Aside from the studies cited in the text, Hadley (1982), Kitagawa and Hauser (1973), Menchik (1993), Rosen and Taubman (1979), and Taubman and Rosen (1982) also provide evidence that there is a significant correlation between mortality and such factors as education and income level in the United States. In addition, numerous studies in the United Kingdom have found that people in lower-paying occupations have significantly higher mortality rates. See Wilkinson (1986), Townsend and Davidson (1988), and Whitehead (1988).

41. Duggan et al. (1993a: 11) found that for every additional $1,000 of average income (in constant 1988 dollars) between ages 41 and 45, men experienced a 0.97 percent increase in life expectancy, while women experienced a 0.78 percent increase.

42. To adjust for the impact of income on mortality, we constructed new mortality tables that will result in desired level of life expectancy at age 21 for people at each income level, using the SSA's cohort- and gender-specific mortality tables (SSA, Office of the Actuary 1992) as a base. We constructed each table according to the formula:

$$Q_x^{1} = Q_x R_x^{B}, \tag{5.1}$$

where Q_x^{1} is the constructed mortality rate at each age x for a given cohort and gender after adjusting for the effects of income; Q_x is the SSA's standard mortality rate for that age, cohort, and gender; R_x is the ratio of black to white mortality rates at that age and gender in 1989; and B is a parameter, found by iteration, that results in the desired life expectancy. For low-income persons, B is between 0 and 1, whereas for high-income persons, B falls between 0 and -1. The black-to-white mortality ratio at each age is thus used as a rough proxy to simulate the strength of income's influence on mortality at each age. Mortality rates after age 85 are assumed to be unaffected by income.

43. In the case of years of work, horizontal equity is also an important issue. That is, two individuals with the same annual income levels may work a very different number of years, contribute very different amounts to the system, and yet still receive the same value of benefits. The issue of how Social Security counts years of work is discussed later in chapter 8.

Chapter Six

WELL-BEING AND DIVERSITY AMONG THE ELDERLY

One of the greatest dangers in creating or reforming any social program is to structure it only around the stereotype of some "typical" participant. Not every recipient of Old-Age Insurance is poor, old, and frail, and not every Social Security taxpayer is better off than those whom he or she supports. The elderly are a group that is far from homogeneous. They face different risks in life, their needs vary widely, and their means of supporting themselves are diverse. Since the fundamental rationale of Social Security is to provide for the special or extraordinary needs that often accompany the aging process, it is important that we reflect on the resources and needs of the elderly relative to the nonelderly, and relative to each other.

In defining what it means to be old or elderly, one dictionary suggests that relative comparisons, especially to the time when death might be expected, are appropriate. It defines the elderly as being "somewhat old" or "between middle and old age." It makes the further distinction that "an old person has lived long, *nearly to the end* of the usual period of life," whereas an "elderly person is somewhat old, but usually has the mellowness, satisfactions, and joys of age before him."[1]

Although one might quibble with this dictionary's distinction between being elderly and being old, it does emphasize that the needs and capabilities of senior citizens are likely to vary with age. It also implies that the definition of being old—that is, of being "near to the end"—would change as expected life spans increase. If, at one point in history, someone who was 60 had an expected remaining life span of 10 years, that person might be considered near the end of the usual period of life. When those aged 60 can expect on average to live to 80, they are much less likely to meet the same criterion for being "old." Put another way, if the age at which elderly status were reached were to be defined by remaining expected life span, those who are 65 today would demonstrate characteristics similar to those who were, say, 57 a few decades ago.[2] Add to this the decline in the typical retirement age, and the retired population becomes younger still in both absolute, as well as relative, terms.

To clarify some of the distinctions among senior citizens, we find it useful to divide them into three groups: the near-elderly, the younger-elderly, and the older-elderly. Given life expectancies of about 18 to 22 years at age 62 today, the near-elderly might be considered those still in their sixties, the younger-elderly those in their early- to mid-seventies, and the older-elderly those in their late seventies and beyond. The division, of course, is somewhat arbitrary and a medical definition might not divide years so evenly but put more emphasis on points when impairments become more dominant. The main point, however, is that the definition should change as life spans increase.

ECONOMIC STATUS OF ELDERLY

Income and wealth vary both over time and among different age groups. Two trends especially are worthy of note. First, throughout most of modern history, each cohort of workers and of retired persons typically has been better off than those that preceded it. Second, at a given point in time, income is closely related to age, with peak incomes typically occurring when the head of household is 50 to 55 years old, then declining once again as retirement age is reached and, especially, as one reaches very advanced ages.

Median Incomes

Table 6.1 demonstrates both how income varies over the life cycle and how it tends to grow from cohorts born at one point in time to those born later. Median income represents the midpoint in the income distribution, that is, half of all family units have incomes above this point and half fall below.[3] There is, of course, great variation around the median within each age group. The measure of money income depicted here includes forms of income such as wages and salaries, interest, pensions, Social Security, and other cash transfers from the government, but excludes the effects of taxation. Income for each household or family is also adjusted modestly to account for differences in living expenses depending on the number of persons in the unit and the age of its head.[4]

Table 6.1 MEDIAN MONEY INCOME ADJUSTED FOR UNIT SIZE
AND AGE, BY AGE OF UNIT HEAD (IN CONSTANT 1993
DOLLARS)

Age of unit head	1979	1990
20-24	$15,490	$12,436
25-29	20,467	19,458
30-34	21,606	21,215
35-39	21,690	23,062
40-44	22,764	25,241
45-49	25,347	29,103
50-54	25,959	28,746
55-59	26,193	27,530
60-64	21,269	22,710
65-69	15,968	20,474
70-74	13,566	17,249
75-79	11,726	14,909
80-84	10,653	12,723
85 or older	9,654	11,307
Under 65	21,524	22,571
65 or older	13,011	16,354
All ages	19,714	21,213

Sources: Radner (1987 and 1992), based on tabulations from March
1980 and March 1991 Current Population Survey (CPS).
Notes: Income is adjusted according to weights in the poverty equivalence scale. "Money income" includes cash transfers from the government, but not the effects of taxation. "Under 65" and "all ages" include
persons older than 15.

For those aged 60–64, median income falls somewhat relative to
the peak earning years, but it still remains higher than median income
for the overall population. Those aged 65–69 have median incomes
just below the median for the entire population (although still above
that for families in their twenties). Median incomes drop sharply
thereafter (see table 6.1). Among those 85 or older, median incomes
are a little more than half the level for the population as a whole.

The older-elderly are worse off than the younger- and near-elderly for a number of reasons. Obviously, the older-elderly are less likely or able to work. Many nonwork forms of income, such as private pensions that are not adjusted for inflation, also tend to erode in value as one ages. In addition, each successive cohort of retirees benefits from income growth in the economy. As each new generation earns more and saves more for retirement, it eventually receives higher levels of interest and pension payments. Social Security itself is also designed to provide benefits that rise from one cohort to the next; as each generation earns higher wages during working years, it is granted a higher level of Social Security benefit.[5] Thus, for any given age group such as 65–69-year-olds, incomes tend to be higher as each new cohort replaces an older cohort.

In recent years in the U.S. economy, wage growth has been weak for young workers. Although the elderly in 1990 had significantly higher real median incomes than their counterparts in 1979, people in their twenties and early thirties actually tended to have slightly lower median real incomes. As a result, the typical well-being of the elderly improved markedly relative to that of younger persons during this period.

Other Sources of Economic Well-Being

Although median money income provides a general picture of changes in income over the life cycle, it tends to understate the relative economic well-being of the elderly for a number of reasons. Among the most important factors are the preferential tax treatment given to the elderly, differences in household size, underreporting, the fact that the potential earned income of the elderly is generally much higher than actual income, and the additional economic security provided by accumulated wealth.

Most of the income received by retired persons is nontaxable. Only income from work, which provides an average of just 22 percent of total income for those aged 65 or more, is subject to the Social Security payroll tax. Most Social Security benefits, which account for an average of 35 percent of income for those aged 65 or over, are exempt from all taxation.[6] Some elderly do begin to pay income tax on Social Security benefits when income exceeds $25,000 for a single individual or $32,000 for an elderly couple. Even for those at the highest income levels, however, at most 85 percent of cash Old-Age and Survivors Insurance (OASI) benefits, and no Medicare benefits, are now subject to income taxation. Other forms of income often remain

Table 6.2 EFFECTIVE FEDERAL TAX RATES BY
QUINTILE AND AGE OF UNIT HEAD, 1992
(IN PERCENT)

Income quintile	Age 65 or over	Under age 65
Lowest	3.1	10.3
Second	4.9	18.4
Middle	7.9	22.1
Fourth	12.4	23.9
Highest	23.1	27.5
All quintiles	16.3	24.7

Source: Sammartino and Williams (1991), based on Congressional Budget Office tax simulation model.
Notes: Income quintiles are for the total U.S. population.
Table includes all federal taxes.

nontaxable because of various features of the income tax such as personal exemptions, standard deductions, and a special standard deduction for those aged 65 or older.

Table 6.2 compares the total federal tax burdens of elderly and nonelderly families in the same income classes. The average federal tax rate for all family units under age 65 is nearly 25 percent, compared to about 16 percent for those aged 65 or over. Among those in the middle income quintile, the elderly pay approximately 8 percent of their incomes in taxes, while the nonelderly pay over 22 percent. At each income level, tax rates on the nonelderly are significantly higher. Increased taxation of Social Security benefits, enacted in 1993, will have little immediate effect on those calculations and almost no effect except in the higher quintiles.

Younger families on average are also likely to contain more members than are the families of the near-elderly and elderly. For families with children, however, there is only very modest help from the government in the form of an additional dependent exemption (typically worth less than $350) or, for certain low-income individuals who work, an earned income tax credit. The cost of raising children certainly means that younger families need more income than older families to support the same level of life style or consumption. Although median incomes shown in table 6.1 are adjusted modestly

Table 6.3 RATIO OF AVERAGE INCOME OF ELDERLY TO AVERAGE INCOME OF NONELDERLY UNDER ALTERNATIVE MEASURES, 1979

Measure of income	Income				Income adjusted for underreporting			
	House-hold	Poverty Line Index	Budget Share Index	Per Capita	House-hold	Poverty Line Index	Budget Share Index	Per Capita
Conventional money income	0.52	0.64	0.84	0.90	0.66	0.82	1.07	1.16
Conventional money income plus employment benefits and income in-kind less taxes	0.65	0.80	1.04	1.14	0.79	0.99	1.28	1.40

Source: Hurd (1990), based on data from Smeeding (1989).

for household size, academic studies have suggested that this type of adjustment is inadequate to account for the needs of caring for children.[7] If incomes were counted on a per capita basis—an even stronger family size adjustment—then older persons would appear much better off relative to the rest of the population.

The median income numbers depicted in table 6.1 also obscure underreporting of income. Property income tends to be substantially underreported in surveys such as the one used here. Since property income comprises a much larger percentage of the income of the elderly, survey data tend to understate the relative well-being of the elderly. One validation study of a 1973 Census Current Population Survey found that those under age 65 underreported their income by an average of 3 percent, while those 65 or over underreported by an average of 37 percent.[8]

Table 6.3, from Hurd (1990), offers a rough picture of the effect of these various additional sources of well-being on the relative mean incomes of the elderly and nonelderly. The top line in the table shows the ratio of the average income of the elderly to that of the nonelderly, using the same conventional measure of income underlying table 6.1. The figures in table 6.1 are adjusted for household size and age according to the weights implicit in the official U.S. poverty thresholds (the "poverty line index"). The ratio of elderly to nonelderly average incomes under this measure was 0.64 in 1979. The "budget share index," developed by Van der Gaag and Smolensky

(1982), offers an alternative method of adjusting for household size and age. It arguably provides a better approximation of the relationship between living expenses and household size. Under this adjustment, the elderly to nonelderly income ratio rises to 0.84. On a per capita basis, it rises to 0.90. When adjustments are made for underreporting, the budget share index and per capita measures actually indicate that the elderly have a *higher* average money income than the nonelderly.

The bottom line in table 6.3 further adjusts these figures for the estimated value of employment benefits, in-kind benefits such as Medicare, and the effects of taxation. These adjustments make the elderly look even better relative to the nonelderly. Adjusting for all factors results in the average aftertax, aftertransfer, income of the elderly varying between 99 percent and 140 percent of the average income of the nonelderly, depending upon the method of family size adjustment chosen.

An important distinction must also be made between actual income and potential income. Two persons in equal health and equal circumstances, one of whom has retired and one of whom works, may have equal ability to pay tax or equal needs for government help. The former, however, will be measured as being worse off if we confine our measures of well-being to income alone. Among groups that have the choice of working, income becomes a very poor measure of capability to pay tax or relative ability to support oneself. We know from historical experience that many people in their sixties are quite capable of working, even though they have decided to retire at younger ages. Their choice to retire at younger ages should not necessarily imply that they are worse off than if they didn't retire.

When one turns to measures of wealth, the relative status of the elderly appears even better (see table 6.4). According to the 1988 Survey of Income and Program Participation, the median net worth of those aged 65 or over in 1988 was *twice* the median for the population as a whole. Median wealth for those aged 65 to 69 was the highest of any age group, and was more than 2.3 times as high as the median for the overall population. Even those aged 75 or more had a median net worth much higher than that for the population as a whole. These calculations, by the way, do not account for the additional wealth contained in most pension plans nor for the lifetime value of Social Security or Medicare.

One advantage of greater wealth, of course, is that it reduces the amount of income needed to sustain a given life style. The most obvious reason is that wealth itself—independently from any income

Table 6.4 MEAN AND MEDIAN NET WORTH OF
HOUSEHOLDS BY AGE OF HEAD, 1988

Age of household head	Mean Net worth	Median Net Worth
Under 35	26,493	6,078
35-44	76,922	33,183
45-54	119,536	57,466
55-64	147,679	80,032
65-69	149,495	83,478
70-74	155,795	82,111
75 and over	112,645	61,491
Total, all ages	92,017	35,752
65 and over	136,013	73,471

Source: U.S. Bureau of the Census (1990), based on
Survey of Income and Program Participation.

it produces—is also available to support retirement. A second reason, however, has to do with the understatement of the income due to wealth ownership. Most important here is the rental value of a residence that is owned. Those who own their own home—those over 65 are more likely to own their own home than are younger families—have no rental payments to make. Many have long since paid off their mortgages and owe no interest either. Hence, the income they need to support themselves is less than that needed by someone who owes rental payments or interest on mortgage debt. In economic terms, there is a return to homeownership that does not show up in cash measures of income.

Poverty Rates

Poverty rates give us yet another way to make comparisons among different age groups and within the elderly population itself. Although the official definition of poverty is somewhat arbitrary, it still can provide a rough picture of the proportion of the population that suffers significant privation.[9] Official poverty thresholds are adjusted for family size and age, and are indexed every year to keep

Figure 6.1 PERCENTAGE OF PERSONS BELOW POVERTY AND NEAR POVERTY
THRESHOLDS, BY AGE, 1990

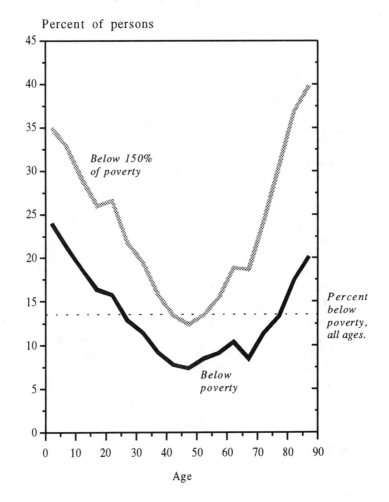

Percent of persons

Below 150% of poverty

Below poverty

Percent below poverty, all ages.

Age

Source: Radner (1992), based on tabulations from March 1991 CPS.

pace with inflation. Income thresholds for 1991 were $13,812 for a
family of four with two children, $8,233 for an elderly couple, and
$6,532 for a single elderly person.[10]

Although poverty rates for those over age 65 used to be among the
highest in the nation, they are now lower than that of the nonelderly
population (see figure 6.1). In 1990, 12.2 percent of people 65 or over

were poor, compared to 13.7 percent of people below 65. Children, in fact, have become the poorest age group in the U.S. population. The poverty rate for people in their sixties is less than half of that for children.

Here, again, it is important to make distinctions among the elderly. The older-elderly are much more likely to be in poverty than are the near-elderly or the younger-elderly, and have poverty rates significantly higher than the overall population. For example, 20.2 percent of those aged 85 or over fell below the poverty threshold in 1990 (see figure 6.1). Poverty rates are also quite high in certain subgroups of the elderly. Among blacks aged 65 and over, 33.8 percent had incomes below the poverty line in 1991. The poverty rate for women aged 65 or over who live alone was 23.6 percent, with many of these individuals, again, being at more advanced ages.[11] These high poverty rates persist despite the existence of the Supplemental Security Income (SSI) program. SSI provided means-tested income assistance to only about 4.5 percent of the population aged 65 or over in 1991, and was often insufficient to push recipients above the poverty line.[12]

Although Social Security helps keep many elderly people out of poverty, these individuals often do not rise far above this line. Among those aged 65 or over, 26.3 percent had incomes below 150 percent of poverty in 1990. Almost 40 percent of people aged 85 or over had incomes below 150 percent of poverty. The rate for all ages was 22.7 percent. Many elderly and nonelderly have to struggle to make ends meet—even when they are not technically in poverty. Radical steps such as the elimination of Social Security, moreover, would once again greatly increase the poverty rate for the elderly, above that for many other groups in the population.

Expenses for Long-Term Care

One example of the widely varying needs among the elderly, particularly the older-elderly, is long-term care. Long-term care includes a broad range of services for chronically disabled persons that are necessary to carry out basic activities of daily life. It is usually provided either through in-home assistance by family members or visiting nurses or through professional care in a nursing home. Zedlewski and colleagues (1990: chap. 4) estimated that about 20 percent of people in the United States aged 65 or over, or about 6.5 million persons, required long-term care services in 1990. About 28 percent of these were cared for in nursing homes, while the bulk of the rest were cared for in the home by family members. The need for long-term care is, of course, much more prevalent at very advanced ages. For instance, it has been estimated that in 1984, about half of all persons aged 85 or over had at least one limitation in an "activity of daily living" such as bathing, dressing, or eating, compared to about 11 percent of those aged 65 to 74.[13] In 1985, 22.1 percent of persons aged 85 or over were in nursing homes, relative to just 1.2 percent of those aged 65 to 74.[14]

Using the Urban Institute's DYNASIM microsimulation model, Zedlewski and colleagues (1990) projected that the number of persons aged 65 and over who require some form of long-term care will rise from 6.5 million persons in 1990 to 9.2 million in 2010, and to 14.4 million by 2030. This growth arises mainly from the increase in the size of the elderly population, and in particular, the large projected growth in the number of people aged 85 and over.[15]

Long-term care expenses can impose a serious financial burden on the elderly and their families, as well as on the nation. The average annual cost of a nursing home stay, for example, is currently around $30,000, and this cost is rising rapidly.[16] Total national expenditures on nursing home care have been estimated at about $65 billion in 1992, and are projected to rise to $86 billion in 1995 and to $131 billion by 2000.[17] An expense that is probably even larger, but not measured, is the work of informal care providers in the home.

Most government support for long-term care problems comes from Medicaid, which now covers about 46 percent of nursing home expenses.[18] Medicaid, however, has many of the classic problems of welfare programs and complicates the attempt to measure relative well-being within the population. Some families game the system by transferring assets from elderly to younger family members, allowing the elderly to qualify for Medicaid.[19] Medicaid also provides an incentive for the younger-elderly to spend all of their assets and avoid saving or insuring themselves.

Economic Resources Decline as Needs Increase

It is clear that the economic resources of the elderly tend to decline as they proceed toward very old age. Unfortunately, the lower incomes of the older portion of the elderly population coincide with a dramatic increase in economic pressures arising from greater health care costs and increased need for assistance with everyday activities.

Figure 6.2 demonstrates the nature of the problem. The principal source of income for most retired persons is Social Security. After retirement, Social Security benefits are indexed to keep pace with

Figure 6.2 COST OF A NURSING HOME RELATIVE TO THE VALUE OF OASI
BENEFITS AND AN UNINDEXED PENSION
(VALUE AT AGE 65 = 100)

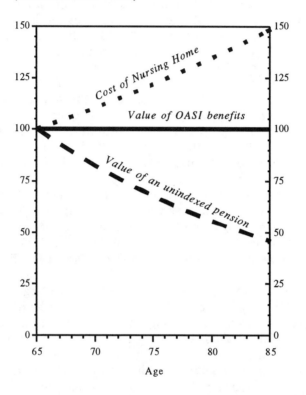

Note: Figure assumes 4 percent annual inflation rate and 2 percent annual increase
in real cost of nursing home care.

inflation, and remain constant in real terms. The second major source
of income is private pensions. In a number of cases, however, these
private payments are not indexed for inflation.[20] The cost of many
types of services received by the elderly—in particular, long-term
health care—is likely to increase considerably faster than inflation.
Since these services are labor intensive, their costs will typically
increase at least as fast as wages in the economy. In figure 6.2, this
is shown by allowing nursing home costs to rise by 2 percent in real
terms per year.[21] In reality, nursing home costs have been rising at
a much faster pace.

If individuals retired with only a few years likely until death, the gradual decline in pension benefits and the decreasing ability of Social Security to cover nursing home costs might be unimportant. Note, however, what happens if there is a 20-year lapse and the retiree is still alive—a common situation today. Private pension benefits have declined by half simply because of inflation and by almost two-thirds relative to the cost of a nursing home. Even Social Security has dropped in value by about one-third relative to the cost of a nursing home.

Individuals who retire in their early sixties believing that their current income is more than sufficient for a variety of emergencies, therefore, are deluded when they do not take into account the number of years they are likely to live. Social Security and private pension plans add to this delusion by encouraging earlier and earlier retirement relative to life expectancy. For example, the OASI system currently allows workers to retire at age 62 and then reduces their annual benefits over the entire retirement span to 80 percent of the level they would have received if they had retired at age 65. With increases in normal retirement age now scheduled, the reduction in annual benefits will be even greater for those retiring at age 62. As a result, many individuals will be able to live moderately well early in retirement, but then face serious financial difficulties later in life.

Role of Pensions

At one point in the development of the Social Security system, many believed that the private pension system might eventually play an important role in supplementing the incomes of most of the elderly. Today, however, it is unclear whether private pensions will ever provide a significant second tier of benefits for most of those elderly at low- and moderate-income levels.[22]

In 1990, approximately 44 percent of couples and individuals aged 65 and older were receiving pension income, including both private plans and government-employee pensions. About two-thirds of these were receiving at least some income from private plans. Pensions and annuities accounted for an estimated 18.3 percent of total income of families and individuals aged 65 or over (Grad 1992).

Those with few or no employer-provided pension benefits, however, are mainly concentrated among the lower-income classes. In 1990, pensions were received by only about 8 percent of elderly families and individuals in the lowest income quintile and about 26 percent of those in the next poorest quintile. Meanwhile, about two-thirds of those in the highest two income quintiles received pension income. Those low- and moderate-income elderly people who were covered by pensions typically received only very small payments. Private pensions and annuities and government-employee pensions together provided only about 3.4 percent of income for those in the poorest income quintile and 7.9 percent for those in the next poorest quintile. Those in the richest income quintile, by contrast, received about 20.1 percent of a much higher base of income from pensions.[23] Thus, pensions and annuities seem to be doing a much better job of supplementing the incomes of middle- and upper-income retirees than of helping those at the lower end of the income scale.

Given the concentration of pension participation in middle- and higher-income categories of current workers, this distribution is likely to persist in the future. In 1991, about 10.1 percent of workers with annual earnings of less than $10,000 participated in employer-sponsored plans; the percentage rose to 43.1 percent for those with earnings between $10,000 and $24,999, and climbed to over 70 percent for those with earnings more than $25,000.[24] Over a lifetime, of course, the percentage of low-earnings individuals who will participate for at least a few years will increase.

On the positive side, *overall* private pension coverage rates can be expected to increase for future retirees. The percentage of workers covered by employer-sponsored pensions increased greatly between 1950 and the end of the 1970s. Federal laws in the 1970s and 1980s also required a number of reforms in private pension plans, such as shorter vesting periods. As a result, a larger share of people who were covered for at least some period of time will eventually be eligible for at least some benefits. In addition, higher labor force participation rates among females mean that a growing number of women will be eligible for pension benefits in their own right. Largely because of these factors, some projections suggest a significant increase in pension coverage among future retirees. For example, projections using the Urban Institute's DYNASIM microsimulation model (Zedlewski et al. 1990) estimated that the proportion of married couples aged 65 and over who receive at least some pension income would rise from 60 percent in 1990 to 86 percent in 2010. Among unmarried or widowed elderly women, the increase would be from 26 percent to 50 percent.[25]

These projections, however, do not conflict with the basic conclusion that lower-income individuals will still be likely to receive *very little* in the way of pension benefits. Some newer trends, not taken into account in these projections, are also disturbing. Many individuals with defined contribution pension plans have begun to withdraw their accumulated funds in lump-sum amounts—leaving themselves without annual income later in their lives. Between 1979 and 1989, moreover, the proportion of workers covered by private employer pension plans declined across all earnings groups, with the sharpest declines occurring among individuals in lower quintiles (Acs and Steuerle, forthcoming).[26] The bottom line is that when the baby boom population begins to swell the ranks of the elderly, half of all retirees are still likely to be without significant employer-provided pension benefits or other income sources and will be dependent largely upon Social Security.

Both the Social Security and the private pension systems must be reformed to fill important gaps in their combined ability to provide adequate retirement income for the elderly. The failure of the private pension system to provide significant benefits to most low- and moderate-income elderly persons argues for either a reform of that private system to expand coverage and participation or for the creation of some higher minimum benefit level in Social Security.

HEALTH AND ABILITY TO WORK

As noted earlier, well-being—especially for those with some choice as to whether to stay in the work force—is better defined by ability than by income. An important issue concerns the extent to which income measures understate true levels of well-being among the elderly and near-elderly. Although ability is very difficult to measure, some facts are known. In particular, life expectancy among the elderly has improved dramatically since the inception of the Social Security system (see chapter 3). Advances in the quality and availability of health care, less strenuous jobs, better diets, and more exercise, are probably responsible for much of this improvement. Judging from improvements in longevity, one would expect that the health of people at any given age has been improving from one generation to the next (i.e., today's 60-year-olds are probably healthier on average than their counterparts a few decades ago). Indeed, Victor Fuchs (1984), among others, has argued that the health status of the elderly is better measured as a function of years remaining until death than of years since birth. Thus, a female aged 65 today might be expected to exhibit the health characteristics of a woman aged 57 when Social

Security was first established, since the remaining life expectancy for each is about 20 years.

The Fuchs argument makes intuitive sense, but it is difficult to verify empirically. No reliable statistics are available that provide a complete or objective assessment of the health status of different individuals over time. Fuchs (1984) did observe that the vast majority of health care expenditures are typically concentrated during a person's last year or two of life. As life expectancies lengthen for each successive cohort, that year or two of severe health problems immediately preceding death has moved further away for people at any given age. It has proven difficult, nonetheless, to derive more complex measures of physical well-being or illness that can be compared over time from one person to the next. Some authors, including Manton (1982), argued that improved health care services are keeping alive many frail elderly persons who would have died in an earlier era. If the main impact of health technology is to extend the lives of very sick elderly persons, rather than to improve the general health of all elderly persons, then the average health of the elderly population may actually be stagnant or declining. Since much technology clearly improves health, rather than merely delaying death, this represents an extreme case.

A statistical analysis of the Retirement History Survey performed by Poterba and Summers (1987) suggested that both general improvement in health at any given age and prolonged lives for very sick elderly people are occurring. The latter factor is considered much more likely to affect the average health status of the older-elderly than that of the younger-elderly, since a much larger proportion of the older-elderly owe their survival to improvements in mortality rates over time.[27] They conclude that the average health of the elderly is probably at least remaining steady. In a comment on their research, Joseph Newhouse (1992: 57) suggests that improvements in health status at, say, age 65 must eventually overtake the countervailing growth in the proportion of persons at that age who are frail survivors. The latter trend is necessarily bounded, since the decline in mortality rates before age 65 must eventually approach a limit. Improvement in the quality of health care, however, is not necessarily bounded, so that the average health status of people at age 65 would eventually improve unambiguously.

Although there is plenty of room for debate and further research on this topic, it seems most likely that the tremendous improvement in life expectancy among the elderly must reflect some improvement in their general level of health and well-being. In particular, the near-

and younger-elderly on average are probably more healthy and at least as capable of working as their counterparts a few decades ago.

In the meantime, the economy has been undergoing a major shift away from goods-producing industries such as manufacturing, construction, and mining. Between 1946 and 1990, jobs in goods-producing industries declined from 41 percent of total employment to 23 percent, whereas service sector jobs climbed from 59 percent to 77 percent of total employment. The U.S. Department of Labor projects that by 2015, goods-producing jobs will account for just 19 percent of employment; 81 out of 100 jobs will be in service industries.[28]

When all these factors are taken together—tremendous increases in longevity, improvements in the quality of health care, and the increasing prevalence of jobs that do not require great physical exertion— the younger portion of the elderly and near-elderly (i.e., those in their sixties) seem more capable of working now than at any time in the past. Indeed, examining more recent data, Manton (1993) concludes that "[i]t seems clear that, physically, most persons should be capable of working at age 65, i.e., the incidence rates for chronic disability for persons 65–74 are low and declining." As pointed out in chapter 3, however, the labor force participation rates of the near-elderly and younger-elderly have declined dramatically since the inception of Social Security.

Table 6.5 offers a more detailed look at labor force participation by age group. The most dramatic declines in participation have occurred among males, since they started at much higher levels. Among males aged 65 to 69, participation rates dropped from 52.6 percent in 1957 to only 25.9 percent in 1992. The rate for males aged 60 to 64 fell from 82.9 percent to 54.7 percent over this period. Among males aged 55 to 59, the rate dropped from 91.4 percent in 1957 to 78.9 percent in 1992. Older males also reduced their participation rates substantially over these years. Participation rates for older women remained at very low levels throughout the period, despite the fact that younger women were dramatically increasing their role in the labor force. Although it is too early to tell, this period of declining participation rates may just now be drawing to a close. Since the mid-1980s, labor force participation rates among older men and women have leveled out or even increased slightly, although they still remain well below the levels of a few decades ago.

Whereas a large portion of the near-elderly and younger-elderly are clearly able to work, but choose not do, we must again caution that there is tremendous diversity within all age groups. Many in their sixties are not capable of working at full-time or even part-time

Table 6.5 CIVILIAN LABOR FORCE PARTICIPATION RATES AT AGE 55 AND OVER

Year	MALES					FEMALES				
	55-59	60-64	65-69	70-74	75+	55-59	60-64	65-69	70-74	75+
1957	91.4	82.9	52.6	*	*	38.2	30.3	17.5	*	*
1965	90.2	78.0	43.0	24.8	14.1	47.1	34.0	17.4	9.1	3.7
1970	89.5	75.0	41.6	25.2	12.0	49.0	36.1	17.3	9.1	3.4
1975	89.4	65.5	31.7	21.1	10.1	47.9	33.2	14.5	7.6	3.0
1980	81.7	60.8	28.5	17.9	8.8	48.5	33.2	15.1	7.5	2.5
1985	79.6	55.6	24.5	14.9	7.0	50.3	33.4	13.5	7.6	2.2
1990	81.2	56.2	24.6	14.5	7.4	56.1	36.0	15.8	8.9	2.7
1992	78.9	54.7	25.9	15.0	7.3	56.8	36.5	16.2	8.2	2.8

Sources: Hurd (1990: 572) updated by U.S. Bureau of Labor Statistics (1991, 1993).
Notes: Data reflect percentage of civilian noninstitutional population in the group specified who are working or actively seeking work. Asterisks (*) denote data not available.

jobs. Disability becomes a much more common problem as workers approach old age. For example, about 10.5 percent of males aged 60 to 64 were on the Social Security Disability Insurance rolls in 1991, as opposed to just 2.4 percent of all males aged 16 to 64.[29] Many individuals also no longer qualify for jobs they held late in their careers, and their potential earning power, even if positive, may be declining.

IMPLICATIONS FOR THE SOCIAL SECURITY SYSTEM

As demonstrated in chapters 3 and 5, a significant portion of growth in the cost of Social Security has been caused by increases in the average length of retirement. Much of the additional spending has been devoted, therefore, to those who are further and further from being old in the dictionary sense of being "near to the end." Relative to life spans, an increasing share of Social Security payments has gone to a younger and younger population, or to those with more years of life expectancy remaining.

In recent years, a number of different problems have come to the fore in the public policy debate. Children are now the poorest group in the population. Among the elderly, long-term care needs have become a greater concern and Medicaid expenditures have skyrocketed in part because of these rapidly rising costs. Meanwhile, private pensions do not seem to be meeting the job of supplementing the retirement incomes of low-income persons.

An additional problem arises when Social Security encourages retirement among relatively young people who are in good health and fully capable of working. The near-elderly and younger-elderly withdraw useful skills and experience from the work force when they retire. The upcoming decline in the ratio of workers to retired individuals makes the loss in output—and the corresponding increase in the share of the output of the young that must be spent on the elderly and near-elderly—more acute.

We do not mean to imply that there are any easy solutions to these problems. Social Security, however, must adapt to the changing nature of both old age and the broader economy. It cannot do so without a firm understanding of the well-being of all its beneficiaries.

Notes

1. *The Random House College Dictionary*, New York: Random House, 1973.
2. The average remaining life expectancy at age 65 for the cohort born in 1935 was

20.1 years for females and 15.8 years for males. For the cohort born in 1875, similar life expectancies occurred at age 57 for females and at age 59 for males. (SSA, Office of the Actuary 1992a), and unpublished tables furnished by the SSA.

3. This median is often a better indicator of the typical characteristics of a group than is the arithmetic mean, since the former is not affected strongly by extreme values.

4. Income is adjusted here according to the weights implicit in the official poverty scales. See Radner (1992).

5. Because of the way the formula is indexed, more real income is eligible for higher rates of return over time. Accordingly, a worker who retires with an average real income of $25,000 a year 20 years from now will receive higher real OASI benefits than one who retires with the same level of real income today. The only requirement is that wage growth be positive on average between the cohorts of retirees.

6. Figures on composition of elderly income are from Radner (1991: 14).

7. The poverty-equivalence weights commonly used to adjust family income probably overstate the economies of scale (or understate the additional cost) associated with a larger family size. See Van der Gaag and Smolensky (1982) for an alternative utility-based weighting scheme for measuring economic well-being. Poverty measures are used in most government studies to adjust for family size, however, because they are "official" and many government programs attempt to measure what happens to those in "poverty" according to this measure.

8. See Hurd (1990) and Radner (1993). The validation study used records from the Social Security Administration and the Internal Revenue Service to check the accuracy of income as reported in the 1973 CPS.

9. See Ruggles (1990) for a discussion of issues surrounding the poverty line.

10. Although these figures are unadjusted for underreporting and taxes, both should be of less concern with those near poverty, since there is less capital income to report and fewer taxes are due.

11. Source: U.S. Bureau of the Census (1992b: 16–18).

12. See Zedlewski and Meyer (1989) for further discussion of this topic.

13. Zedlewski et al. (1990: 48). This estimate is based on data from the 1984 National Health Interview Survey/Supplement on Aging and the 1985 National Nursing Home Survey.

14. U.S. Congress, House Committee on Ways and Means (1992: 266). These percentages are based on Congressional Research Service analysis of the 1985 National Nursing Home Survey and the U.S. Bureau of the Census Current Population Surveys.

15. These projections assume that future disability rates by age remain about the same as in 1993.

16. U.S. Congress, House Committee on Ways and Means (1992: 282).

17. Estimates by the U.S. Health Care Financing Administration, published in Sonnefeld et al. (1991: 17).

18. U.S. Congress, House Committee on Ways and Means (1992: 280).

19. Although legal restrictions have been placed on this sort of maneuver, clever families often find ways around them. One can legally transfer assets if done enough years before entering a nursing home. Even in later years, the transfer of assets is usually difficult to trace or prove.

20. Ad hoc increases are sometimes given in private defined benefit pension plans. Government-employee pension plans more often are indexed for inflation, and some private defined-contribution plans receive at least partial indexing or offer it as an option.

21. In an economy with real growth, of course, these rising service costs would also

reflect improvements in amenities in nursing homes and in the productivity of nurses and others who work there.

22. See Reno (1993) for a more detailed discussion of these issues.

23. Grad (1992).

24. These data are drawn from Employee Benefit Research Institute tabulations from the March 1992 Census Bureau Current Population Survey, in Silverman and Yako-boski (1993).

25. Another set of projections using the ICF PRISM microsimulation model came to similar conclusions about growth in the proportion of future retirees receiving pension income (Advisory Council on Social Security 1991).

26. The proportion of workers in the lowest earning quintile who were offered pension coverage declined by 5 percentage points between 1979 and 1989; in 1989, only 41.7 percent had a plan offered to them, and less than one-third actually participated.

27. Poterba and Summers (1987) also estimated the portion of people in different age groups who are "marginal survivors" (i.e., they owe their survival to improvements in mortality rates over time). Their analysis examined only people who had survived to age 50; improvements in mortality at younger ages were not taken into account. They found that about 5.4 percent of men and 3.6 percent of women who were alive at age 60 in 1980 would not have been alive had mortality rates remained constant over the preceding 30 years. By contrast, about 15.1 percent of men and 35.2 percent of women aged 80 in 1980 owed their survival to improvements in mortality rates that occurred between 1950 and 1980. A far greater proportion of the older elderly were therefore marginal survivors. Does this survivor fit the possible profile described by Manton (1982)? The evidence is still limited and the implications different for different age groups.

28. Historical figures are from the U.S. Department of Labor, Bureau of Labor Statistics, cited in *Economic Report of the President* (1992: 344–45). Projections are from Kutscher (1991: 7).

29. These percentages are from Bakija and Steuerle (1993: 9), based on data from the SSA, Office of the Actuary (1993).

Part Three

OPTIONS FOR REFORM

Chapter Seven

OPTIONS FOR REFORMING THE SOCIAL SECURITY PAYROLL TAX

To this point in this volume we have provided background on the Social Security program: the principles, sometimes conflicting, under which it operates; its promises of benefit and tax levels that together cannot be met in the future; the extent to which redistribution occurs among different groups over time; and the changing economic status and patterns of needs of the older-elderly, younger-elderly, and near-elderly.

This background allows us to develop more informed judgments on a variety of options to reform Social Security. By examining the economic status of the elderly, for instance, we can better assess how well the program meets the principle of progressively redistributing income from those with greater means to those in greater need. The information provided so far will prove sufficient to draw some strong conclusions: in particular, some options will be shown to fall outside the bounds of what is reasonable under almost any principle. Other proposals cannot be determined as bad or good per se without reference to some further value judgment, such as the extent to which higher-income individuals should support redistribution by paying Social Security taxes in excess of benefits received. Given that value judgment, however, some options are able to achieve the redistribution more efficiently or in ways more consistent with a goal such as equal treatment of equals. The first four chapters in Part Three closely examine a variety of reform options, with reference to various principles of Social Security and the extent to which a reformed system would follow those principles. Chapter 11, the final chapter in the volume, summarizes our conclusions about principled approaches to reform. We begin in the current chapter with options for reforming the Social Security payroll tax.

For many years the Social Security tax was either a small or moderate-sized item in the array of taxes assessed in the United States. In 1950, for instance, Social Security tax receipts amounted to only 1.1

Table 7.1 FEDERAL TAX RECEIPTS, 1950–91

| Year | As a percentage of GDP | | | Social security taxes as a % of total fed. taxes |
	Social security taxes	All other federal taxes	Total federal taxes	
1950	1.1	15.4	16.5	6.8
1955	1.6	15.7	17.3	9.3
1960	2.5	15.3	17.8	13.8
1965	2.6	14.1	16.7	15.6
1970	3.9	14.1	18.0	21.9
1975	4.9	12.2	17.1	28.5
1980	5.3	13.5	18.7	28.1
1985	6.0	11.7	17.7	34.0
1990	6.6	11.9	18.5	35.8
1991	6.8	11.4	18.1	37.3

Source: Authors' calculations based on data from U.S. Bureau of Economic Analysis.
Notes: Social Security taxes include payroll contributions for OASDI, HI, and railroad retirement. Nontax receipts, SMI premiums, and contributions to federal employee retirement plans are not counted as taxes.

percent of GDP, while all other federal taxes consumed 15.4 percent of GDP (see table 7.1). Over the succeeding decades, the Social Security payroll tax has grown steadily in importance while other federal revenue sources have waned. By 1991, Social Security tax receipts had increased to 6.8 percent of GDP, while all other federal taxes had declined to just 11.4 percent. Now the second largest of all revenue sources, the Social Security tax accounts for over 37 percent of total federal tax receipts and is 83 percent as large as the far more visible federal individual income tax.

Along with the growth in the Social Security tax has come greater attention to the way it operates, to its incentive effects, and to its impact on the income distribution. Long gone are the days in which changes in the Social Security tax generated little controversy or when fiscal imbalances could be easily remedied by increasing tax rates. By the time of the 1983 Social Security Amendments, for instance, reform meant benefit reductions as much as it meant tax increases. Those reforms, in fact, were fashioned in a way that would avoid increasing the maximum scheduled tax rate (for 1990 and beyond).[1]

CHANGING THE TAX RATE

At first it may appear that the most straightforward of all options for restoring long-run balance to the Social Security system is once again to increase the payroll tax rate. For the first time since the early inception of Social Security, however, serious attention has been given in recent years to proposals to reduce, rather than increase, payroll tax rates. Both courses of action raise a number of concerns in terms of both equity and efficiency.

Tax Rate Increases

We have already seen that Social Security's basic rationale begins with the notion that progressive redistribution is required to address some of society's most pressing needs. Although the term *Social Security* is now used mainly when discussing programs for the elderly, the original Social Security Act provided various types of assistance for all age groups. It is in the broader context of social needs throughout the population that tax rate changes must be considered. The historic rise of about 3 percentage points per decade in the Social Security tax rate between 1950 and 1990, moreover, almost certainly cannot be repeated. This does not mean that some further rate increase might not be used to help restore balance to the system; only that it will be modest at best relative to past increases.

Recent enactments by Congress indicate that already there is special concern with the taxes faced by the nonelderly. The 1983 Social Security Amendments did not increase the tax rate over the long term, and a 1988 law to provide catastrophic health insurance for the elderly—a law repealed in 1989—was designed by Congress with a self-imposed constraint that the financing for those increased benefits should not be paid by those under age 65.

The increased concern with the payroll tax rate derives partly from the recognition that growth in the Social Security tax has already been replacing more progressive parts of the tax system. More importantly,

Table 7.2 EFFECTIVE RATES OF SOCIAL SECURITY TAX AND FEDERAL
INCOME TAX FOR FOUR-PERSON FAMILIES AT VARIOUS
INCOME LEVELS, 1955–91

Year	Half Median Income			Median Income			Twice Median Income		
	federal income tax	social security tax	total	federal income tax	social security tax	total	federal income tax	social security tax	total
1955	0.0	4.0	4.0	5.6	3.4	9.1	10.8	1.7	12.5
1960	0.2	6.0	6.2	7.8	4.6	12.4	12.1	2.3	14.4
1965	2.2	7.3	9.4	7.1	4.5	11.6	11.1	2.2	13.4
1970	4.7	9.6	14.3	9.4	6.7	16.1	13.5	3.4	16.8
1975	4.2	11.7	15.9	9.6	10.4	20.0	14.9	5.2	20.1
1980	6.0	12.3	18.3	11.4	12.3	23.7	18.3	6.5	24.8
1985	6.6	14.1	20.7	10.3	14.1	24.4	16.8	8.5	25.3
1990	5.1	15.3	20.3	9.3	15.3	24.6	15.1	9.5	24.6
1991	4.8	15.3	20.1	9.2	15.3	24.5	15.0	10.6	25.6

Sources: U.S. Department of Treasury Office of Tax Analysis (Allen Lerman), U.S. Census Bureau Current Population Reports (various issues), U.S. Internal Revenue Service Statistics of Income (various issues), and authors' calculations.
Notes: Effective tax rates are expressed here as the total amount of tax paid as a percentage of cash wages. Table includes both employer portions of the Social Security tax. All amounts are rounded to the nearest tenth of a percent. The median income among four-person families was $43,056 in 1991. Table assumes all income is earned by one spouse. Itemized deductions are assumed to equal 23 percent of income through 1986 and 18 percent thereafter.

postwar tax changes have placed a particular burden on low- and moderate-income working families with children, who have also fared poorly in the income tax. A four-person household earning about one-half the median income for that size family (about $21,500 in 1991) faced a federal income tax and employer-employee Social Security tax bill equal to more than 20 percent of its income in 1991 (see table 7.2). This represents a dramatic increase from 1955, when the two taxes consumed only 4 percent of such a family's income. For a four-person family of median income (approximately $43,000 in 1991), the combined federal income tax and Social Security tax rate rose from 9.1 percent in 1955 to 24.5 percent in 1991. Such a family now faces nearly the same combined tax rate as a similar size family with twice as much income.

The overall federal tax burden, on the other hand, did not change much over this period; it rose from 16.5 percent of GDP in 1955 to 18.1 percent in 1991. The increases depicted in table 7.2, therefore, reflect a substantial shifting of the federal tax burden toward low- and moderate-income working families with children. This shift was due mainly to increased Social Security payroll taxes, but also to a dramatic decline in the value of dependent exemptions in the income tax system.[2]

The principle of progressivity requires that the needs of the people who pay taxes be compared to the needs of those who receive the benefits financed by the taxes. Many workers today have life-styles and consumption levels below those of many of the Social Security recipients they are supporting. As discussed in chapter 6, there is substantial evidence that people in their sixties are typically better off economically than young families with children. Reducing the after-tax income of low- and moderate-income families through further Social Security tax rate increases cannot help but have an impact on children, the age group with the highest poverty rate in the United States. From an efficiency standpoint as well, policymakers must be concerned with the degree to which additional payroll taxes reduce investment in children to finance additional consumption by the near-elderly and younger-elderly. To the extent that higher payroll taxes support higher benefits to the younger, better-off portion of the elderly population, they are difficult to justify.

One might argue to the contrary that although low- and moderate-income families have been facing a steadily growing tax burden, they still pay lower tax rates than their counterparts in most other industrialized countries. In that context, an increase of a few points in the payroll tax rate might not seem inappropriate. This argument, however, is incomplete. Even if taxes can be raised, the United States still has an obligation to determine where needs are greatest and where the funds can best be spent. Many of these other countries also have generous child allowances that do a much better job of reducing tax burdens on low- and moderate-income families than do personal exemptions and standard deductions in the U.S. income tax.

In a growing economy, each generation achieves a consumption level on average that is above that of the previous generation. Another argument in favor of higher payroll tax rates might be that transfers from today's moderate-income workers to elderly people in equal or better circumstances would simply recognize the generational gains that will probably be obtained by workers later in life. This argument, however, is dubious. Such a goal goes far beyond that of setting up a Social Security system to address the special needs of old age; indeed, it argues for a transfer system even in the absence of special needs. Carried further, the argument could be used to suggest that education and other investment in children should be forgone in favor of the current consumption of their parents and grandparents, or that we should increase even further the debt burden we leave to future generations.

When considering increases in Social Security payroll tax rates, one must also be concerned with economic efficiency. In economic terms, there is much more efficiency loss associated with raising the tax rate today than when the rate was lower. That is, a tax rate increase of 1 percentage point generally causes more economic disincentives and distortions when rates are already high than when they are low. One reason is that each 1 percentage point rate increase represents a much larger share of a worker's *disposable* income when rates are already high. An exaggerated example illustrates this point. When the tax rate is zero, a 1-percent rate increase reduces disposable income by only 1 percent. The same increase when rates are raised from 98 percent to 99 percent reduces disposable income by 50 percent.

With that said, changing demographics make it unlikely that we will be able to completely avoid increases in the tax burden necessary to support programs for the elderly. The upcoming retirement of the baby boom generation will make it very difficult to hold the line on taxes and to force the entire additional burden of an aging population onto the aged themselves through lower benefits. This issue, of course, extends beyond cash retirement benefits. Even if the government is highly successful in its efforts to control rising health care costs, we have seen that demographic trends alone will cause the medical bill for the elderly to rise dramatically as a share of GDP during the next century.

The principles of progressivity and efficiency both provide justification for shifting government resources over time toward areas where needs are greatest. Those who live during a period of war bear sacrifices that are not required of those in other times. When crime rates are especially high, the cost of police protection will rise. Our children are a current need. In a period where the old-elderly come to comprise an unusually high percentage of the population, those needs in turn cannot help but become relatively more dominant. Some Social Security tax rate increases, therefore, cannot be taken out of the picture as a response to those needs.

Reducing the Payroll Tax

In 1990 Senator Daniel Patrick Moynihan (D.-N.Y.), now chairman of the Senate Committee on Finance, made a proposal that would, at least initially, reverse the historical trend toward ever-higher Social Security payroll tax rates. His proposal would reduce the current combined employer and employee Social Security tax rate from 15.3 percent to 13.1 percent, in exchange for much higher rates during much of the first half of the next century. The system would be returned to pay-as-you-go financing, eliminating the buildup of large trust funds.

Moynihan's proposal was motivated by two concerns, both legitimate. First, as just noted, increases in the Social Security tax rate have been reducing the progressivity of the tax system slightly and, more particularly, have been placing a heavier burden on young working families.

A second problem is that the buildup in Social Security trust funds is arguably being spent to finance other parts of the federal budget. Without the positive cash flow provided by the Social Security surpluses, the government would have to raise other taxes, cut spending, and/or borrow more from the public. Senator Moynihan, among others, has argued that the Social Security surplus primarily provides an excuse for legislators to avoid other tax increases or spending cuts, thereby enlarging the non–Social Security deficit.

While returning Social Security to pay-as-you-go financing might be viewed as a response to both of those situations, it carries with it several excess pieces of baggage—pieces so large that the load has become insupportable to many. In truth, some supporters of lower rates, including Senator Moynihan, are probably aware of and concerned with these problems, but see no advantage in trying to address them unless rate reduction becomes more likely to be enacted.

The first difficulty is that the proposal would increase the deficit over the near term—requiring more borrowing by the government from the public and an exacerbation of America's fiscal crisis. Some proponents have argued that reducing the current payroll tax would force legislators to act more aggressively to reduce the non–Social Security deficit. However, if the payroll tax were reduced by 2.2 percentage points, as proposed by Moynihan, the government would

Table 7.3 PROJECTED SOCIAL SECURITY TAX RATES
REQUIRED UNDER PAY-AS-YOU-GO FINANCING

Year	OASI	DI	Total OASDI	HI	Total OASDHI
1993	10.1	1.3	11.4	3.2	15.3
2000	9.7	1.7	11.4	3.9	15.3
2010	9.4	2.0	11.3	5.1	16.4
2020	11.5	1.9	13.4	6.8	20.2
2030	13.6	1.9	15.5	8.8	24.3
2040	14.0	1.9	15.8	10.1	25.9
2050	14.1	2.0	16.1	10.6	26.7

Sources: Board of Trustees, OASDI and HI (1993), intermediate assumptions, adjusted by authors to reflect estimated impact of 1993 enactments, including removal of HI tax cap. Tax rates are set at the cost rate minus revenues from income taxation of benefits (assuming that additional revenues from 1993 increase in benefit taxation are credited to general funds).

have to come up with nearly $60 billion in additional spending cuts and increases in other taxes per year simply to keep the overall federal deficit from expanding.[3] Efforts to effect any real reduction in the overall federal deficit would require even more stringent measures. Even if a case might be made for a Social Security payroll tax cut that was offset by other tax increases or spending reductions, the Moynihan plan did not provide for such offsets.[4]

Second, the Moynihan plan, without any other change, would schedule significant payroll tax increases in the future. Table 7.3 illustrates an estimate of the payroll tax rates that would be required if Social Security were returned to a pay-as-you-go basis.[5] Under current law, the combined OASDI rate is scheduled to remain at 12.4 percent for the indefinite future. Under the Moynihan plan, the OASDI tax could be kept a point or two below the current rate for the next two decades or so. After that, demographic changes would force the OASDI rate to climb steadily, to 15.49 percent in 2030 and 16.06 percent by 2050 (see table 7.3). Much of this increase results from rectifying the imbalance that already exists under current law, but a significant amount would be due to the proposed elimination of a buildup in the Social Security trust funds.

Note also that this future increase in OASDI payroll tax rates would come on top of an HI tax rate that is already expected to climb significantly. Table 7.3 shows the Health Care Financing Administration's (HCFA's) best-estimate projections of the HI tax rates that would be required to support currently promised HI expenditures. Rates would have to rise rapidly even under a much more optimistic scenario. The total Social Security tax rate, therefore, could reach well above 20 percent by the middle of the next century under pay-as-you-go financing, even assuming slow growth in Medicare. Still other tax increases, moreover, will be required to support Medicare Supplementary Medical Insurance and other programs that meet the needs of the elderly.

Another argument for cutting payroll taxes today goes as follows. Future generations will end up paying higher taxes either way—with or without the trust funds. After all, the Social Security trust funds are essentially IOUs that will have to be redeemed by future taxpayers. If the system relies on trust fund financing, future workers will probably end up paying higher income taxes or sacrificing in some other way to repay the trust funds in an amount sufficient to support future benefits. If, on the other hand, the system converts to pay-as-you-go status, future taxpayers will bear essentially the same burden through the payroll tax system. As a result, it might be argued, the trust funds are irrelevant and misleading, and ought to be eliminated.

In fact, this argument holds only if current reductions in payroll tax revenues are offset concurrently by spending reductions and tax increases elsewhere. If a payroll tax cut were to increase the current budget deficit, the burden on future taxpayers would unambiguously rise, since the national debt and corresponding interest payments would be increased substantially.

Advocates of pay-as-you-go financing have also argued that by setting future payroll tax rates such that they reflect the true costs of the system, the public may become more conscious of the need to restrain the program's costs at that time. This argument remains suspicious so long as the proposal would provide a windfall to today's voters, push the difficult decisions off onto the shoulders of future generations, and establish in law a preference for raising tax rates (which would already be enacted) over benefit reductions (which would require new legislation) as a means of restoring fiscal balance in the future.

Reduction of Social Security payroll tax rates is certainly appealing to those concerned with progressivity, as well as to those who wish to remove some of the tax disincentives to work. Considering the large burden future taxpayers are already expected to bear, however, one wonders whether there is much justification for lowering tax rates today if it merely means shifting onto our children an even greater burden through higher future tax rates. To avoid such a shift, once again, any reduction in rates would need to be offset by specific spending cuts or tax increases elsewhere.

A payroll tax cut, of course, could be implemented gradually, if matched by reductions in the rate of benefit growth so that the system would be returned to long-run actuarial balance. Given the large spending cuts and tax increases that will already be required to keep the existing federal deficit under control and restore balance in the Social Security system, however, a responsible plan of this sort would have to be considered as an add-on to an already difficult task.

CHANGING THE LIMIT ON TAXABLE EARNINGS

For each individual, the total amount of annual earnings that can be subject to Social Security tax is limited.[6] Recall from chapter 4 that in 1993, the cap (or taxable earnings limit) was set at $57,600 for Old-Age, Survivors, and Disability Insurance taxes, and at $135,000 for the Hospital Insurance tax. Beginning in 1994, the HI cap will be eliminated entirely. The dollar limit in OASDI is increased each year by the rate of increase in average wages.

One common proposal for improving the fiscal balance of Social Security and increasing progressivity is to raise or even eliminate the limit on taxable earnings for OASDI. Because about 87 percent of wages and salaries in covered employment already fall below this cap, the amount of revenues that can be raised in this way is modest. Even if the cap were completely eliminated, so that all wages in covered employment were subject to taxation, revenues would rise only about one-ninth above their current level.

Under the current Social Security system, any increase in the cap leads in turn to an increase in future benefit payments to those high-income workers who pay the higher taxes. The long-term benefit increase would not fully offset the revenue gain, largely because the top bracket of the current benefit formula provides a small replacement rate (15 percent of the average monthly earnings subject to tax in that bracket). Nonetheless, benefit gains for those with very high incomes would be significant. With lifetime Social Security benefit amounts already growing to several hundred thousand dollars for future high-income retirees (see chapter 5), it is not clear that any social goal is served well by increasing benefit amounts even further.[7]

If the purpose of a base increase is to raise net taxes from high-income individuals, it might be better to find alternative means of achieving that end without raising benefits. One could adjust the benefit formula so as to limit benefit increases going to higher-income persons, perhaps by lowering below 15 percent the top rate in the formula that relates benefits to past earnings.[8] This, of course, would reduce the returns that future high-income retirees receive from the system below levels that are already expected to be negative. Alternatively, if progressivity is the principal goal, it would be simpler—and require a smaller increase in tax rates—to increase *income* tax rates in this income range than to increase the Social Security tax limit.

A second problem with raising the taxable earnings limit is a technical one related to the efficiency and horizontal equity of the tax base: those who are self-employed include capital income in earnings subject to Social Security taxation, whereas corporations and some partnerships include returns to capital as dividends or other payments that are not subject to Social Security tax. This problem is accentuated at higher-income levels where larger percentages of income represent returns to capital. The higher the Social Security earnings limit, therefore, the more likely it is that those who are self-employed in the noncorporate sector would face increased discrimination relative to those who are employed but do not have their returns to capital subject to Social Security tax. Whereas the self-employed might circumvent this problem by incorporating themselves, this type of tax-induced behavior is inefficient and breeds disrespect for the tax system as a whole. In this regard, the current separation of the HI tax base from the OASDI tax base already discriminates against the self-employed. It also adds considerable complexity to the Social Security tax system and is not easily explainable to most taxpayers.

In sum, since most wages are already subject to Social Security taxation, an increase in the maximum amount of wages subject to OASDI tax would increase revenues only modestly. Continually increasing the limit on taxable earnings distances the Social Security system from three of its underlying principles: there is almost no "need" to increase benefit levels for high-income beneficiaries; there would be a decrease in horizontal equity between the self-employed and those who invest capital through corporations; and some self-employed would engage in inefficient shifts in form of business organization. If anything, the tax base for OASDI and HI ought to be brought back into line.

EXPANDING THE TAX BASE BY ELIMINATING TAX PREFERENCES

Broadening the tax base and eliminating special preferences for certain types of income or expenditure have been principal goals of tax reformers for decades. Although these efforts have usually been centered on the individual income tax, uneven taxation can cause distortions and inequities in any tax system. Given the size of the Social Security tax and its long-run imbalance, traditional tax reform—expanding the tax base to include items of income that are now favored—is a way of both reducing the long-term deficit and increasing the efficiency and horizontal equity of the tax system without raising tax rates.

A strong case can be made that two workers with equal economic resources should pay the same amount of tax. Why should one worker earning $30,000 in cash wages pay $4,590 in combined employer and employee Social Security tax, while another, receiving exactly the same amount of employment compensation but receiving $8,000 in nontaxable benefits, pay only $3,366 in tax? If those differences hold up for years, the first worker can end up with a tax burden tens of thousands of dollars greater, despite an identical ability to shoulder the burden of government.

Who are the victims of this tax discrimination? Typically, they are people who have greater need of cash or who are less likely to work for firms with substantial nontaxable employee benefits, most of which are in the form of health insurance or private pension insurance. Women traditionally have been subject to such discrimination because they have been less likely to work in jobs providing employee benefits. In addition, when one person in a family already receives benefits such as health insurance, the secondary worker (often female) will receive little or no additional gain from provision of similar insurance. Hence, not only does the secondary worker receive less total compensation, counting employee benefits, for similar work, but the tax system adds to the discrimination against her.

The Social Security system does mitigate this uneven treatment by granting higher retirement benefits to those with greater tax contributions. That is, those who put in fewer tax dollars receive fewer benefits down the line. Because the benefit formula is progressive, however, the benefit loss is typically much smaller than the tax saving. Thus, the benefit offset to the tax discrimination is only partial.

Social Security tax discrimination is not only unfair, but it causes a number of distortions in the economy. The tax-free status of employee benefits induces people to take a greater share of their compensation in this form. In the case of tax-free employer-provided health insurance, for instance, taxpayers are induced to accept lower cash wages to buy more insurance than they would otherwise purchase. Suppose a firm is willing to provide an additional dollar of compensation to an employee who faces a 50 percent marginal tax rate (e.g., the combination of 28 percent federal income tax, 15.3 percent Social Security tax, and a high state income tax rate).[9] If the firm provides the dollar in the form of cash wages, the employee receives only 50 cents after taxes. If, on the other hand, the employer provides a dollar in the form of additional health insurance, the employee receives the full dollar. The tax system, therefore, provides incentives to both employers and employees to purchase insurance plans that are more generous than they otherwise would be. These incentives encourage higher prices and excessive consumption of health care services.

Growth in employee benefits has slowly eroded the Social Security tax base, leading to increased pressures to raise tax rates. Employee benefits increased from about 2.4 percent of total compensation in 1950 to 8.4 percent in 1991 (see table 7.4).[10] The SSA actuaries project that this trend will continue, and that taxable payroll will decline steadily from 43.0 percent of GDP in 1990 to just 38.6 percent of GDP in 2050.[11] Such an erosion of the tax base will require tax rates to be higher than they would otherwise have to be to raise the same amount of revenues.

Social Security taxation of employee benefits, or at least capping the growth of the amount that can be excluded, could provide a significant reduction in the long-term actuarial deficit of Social Security. Such a reform, of course, faces some of the same problems as raising the limit on taxable earnings. By increasing the amount of earnings credited on workers' Social Security records, benefit levels will rise in the long run, offsetting some portion of the revenue gains. Because an expansion in the tax base would improve the efficiency and fairness of the tax system, however, such a reform would be desirable even if it didn't provide any improvement in the system's

Table 7.4 WAGES, SALARIES, AND EMPLOYEE BENEFITS AS
PERCENTAGE OF TOTAL EMPLOYEE
COMPENSATION

| Year | | Employer contributions to: | | | | Total Comp- ensation |
	Wages & salaries	Social insurance	Private health insurance	Pensions & profit sharing	Other	
1950	94.7	2.9	0.5	1.1	0.8	100.0
1960	91.9	4.2	1.1	1.7	1.0	100.0
1970	89.2	5.5	2.0	2.1	1.2	100.0
1980	83.8	7.8	3.6	3.3	1.5	100.0
1990	83.3	8.4	5.3	1.5	1.5	100.0
1991	82.9	8.6	5.5	1.4	1.5	100.0

Source: Authors' calculations based on data from U.S. Bureau of
Economic Analysis.
Notes: Social insurance includes OASDI, HI, railroad retirement,
government employee retirement, unemployment insurance, and
public worker's compensation. The "Other" category consists
mostly of life insurance and private workers' compensation.

long-run financial balance. To strengthen its fiscal impact, the reform
could also include a compensating adjustment in the benefit formula
so that long-run benefits would not increase.[12]

In any event, eliminating the special tax preference for employee
benefits is likely to be a fairer and more efficient method of raising
additional revenues than either increasing the payroll tax rate or
eliminating the cap on taxable earnings.

ALTERNATIVE METHODS OF FINANCING SOCIAL SECURITY

This chapter has so far emphasized options that rely on the existing
payroll tax format to address the long-term deficit in Social Security.
More fundamental shifts in the way the system is financed must also
be mentioned. The number of alternatives, however, is countless,
and issues raised in some of these alternatives move well beyond
the scope of this study toward broader issues such as general tax
reform.

How Much General Revenue Financing?

The current Social Security system requires that a significant portion of Social Security health care benefits—in particular, insurance for doctors and other care outside of hospitals (Medicare Part B, or Supplemental Medical Insurance)—be financed out of general revenues of the federal government. Contributions from general revenues for SMI are currently *larger* than the more widely recognized surplus of OASDI payroll taxes over spending.[13] In addition, income taxes collected on Social Security benefits are redeposited directly into the OASDI trust funds.[14] Thus, the nonelderly must pay income tax to support defense, public works, and other governmental efforts, while the elderly, to the extent that their income taxes are designated to cover their own benefits, forgo bearing a share of the former burden.[15]

If payroll taxes are not raised to cover future Social Security deficits, should the system rely even more heavily on general revenue financing? Probably not. Such shifts would make even weaker the tie between benefits and taxes—a tie that at least provides some fiscal discipline to the program. A hybrid financing system that relies partly on earmarked payroll taxes and partly on general revenues gives a misleading impression of the amount we are actually spending on programs for the elderly, since people tend to focus only on the earmarked taxes.

Following the approach used when the system was originally adopted, one might move in the opposite direction—requiring elimination of general revenue financing of Social Security that occurs through Medicare, Part B, and the ways in which the trust funds are reimbursed for income taxation of Social Security benefits.[16] This might help to force more fiscal discipline on programs for the elderly. Equally important, it would probably lead to a policy process in which trade-offs among the different programs for the elderly would more likely be considered.

If one moves in the direction of general revenue financing, one intriguing possibility is to substitute another tax for part or all of the Social Security tax. For instance, some would argue that value-added taxation should displace some Social Security taxation. This type of shift would generally increase the reward from work and reduce the reward from consumption—although for most workers who consume their wages, the net change is likely to be small.

There are several difficulties. Adoption of a value-added tax can add significantly to tax filing and tax administration burdens. It should not be undertaken lightly. Such a tax shift also requires reconsideration of the trust fund concept and loosens even further the tie between contributions and eventual benefits (although one could also argue that benefits were always related to earnings subject to tax, rather than taxes paid).

Japan recently adopted a value-added tax (VAT), in part because it wanted the increasing burden of an aging population to be placed on the entire population, not simply on nonelderly workers. Japan's population has aged much faster than that of the United States because Japan did not have a large postwar baby boom and has lower immigration and mortality rates. Accordingly, debates over the aging of the Japanese population are likely to be repeated in the United States in the beginning of the next century. Of course, revenues from a VAT could also be placed into general revenues rather than into the Social Security trust funds.

Any major shift in source of funds, therefore, is a question that extends beyond Social Security and requires consideration of more fundamental issues of the design of the entire tax structure. Although we do not want to discount the possibilities that could be examined, the considerations move far beyond the focus of this book.

Increasing Progressivity in Tax Rate Schedule

Social Security achieves progressivity mainly through its benefit formula. We have noted, however, that people with low incomes typically face higher mortality rates, mainly during their working years. A larger-than-normal share of the low-income population, therefore, dies before reaching retirement and receives little or no return from Social Security contributions. Their loss of old-age benefits is only partially offset by relatively higher disability and survivors benefits.

A possible goal of Social Security reform could be to try to attain the levels of progressivity that would apply even in absence of life expectancy differentials. As noted in chapter 5, the Social Security system is already expected to become more progressive on a lifetime basis for those retiring during the next century. One might argue, nonetheless, that a further offset for differential mortality rates should be provided anyway. One means would be to require that taxes, rather than benefits, be adjusted by excluding the first dollars of earnings from Social Security taxation, as, for example, Canada does now.[17] After all, for those who die before retirement age, adjustment in the benefit formula will typically make little difference.

In one sense, this type of change has been implemented in recent years, but not directly in the Social Security system itself. The Earned Income Tax Credit (EITC), first enacted in 1975, will by 1995 offer as much as $3,032 of tax credit to many low-income workers with children. This credit, of course, is crude as a Social Security offset. For instance, it imposes large marriage penalties on two-earner couples, who receive much less EITC than if they could file separately. The credit also provides at most $306 to low-income persons without children.[18] Nonetheless, it may be simpler to rely on adjustments in the EITC than to alter the Social Security tax rate schedule.

Simulations presented in chapter 5 warned us that differences in life expectancy may not make as much difference as may have been expected in the redistributive patterns of Social Security. Our simulations, however, were based upon the limited information available to the public. Before any legal changes are proposed, therefore, the Social Security Administration should make more elaborate and detailed calculations of exactly who wins and who loses because of differential mortality. The appropriate amount of adjustment, for instance, could be a function of labor force participation over the years, marital status, and other variables that we are unable to examine. Such an effort should also attempt to account for welfare programs, earned income credits, and other programs that may act as compensating mechanisms.

CONCLUSION

Even independently from the need to bring Social Security into long-run balance, a strong case can be made for expanding the Social Security tax base to include employee benefits. The exclusion of health insurance premiums and other forms of nonwage compensation from taxation creates a number of problems of both equity and efficiency. Whatever the level of revenue to be collected, a broader base has the advantage of allowing a lower rate to be applied.

Raising the limit on maximum earnings subject to tax, on the other hand, is a relatively weak option. There are other ways of adding to the progressivity of the system, if that is the goal, without discriminating against the self-employed and without raising the benefits already received by high-income persons. This option involves only modest revenues, in any case. Indeed, there is a strong case for bringing the OASDI and HI tax bases back into line.

Increasing the tax rate in one sense is a last-resort means of correcting the Social Security imbalance, but cannot be ruled out entirely. Once benefit levels and the tax base are established in equitable and efficient ways, then some rate of tax must be applied—so it is point-less to act as though current rates are immutable and that program changes can always be handled through expenditure and tax base changes. A large payroll tax rate increase used to finance retirement benefits, however, would clearly be both inequitable and inefficient. The tax rates on low- to moderate-income workers with children are quite high already, especially given their economic status and the relative well-being of other parts of the population.

The problems of lower-income working families certainly provide an argument for lowering the Social Security tax rate. As a practical matter, however, any attempt to lower the rate of Social Security tax must be done in a way that does not add to the long-run imbalance in Social Security or to the nation's fiscal problem. A simple Social Security rate cut by itself would not be appropriate, since it would only exacerbate these problems.

Other adjustments in tax rates—such as excluding the first dollars of Social Security earnings from tax—might be worthy of consider-ation as a matter of individual equity to those who are more likely to die before reaching retirement, or out of concern for the well-being of low-income workers. For a variety of reasons, including administrative simplicity, however, it may be easier to keep the Social Security tax essentially a flat rate tax, and make adjustments else-where. The Earned Income Tax Credit provides an example of an alternative mechanism.

Other shifts in sources of revenue cannot be dismissed out of hand, although this takes us far beyond the issue of Social Security by itself. Although a value-added tax might be superior to taxes on earnings as a means of assisting the elderly, for instance, simply adding a VAT onto current law could make even vaguer the net amount of transfers made and could weaken the fiscal discipline that does exist. As a matter of both fiscal discipline and simple honesty in policy, moreover, the current use of various sources of general revenue financing in Social Security tends to present a misleading picture of the cost of the system, tends to deter trade-offs among programs for the elderly that could improve their own well-being, and violates the fiscal integrity supposedly imposed by trust fund financing.

Notes

1. The two major long-run changes in the amendments were to increase the retirement age and to begin taxation of benefits. As discussed later, many considered the latter to be a form of net benefit reduction.

2. For further discussion of the decline in the personal exemption, see Bakija and Steuerle (1991).

3. Taxable payroll in 1993 is estimated at $2,658 billion (Board of Trustees, OASDI 1992: 177). A 2.2 percent tax rate reduction thus costs about $58.5 billion.

4. Senator Moynihan's proposal was eventually amended to increase the maximum wage subject to Social Security taxation. This provision would offset a small portion of the revenue loss due to the tax reduction.

5. In table 7.3, pay-as-you-go OASI and DI tax rates are equal to total OASI and DI costs, less revenues from income taxation of benefits, as a percentage of taxable payroll. Projections are based on the intermediate assumptions in the 1993 Board of Trustees reports. Revenues from increased taxation of benefits enacted in 1993 are assumed to go into general funds of the federal government, rather than the trust funds. Crediting them to the trust funds would probably reduce the required OASDI tax rate by about 0.5 percent or 0.6 percent in 2030. Tax rates for HI are adjusted for the estimated impact of 1993 enactments, including the removal of the HI tax cap.

6. If an employed worker has more than one source of earnings, the combined employee and employer taxes can exceed the cap. The employee tax on earnings in excess of the cap, however, is refundable to the employee. In the case of a self-employed person, no additional tax is owed if earnings from other employment adds up to the cap.

7. One could enact benefit reductions at the same time, for instance, by lowering the rate of return for the last dollars of contributions.

8. Technically, the formula relates the Primary Insurance Amount (PIA) to Average Indexed Monthly Earnings (AIME).

9. The tax rates are not fully additive, as portions of different taxes are deductible against each other.

10. Employee benefits remained roughly constant as a percentage of compensation in the 1980s, as a decline in pension contributions roughtly offset continued rapid growth in health insurance contributions. The decline in pension contributions resulted partly from a stock market boom that increased the real value of underlying pension assets and reduced contribution requirements. The share of compensation exempt from taxes, nonetheless, remains large and is expected to grow in the future.

11. Board of Trustees, OASDI (1992: 191).

12. The technical details of such an adjustment need close attention. In particular, one would have to pay special attention to the wage index. If employee benefits were suddenly to be included in this index measure, the index would jump upward abruptly, causing windfall increases in OASDI benefit levels for new retirees. A separate index would have to operate for wages earned before the reform went into effect.

13. In fiscal year 1992, federal government general revenues made $38.7 billion in direct payments and $1.7 billion in interest payments to the SMI trust fund. By contrast, OASDI payroll taxes exceeded disbursements by only $20.9 billion. If revenues from income taxation of benefits and net interest are included, the OASDI surplus rises to $50.7 billion. This larger figure can be misleading, however, since interest payments and money from income taxation of benefits may be regarded as transfers from general revenues of the federal government.

14. The calculation of income taxation of Social Security benefits is also done in a way that maximizes the turning over of receipts to the Social Security trust funds. Social Security benefits are treated as if they are the last items of income taxed— hence allowing zero and lower rates of income tax to be applied to other sources of income, and the highest rates of tax to be imputed to the taxation of Social Security benefits.

15. One can also view the income tax as subsidizing Social Security because the employer portion of Social Security is exempted from income tax. If such an exclusion

were not available, of course, then the case for taxing benefits would be much weaker. In effect, to find the income tax subsidy for Social Security benefits, one has to look at the treatment both of deposits of taxes and withdrawals for benefits simultaneously.

16. It should be noted that one of the rationales for subsidizing the SMI system out of general revenues is that it is a voluntary program paid for by the elderly themselves through premiums. If the premiums reflected 100 percent of SMI's costs, a large share of the elderly might opt out of the system either out of preference or necessity. An adverse selection problem would be more likely to result as those who were relatively more healthy chose not to join the system. This problem could be reduced or avoided by making the program mandatory, financing part of it through an earmarked payroll tax, as is currently done with HI, or requiring that any health insurance for the elderly, private or public, set a "community rate" available to all who want to participate.

17. This could cause some administrative problems with regard to people who work multiple jobs.

18. The 1993 budget agreement increased the maximum credit to these new, higher levels, and added, for the first time, a credit for households with no children.

Chapter Eight

BENEFIT OPTIONS

During Social Security's early decades of growth, practically all major legislation led to increases in cash or health benefits. By the late 1970s, this was no longer true. Legislation enacted in 1977 slowed the rate of future cash benefit growth. Although this reduction mainly eliminated a technical flaw with the way benefits were indexed in previous legislation, the bill still represented a departure from the past.[1] In 1983 Congress went even further and reduced the rate of benefit growth by raising the Normal Retirement Age (NRA) above 65 for those who begin to retire after the turn of the century, delaying each year's cost-of-living adjustment (COLA) by six months, and subjecting some of the benefits of higher-income Social Security recipients to income taxation.

Benefit cuts for retirees are an extremely sensitive issue. Even beyond the obvious politics of the situation is a timing problem. In the short run, a benefit cut requires a much larger sacrifice from a much smaller group of people to achieve the same initial fiscal impact as an increase in the payroll tax. Taxable payroll (estimated at $2.66 trillion in 1993) is about 10 times the size of total OASI benefit outlays (estimated at $268 billion in 1993).[2] Accordingly, increasing the OASI tax rate by 1 percentage point (i.e., taxing an additional 1 percent of taxable payroll) raises about as much revenue as is saved by a 10 percent cut in OASI benefit payments.[3] The tax increase reduces before-tax earnings by exactly 1 percent—a modest burden for most workers. An across-the-board benefit cut of 10 percent, on the other hand, would be a real hardship for many retirees, especially poor and near-poor elderly persons who rely on Social Security for much or all of their income. If not implemented carefully over time, benefit changes can have an immediate and significant adverse impact upon the lives of those affected. The best strategy for benefit cuts is thus to plan for the long term so that cash flow crises are avoided and so that individuals can approach retirement with reasonable expectations.

When one considers problems of fiscal imbalance in Social Security, the continually increasing share of the federal budget devoted to the elderly, and the already large burden of payroll taxes on moderate-income households, it remains clear that options for restraining the growth in benefit outlays must be examined. Unless we are willing to allow the tax burden for supporting the elderly to climb significantly, reform of the benefit structure almost inevitably will be required.

Benefit reductions can come in almost any size or shape. This chapter examines the principal options most often discussed when considering Social Security legislation.

CHANGES IN INDEXING

Social Security benefits are indexed to adjust automatically for changes in wage and price levels. Since recipients see their checks rise with inflation each year, the COLA is perhaps the best known of the various indexing procedures. As outlined in chapter 4, various parts of the benefit calculation process also involve automatic indexing to keep new benefit awards growing along with average wages in the economy. Here we focus on common proposals to change the indexing rules—proposals that can have a dramatic impact on the cost of Social Security for the long run.

Cost-of-Living Adjustments

Perhaps the most common proposal for restraining the growth of Social Security spending is to reduce, delay, or eliminate cost-of-living adjustments, which index social insurance benefits for inflation. Because deficit reduction efforts now dominate so much of federal policymaking—with major legislation passed in 1982, 1984, 1987, 1990, and 1993—COLA cutbacks for Social Security and other programs have been suggested frequently in Congress in recent years. When the idea of paring COLAs is examined more carefully, however, it becomes clear that such a policy would represent a major step backward for Social Security and would be inconsistent with the fundamental purposes and principles of the system.

Among the most important reasons for indexing of benefits is that it maintains a recipient's benefit level at a constant real value, or purchasing power, from age of retirement to age of death. As a matter of retirement policy and of helping individuals to plan for their future, indexing represents sound policy. After all, why should real benefit levels vary with the whims of inflation?

During the aging process, the incomes of the elderly already tend to fall relative to average incomes in the economy. Recall that while the nonelderly often receive real wage increases, a large portion of the elderly are dependent mainly upon Social Security, which is indexed only for inflation, and upon private pensions, many of which are not indexed at all. Reducing or eliminating COLAs would cause the incomes of the elderly to fall even faster as they aged. Proposals to reduce COLAs to a point or two below inflation every year are particularly bad in this respect. Since needs tend to increase and abilities tend to decrease at older ages, one would expect that a progressive need-oriented system like Social Security would attempt to *increase* real benefit levels over the aging process, rather than decrease them. Cutting back on COLAs moves the system in exactly the opposite direction.

A COLA reduction is also at odds with Social Security's progressive goals because it would hurt many elderly persons who are truly needy. The primary rationale for Social Security was to provide benefits adequate to prevent destitution and dependency among the elderly. A COLA reduction is essentially an across-the-board cut in benefits for all recipients, regardless of their economic circumstances. For example, suppose the COLA were canceled for a year in which there was inflation of 4 percent. This would effectively cut the real value of all current recipients' benefits by 4 percent. Benefits in each subsequent year would also be 4 percent lower than they would have been otherwise. Although this might represent only a small burden on middle- and upper-income retirees who receive substantial pensions and property income, it could be a true hardship for low-income elderly people who depend almost entirely on Social Security for their sustenance.

Some COLA-cut proposals would deny price adjustments for one year only. This particular variation, unless accompanied by other benefit formula changes, would do nothing to affect the benefits of those who have not yet retired. As a result, the long-run costs of Social Security would be changed little. It would also have the perverse effect of increasing the gap between those already retired and the richer, younger generations yet to come into the system.

The costs to the government of inflation indexing are often misperceived. COLAs do not increase the real costs of the Social Security system; they merely keep benefit amounts at a constant level relative to prices in the economy. Since wages and national income almost always rise faster than prices, tax revenues automatically increase by more than enough to cover the cost of the COLAs.[4]

Sometimes it is asserted that the historic decision to index benefits added significantly to the overall cost of the system. This is misleading. Before indexing was introduced, lawmakers responded to the effects of inflation by periodically enacting benefit increases. Because these ad hoc increases occurred at irregular intervals and were not directly tied to any measure of price or wage growth, real benefit levels continued to fluctuate erratically over time. Many of these legislated increases, however, more than compensated for the effects of inflation and amounted to real benefit increases. The decision to index benefit payments by formula was in large part an effort to make planning more exact and to replace discretionary indexing with automatic indexing. Whether over the long run these cost-of-living adjustments turned out to be any more expensive than ad hoc increases is a matter of conjecture.[5]

If the Social Security system had been considered too expensive at the time that indexing was approved, then it would have been quite possible to cut back on the basic benefit level or to increase the retirement age (see further discussion on these options later in the chapter). Regardless of the basic benefit level, an indexed system with a lower initial benefit would almost always be superior to an unindexed system with a higher initial benefit and a lower final benefit. It was not so much the decision to index, as the unwillingness to pay for indexing through other benefit adjustments, that added to the cost of the system—and, even then, only to the extent that explicit indexing was in excess of the ad hoc indexing that would have occurred anyway.[6]

Perhaps the only case to be made for cutting back on the COLA is that the index used is imprecise. Social Security bases its COLA on the consumer price index for urban wage and clerical workers (CPI-W). For a variety of technical reasons, this index tends to display slightly more inflation than do some other indexes, such as those used to calculate national income.[7] The annual difference today is usually only a small fraction of 1 percent. Only a very modest cut today could be justified by an appeal to other indexes.[8]

In sum, there appears to be little justification for cutting back on cost-of-living adjustments. Inflation-induced benefit cuts could have too dramatic an impact upon the neediest portion of the elderly population and would tend to violate the need-based rationale for the system. Only a minor adjustment for the tendency of the CPI-W to overstate inflation relative to other inflation indexes might be warranted.

Indexing of Measure of Lifetime Wages (AIME)

Recall from chapter 4 that the level of one's Social Security benefit is based on a measure of one's lifetime earnings, or more precisely, the average indexed monthly earnings (AIME). The AIME calculation uses a "wage index" to adjust earnings from each year before age 60 for the effects of inflation and real wage growth. This makes earnings from many years ago comparable with wages earned at age 60. In many ways, this type of formula appears far superior to those used in many private pension plans, especially those where pension benefits are based upon the highest few years (typically three) of earnings within the firm. One consequence of this latter type of formula is that younger and middle-age employees who leave a firm many years before retirement usually end up with very little in the way of retirement benefits. Inflation and real wage growth reduce enormously the real and relative value of income earned in the "high-three" years when those years occurred long ago.

The question of how wages should be measured in the calculation of average monthly earnings is totally separable from how high benefit levels should be. One could achieve the same basic benefit levels under almost any method for calculating average earnings merely by adjusting the benefit formula. AIME indexing simply tells us how wages from the past should be weighted relative to more recent wages when determining benefits.

The wage-indexed AIME was actually introduced in 1979 to *restrain* the growth in Social Security costs. Between 1974 and 1979, benefits were "overindexed" for inflation—that is, when inflation rose, benefits rose even faster. This resulted largely from the combination of an indexed benefit formula with an average wage measure that rose with inflation and economic growth over time. Introduction of the new benefit formula and indexed AIME eliminated this problem and returned benefit growth to a slower and steadier pace.[9]

Aside from its advantage of promoting stability in benefit growth, wage indexing in the AIME also promotes fairness and efficiency in the way wages from different years are counted. The principles of horizontal equity and individual equity suggest that contributions of equal value made in different years should be granted the same weight in determining benefit levels. Comparing the true value of contributions (or wages) from different years requires an adjustment for the effects of both inflation and interest. Wage indexing roughly accomplishes this by adjusting not only for growth in nominal prices but also for a real rate of return on contributions (equal to the rate of real wage growth).

The current method of calculating AIME, therefore, helps maintain equality between people who received approximately equal real wages over a lifetime. Consider two women with identical earnings histories, except that one woman is employed for 35 years from ages 20 to 54, whereas the other is employed from ages 30 to 64. In an unindexed system, as is typical of most private pension plans, the woman who was unemployed after age 55 would fare much worse because the extra wages she earned during her twenties would be counted at a very low value, while the wages the other woman earned at ages 55–64 would be counted very heavily. This unequal treatment would be unwarranted, because the two actually had almost identical earnings profiles and contributions when one considers the effects of inflation and interest. Wage indexing in the AIME helps prevent such inequities.[10]

The AIME's indexing procedure also adds to the efficiency of the system by making the worker more indifferent as to when contributions are made. In an inflationary economy and an unindexed system, contributions in early years will be worth almost nothing, yet bear the full Social Security tax rate. Contributions in later years, on the other hand, will reap huge benefits because they will dominate the calculation of average lifetime earnings. With wage indexing, such perverse incentives for timing years of contribution are avoided.

In sum, there seems no good reason to cut back on the indexing of the AIME. Failing to adjust the value of past wages for inflation and real wage growth would result in arbitrary fluctuation of benefit values, inefficiency, and horizontal inequity, without necessarily saving any money for Social Security.

Indexing of Benefit Formula for Real Wage Growth

Once average lifetime earnings are calculated, Social Security determines a primary insurance amount (PIA) on the basis of a progressive formula. Recall, from chapter 4, that the PIA represents the basic monthly benefit level before adjustments for factors such as early or delayed retirement and spousal benefits. The formula for determining benefits is progressive in the sense that it applies a considerably higher rate of replacement or return to the first dollars of AIME than to the last dollars.

As noted before, the bend-points, or dividing lines between the different brackets in the PIA formula, are "wage indexed." This practice causes benefit levels to grow from one cohort of retirees to the next at about the same rate as average wages in the economy.[11] It also has the consequence of maintaining a fairly constant "replacement rate" over time at different relative levels in the income distribution. A person who earned the average wage every year until retirement in 1990, for instance, will receive approximately the same replacement rate as a person who earned the average wage every year until retirement at the same age in 2000. So long as there is real wage growth between those years, there will be real benefit growth as well.

If the PIA formula bend-points were unindexed or indexed at a rate slower than wage growth, on the other hand, each successive cohort would find that a larger and larger share of their earnings fell in portions of the benefit formula that provided lower rates of return. A few decades from now, almost all earnings of all new retirees would fall in the least favorable bracket in the benefit schedule, and everyone would receive approximately the same rate of return— which would be the lowest rate of return possible under the current system. This would gradually result in a fundamental change in the character of the Social Security system.

The indexing of the benefit formula, therefore, plays a crucial role in determining the growth of the Social Security program over time. It causes benefits for each new generation of retirees to grow in real terms and to keep pace with earnings in an economy. Such a system would consume a fairly steady share of the national economy if the age distribution of the population itself were to remain stable over time. As demonstrated in chapter 3, when the proportion of the population that is retired increases dramatically, a system set up in this way will automatically consume a much larger share of the national economy.

At a minimum, price indexing of the formula seems easy to justify. Benefits—and the planning ability of those approaching retirement— should not be subject to the caprices of inflation. Merely indexing for prices helps ensure that Social Security provides at least the same real benefit to each generation.

Indexing for real wage growth, not just inflation, also seems reasonable, but the case here is less clear-cut. The current system's practice of increasing real benefit levels over time, in order to maintain recipients' relative standing in the income distribution, is open to debate. If the government were to index every program so that it grew in line with real economic growth, then new revenues deriving from a growing economy would almost always be precommitted, absent higher and higher tax rates.[12] Congress would have little ability to adjust to new demands, new needs, and new emergencies. Indeed, on a wider scale, this is part of the problem facing the government today and helps explain why Congress feels it has little control over policy even as real taxes and real expenditures increase with an expanding economy.

An alternative to wage indexing, therefore, might be merely to maintain benefits at a certain level of purchasing power over time and provide a floor of protection comparable to the one we provide today. To the extent that people are additionally concerned with maintaining their preretirement standards of living, they would have to rely increasingly on their own private provision for old-age under such an alternative. This, however, would represent a clear departure from the current approach, and would gradually shrink Social Security's role in retirement protection over time.

Another option for restraining future growth, without hurting the needy, would be to apply indexing differently at different wage levels in the benefit formula. Minimum benefits or benefits for low-income individuals could be indexed to keep pace with earnings or wages, while growth in benefits to higher-income individuals could be restricted closer to price inflation.[13] Note that this need not be a permanent change; for instance, indexing of the top bracket for more than prices could be deferred for a number of years.

Given the uncertainties surrounding the adequacy of pension coverage in the future, and the apparently low propensity of today's workers to save by themselves, one must be very cautious about the effect of such approaches, particularly for low- and moderate-income workers. Questions of individual equity should also be considered. As discussed in chapter 5, many workers retiring during the next century can expect to receive considerably less than a fair actuarial return on their contributions. Reducing the rate at which bend-points are indexed would significantly reduce benefits for those retiring in the distant future relative to current law, without significantly affecting the benefits of current or near-future retirees. Such a plan might be viewed as further weakening the individual equity element of the program for today's young workers.

DROPOUT YEARS

The use of wage-indexing in the calculation of average lifetime earnings (AIME) helps promote equity and efficiency by providing approximately equal credit for contributions made in different years. Another feature of the calculation process, however, moves in just the opposite direction and tends to violate the same principles that tend to justify this wage indexing. The current method for calculating the AIME for retirement benefits includes only the 35 best years of earnings for individuals, even though many are likely to participate in the work force for 45 years or longer, especially when years of part-time work are counted.[14] Years excluded from the calculation are known as "dropout years"; contributions made in these years receive no return whatsoever.

The restriction on the number of years included in the benefit calculation is at odds with most of the basic principles underlying Social Security. The deletion is hardly progressive. Among its beneficiaries are those who delay their entrance into the full-time labor force in order to attend college and graduate or professional school; these are the people who typically earn high wages over their lifetimes. Dropout years especially tend to discriminate against those lower-wage workers who enter the labor force at a younger age and stay in the labor force throughout most of their adult lives.[15]

The current dropout year requirement also violates the individual equity principle, since no return is provided for contributions made in many years. As for horizontal equity, suppose that two individuals have the same earnings patterns for 34 years. Taxpayer A works a 35th year at $40,000, whereas taxpayer B works two more years at $20,000 each. Current law will normally provide a greater benefit to taxpayer A even though she has contributed no more in taxes.

The failure to include more years adds to the inefficiency of the program. In effect, this programmatic feature helps ensure that many workers get almost no marginal increase in old age insurance benefits for working an additional year.[16] Earlier in this volume, we pointed out how the efficiency cost of a universal Social Security program could be less than it might at first appear, especially if one calculated the net rate of tax—taxes less benefits—rather than the gross rate of tax.[17] Now it turns out that for many individuals the net and gross rate of tax for additional work are often the same after all. Since many individuals will have more years in the labor force than are included in the formula, they often receive little or no return *at the margin* for contributing in any one year. Correspondingly, the gain from working off the books or illegally underreporting income is greater, since one can engage in such noncompliance for many years without losing benefits.

Dropout years might be considered a backdoor way of compensating those who leave the labor force to engage in child-rearing, but, if so, it is an extraordinarily crude method—the same benefit is granted to those who engage in child-rearing as to those who go to graduate or professional school or simply drop out of the labor force. A strong case, therefore, can be made for including more years in the AIME calculation, and, if necessary, providing compensation through some other means for those engaged in child-rearing.[18]

OTHER CHANGES IN BENEFIT FORMULA

The benefit formula theoretically can be changed over time to meet any particular benefit or cost target. One could continue indexing or make ad hoc adjustments, alter the number of dropout years, or make any number of other amendments and still achieve the same costs over time by making compensating changes in the benefit formula. Real benefit increases, for example, could be achieved through ad hoc changes in the benefit formulas even if wage indexing were abandoned. Correspondingly, real benefits could be lowered while maintaining all of the current indexing mechanisms.

Outside of ad hoc increases or decreases, changes in indexing methods, and including more years of contributions, the most straightforward structural change is to revise brackets or rates in the benefit formula. Adjusting the rates of return to different levels of lifetime earnings is analogous to changing the tax rates in a progressive income tax. Arguments for and against these types of changes are similar in both systems. If Social Security rates are changed, they will affect the balance between progressivity and individual equity. Of course, there is no reason for any particular rate structure— whether in Social Security or an income tax, or in any other government policy—to be permanent for all time.

Two-Tier or Double-Decker Social Security System

A more fundamental structural reform of Social Security benefits would be to replace the current system with a system that has two "tiers" or "decks." Recall that the current benefit formula essentially has three rates of return that apply at different earnings levels. In a two-tier or double-decker system, a clearer separation is made between the transfer (progressive redistribution) and pension (individual equity) components. Within the pension component, all contributions would receive relatively equal rates of return, usually based upon current market interest rates.[19] The separate transfer component ensures adequate benefit levels for low-income persons. It might take the form of a universal flat benefit that is uniform for all retirees—a procedure followed in a number of other countries; this is usually referred to as the double-decker approach. Transfers might be provided as part of a broader negative income tax or universal assistance program that applies to all households (see Pechman et al. 1968). Alternatively, they might be targeted on the basis of needs of the elderly, through a means test; this is sometimes called the two-tier approach (Boskin 1986).

There are variations on a two-tier or double-decker structure in many other industrialized nations, including Canada, Japan, Great Britain, France, and Sweden.[20] Often there is an identifiable "individual equity" component, in that a common rate of return is applied to certain contributions. Usually this is supplemented by a minimum benefit component, and sometimes a maximum benefit limitation. Although some may fear that movement toward this type of structure would decrease progressivity, international evidence does not support that view. In some of these other countries, old-age benefits are arguably more generous and more progressive than in the United States. Movement to a two-tier or double-decker system, therefore, need not imply either a more liberal or a more conservative stance toward social insurance.

This type of reform is aimed partly at the decision-making process, regardless of overall levels of benefits. Making the transfer and pension portions of Social Security more explicit would allow policymakers to decide on the relative size desired for each of them without confusing objectives. The distribution of benefits within each system could also be based more directly upon the set of standards or principles within each system separately.

A related advantage is that *within* the pension component, a number of problems fall by the wayside. If all contributions to the earnings-related component are to be given approximately equal treatment, then all years of work could easily be included. Secondary workers could be given equal returns with primary workers. Dependents' allowances would be handled more within the transfer portion of the system.

Without complete specification of the design of the two parts, however, it is hard to draw any hard and fast conclusions, other than procedural, between this alternative approach and the more traditional method adopted in the United States. For instance, even if the pension component provides an equal return to all contributions—and, hence, makes it easier to include all years or to treat contributions of secondary workers equivalent to those of primary workers—the transfer component or flat-benefit component could completely offset those effects.[21]

It is easy, in fact, to approximate a double-decker Social Security system simply by reducing the number of brackets in the current benefit formula from three to two. The first deck might be designed essentially to provide a minimum benefit to all workers. Suppose one designated or labeled a portion of the current Social Security payroll tax as supporting the first (transfer) deck, and the remaining portion of the tax as supporting the second (pension) deck. The division of portions could be determined so that the taxes labeled as supporting the second deck received a market rate of return. Whether this double-decker system would be less or more progressive than the current system—which might be labeled a "three-deck system"—would depend mainly upon the rates of payment or return established in each deck.[22]

One approach to a two-tier system creates a transfer tier outside the Social Security system through a means-tested program financed out of general government revenue (Boskin 1986). This would require higher income tax rates, rather than higher Social Security tax rates, to finance the redistribution. Another consequence of this approach is that need becomes measured on the basis of current income rather than lifetime earnings. In explaining some of the rationale behind a more universal Social Security system in chapter 2, we pointed out some of the problems of basing redistribution in retirement on current, rather than lifetime, income. In particular, those with substantial lifetime ability to cover their own costs of retirement could easily avoid saving for retirement or could transfer their assets to their children and then turn unnecessarily to other taxpayers for support. This leads us to conclude that even if a system with a more explicit pension tier or deck is adopted, an approach closer to current law— where the bottom bracket in the Social Security benefit formula essentially establishes a minimum benefit for almost all elderly—may be more appropriate.

Minimum Benefits

As suggested in chapter 6, it is highly unlikely even many decades into the future that more than half of all retirees will have significant employer-provided pension income. The ones who do not will be among the poorer elderly—those dependent mainly upon Social Security for their retirement income.

It is not possible within the scope of this book to deal adequately with potential reform of the employer-provided pension system for workers in private business and government. We have already seen that this system creates problems when it provides lower real benefits as a person ages, when it discriminates arbitrarily among workers depending upon age and rates of inflation, and when it too easily allows early withdrawals and borrowing that decrease resources available later in retirement. Even if these latter items were to be reformed, it is still doubtful that the basic structure of today's private pension system would supplement the incomes of most retirees sufficiently. Mandatory private pensions might be one way to go—in Chile, such pensions now provide the second deck of a double-decker system—but, in their absence or until such a system would mature, a compelling argument can be made for increasing minimum benefits in Social Security.

We also suggest in this book a number of areas where benefits may be cut back—for example, by eliminating most dropout years, by changing formulas, or by increasing the retirement age. We reemphasize that simultaneous increases in minimum benefits can be used to assure that low-income individuals not be hurt by these other changes.

There are, of course, different ways to increase benefits at the bottom of the income distribution. One can increase the special minimum benefit, raise the high rate of return provided to the first dollars of earnings, or increase benefits in Supplemental Security Income (SSI)—the program that provides income-related benefits to the elderly. Our preference would simply be to increase the special minimum benefit in Social Security and decrease dependence upon SSI.

TAXATION OF BENEFITS

Prior to passage of the 1983 Social Security Amendments, all Social Security benefits, no matter how large or how well-off the recipient, were free from income taxation. Legislation in 1983 reversed over 40 years of history and required that up to one-half of OASDI benefits be made subject to income taxation for people whose incomes (including half of OASDI benefits) exceed certain thresholds—$25,000 for a single person and $32,000 for a married couple. In 1993, Congress accepted, with some modification, the Clinton administration's proposal to tax benefits further. At higher income levels, up to 85 percent of benefits now are taxable. None of the income thresholds related to the taxation of benefits are indexed. As the thresholds gradually decline in real value over time, more and more retirees will find that at least some of their Social Security benefits are subject to income taxation. As we will demonstrate, taxation of benefits has been one of the more reasonable Social Security reform options, and modest further movement in this direction may be advisable in the future.

Whether taxation of benefits is regarded as a net reduction in benefits or an increase in taxes is arbitrary. A nontaxable benefit of $10,000 is worth the same to a recipient as a taxable benefit of $12,500 on which $2,500 of tax is paid. Whether the net amount of money being transferred to a retiree is decreased through taxes on benefits or through a direct reduction in payments, the consequences for the retiree, the budget, and the economy are all essentially the same. We chose to discuss the taxation of benefits in this chapter, rather than in chapter 7, mainly because taxation places a burden on Social Security beneficiaries, rather than on workers or the population as a whole. (As an aside, President Ronald Reagan threw his support behind taxation of benefits in 1983 because he was persuaded that it was effectively a "spending reduction," rather than a "tax increase," which he opposed. President Bill Clinton also labeled increased taxation of benefits as a spending reduction when trying to show the balance between spending cuts and tax increases in his budget proposals.)[23] The U.S. government itself classifies the favorable tax treatment of Social Security benefits as a hybrid—a tax expenditure—that is, an expenditure administered through the tax system. The issues addressed here, however, are not dependent upon how one classifies the net reduction of after-tax income that would result from increased taxation of benefits.

Justifications for Taxation of Benefits

One important advantage of taxing Social Security benefits over other benefit reduction options is its progressivity: it mainly affects the better-off portion of the elderly population. Under current law, those for whom the sum of non–Social Security income and one-half of OASDI benefits is below the initial $25,000 and $32,000 thresholds, respectively, are completely unaffected by taxation of benefits. Even people with incomes several thousand dollars above the thresholds face a very small burden because taxation is phased in gradually and the 15 percent income tax bracket remains in effect until higher income levels are reached.

Even if the special income thresholds were reduced or eliminated, elderly people in poverty would remain unaffected, while those with moderate incomes would be affected only slightly. Elderly couples with incomes below $12,000 in 1993, for instance, would still be exempt from federal taxation because of personal exemptions, the standard deduction, and the special deduction for the elderly. Many moderate-income elderly persons also qualify for a special tax credit that increases their tax-exempt threshold to well above $16,000.[24] Those with still higher incomes would find only a portion of their benefits taxed and, for most, only at a 15 percent rate.

A related advantage of taxing benefits is that it affects the elderly at a point in the life cycle when they are best able to afford it. Progressive income taxation typically has a diminishing impact as an elderly person ages. Total income, including work earnings and unindexed pensions, often declines in later years of retirement. Meanwhile, exemptions, standard deductions, and rate brackets in the income tax increase because they are indexed for inflation. Accordingly, a larger share of income falls into a lower tax bracket or becomes exempt from taxation. Thus, income taxation allows retirees to keep more of their benefits when their needs are likely to be greater. By contrast, most other benefit reduction options, such as a cutback in cost-of-living adjustments or an across-the-board reduction in benefits, would tend to have a proportionate or even increasing effect throughout the remaining life of the retiree.

In light of the redistributional patterns illustrated in chapter 5, taxation of Social Security benefits for current and near-future retirees can also be justified in terms of individual equity. Most current retirees who earned very high incomes during their careers are receiving large transfers beyond the fair annuity value of their contributions. Many are even receiving net transfers beyond what many poor elderly and nonelderly are receiving or ever will receive. These subsidies are clearly difficult to justify under any principle. Since benefits exceed the fair annuity value of contributions, they cannot be justified by appealing to the insurance or "individual equity" principle. To the extent the system was meant to be progressive or need-based, these transfers are even more unwarranted.

This compelling rationale for taxing the benefits of current and near-future retirees is less applicable to those retiring during the next century. Most high-income workers retiring a few decades into the next century can be expected to receive considerably less than a fair actuarial return on their Social Security contributions. Any additional taxation of benefits at that time will simply make an already progressive system that much more progressive.

Taxation of benefits is also appealing on horizontal equity grounds. As noted in chapter 6, elderly persons typically face much lower tax rates than younger families with identical incomes. Consider, for example, a 65-year-old retired couple with $10,000 in Social Security benefits and $15,000 in pension and interest income in 1993. Since almost all of their income is exempt from taxation, their federal tax bill will be at most $450. A young four-person family with $25,000 in work earnings, by contrast, typically faces a federal tax burden more than 10 times as large, at $5,235. All of their earnings from work are subject to the 15.3 percent Social Security tax, and $9,400 of their earnings are also subject to the 15 percent income tax rate. The younger family must shoulder a much larger share of the burden of supporting our national government, despite the fact that their income is identical and the needs of four persons are likely to be greater than those of two persons. Including at least some Social Security benefits in taxable income helps mitigate this disparity at higher-income levels. Raising Social Security payroll tax rates, on the other hand, would only exacerbate the disparity between the two families.

Another horizontal equity argument is made by comparing Social Security with private pensions. This argument was cited by President Clinton to support his 1993 proposal to increase taxation of benefits. Contributions to private pensions and Social Security receive fairly similar income tax treatment; employee contributions are taxable, whereas contributions made by a firm on a worker's behalf are exempt from taxation. Interest on all contributions is also deferred from taxation while it is accumulating. Except for previously taxed employee contributions, however, all private pension benefit payments are subject to income taxation. As a general rule of thumb, it is usually argued that 85 percent of OASI benefits would have to be included in taxable income to achieve comparable treatment with other public and private pensions. This figure, of course, is only a rough approximation.[25] For those retiring in the future, the 85 percent rate could turn out to be slightly too high for some upper-income workers, who will have contributed more than 15 percent of the cost of their benefits.[26]

One must also be careful with the private pension analogy. For the most part, Social Security does not accumulate funds. If one thinks of the system purely as an income transfer system, then income should be taxed either to the transferor (the taxpayer) or the transferee (the recipient), but not necessarily both. This logic was applied in the 1983 amendments to justify taxation of one-half of benefits. That is, one-half of Social Security transfers would be taxed to employees, while transfers from employers would be treated as taxable to recipients. Under that theory, only the generous income thresholds remained a source of special tax treatment.

The savings to be achieved through taxation of benefits are significant, although not a panacea. Legislation passed by Congress in 1993 increases the portion of benefits subject to tax for those with incomes above a second set of thresholds ($34,000 for singles and $44,000 for joint returns), and raises the maximum taxable portion to 85 percent (see chapter 4 for further detail). This is expected to raise an extra $4.6 billion in 1995. The extra revenues over the next 75 years is expected to improve actuarial balance by an amount equivalent to a tax increase of between 0.3 and 0.4 percent of OASDI's taxable payroll; legislators in 1993 proposed crediting this to the financially troubled HI trust fund.[27] Taxing 85 percent of benefits *plus* eliminating the income thresholds would have a much larger impact in the short run, raising about $24 billion in 1995.[28] The difference over the long run would be smaller, however, since the thresholds are already scheduled to decline in real value over time.

For a variety of reasons, therefore, taxation of Social Security benefits is one of the more appealing choices among an array of unpleasant benefit reduction options. It does, of course, have drawbacks associated with basing taxation on an annual income measure. For instance, it will reduce slightly the incentive to save for retirement or to work during retirement, since either activity will increase annual retirement income and result in a slight reduction in one's net Social Security benefits.

Further Reforms in Taxation of Benefits

The debate over taxing OASDI tends to obscure the issue of how to treat Medicare insurance. Here, too, much of the transfer escapes tax altogether, as recipients never recognize as income the Medicare benefits received. Again, this is more generous than the treatment of private insurance. If one puts aside money to buy health insurance in retirement, the money would have been subject to tax when earned. Interest on that money would also have been taxed over time.[29]

As a practical matter, it is difficult to explain to taxpayers the mechanics of taxing Medicare benefits. The value of benefits would have to be "imputed" to them. It would be simpler to combine additional taxation of Social Security cash benefits and Medicare benefits in a simple formula. For instance, taxation of 100 percent of cash benefits might be a very crude way of taxing Social Security cash benefits (implicitly at an 85 percent rate) and Medicare benefits (implicitly at a rate equal to 15 percent of cash benefits). Another alternative is simply to charge higher-income taxpayers more for their Medicare benefits, as discussed in chapter 11.

Another problem with the current design is that taxation "phases in" in a way that significantly increases the marginal tax rate on earned income in the phase-in range, thereby reducing the incentive to work. Within one part of this phase-in range, for every dollar earned, an additional $1.85 becomes subject to taxation (one dollar of earned income plus 85 cents of Social Security benefits). For those in the 28 percent income tax bracket, the marginal tax rate on earned income in this range is effectively increased to 51.8 percent (1.85 × 28 = 51.8). To this tax rate must be added Social Security tax rates, state income tax rates, and any reduction in net benefits that may derive from the earnings test in Social Security.[30] The problem could be remedied by simply eliminating the special thresholds and phase-in range, so that a fixed proportion of Social Security benefits would be included in taxable income regardless of how much one earned. To ease the impact on low- and moderate-income elderly persons, this change could easily be offset by a compensating alteration in the benefit formula or by the maintenance of a tax credit for the elderly. As noted earlier, the current thresholds are justified almost entirely on political grounds and leave moderate-income elderly persons with much lower rates of taxation than nonelderly individuals with equal or lower incomes.

An additional problem is one of accounting. When taxation of benefits was first introduced in the 1983 legislation, the revenues were designated for the Social Security trust funds. Income taxes, however, are generally designated for general government purposes. The 1983 legislation, therefore, set a precedent that the elderly's income taxes would be devoted to the elderly, while other individuals' income taxes would cover government expenses, such as defense and interest on the debt, that served everyone. President Clinton's proposals in 1993, therefore, would have designated the revenues from the increased taxation of benefits for the general funds.[31] Putting the revenues in general funds would indicate lower non–Social Security deficits, but would not show any improvement in the long-run imbalance within the Social Security trust funds. In the version finally enacted by Congress, the increased revenues were to be credited to the Medicare HI trust fund. This issue is arguably a mere technicality, however, since any of these options will have the same real effect of improving government finances.

Taxing Benefits versus Other Benefit Changes

Of course, if one's goal is to reduce the cost of Social Security in a progressive manner, there have always been alternatives to taxing benefits. A straightforward increase in the progressivity of the benefit formula, for instance, accomplishes many of the same goals. Adjusting the benefit formula can reduce net benefits according to one's level of lifetime wages, rather than one's income measured in a single year of retirement. As a result, the former has little impact on decisions regarding lifetime savings levels or whether or not to work during old age.

On the other hand, taxing benefits does have the advantage of adjusting payments according to one's actual level of economic well-being during retirement, and takes into account all forms of income, including private pensions and capital income. Remember also that the impact of income taxation tends to decline as one ages and, therefore, adjusts according to needs and abilities at different stages of old-age.

Neither basis for measuring well-being—lifetime earnings or annual income—is perfect. On balance, there is justification for using *both* in attempting to adjust benefit payments in a progressive fashion.

RAISING THE RETIREMENT AGE

So far we have discussed a wide range of options that could affect in different ways the level of annual benefit that might be received by the elderly. Now we must return to a more basic issue. For how many years should Social Security old-age benefits be provided?

More specifically, if there is to be a cutback in benefits, would it be preferable to reduce the level of benefit or the number of years benefits are provided?

As noted in chapter 3, longer retirement spans have greatly increased the cost of old-age assistance since the inception of Social Security. For a 62-year-old single retiree in the 1990s, the system can already be expected on average to provide a pension lasting around two decades and, for a couple of that age, a pension will last on average one-quarter of a century. Suppose Social Security were to be enacted anew and that its drafters accepted the same basic goals put forward in 1935: to meet the needs of those in their last years of life. Given what we now know about the relative well-being of the near-elderly and the younger-elderly, it is highly doubtful that such a large share of total resources would have been devoted to those groups who are so well-off. As originally designed, most individuals received benefits for fewer years of retirement than today, allowing scarce resources to be devoted where they appeared to be needed the most.

Among various benefit options, therefore, an increase in the retirement age is one of the easiest to justify under Social Security principles. The near-elderly and younger-elderly are relatively well-off. Their average current income is much higher than that of the older-elderly. Moreover, their income on average is as high, if not higher, than that of the nonelderly population—not even taking into account the potential earnings ability of those who are retired. In terms of wealth, they are among the richest of all age groups.

It is hard to argue that individuals today need assistance for many more years of retirement than they did about 60 years ago, when Social Security was first enacted. Jobs today are much more likely to be in the service sector, while even those in manufacturing and agriculture utilize better technology and are less likely to require heavy lifting and other physical exertions that might diminish one's work capacity as one becomes older. If anything, a program based upon a constant definition of both capability and need would likely require fewer, not more, years of retirement support as decades pass.

In response to improvements in longevity and rising costs, the 1983 Social Security Amendments scheduled an increase in the Normal Retirement Age from 65 to 67, to be phased in gradually over approximately two decades at the beginning of the next century (see table 8.1). The scheduled increase in the NRA will roughly offset projected increases in longevity between passage in the early 1980s and the

Table 8.1 SCHEDULED CHANGES IN NORMAL RETIREMENT AGE AND ADJUSTMENTS FOR EARLY AND LATE RETIREMENT

Year cohort turns 65	Normal Retirement Age	Benefit as a percentage of PIA, rounded to the nearest percentage point, if retiring at age:			
		62	65	67	70
1994 - 95	65	80	100	109	123
1996 - 97	65	80	100	110	125
1998 - 99	65	80	100	111	128
2000 - 01	65	80	100	112	130
2002	65	80	100	113	133
2003	65, 2 mo.	79	99	112	131
2004	65, 4 mo.	78	98	112	133
2005	65, 6 mo.	78	97	111	132
2006	65, 8 mo.	77	96	110	133
2007	65, 10 mo.	76	94	109	131
2008 -19	66	75	93	108	132
2020	66, 2 mo.	74	92	107	131
2021	66, 4 mo.	73	91	105	129
2022	66, 6 mo.	73	90	104	128
2023	66, 8 mo.	72	89	103	127
2024	66, 10 mo.	71	88	102	126
2025 +	67	70	87	100	124

Source: U.S. Congress, House Committee on Ways and Means (1992: 9–13)

time the change is fully phased in, but will not provide any offset for growth in life spans before or after.[32]

Raising the retirement age improves the actuarial balance within Social Security significantly. The increase in the Normal Retirement Age to 67 alone was estimated to improve the 75-year actuarial balance of the combined OASDI trust funds by 0.71 percent of taxable payroll, even though the change is not fully phased in until late in that 75-year period.[33]

Further changes in the retirement age can be implemented over time so that no current retiree suffers a benefit loss. They can be timed so that most of the impact is felt when the demographic hump—the retirement of the baby boom population—reaches its peak. The Normal Retirement Age, for example, could be scheduled to rise gradually until it ultimately reaches age 69 for those turning 65 in 2026. The SSA estimates that this particular plan would improve the 75-year actuarial balance in OASDI by 0.77 percent of taxable payroll. If the NRA were further raised to age 70 for those reaching age 65 in 2032, the long-run actuarial balance would be improved by a total of 0.97 percent of taxable payroll.[34] Under the latter approach, the average remaining life expectancy at the Normal Retirement Age, when fully phased in, would be about 18 years for a female and 14 years for a male.[35] Thus, average retirement spans would still be longer than they have been over most of Social Security's history (recall table 3.1). Such a change would go a long way toward bringing benefit outlays closer to tax revenues.

A policy of increasing the Normal Retirement Age might also be implemented by fixing a target number of years for support in old age and then "indexing" the retirement age for longevity. Currently, life expectancy at age 65 is about 15½ years for a male and a little less than 20 years for a female, for an average of roughly 18. Since many retire early (the average retirement age is close to 63), the average retirement span is closer to 20 years. The retirement age, therefore, could be gradually adjusted upward so that the average number of supported years was reduced, say, to 15, and then indexed thereafter for increases in longevity.[36] This might be accomplished roughly by implementing a plan like the ones previously discussed, and then continuing the gradual rise in the retirement age for as long as improvements in longevity persist.

Currently scheduled law retains an early retirement age of 62 even as the Normal Retirement Age increases. An increase in this early retirement age should also be seriously considered. Table 8.1 illustrates the percentage of the primary insurance amount paid for retirement at various ages. People who retire at age 62 in the future will face a larger reduction in benefits than today. Those retiring at 62 in 2022 or later will face five years', rather than three years', worth of actuarial reductions, so that their benefits will be equal to just 70 percent of their PIA for the rest of their lives. These lower benefits only increase the probability that when very old they will have inadequate income and will need to rely on the government for additional support. Gradually raising the earliest age at which OASI benefits can be obtained would help maintain benefits at an adequate level when they are really needed, at more advanced ages.

Retirement Age and Labor Force Participation

As discussed in chapter 3, retiree-to-worker ratios are projected to increase significantly during the next century. Greater labor force participation among older workers would help ameliorate this growing burden. An open question is the extent to which changes in Social Security retirement ages will affect these decisions.

In a pure economic sense, one might argue that it is the value of total benefits in retirement that should mainly influence the economic choice of when to retire. If one increased the early retirement age in a way that left individuals with the same amount of Social Security wealth, for example, they could always compensate temporarily by borrowing against the future (e.g., by remortgaging their houses). Because people cannot borrow against accumulated Social Security wealth, however, many are "liquidity constrained" and must rely heavily on current income for their consumption. Social Security's retirement ages will have real economic effects for such people. Social Security's "early" and "normal" retirement ages of 62 and 65 are also very important symbolically. They send signals about when people "ought" to retire, and a wide range of private programs, including private pensions, are often designed around Social Security retirement ages. Traditionally, retirements have been bunched around these two ages.[37] Raising these statutory retirement ages would probably have at least some positive impact on the labor force participation of those in their sixties.

Although signals and symbols can be powerful in their effect, other influences could certainly offset any potential increase in labor supply among older workers. For example, other sources of retirement income, such as pensions, private savings, and wealth, will influence work choices. The practices of private companies are developed over many years in response to a variety of incentives, not just those set by the government.

If people have a preference for early retirement and have the economic resources to do so, government should leave them free to make their own decision—as it is a choice based on private incentives and resources. There is no reason, however, why our public policies should be encouraging early retirement if there are greater needs in society.

Increasing the retirement age for Social Security raises again the issue of rules regarding private pensions, IRAs, and related plans, which often allow participants to begin receiving retirement benefits even before age 62 or to withdraw funds in a lump sum at an early age. Policymakers need to consider both limiting the tax benefits available to private and government plans that encourage early retirement, and increasing the minimum ages at which tax-preferred pension benefits can be received.

Easing Potential Impact on Needy and Impaired

Although gradually increasing the retirement age appears to be one of the more equitable and efficient options for reducing the costs of the Social Security system, two caveats must be noted. First, low-income individuals have been found to have shorter life expectancies than do high-income individuals. Accordingly, increases in the retirement age by itself might be viewed by some as affecting low-income individuals too harshly.[38]

An increase in the retirement age, however, need not be a stand-alone policy. If one wants to target benefits on lower-income and impaired individuals, supporting many years in retirement is a rather crude and arbitrary means of achieving this goal. Any increase in the retirement age could easily be tied to other specific measures that maintain the progressivity of the system.

A couple of possibilities have already been suggested. The tax system itself might be adjusted so that those with lower earnings are taxed at lower rates. Current efforts to increase the Earned Income Tax Credit (EITC) for low- and moderate-income workers could serve this purpose. Minimum benefits might also be raised for retirees.

A second difficulty with raising the retirement age is that while the average person in his or her sixties might be economically better off than the average person in the rest of the population, not everyone is average. The near-elderly and elderly are a heterogeneous population. There are many among the near-elderly who are needy and have reduced work capacity. Some near-elderly workers are the victims of "downsizing" in firms. Others suffer from reduced capability and are removed from current jobs because their salaries no longer match their productivity. Still others expect larger salaries than younger workers with comparable skills, causing a further deterrent to employment.[39]

These problems, unfortunately, are not unique to the near-elderly. They also apply to many workers in their fifties. Why isn't the retirement age lowered even further, then, to age 60, 55, or 50? Why are those in their late fifties who lose their jobs expected to try to find work, even if it is for lower pay? The answer, we believe, is clear. A program of support for everybody is a rather expensive way of trying to meet the needs of some. If the needy, unemployed, or disabled are only a minority of any age group, then there is little justification for entitling all members of this group to benefits required by that minority. It is not a question of whether need exists, but, rather, which needs most demand society's resources.

Although they are certainly not without their own problems, various unemployment and disability programs, including the disability portion of Social Security, do provide mechanisms to deal with some of these problems. Relying on these types of programs to meet the needs of the near-elderly would be far less costly than granting benefits to everyone in this group. As Social Security becomes retooled for the 21st century, it is also necessary to give serious attention to other institutional changes that may ease the impact on all affected groups.

Partial Benefits and Other Barriers to Early Retirement

There is an additional possibility for those who have not yet reached the full retirement age but have reduced earnings capacities. Rather than expect individuals to be able to maintain the same jobs on a full-time basis as they age, a partial benefit could be established. This would allow the younger-elderly to switch to less-strenuous jobs or a reduced work schedule. A program of this sort is currently offered in Sweden.[40]

There are several ways this type of change might be implemented. One alternative would simply require that only partial benefits be available to those who want to claim Social Security benefits before a Normal Retirement Age. For instance, those claiming benefits between age 62 and the Normal Retirement Age could be restricted to benefits that are only 50 percent of the level they currently can claim. After the Normal Retirement Age, benefit levels would be increased closer to full value of the PIA. The actuarial value of benefits over a lifetime, however, could be kept at whatever level was desired.[41]

CONCLUSION

A broad array of options is available to restrain the long-term rate of growth in Social Security spending to a sustainable level. A cost-reduction plan could easily be implemented in a way that maintains or increases protection for the truly needy portion of the elderly population. Real benefits, moreover, could still be allowed to increase over time. The current structure of the program would be retained under most options being discussed today. Many of these benefit-reduction options are merely extensions of the approaches used in 1977 and 1983 amendments to Social Security. Together, these two bills cut back on the ways in which benefits were (unintentionally) indexed to increase over time, delayed price indexing by six months, began to tax Social Security benefits, and increased the retirement age.

Among the options that are most consistent with the underlying principles of Social Security are an increase in the retirement age, the elimination of dropout years so that all contributions to Social Security are counted in the benefit formula, and the taxation of benefits (especially for those who have received substantial windfalls or net transfers from the system). Among the benefit options least consistent with underlying principles are a cutback in the COLAs or price adjustments granted to those already retired and an elimination of the way in which wages are indexed in the benefit calculation. A number of broader reform options can also be designed in a way consistent with underlying principles.

The significant rise in Social Security outlays scheduled for the early part of the next century, of course, provides a major impetus for further benefit reform. Principled benefit reduction must occur in a way that truly balances the needs of the elderly with other needs of society. Often this means maintaining or increasing benefits for the poor or older-elderly even if other Social Security benefits are required to grow at a slower rate.

Notes

1. Robert J. Myers (1986) pointed out that under some alternative inflation rates and annual increases in earnings, the technically flawed procedures adopted in 1972 would not have forced benefits to grow faster than wages. The 1972 amendments essentially put into law the procedure implicit in the ad hoc changes adopted in the 1950s and 1960s. Very high inflation rates in the 1970s, however, caused this procedure to go awry.

2. Board of Trustees, OASDI (1993: 104, 181).

3. In this example, Social Security taxes are raised by about the same percentage as

Social Security benefits are cut. The difference is that the taxes represent a much smaller portion of the income of taxpayers than do the benefits of the income of most beneficiaries.

4. Indeed, if the system were indexed only for inflation, with no increases in real benefit levels for new retirees, we would find that Social Security would gradually decline as a share of GDP over time.

5. It is also sometimes argued that because Social Security benefits are indexed, they are more generous than private pensions. This comparison is misleading. As demonstrated in chapter 5, evaluating the generosity (or cost) of a pension requires a measurement of its value over a retiree's entire expected lifetime. If Social Security is deemed too generous on this basis, then its basic benefit level should be reduced or retirement ages increased; there is no reason to remove indexing. Indeed, private pensions would accommodate retirement needs better if they started at a lower level and then were indexed to keep pace with inflation.

6. As noted previously, the technical flaw in indexing during the mid-1970s caused benefits to grow at a much faster rate than intended. The problem was not with indexing per se, but rather with the way in which the indexing was designed.

7. The CPI keeps constant for a number of years the relative weights given to the goods and services comprising the index. Many would argue that as expenditures on one good decline from, say, 10 percent of the household's budget, any inflation in the price of that good should gradually be given a weight of less than 10 percent in deriving the overall index. Such an adjustment would reduce the measured amount of inflation slightly.

A related question is whether goods and services consumed by the elderly experience greater or lesser inflation than those consumed by the general population. Boskin and Hurd (1985) found that for the preceding 20 years, "the cumulative rise in cost of living was virtually identical for the general population and for the elderly." Although some have argued that the elderly face lower inflation rates because they spend less on items such as housing, their large out-of-pocket spending on other items as health care may make up for this. See also Boskin (1986) and Myers (1993a).

Also note that the CPI-W displayed somewhat higher rates of inflation than indexes such as the GDP deflator of personal consumption expenditures index, but slightly lower inflation than the CPI-U. See Myers (1992 and 1993b: 101) for a more detailed discussion of these issues.

8. Legislation would need to deal with some technical problems in switching indices. The CPI, when posted, is treated as a permanent index (i.e., past years are not revised). Other indices do not claim such preciseness and are amended over time. From an administrative standpoint, it is easier not to have to try to reverse benefit changes that have already been implemented. Still, there are some easy ways of dealing with this issue—such as adjusting benefits by the CPI, less an amount estimated to reflect the extent to which the CPI will overstate inflation relative to other indexes.

9. The AIME's predecessor was the unindexed "average monthly wage" (AMW). Beginning in 1975, the benefit formula was indexed in such a way that benefit levels based on a given AMW would automatically increase at the same rate as inflation. The AMW, however, was still based on nominal wages, and gave a very heavy weight to the last few years of earnings before retirement. As a result, inflationary increases in nominal wages caused AMWs to rise dramatically from one cohort of retirees to the next. Indexing benefits fully for inflation for a fixed AMW while AMW levels were also rising effectively resulted in "overindexing," and benefit levels rose sharply. Under some economic conditions, this problem might not have arisen; the accelerating inflation of the 1970s, however, made the overindexing problem quite strong. See GAO (1988) and National Academy of Social Insurance (1988) for a more detailed explanation of the overindexing problem.

10. This argument holds best when tax rates are constant over time. Obviously, when

tax rates vary, a system designed strictly according to the individual equity principle would index tax contributions, rather than the wage base upon which the taxes were based, to determine final benefit levels.

11. One issue to consider with respect to wage indexing is which measure of average wages to use. The current wage index is derived simply by dividing an estimate of the total amount of employment earnings in the United States by an estimate of the total number of employees. As a result, the series is affected by such factors as the increasing prevalence of part-time work. A series that was based on the average wage per full-time or full-time equivalent worker would result in higher measured wage growth, and correspondingly higher benefit growth over the long run. See Sandell (forthcoming) for a discussion of this issue.

12. In this simple example, we are assuming that revenues grow at about the same rate as the economy, as in a system with a constant tax rate. Continually higher rates of tax, of course, could finance new programs.

13. Thus, it is not necessary to index all bend-points by the same index. The PIA bracket with the highest rate of return, for instance, can be viewed as supporting some "minimum benefit" amount that should rise with earnings.

14. The number of years included in the AIME calculation was less than 35 for those reaching age 62 before 1991.

15. Some offset is provided by the fact that lower-income workers may be more likely to suffer spells of unemployment or to retire early owing to poor health.

16. Only if earnings in these additional years are higher than indexed earnings in prior years will the additional taxes paid add to benefits. Even then, the amount is likely to be small, as the additional year merely "replaces" one of the earlier 35 years in the benefit computation.

17. Martin Feldstein and Andrew Samwick (1992) recently published a study reaching similar conclusions about dropout years in Social Security. Their study also provides some measures of net marginal tax rates (inclusive of benefits) in OASI.

18. The progressive benefit formula by itself—even without any dropout years—provides some compensation for dropping out of the labor force. Although the AIME is reduced, the average dollar of earnings now falls in a higher rate of return bracket.

19. In the Pechman et al. version (1968), replacement rates would be maintained at existing levels for an extended transition period, implying that significant redistribution toward current and near-future retirees would persist.

20. SSA (1992). See Appendix table A.13 for summaries of Social Security provisions in a few selected countries.

21. An analogy here with one type of reform of the income tax is sometimes suggested: reducing the number of rate brackets. Reducing the number of rates of taxation does not necessarily change the progressivity of the system, the size of the system, or its simplicity. If the top rate in a two-tier income tax system is higher than in a multi-tier system, for instance, the tax may become more progressive.

22. It would probably also be necessary to base the rates of return on taxes paid, rather than on earnings subject to tax. In theory, there is no difference if the rate of tax is constant over time, but political and demographic factors make it difficult to contemplate a tax rate forever constant.

23. Neither president was necessarily consistent. If cutting back on a tax expenditure can be treated as an expenditure cut, then increasing other tax expenditures should be treated as expenditure increases. Neither was willing to go this far.

24. The design of this credit presumably would be reexamined if the thresholds for taxing Social Security were eliminated.

25. Remember that we are comparing Social Security benefits here with nominal contributions, before the accumulation of interest or adjustment for inflation, since this is the basis used for taxing pension benefits where previously taxed employee contributions are involved.

26. Myers (1993a) argues that the 85 percent guideline is already a bit high for some high-income workers retiring today. He suggests a rate of 80 percent today, declining gradually over time to 72 percent by 2027. The SSA Office of the Actuary, however, has pointed out a source of disagreement with these calculations (Memorandum by Stephen Goss, April 7, 1993). A strict comparison of the treatment of OASI benefits with a similarly designed private pension (with after-tax contributions of employees similar to the employee portion of the Social Security tax) requires a calculation of the *nominal* employee contributions as a percentage of *nominal* lifetime benefits. According to Goss, Myers calculated nominal contributions as a percentage of the *present value* of lifetime benefits at retirement age, thus excluding from taxation both employee contributions and the interest earned on accumulated contributions after retirement. In any event, there are many other arguments for taxing benefits, each of which would lead to a different conclusion about the proper portion to be taxed.

27. Extra revenues for FY 1995 are Joint Committee on Taxation estimates, August 4, 1993. The improvement in the 75-year actuarial balance of OASDI under President Clinton's plan was estimated at 0.4 percent by the SSA Office of the Actuary (Memorandum by Stephen Goss, May 14, 1993). The version finally passed by Congress will have a somewhat smaller impact.

28. U.S. Congress, Joint Committee on Taxation, estimates published in CBO (1993: 358).

29. Of course, private health insurance for the nonelderly is currently tax favored, although many believe that this provision is also inequitable. See the discussion in chapter 7 on its effect on reducing the tax base for Social Security.

30. See Forman (1993a and b), Steuerle (1993b), and Chambers (1993).

31. In early 1993, one of the authors, as well as Robert Ball, a former commissioner, and Robert Myers, a former chief actuary, testified in response to a question before the Senate Committee on Finance that income taxes in principle should be devoted to general revenues. Putting these taxed benefits in general revenues, however, does reduce the actuarial balances in Social Security—an issue that would have to be addressed.

32. People turning 65 in 2003 will be the first to be affected, as the Normal Retirement Age (NRA) rises to age 65 and two months. The NRA will rise by an additional two months for cohorts turning 65 in each successive year until 2008, when it reaches 66. After remaining at 66 for people turning 65 between 2008 and 2019, the NRA will once again rise by two months per cohort for those turning 65 from 2020 to 2025. Cohorts turning 62 in 2025 or later face a NRA of 67.

33. Estimate by SSA from 1984, cited in U.S. Congress, House Committee on Ways and Means (1992: 33).

34. Memorandum from Stephen Goss, SSA Office of the Actuary, December 23, 1992. Based on intermediate assumptions of the 1992 Board of Trustees report.

35. Under the intermediate projections used by the SSA for the 1992 Board of Trustees reports, the average life expectancy at age 70 in 2040 will be 18.12 years for a female and 14.11 years for a male.

36. Indexing of the NRA was included in the majority recommendations of the 1983 National Commission on Social Security Reform and the original 1983 Senate bill on the subject, but was not enacted in the final legislation.

37. Leonesio (1991: figure 1) illustrates the double-peaked pattern of retirement ages, with peaks at ages 62 and 65.

38. Survivors and disability benefits offset some of the effect of earlier death.

39. For a discussion of the labor market problems faced by older workers, and some approaches that could help improve the situation, see Sandell (1987).

40. SSA (1992: 268).

41. This rule would apply even to those who do not work past an early retirement date. For those who work and have sufficient earnings, current law already can force a reduction in partial benefits. See chapter 9 for a further discussion of appropriate adjustments for recipients who both work and claim early benefits.

Chapter Nine

SPOUSAL BENEFITS AND RULES FOR EARLY AND DELAYED RETIREMENT

In previous chapters we have touched only briefly on two important features of Social Security: the ways in which it treats married couples and the rules it applies to those who retire both before and after the Normal Retirement Age (currently 65). Of the many reforms of these features that have been discussed over the years, most are directed at removing perceived inequities and labor market distortions among beneficiaries and taxpayers. Few proposed changes, if any, are likely either to increase taxes or reduce benefits dramatically. Neither feature, therefore, plays prominently in the effort to bring Social Security back into long-term balance. It is the second major impetus for reform—adapting the system to the needs and conditions of the time and improving its equity and efficiency—that make it likely that legislators will also address these issues in upcoming reform efforts.

SPOUSAL BENEFITS AND RETURNS TO SECONDARY WORKERS

Social Security contains a number of provisions that affect the benefits received by spouses and survivors of insured workers. As we saw in chapter 5, these rules play a large role in the distribution of benefits and the returns workers receive for their contributions. The basic framework for these provisions was developed during Social Security's early years, when women played a much smaller role in the formal marketplace for workers. At that time, issues of equity among one-earner and two-earner couples and of returns to the contributions of secondary workers did not arouse substantial concern. As women's participation in the paid labor force has grown dramatically, however, these issues have received greater attention. Historical and projected increases in women's work-force participation suggest that within a few decades, the majority of women will have earned substantial Social Security benefits in their own right.[1] Now is thus a propitious time to reexamine Social Security's provisions for spousal and survivors' benefits.

Spousal Benefits

Recall from chapter 4 that Social Security offers supplemental benefits to the spouses and survivors of insured workers. These benefits are directly proportional to the size of the primary worker's benefit. The spouse of a retired worker is eligible to receive a benefit equal to 50 percent of the primary worker's basic monthly benefit (primary insurance amount, PIA). In addition, a retired widow or widower is eligible to receive a survivor's benefit equal to 100 percent of a deceased worker's benefit. Both of these benefits are subject to an actuarial reduction (explained later in this chapter) if the dependent spouse begins collecting benefits before the Normal Retirement Age. Suppose a spouse also has a worker's benefit, based on his or her own earnings record, that is less than the available spousal or survivor's benefit. Then his or her own benefit will be supplemented until it reaches the level of the higher spousal or survivor's benefit.

Upon what principles are spousal benefits based? The basic justification must be the same as that for the program as a whole: the needs of the elderly. Households with two people need more money to support themselves than households with one. Many elderly couples—in particular, those alive in the early years of Social Security—were removed from poverty thanks partly to spousal benefits. Many widows would also fall into poverty if they did not gain access to survivors' benefits earned through their spouses' earnings history.

If spousal benefits were based mainly on need, however, they would be governed by the progressivity principle and would be targeted where the needs are greatest. In the American system, however, just the opposite occurs: *the size of spousal benefit is related inversely to need*. How does this occur? Because the spousal benefit is set at 50 percent of the primary worker's PIA, the two rise in tandem. The higher the income of the worker, the greater will be the value of the spouse's benefit. Survivors' benefits work the same way. Consider male workers in the cohort turning 65 in 1995 who have a nonwage-earning spouse and two children. The annuity value of lifetime spousal and survivors' benefits is approximately $76,900 if the worker has low wages, but rises to $127,700 if he has average wages and $171,800 if he has high wages (see chapter 5, table 5.1).

Certainly such a transfer to higher-income individuals cannot be justified on the basis of need. Perhaps, therefore, appeal might be made to one of the other Social Security principles. How about individual equity or an analogy to private insurance? Here, again, no rationale can be found. For example, two male workers with identical earnings histories will pay the same amount of tax contributions. If one of these workers has a nonwage-earning spouse, however, he will receive a far greater return on his contributions. As we saw in chapter 5, if he retires in the near future his family's benefits will greatly exceed the annuity value of his contributions, regardless of his income level, whereas a worker without dependents may receive less than a full market return on his contributions. Following a principle in which benefits are related directly to contributions, the existing benefit distribution could only be justified if workers who wanted to receive spousal benefits were required to pay higher premiums during their working years.

Horizontal equity likewise does not justify the observed redistributive patterns. The spousal benefit does not treat equally those in equal need, provide equal rates of return on past contributions, or even treat all spouses equally. The efficiency of the system is not enhanced by this regressive redistribution, either. Benefits are not related to taxes, and taxes on workers are higher than would be required if there were less redistribution to spouses at the top of the income scale.

Suppose we take the spousal benefit outside of the employee insurance world and treat it as a type of "family" benefit. Could the current structure of spousal benefits be justified by some societal desire to compensate people for the costs of raising children? No. Here, too, the structure would be found wanting. Suppose, for instance, that the spousal benefit is viewed as one based on "shadow wages" for uncompensated work raising children in the home. The implication of larger spousal benefits for upper-income households would then be that society places a much higher value on child care given in high-income households than in low-income households. High-income parenting would be valued more than low-income parenting. Single parents and many two-earner couples, moreover, receive no spousal allowance despite their efforts at raising children.

Since no principle has been found that justifies this particular pattern of distribution, perhaps it may be thought that a last appeal can be made to some "natural" order in the design of pension plans (i.e., that spousal benefits are often a given percentage of the worker's benefits). In a private insurance scheme, however, those who wanted to receive spousal benefits of this sort usually would either have to pay higher premiums or have their own benefits adjusted in such a way that the total actuarial value would not rise. International experience also calls this line of reasoning into question. Many comparable nations, including Canada, France, Sweden, the United Kingdom, and Japan, provide support to spouses that is unrelated to the income of the higher-earning spouse. These other countries typically aid nonwage-earning spouses through either a uniform universal benefit or a flat spousal benefit.[2]

Returns to Secondary Workers

Because the spousal benefit provides a return that is unrelated to past contributions of the spouse, it interacts with the normal rules for workers to create some additional problems when a spouse enters the work force and makes contributions to Social Security. The lesser-earning spouse in a family may contribute a substantial amount to Social Security over a lifetime, but receive little or no marginal increase in retirement benefits over what would have been obtained anyway. Many spouses, particularly women, don't earn enough over their careers to yield Old-Age and Survivors Insurance (OASI) benefits greater than half of the primary worker's benefits. These spouses receive no marginal return on their contributions. Even those secondary workers who earn benefits much larger than the available spousal benefit typically receive only a small marginal return on their contributions.

Table 9.1 illustrates the very small returns that working women often receive. It demonstrates the percentage increase in a family's lifetime OASI benefits and contributions when a wife works, compared to a situation where the wife does not work for wages at all. The calculations are derived directly from the actuarial analysis we presented in chapter 5, and are adjusted for the chance of death and value of survivors' benefits in all years after age 21. We use couples from the cohort turning 65 in 2030 (currently in their late twenties) as an example, although the results would be similar for almost any cohort.

Consider, first, a family where the husband earns at least the maximum wage subject to Social Security tax in every year ($57,600 in 1993). If the wife earned the average national wage every year for 46 years, the family's lifetime Social Security contributions would

Table 9.1 MARGINAL RETURNS FROM OASI FOR WAGE-EARNING WOMEN
TURNING 65 IN 2030

FAMILY TYPE	Percentage increase in family OASI contributions due to wife working	Percentage increase in family OASI benefits due to wife working	Net increase in benefits as a % of net increase in contributions
High-wage husband & average-wage wife	43.3%	1.0%	2.5%
Average-wage husband & low-wage wife	46.6%	1.2%	4.1%
Low wage husband & low-wage wife	103.6%	15.2%	31.2%

Notes: All amounts are converted to constant 1993 dollars, discounted to present value at age 65 using 2 percent real interest rate, and weighted according to probability of survival from age 21. Includes actuarial value of all OASI worker's, spousal, and survivors' benefits payable over a lifetime. Table includes both employer and employee portions of OASI payroll tax. Couples are assumed to be the same age and to have two children born when the parents are aged 25 and 30. Assumes retirement at OASI Normal Retirement Age. Projections are based on intermediate assumptions of 1993 OASDI Board of Trustees report. OASI tax rate is assumed to be set at 10.65 percent after 1992.

increase by about 43 percent. The value of the family's lifetime OASI benefit, however, would only increase by 1 percent compared to what would be received if she never worked at all. Almost exactly the same story holds true in a family where the husband earns the average national wage and the wife earns low wages. In both these types of families, the net marginal tax rate imposed on the wife is close to the full OASI tax rate. This net marginal tax rate would be reduced slightly if the wives were to earn wages much closer to their husband's throughout their careers, but even then would be quite high.[3]

When a wife works in a family where both spouses earn a low wage equal to 45 percent of the average national wage, the actuarial value of the family's lifetime contributions approximately doubles.[4] Her additional contributions only increase the family's lifetime benefit by about 15 percent. The net increase in lifetime benefits amounts to less than a third of the wife's additional contributions (see table 9.1).

Another consequence of the current spousal benefit scheme is that two couples with exactly the same lifetime incomes and contribu-

Table 9.2 TWO COUPLES WITH IDENTICAL CONTRIBUTIONS
CAN RECEIVE DIFFERENT BENEFITS
(ANNUAL BENEFITS FOR COUPLES TURNING 65 IN 1995, IN
CONSTANT 1993 DOLLARS)

	One-earner couple, husband earns maximum wage subject to OASI tax ($57,600 in 1993)	Two-earner couple, each earns half of maximum taxable wage ($28,800 in 1993)
Benefit when both spouses are alive	20,399	18,229
Benefit when only one spouse is alive	13,599	9,115

Note: Couples are assumed to be the same age and to retire at age 65.

tions to the Social Security system can receive very different benefits (see table 9.2). In these cases, a two-earner couple will almost always fare worse than a one-earner couple. For example, compare two couples turning 65 in 1995, each of which has family incomes equal to the maximum earnings subject to OASI tax ($57,600 in 1993).[5] For our purposes here, we assume they are identical in all respects except that in the first household, the husband earns all of the income, while in the second, each spouse earns half of the income.[6] The one-earner couple will receive an annual benefit of $20,399 (in constant 1993 dollars) while both spouses are alive. In the likely event that the husband dies before the wife, she will receive a survivor's benefit worth $13,599 annually. The two-earner couple, by contrast, receives an annual benefit of $18,229 while both are alive, and just $9,115 when only one survives. Thus, the one-earner couple's benefit is 12 percent larger than that of the two-earner couple when both are alive, and 49 percent larger when only one is alive. Since the two couples made identical contributions to the system, and presumably the two-earner couple has at least identical needs, this is a clear case of horizontal inequity.

TREATMENT OF DIVORCE

A closely related question in Social Security is how to treat those who are divorced. Under current law, a divorced spouse who does not remarry is eligible for exactly the same spousal and survivors' benefits as if he or she were still married, so long as the marriage lasted at least 10 years. Those who were married fewer than 10 years are not eligible for any spousal or survivors' benefits. A divorced person who remarries loses eligibility for benefits based on his or her ex-spouse's record while his or her new spouse is still alive. If the divorcée becomes widowed, however, he or she is eligible for the largest survivors' benefit available based on the earnings record of any of his or her deceased spouses.

Here again, goals seem to be confused. The purpose of the benefit to divorced persons seems to be twofold: (1) to entitle them to some appropriate share of their spouse's benefits and (2) to provide help on the basis of need. The program's crazy-quilt design for dealing with divorce, however, does not directly address either of those issues. The former problem, for instance, might be met by splitting the earnings credits of a divorced couple, or entitling each of them to some share of the benefits earned by the other. Variations of these approaches are already offered in Canada and Germany.[7] The latter problem might be met by guaranteeing some minimum benefit to all persons, or by providing some credit or minimum credit for years engaged in meaningful nonmarket efforts such as child care. U.S. policy does not relate benefits for divorced spouses to need, nor does it share earned benefits among divorced spouses. Thus, a spouse of 40 years who has raised the children of the worker is granted no greater share of benefits than a spouse of 10 years who has performed no child-raising and could more easily have earned taxable wages. By marrying several times, moreover, one person can sometimes generate substantial benefits for multiple wives or husbands.[8]

Earnings Sharing and Other Options

We do not wish to imply that spousal and divorce issues can be dealt with simply; rather, that the rules should be modified to adhere more closely to the principles that ought to guide the Social Security system. Any such change would require some trade-offs. In the case of married couples, not only must there be a trade-off between progressivity and individual equity, but the definition of "equals" must be clarified. Are all individuals with equal earnings or all couples with equal earnings to be treated equally? If needs are not perfectly proportionate to the number of persons in the family, for instance, then some would argue that progressivity requires that the benefits given to two separate single-person households should be greater than the benefits given to a married couple.[9]

Among the options sometimes proposed to deal with the problems of married couples has been to allow for "earnings sharing." Although the proposal may take various forms, its essential ingredient is the splitting of earnings of each member of a couple and the generation of separate earnings records for all individuals. For example, if a husband earns $40,000 in a year and his wife earns $20,000, each might be credited with $30,000 of earnings for Social Security purposes. Each would eventually receive a benefit calculated separately on the basis of his or her own earnings credits. Some proposals would also give special credits for nonworking years when child care is involved.

A variety of studies (CBO 1986; Center for Women Policy Studies 1988; SSA, Office of Legislative and Regulatory Policy 1985; Zedlewski 1984) have examined the potential winners and losers under an earnings-sharing approach. These studies come to the common conclusion that relative to the current system, two-earner couples would gain a greater share of total Social Security benefits under an earnings-sharing approach. This should not be surprising, since nonworking spouses of high-income workers receive very large net transfers that are unrelated either to earnings or to need, whereas an earnings-sharing system would tend to guarantee that benefits are related more closely to earnings.

Whether one goes all the way toward an earnings-sharing approach or not, both the need-based nature of Social Security and its individual equity components could simultaneously be improved by redesigning the ways in which couples are treated. The basic principles of the program—essentially that some minimum or need-based grant be made to almost everyone and that all contributions should receive some rate of return—can be carried over to the treatment of spouses. To begin to achieve this goal, initially the spousal benefits of the richest spouses could be capped—for instance, not be allowed to grow in the future—and the revenues used gradually to provide some rate of return on those contributions for which no return is currently provided.

As for providing credit for years spent caring for children, we believe that this can best be done either by allowing some adjustment to a minimum benefit for years of child-rearing or by providing a flat minimum earnings credit for all spouses during years in which children are being raised in their homes.[10] Eventually, this might come to replace the spousal benefit altogether. Such an approach would tend to give equal treatment to all who provide child care. One proposal—to provide extra "dropout years" in the calculation of average indexed monthly earnings (AIME) for those who raise children—creates several problems. It tends to give higher earnings credits in years of no work to higher-income individuals—once again, valuing their child care more than that of low-income individuals. Increasing the number of dropout years also reduces the marginal incentive to work and contribute to the system in any given year. Many Social Security contributions would continue to receive no return. For instance, the many people who work part-time during child-rearing years would often find that they received no additional benefit for the extra contributions they made.[11]

With respect to cases of divorce, a decision must be made regarding the rights accorded the divorced spouse. Earnings sharing implies that Social Security benefits should be treated as earned equally during years of marriage. One doesn't need to wait for earnings sharing to apply such logic. The worker's basic benefit, plus any spousal benefit deemed earned (however calculated), could be shared equally with a spouse of many years, or spread proportionately according to number of years of marriage, especially in the case of several spouses.[12]

For administrative reasons, as well as problems of transition, these changes would need to be phased in over time.[13] The longer the delay, however, the longer the existing system will tend not only to provide significant welfarelike transfers to high-income individuals but to imply that high-income parents provide child-raising services more valuable than low-income parents, and to sustain unnecessarily high poverty rates for divorced persons.

Survivors' Benefits and the Very Old

Under current law, many retired couples are granted Social Security benefits that are 1.5 times the benefits that will be received when one of the spouses dies. The changeover occurs when the combined worker and spousal benefit is reduced to just a worker or survivor benefit for the remaining spouse. When this switch occurs, some individuals who formerly had incomes above the official U.S. poverty line now fall below that line. Partly as a result, the poverty rate for women aged 65 and over who were living alone was 26.6 percent in 1991; 50.8 percent of these women had incomes below 1.5 times the poverty line.[14]

The reason for the movement into "poverty" is partly technical. The poverty line for a single person is more than two-thirds of the poverty line for a married couple. Thus, when a couple lives on Social Security just above the poverty line, the death of one spouse will make income fall more than the poverty line falls.

These poverty lines are determined according to a standard that implies significant economies of scale in housing, automobiles, use of appliances, and so forth. Although the poverty measure (and the accuracy of its assumed economies of scale) might be called into question for a variety of reasons,[15] it does remind us that many very old persons, particularly widows, do live on very little income. We have consistently noted the relatively poorer status of the very old and the reasons for reorienting Social Security toward their needs. These surviving spouses face additional problems when various infirmities and disabilities of old age occur, since there is now no spouse there to help them. They are much more likely to require outside assistance in daily living than are married couples.

A number of options for dealing with this problem are available. One approach would be to make an actuarial adjustment at the time OASI benefits start, so that benefits would not decline so much when one spouse dies.[16] On an optional basis, benefits could even be held constant throughout years of receipt, regardless of whether both spouses or one spouse was living.[17] If done in an actuarially "fair" manner, the net cost to the system would be zero over time, and the net change in benefits for the couple would be zero. A greater share of total benefits, however, would be available in very old age, rather than at younger ages. Remember that a couple retiring at about age 62 is likely to receive benefits for about one-quarter of a century, and the ability of Social Security benefits to cover costs at the beginning of that quarter-century is a misleading indicator of its ability to meet needs at the end of that period of time.

Note that this simple actuarial adjustment can be performed under almost any system for providing benefits, including either current law or an earnings-sharing approach. Private pensions and insurance companies commonly provide these types of adjustments for annuitants as well.

Increases in minimum benefit levels and the Supplemental Security Income (SSI) program could also be used to help the poorest of widows.[18] Indeed, this would be a useful means to assure that some married couples, who would receive lower initial benefits, would not fall into poverty because of the change.

EARLY AND DELAYED RETIREMENT

If the elderly had no special needs, Social Security would not exist in its current form. The primary problem that Old-Age Insurance in Social Security was meant to address was obviously the reduced income that derived mainly from a reduced capacity to work. Identifying exactly who is incapacitated or disabled, however, can be an extraordinarily difficult and arguably demeaning process. Social Security, therefore, uses age as a much cleaner, although arbitrary, means to identify those who should be eligible for benefits. To accomplish this, it established age 65 as the "normal" age at which people are expected to retire.

The Old-Age and Survivors Insurance system has developed a complex array of rules for adjusting the benefits of those who deviate from the Normal Retirement Age.[19] Even experts are sometimes confused about how all of these rules work and interact, and what their net effects are. Initially, these provisions were designed in a way that clearly produced a strong financial incentive to retire early. In many ways, the system has been trying to amend that initial design ever since. Over time, Congress has adjusted these rules and established new ones in an attempt to reduce the penalties for working. Even today, as we will demonstrate, Social Security continues to provide financial incentives for individuals to stop working before the end of their productive years, and the signals it sends seem to be interpreted the same way they were 50 years ago.

Basic Rules for Early and Delayed Retirement

Social Security allows workers to begin receiving retirement benefits as early as age 62. To prevent early retirement from significantly increasing the lifetime value of benefits, an "actuarial reduction" is applied to the benefits of those who begin receiving OASI before the Normal Retirement Age, currently 65. Those who fully retire at age 65 receive benefits equal to 100 percent of their PIA. For every month before age 65 that someone receives OASI payments, the monthly benefit is permanently reduced by 5/9 of a percent of PIA.[20] For example, people who retire 36 months early, at age 62, receive a benefit equal to 80 percent of PIA for the rest of their lives. Reductions for early retirement will also generally continue to apply to any survivors' benefits based on that worker's record, although no survivors' benefit will be reduced below 82.5 percent of the worker's PIA.[21]

Spousal benefits face a slightly larger rate of reduction; they fall from 50 percent of PIA at the Normal Retirement Age to 37.5 percent for those who retire at age 62.[22] As the Normal Retirement Age increases to 67 during the next century, the rules will gradually be adjusted so that eventually a worker and spouse retiring at 62 will receive benefits equal to 70 percent and 32.5 percent of PIA, respectively.

To reduce benefit payments to those who are not fully retired, Social Security applies an "earnings test" (also known as the "retirement test"). In 1993, the earnings test reduces Social Security benefits by 50 cents for every dollar earned over a basic exempt amount of $7,680 below age 65, and 33 cents for every dollar earned above $10,560 between ages 65 and 70.[23] Workers aged 70 and over are exempt from this earnings test.[24] During Social Security's early decades, the earnings test was much more strict. Over the years, exempt amounts have gradually been increased and benefit reduction rates have been lessened in an effort to reduce penalties against work.

To further offset some of the work disincentives created by the earnings test, Congress established a "delayed retirement credit" (DRC) in 1972 and has increased it gradually over time. The DRC causes any loss of benefits occurring between the Normal Retirement Age and age 70 to be at least partially compensated with an increase in later benefits. Those in the cohort turning 65 in 1995 will receive a permanent benefit increase of 4.5 percent of PIA for each year's worth of benefits that they forgo (or lose owing to the earnings test). For example, people in this cohort who fully retire at age 67 and do not receive any benefits beforehand will get benefits equal to 109 percent of PIA for the rest of their lives.[25] The delayed retirement credit will be gradually increased for future retirees, eventually reaching 8 percent per year for the cohort turning 65 in 2008.[26] Benefits for widows and widowers are also subject to the DRC, although spousal benefits are not.

The way Social Security relates benefit amounts to past earnings also has a significant impact on how people who retire at different ages are treated. Delaying retirement for a few years will typically increase an individual's total tax contributions to Social Security by a large amount. These extra contributions, however, usually result in but a small increase in benefit levels. One reason is that only a limited number of years (currently 35 for most new retirees) are included in the calculation of average earnings (AIME). Only if wages are high enough to "replace" other years of earnings in the AIME calculation might the AIME increase through additional years of work late in life. Even then, the effect is extremely small. The progressive nature of the benefit formula also reduces the returns from delayed retirement for many middle- and upper-income workers. When extra years of work do cause the AIME to increase by a few dollars, these additional dollars usually fall into those brackets of the benefit formula that provide lower rates of return.

Finally, income taxation of benefits can also cause a disincentive to work. A person's wages and other income are used in the test to determine whether Social Security benefits are subject to taxation. As a result, additional wages in some income ranges may cause benefits that would otherwise be tax-free to become taxable.

Does Social Security Provide an Incentive to Retire Early?

Financial rewards for early retirement and penalties for delaying retirement are both inefficient and inequitable. Incentives to retire before the end of one's productive years may induce experienced and talented workers to withdraw from the labor force. As a consequence, the economy may shrink and younger workers may be forced to bear greater burdens in meeting the needs of society.[27] By imposing different treatment on people with identical economic resources and abilities, but different preferences between labor and leisure, these rewards and penalties can be horizontally inequitable as well.

Because so many complex rules are involved, it is not immediately apparent whether Social Security actually offers a financial reward or penalty for retiring early or late. To examine this question, we have calculated the effect various retirement decisions would have on the expected actuarial value of OASI contributions and benefits for workers in the cohort turning 65 in 1995. All rules that can affect lifetime benefit or tax payments, including taxation of benefits, are taken into account.[28] The methodology here is basically the same as that in chapter 5, except we assume here that the worker has already survived to age 62, and we weight benefits and taxes for the probability of survival only in subsequent years. This provides a reasonable measure of the financial incentives facing a worker about to turn 62 and trying to decide when to retire.[29]

Table 9.3 summarizes the results of this actuarial analysis (more detail is offered in Appendix table A.11). In this table, full retirement at age 65 is considered the "baseline." Changes in the value of benefits and taxes are all shown relative to what would happen if the worker fully retired at age 65. Three possible retirement options are displayed: (1) fully retire and register for benefits at age 62; (2) register for benefits at 65 but continue working until 67; and (3) register for

Table 9.3 EFFECTS OF ALTERNATIVE RETIREMENT DECISIONS ON VALUE
OF OASI
(WORKERS TURNING 65 IN 1995; AMOUNTS IN THOUSANDS OF CONSTANT
1993 DOLLARS)

Retirement decision	MALE WORKER			FEMALE WORKER		
	Low wage	Average wage	High wage	Low wage	Average wage	High wage
Retire at 62						
Change in benefits	- 0.2	- 0.5	- 4.6	- 3.6	-6.2	- 13.3
Change in contributions	- 3.2	- 7.2	- 17.7	- 3.3	- 7.3	- 17.9
Net gain (+), or loss (-)	+ 3.1	+ 6.7	+ 13.1	- 0.3	+ 1.1	+ 4.6
Retire at 67						
Change in benefits	+ 0.4	- 2.8	- 8.0	+ 0.5	- 1.7	- 4.3
Change in contributions	+ 2.0	+ 4.3	+ 10.5	+ 2.0	+ 4.5	+ 10.9
Net gain (+), or loss (-)	- 1.6	- 7.2	- 18.5	- 1.5	- 6.2	- 15.2
Net OASI tax rate on wages after age 65	8.7 %	17.6 %	18.8 %	8.0 %	14.6 %	14.8 %
Retire at 70						
Change in benefits	+ 1.0	- 7.4	- 22.5	+ 1.5	- 4.7	- 13.9
Change in contributions	+ 4.6	+ 10.2	+ 24.7	+ 4.9	+ 10.8	+ 26.1
Net gain (+), or loss (-)	- 3.6	- 17.6	- 47.2	- 3.4	-15.5	- 40.0
Net OASI tax rate on wages after age 65	8.3 %	18.4 %	20.3 %	7.4 %	15.3 %	16.3 %

Notes: Table reflects change in actuarial present value of OASI benefits and taxes
relative to retirement at age 65. All amounts are converted to present value at age
62, using 2 percent real interest rate. Includes impact on worker's benefits only.
Those who delay retirement are assumed to register to begin receiving OASI benefits
immediately at age 65. Includes both employer and employee portions of OASI
payroll tax. Projections are based on intermediate assumptions in 1993 OASDI Board
of Trustees report. Assumes OASI tax rate is set at 10.65 percent after 1992.

benefits at 65 but continue working until age 70. Workers who delay
retirement are assumed to register to begin collecting at least partial
benefits at age 65, if available, because it turns out they are almost
always better off on an actuarial basis if they do so (see Appendix
for a comparison). That the system offers different benefits to people

in identical circumstances, based solely upon time of filing, raises considerable equity questions, since people may inadvertently reduce the lifetime value of their benefits simply because they do not know the optimal time to apply for OASI.

As table 9.3 indicates, the current OASI system does indeed tend to treat people better the earlier they retire. This is generally true regardless of income level or gender. Incentives for retiring early (or penalties for delaying retirement) are particularly strong for men with average or high lifetime wages. The bias is relatively small for people with low incomes, mainly because they are not hit very hard by the earnings test, and the progressive benefit formula gives them a higher rate of return for their additional contributions. The incentive for earlier retirement is also slightly smaller for women than for men, since the delayed retirement credit would give credits for more years to those with longer lifespans.

If a worker retires at age 62 instead of age 65, the expected value of his or her lifetime OASI benefits will decline slightly. The actuarial reduction for early retirement roughly offsets the extra benefits one receives before 65. Retiring at age 62 instead of 65, however, also means three fewer years of payroll tax contributions. In almost all cases, the reduction in lifetime tax contributions resulting from early retirement is larger than the reduction in benefits. As a consequence, early retirement generally increases net transfers—benefits less taxes—from Social Security. The combined effect is to create an incentive for early retirement.

The penalty for delaying retirement past the Normal Retirement Age of 65 turns out to be quite large for average- and higher-wage workers, since lifetime benefits are reduced while lifetime taxes increase. Consider, for example, a male worker who earns the average national wage. If he decides to continue working until age 67, he will pay about $4,300 more in OASI taxes, yet his lifetime benefits will decline by $2,800, for a net loss of about $7,200 (after rounding). A male worker who earns at or above the maximum wage subject to OASI taxes faces a similar penalty for retiring at 67, losing $18,500 overall. The later one retires, the larger the penalty. For example, if an average-wage male worker waits until age 70 to leave his job, OASI imposes a net actuarial penalty of $17,600. The net loss for a high-wage male worker retiring at 70 is also quite large, at $47,200.

Table 9.3 also expresses the net OASI penalty for delayed retirement as a percentage of all wages earned after age 65. This provides a measure of the effective average tax rate imposed by OASI on post-65 wages. As noted in chapter 5, most people face a net lifetime

OASI tax rate that is considerably below the gross rate of tax, since their tax contributions are offset by later benefits. Those who work past age 65, however, typically face net tax rates much *higher* than the statutory OASI tax rate during those years, since their additional tax payments are accompanied by *reductions* in benefits. If an average-wage male worker delays retirement from 65 to 67, for example, his lost benefits and increased payroll taxes combine to impose an effective average OASI tax rate of 17.6 percent on those two extra years of work effort. A high-wage male worker retiring at age 67 faces a similar tax rate of 18.8 percent. The tax rate increases a bit further for those who choose to retire at age 70. When these tax rates are combined with other federal and state taxes and work expenses, the overall financial gain from choosing to work instead of retiring is reduced significantly. If we were to consider the marginal tax rates on the last dollars earned, the disincentives would often be greater.[30]

The results shown here only consider the impact on a worker's own benefit. If the worker's family also received spousal and survivors' benefits, the penalties for delayed retirement would generally increase. The fact that spousal benefits do not receive delayed retirement credits exacerbates this situation.[31] One qualification to these results is that those who have the option of working past age 62 may be healthier and have a longer life expectancy than average. This would slightly reduce the financial incentives for early retirement, since delayed retirement credits are worth more the greater the number of years those credits are received.

If the delayed retirement credit were immediately increased to 8 percent per year, there would be some improvement. This credit rate is sometimes stated to be actuarially neutral at this level. A net penalty remains, however, because additional taxes paid into the system continue to provide little or nothing in the way of additional benefits (see table 9.4). A second, more technical, problem is that if a delayed retirement credit is to make all retirement choices actuarially neutral, it would have to be applied at an increasing, rather than a flat, rate. Why? The value of the DRC depends on the number of years of remaining life expectancy. Because life expectancy and number of years of receipt of future credits decline so rapidly between ages 65 and 70, a perfectly fair actuarial adjustment would require a higher DRC rate for benefits forgone at, say, age 69 than at age 65.

When we move a decade or two into the next century, the net penalty for delaying retirement past the normal retirement age will be relatively smaller on an actuarial basis. The delayed retirement credit will be more valuable both because it rises to 8 percent and

Table 9.4 EFFECT OF ALTERNATIVE RETIREMENT DECISIONS IF THE DRC
WERE RAISED IMMEDIATELY TO 8 PERCENT PER YEAR
(WORKERS TURNING 65 IN 1995; AMOUNTS IN THOUSANDS OF CONSTANT
1993 DOLLARS)

Retirement decision	MALE WORKER			FEMALE WORKER		
	Low wage	Average wage	High wage	Low wage	Average wage	High wage
Retire at 67						
Change in benefits	+ 0.4	+ 0.2	+ 1.3	+ 0.6	+ 2.3	+ 8.0
Change in contributions	+ 2.0	+ 4.3	+ 10.5	+ 2.0	+ 4.5	+ 10.9
Net gain (+), or loss (-)	- 1.5	- 4.1	- 9.2	- 1.4	- 2.2	- 3.0
Net OASI tax rate on wages after age 65	8.3 %	10.1 %	9.3 %	7.6 %	5.2 %	2.9 %
Retire at 70						
Change in benefits	+ 1.2	- 0.5	- 2.2	+ 1.7	+ 4.4	+ 13.0
Change in contributions	- 4.6	+ 10.2	+ 24.7	+ 4.9	+ 10.8	+ 26.1
Net gain (+), or loss (-)	- 3.4	- 10.7	- 26.9	- 3.1	- 6.4	- 13.1
Net OASI tax rate on wages after age 65	7.8 %	11.2 %	11.6 %	6.9 %	6.4 %	5.3 %

Notes: Table reflects change in actuarial present value of OASI benefits and taxes
relative to retirement at age 65. All amounts are converted to present value at age
62, using 2 percent real interest rate. Includes impact on worker's benefits only.
Those who delay retirement are assumed to register to begin receiving OASI benefits
immediately at age 65. Includes both employer and employee portions of OASI
payroll tax. Projections are based on intermediate assumptions in 1993 OASDI Board
of Trustees report. Assumes OASI tax rate is set at 10.65 percent after 1992.

because people will have longer life expectancies. When the normal
retirement age rises to 67, moreover, the earnings test will continue
to be eliminated at age 70. As a result, those who work beyond the
normal retirement age stand to lose to the earnings test for a shorter
period of time. If the OASI payroll tax rate were to be increased,
however, net penalties for delayed retirement would rise.

How Do People Perceive these Rules and Incentives?

Because of the complexity of actuarial calculations and the various
rules involved, it is unlikely that many people have a good picture
of what the net financial incentives in OASI really are. There is very

good reason to believe, however, that the *perceived* penalties for delaying retirement are even greater than the penalties just described. One reason is that the reduction in benefits caused by the earnings test is immediately visible and relatively easier to understand. Offsets to the earnings test, such as the delayed retirement credit and reductions in the actuarial penalty for early retirement, are less widely known and more diffuse in their impact. Indeed, most newspaper stories attacking or praising the earnings test have enough trouble trying to explain its operation, and rarely even mention the offset provided by the DRC.

A second reason is that people approaching old age often underestimate their remaining life expectancies, perhaps because they compare themselves to parents with shorter life expectancies or because they are unaware that their life expectancy at retirement is to an age considerably beyond the life expectancy at birth. As a result, even if they understood the delayed retirement credit, they would not give it adequate weight. Finally, some younger-elderly may discount benefits in the distant future at a very high interest rate, since they might have a strong preference for extra liquidity, and may prefer to spend the money when they are younger and healthy than when they are older and sick. The DRC, therefore, is likely viewed as even less valuable relative to the benefits lost to the earnings test.

Data on the work patterns of the elderly provide one piece of evidence that the earnings test and other related rules cause confusion among the elderly. A large portion of OASI beneficiaries who work have wages below the earnings test threshold (Leonesio 1991:15). There is a particular clustering within a thousand dollars below the threshold. The number of people earning wages just above the threshold is extremely small by comparison. This occurs despite the fact that, excluding additional taxes, the benefit penalty for working beyond the threshold is extremely small. Between ages 62 and 65, the loss in current benefits would be almost completely offset by a smaller actuarial reduction in the long run. For those aged 65 to 70, the offset provided by the DRC is not complete, but is still large enough that the reduction in lifetime benefits for earning just above the threshold is modest. Some retirees apparently take the simple signals sent by the Social Security system—what is the appropriate age to retire, what is the maximum amount of earnings that will not result in a loss of benefits—and live according to them.

Do These Incentives Affect Behavior?

The previous section provides evidence that the economic behavior of at least some people is affected by OASI rules such as the earnings test. Of more certainty is that the existence of a Social Security system—or, more generally, growth in retirement assets and income—has over recent decades induced people to retire earlier than they otherwise would. Indeed, we have seen that labor force participation rates of older men have declined dramatically, at the same time that Social Security was covering a growing portion of the population and granting increasingly valuable benefits. The availability of private pensions, some of which pay retirement benefits even before age 62 (and which also may be designed around Social Security), also plays an important role.

In the presence of these fairly strong relationships between greater resources near old age and earlier retirement, what is the impact of particular retirement rules of Social Security, such as the earnings test, on the retirement decision? Most statistical studies on this question have examined behavioral responses to marginal changes in the earnings test or related rules, and have typically found only a small impact. In general, they have concluded that retirement decisions seem to be determined mainly by other factors, such as total income available in retirement.[32] The logic is not hard to understand. Most individuals today retire completely and do not even work up to the earnings threshold. Only a small percentage of the population (11.6 percent in 1991) work past age 65 at all, even though the earnings test exempts several thousand dollars' worth of wages. Given the failure to work of many near- and young-elderly even at income levels where no earnings test applies, it is usually concluded that the earnings test has only a minor impact on the choice to work. Recent reductions in the tax rate implicit in the earnings test also seem to have had little effect on the decision not to work.

One difficulty with this literature is that it cannot separate out the "social" effects of the signals sent by the system as a whole from marginal changes in behavior due to marginal changes in tax rates. That is, if people tend to react as a group to the signals they detect, then the issue centers as much upon the type of signal sent by an earnings test as upon the exact tax rates that are employed. If most of one's cohort of workers retire and take up new life styles, one may want to follow them regardless of minor differences in the effective tax rates one faces. On top of this, employers may respond by setting retirement ages and designing pension plans in ways that follow the signals set by both Social Security retirement ages and the apparent penalties in the earnings tests. Social signals, therefore, reinforce one another (see Straka 1992).

These socialization effects, of course, would occur in response to several signals, not just the earnings test. The maintenance of a Normal Retirement Age of 65, for instance, may be the main signal and the earnings test merely a principal reinforcement. Eliminating the earnings test by itself, therefore, might have only a modest effect on labor supply, especially in the initial years.

The fact that most people do not fully understand the subtleties of Social Security rules only reinforces the importance of signals. As noted, OASI beneficiaries who work tend to clump unnecessarily around the earnings test threshold. The clustering of earnings around the earnings limit, by the way, might also be a sign of underreporting of income or cheating—which is often easy to accomplish with self-employment earnings, where the taxpayer, rather than a separate employer, keeps the books of account. This, of course, does not speak well to the behavioral incentives of the earnings test, either.

Rationales for Earnings Test

The original design of the Social Security system included clear and powerful financial penalties for working during old age. Until 1951, for example, a person would lose all of his or her Social Security benefits in any month during which he or she earned $15 or more. Penalties of this sort were tolerated, in part, because there was a naive but strong belief among many that the economy could support only a limited number of workers. Earlier retirement of individuals, therefore, was viewed by some as a way of opening up more positions to the young.

William Graebner (1980) presents a well-documented case that this belief was a crucial source of early political support for the Social Security system. He offers evidence that in the 1930s key congressmen, at least a few members of the Council on Economic Security, and President Franklin Delano Roosevelt shared this view. Councilmember Barbara Armstrong, for example, noted in her memoirs that "the interest of Mr. Roosevelt was with the younger man. And to that extent, I went along." With regard to the strict earnings test that allowed only $15 per month of earned income, she contended that it was in response to the scarcity of jobs during the Depression: "That's why that little ridiculous amount of $15 was put in. . . . Let him earn some pin money, but it had to be on *retirement*. And retirement means that you've stopped working for pay" (quoted in Graebner 1980:186). Councilmember Murray Latimer's testimony before Congress "surveyed the disruptive impact of older workers, employed and seeking employment, on wage rates, efficiency, and work prospects of younger elements in the labor market. He was distressed at the legislation then being considered because the level of pensions provided, 'even if raised considerably above existing standards, would not be high enough to induce any considerable voluntary withdrawals from the labor market; nor would employers be able to retire superannuated employees without friction' " (quoted in Graebner 1980:188).

As we have noted, this represents poor economics. In any case, the rapidly aging population of the 21st century, with its dramatic drop in number of workers per retired person, implies the need for a different type of system than one centered around the Great Depression of the 1930s.

Although few today are willing to defend the earnings test on grounds that early retirement should be encouraged, a number of other rationales are frequently cited by its supporters. One argument made in favor of the earnings test is that Social Security should provide benefits to people because they are *retired*, not just because they are *old*. In our view, this is misleading. Social Security is a program intended to meet the needs that often accompany old age. Both old age and retirement at best are proxies for measuring those needs. Whereas a substantial number of people do cite poor health or disability as reasons for retirement, it is clear that many retirements are voluntary in nature.[33] In these cases, the difficulty with any "retirement test" is that it is totally under the control of the individual, regardless of need.

A political argument is also made that Social Security retirement benefits should only be paid to those who are retired so that the system does not "appear" to be providing benefits to high-income, working individuals. If actuarial adjustments were made properly, of course, this would merely be a fiction, as the returns to high-income individuals would be the same regardless of when actual benefits are paid. The fear, however, is not that the lifetime value of the pension would be too high, but that Congress would respond to benefits going to higher-income individuals by enacting welfarelike means tests. The political argument by itself, it seems to us, is an inadequate justification for the efficiency and equity costs of the current design. In many ways, moreover, this argument turns inward on itself. The earnings test, after all, has all the markings of a means test, although a perverse one based upon earnings rather than total income.

A final argument often used to defend the earnings test is that it enhances progressivity. Elimination of the earnings test is usually shown to increase net income mainly for those in middle- or upper-middle-income ranges. After all, the test doesn't even begin to apply until someone has earned enough to push himself or herself above the poverty level, and an older worker with that amount of earnings typically has other additional sources of income, including Social Security itself.

As applied to the earnings test, the progressivity argument is misconstrued. One could also deny businesses deductions for the cost of running a business or tax individuals three times on their dividend income; since business deductions and dividend income are more concentrated in upper-income groups, the net result would probably be progressive. But it wouldn't make sense because the normal rules for horizontal equity require that we treat equally all persons with equal ability or need and not distinguish on the basis of arbitrary criteria, such as whether their income came from work.[34] Progressivity is no excuse for treating equals unequally.

Not every program needs to be progressive in every provision for government itself to be progressive. There a variety of ways to achieve the same general level of progressivity while improving the system's fairness and efficiency. One could eliminate the earnings test and simultaneously change the benefit formula slightly. Or one could substitute higher-income taxes on all kinds of income for the tax on employment earnings in the current earnings test. Recent estimates suggest that repealing the earnings test would cost about $6 billion per year, with perhaps 10 percent of this cost being offset by higher payroll tax revenues.[35] In the longer run, some of the cost would also be offset by reduced delayed retirement credits and larger actuarial reductions for early retirement. Any remaining costs of eliminating the earnings test could be offset, for example, by increased taxation of benefits at higher-income levels.

Repealing the Earnings Test

The simple fact is that the earnings test is a tattered remnant of a bygone era. Partly because of its ambivalence toward the earnings test, Congress over time has continued to chip away at its application by increasing exempt amounts, lowering benefit reduction rates, and introducing the delayed retirement credit. The test now applies to only a minority of retirement years—albeit the first years, when the signal is most powerful and most likely to have an effect on labor supply decisions.

Eliminating the earnings test at all ages would probably be the simplest way to reduce many of the perverse incentives in the existing system. It would also greatly simplify the administration of the system, since the earnings test is the largest source of errors in benefit calculations. Many corrections of benefit amounts are required as earnings change over time, and taxpayers are extraordinarily confused about what is occurring. The delayed retirement credit would then become unnecessary in most cases, although it should still be made available to those who choose voluntarily to forgo benefits after the Normal Retirement Age.

As we move toward the 21st century, significant changes may need to occur in the work patterns of the near-elderly and the young-elderly. Society may not desire the ratio of workers to beneficiaries to decline so dramatically as now expected. Perhaps even the questionable tendency to define old age with the year 65—a "signal" that can be traced back well over a century—will itself be called increasingly into question. The rising proportion of jobs in service industries and increasing life spans are bound to affect choices. In the end, no one knows for sure how work behavior will change in the future, but it seems unrealistic to maintain an earnings test that announces somewhat loudly that most people should retire at age 65 or 62 and stay retired.

Removing the earnings test, by itself, would probably not have a large impact on behavior. In combination with other similar changes such as increases in the Normal and Early Retirement Ages, however, it could eventually have a significant impact on the work patterns and behavior of the near-elderly and young-elderly. Such reforms, moreover, could serve as an important first step in a transformation of social attitudes. Work, at least on a part-time basis, could once again become a norm for those in their sixties.

WINNERS AND LOSERS WHEN RESOURCES ARE SHIFTED

This chapter has shown how the fairness and efficiency of the Social Security system could be improved significantly by reforms in the rules applying to spouses, working couples, divorced persons, and retirees who work. Such rule changes would almost inevitably increase the returns to work for some of those within the system: first, for working spouses, and, second, for individuals with earnings after the age of 62. They are also likely to be quite popular. Any such reform, however, requires that someone else pay. Who might those persons be? Again, by relying on principles, a strong case can be made that among those who bear the burden should be the spouses of high-income workers, those who increase their net transfers from Social Security by retiring early, and those who have substantial nonwage retirement income but pay lower taxes than those whose income is from work.

Unfortunately, expenditure programs are not amended easily when "losers" become identified. In an earlier day, it was perhaps easier to resolve problems in Social Security by increasing benefits for those who were found to be disadvantaged, but not taking anything away from those who were unduly advantaged. There are, of course, two problems with this approach. First, it retains many inequities. Second, Social Security and the federal budget now face difficult financial constraints that make such an approach irresponsible.

Our view is that the bullet simply has to be bitten. Some of the political fallout from identifying losers more directly can be reduced by the ways in which these changes are phased in over time. The longer the delay, however, the longer will the existing inequities and inefficiencies remain.

Notes

1. Projections using the Urban Institute's DYNASIM microsimulation model (Zedlewski 1984; also cited in Center for Women Policy Studies 1988) predicted that in 2010, 74.9 percent of women aged 62 to 69 will have spent at least 20 years in employment covered by Social Security, whereas 43.2 percent will have worked at least 30 years in such employment. The corresponding figures for women aged 62 to 69 in 2030 are 82 percent and 58.9 percent, respectively.

2. SSA (1992).

3. These small marginal returns for two-earner couples result from the fact that the actuarial value of spousal and survivor's benefits are very large for a one-earner couple where the wife never works. In our two-earner-couple examples, the wife generally collects benefits in her own right while her husband is alive, and then receives survivors' benefits based on her husband's record when she becomes widowed. As noted in chapter 5, we take into account the "switching strategy" often utilized by wage-earning women who are widowed before the Normal Retirement Age. Such women can receive benefits on their own record beginning as early as age 62 (subject, of course, to the earnings test and early retirement penalty), and then switch to their husband's survivors' benefits at the Normal Retirement Age without facing any actuarial reduction on these latter benefits. Even taking these factors into account, the total actuarial value of benefits for our two-earner couples is only slightly larger than what they would have received if the wife never worked.

4. The actuarial value of expected lifetime contributions increases by more than 100 percent when the wife earns wages identical to the husband's, since she is more likely to survive throughout her career.

5. Workers are assumed to remain in the labor force in all years between age 21 and the Normal Retirement Age. Total family earnings are assumed to be equal to the maximum wage subject to OASI tax in all of these years.

6. The one-earner couple is normally better off because of the additional time that can be devoted to nonmarket work. In theory, this implies that the couple has greater ability to pay net taxes, or taxes in excess of benefits, to Social Security.

7. For a discussion of credit and pension-splitting in Canada and Germany, see Brocas, Cailloux, and Oget (1990:94), Reinhard (1988), or SSA (1992). In the United States this could require splitting of the spouse's benefit as well.

8. In practice, spouses of only 10 years will usually generate substantial benefits in their own right or will be entitled to benefits from other spouses, so that this rarely occurs.

9. A good case can be made to base measurement of need on individual status, rather than marital status. The elderly may live together without being married and still benefit from economies of scale in meeting needs. For instance, many elderly today live in group homes and share facilities. The point of the text, however, is that decisions regarding who are "equals" affect the design of the program.

10. Consideration would need to be given to how this provision would be administered. Some, but not all, of those engaged in child care can be identified through individual income tax forms and Earned Income Tax Credits. Since historical data might be hard to verify, this type of change would probably need to be phased in over time.

11. Admittedly, a similar argument could be made against the ways in which minimum benefits were offered, but the group would be more restricted, and the rationale for moving away from individual equity would clearly be need.

12. For example, in the case of one wife married for 30 years, the worker plus spousal benefit would be split 50-50. In the case of multiple wives, the worker plus spousal benefit would need to be split according to number of years of marriage to each. Absent a current reporting system on marital status each year, applications would need to be made to the Social Security Administration and adjudicated. Presumably, once established, the appropriate time to register for future benefits would be at time of divorce. A minimum benefit provision could prevent any individual from falling below basic sustenance levels.

13. The Social Security Administration has argued that it would take several years for it to develop an automated system to implement an earnings-sharing system (SSA, Office of Legislative and Regulatory Policy 1985).

14. U.S. Bureau of the Census (1992b).

15. See, for example, Ruggles (1990).

16. Timothy Smeeding of Syracuse University is one who has made this type of suggestion.

17. A totally flat benefit may be more than is required to deal with specific problems related to the death of a spouse. Hence, it is suggested as an option.

18. Private life insurance offers another means of protection, particularly for middle- and upper-income families. See Auerbach and Kotlikoff (1987) for a discussion of life insurance protection among the elderly.

19. We provide a brief sketch of these rules in the text following. For more detailed descriptions, see Myers (1993b), SSA Office of the Actuary (1990), or U.S. Congress, House Committee on Ways and Means (1992).

20. If benefits before age 65 are reduced owing to the earnings test, the impact of the actuarial reduction will be lessened. For example, if someone begins collecting benefits at 64, but loses half of his or her benefits to the earnings test in that year, he or she

will only be subject to 6 months' worth of actuarial reduction in permanent benefit level.

21. The actuarial reduction for a worker's early retirement does not apply to survivors' benefits in the event that the worker dies before the Normal Retirement Age.

22. Spousal benefits (which start off at 50 percent of PIA) are reduced by 25/36 percent per month of retirement before age 65; if, for example, a spouse retires 36 months early at age 62, his or her spousal benefit will be reduced to 75 percent of one-half of PIA, or 37.5 percent of PIA. In the event an insured worker dies before retirement, a surviving spouse (without any eligible dependent children) may receive early retirement benefits at age 60 or above. These are reduced by only 19/40 of a percent per month of retirement before 65.

23. The exempt amounts are indexed each year to keep pace with wages.

24. A spouse aged 70 or over may have his or her spousal benefit reduced owing to the earnings test if the primary worker is younger than 70.

25. Those who only lose part of their benefits owing to the earnings test after the Normal Retirement Age are eligible for a partial delayed retirement credit. For example, if someone registered for benefits at age 65, but then lost half of his or her benefits to the earnings test during the subsequent year, he or she would be granted six months' worth of delayed retirement credit.

26. Note that the size of the delayed retirement credit depends on the year someone was born, rather than the year in which earnings occur (January 1 births are treated as having been born in the preceding year).

27. The needs of the elderly will be greater when they retire early, since they have fewer private resources available for emergencies, and because their benefit levels will be lower at older ages. By not working, they also contribute less in taxes to support other costs of society, such as those related to defense or poor children.

28. Income taxation of benefits is treated here as a net benefit reduction. Changes enacted by Congress in 1993 are reflected here. We assume the workers have no nonwage income while they are still working.

29. Another study on this question that comes to similar conclusions is that of Gustman and Steinmeier (1989).

30. The marginal tax rate on the extra work effort of people who had already decided to delay retirement varies greatly by income level. Those earning above the maximum wage subject to OASI taxation would typically face a marginal OASI tax rate of zero; they face no payroll taxes on their next dollar of income, and their benefits have usually already been eliminated by the earnings test. People with average wages, on the other hand, would typically face very high marginal rates, since they fall in the 33 percent earnings test range and receive little marginal return on their last dollars of payroll tax contribution.

31. Benefits lost due to the retirement test are prorated between the worker's and spouse's benefits in proportion to the amounts of the two benefits, but the compensatory delayed retirement credit is only applied to the worker's benefit. Consider a worker who has no auxiliary beneficiary, a base benefit level of $8,000, and earnings of $27,000 above the threshold level. He loses his full benefit of $8,000 to the earnings test, but gets compensated in the future with a full year's delayed retirement credit of 4.5 percent, worth $360 per year. If the same worker has a spouse over 65 entitled on his record, then his benefit is reduced by $6,000 and hers is reduced by $3,000. He receives only 9 months of delayed retirement credit (3.375 percent for the year), increasing his future benefit by only $270 per year; her spousal benefit receives no DRC at all. Thus, by working an extra year past the normal retirement age, the household with spousal benefits loses an additional $1,000 to the retirement test above and beyond what a single worker would lose. In addition, the couple receives $90 per

year less in delayed retirement credit in the future, although they are likely to receive it for a longer time.

32. For a good summary of the statistical evidence on the effects of specific Social Security rules on retirement behavior, see Leonesio (1990 and 1991). A large number of articles have been published on the subject, including (among others): Aaron (1982), Bernheim (1988), Blinder, Gordon, and Wise (1980), Burkhauser (1980), Burtless (1986), Burtless and Moffitt (1984, 1985), Crawford and Lilien (1981), Diamond and Hausman (1984), Gordon and Blinder (1980), Hanoch and Honig (1983), Kahn (1988), Packard (1990a and b), Pellechio (1978), Quinn (1977, 1978), Sherman (1985), Straka (1992), and Vroman (1985).

33. Leonesio (1991) has offered a recent survey of economic literature on the role of Social Security in retirement decisions. He noted that "in general, the findings support the view that earlier retirements have been largely voluntary, as workers have been increasingly able to afford to retire" (p. 6).

34. In these cases, individuals should be taxed on their net income, regardless of source and regardless of what types of expenses were necessary to generate that net income.

35. U.S. Congress, House Committee on Ways and Means (1992:21).

Chapter Ten

MEDICARE REFORM: SOME APPLICATIONS OF BASIC PRINCIPLES

The future fiscal imbalance in Social Security—and, more generally, in the overall federal budget—derives even more from growth in health expenditures than from the cost of Social Security cash benefits. In the year 2030, for instance, the gap between Old-Age, Survivors, and Disability Insurance (OASDI) benefits paid and taxes collected is estimated to be about 3.1 percent of taxable payroll. The gap for the Hospital Insurance Trust Fund (Part A of Medicare) alone is expected to be nearly twice that, according to the 1993 intermediate projections of the Health Care Financing Administration. Even if those assumptions are unduly pessimistic—certainly both the government and the private sector inevitably must react to these cost pressures—the future deficit is likely to remain large for two important reasons. First, as the economy has grown, people have demanded that a greater portion of their goods and services be provided in the form of health care. This relationship between income and rising demand for health services could easily continue into the future. Second, the aging of the population creates the same demographic pressures on health insurance as it does on Old-Age and Survivors Insurance (OASI). Even significant cost control will not eliminate these two sources of tension.

Fundamental health reform for the nation as a whole, not just the elderly, is an extraordinarily important and complicated challenge. This study does not attempt to address this broader issue of health insurance reform—an issue that would require at least one more book, if not several. Most suggested health insurance reforms, including those of the Clinton administration, stretch far beyond Social Security. They include proposals such as pushing individuals into health purchasing cooperatives or managed care arrangements, subsidizing lower-income individuals by setting a limit on the percentage of income that they or their employers spend on health insurance, enacting tort reform, creating new risk pools, providing long-term care, and expanding Medicare to everyone. Some would also try to apply cost controls simultaneously on both the private and public health systems, with the broader controls eventually displacing many of the rules now applying to Medicare alone.

Although such broad-ranging issues are beyond the scope of this book, the principles laid out in Part One of this volume do suggest some minimum requirements in Medicare that need to be met over the long term *independently of whether or not health care is comprehensively reformed on a national basis.* Our focus is not on such issues as what health benefits should be covered, but mainly on how health policy for the elderly must be related to broader budget and Social Security policy. Most especially, we are concerned with the budget impact of built-in, rather than legislated, growth in Medicare expenditures. The automatic nature of this growth prevents or at least deters decisions based upon an assessment of where expenditures are most needed. In addition, we consider two issues in Medicare that have a direct parallel in OASI: the age of eligibility for benefits and the use of an earnings test to deter work among the elderly and near-elderly. In our view, all the issues to be discussed here are raised inadequately in most national health reform debates.

We should also note our skepticism toward depending upon any one reform effort, no matter how well designed. The health care market occupies one-seventh of the U.S. economy, is evolving at an extraordinary pace, and will look very different within even a decade or two. The U.S. government's role in medical care is already larger, as a percentage of gross national product, than that of many countries with national health care systems (Steuerle 1993). A large share of government budgets in the U.S. is devoted to Medicare, Medicaid, and other health programs—indeed, adding in tax subsidies, more than is devoted to defense—and that share would likely increase under either current law or most national health reform scenarios. With responsibility for such a substantial portion of a dynamic market, policymakers will be required continually to search for better and more efficient regulatory and expenditure systems. Moderate and necessary reforms of Medicare, such as we suggest here, therefore, should not be held hostage to "waiting for Godot"—the pure reform coming along down the road.

OPEN-ENDED MEDICARE EXPENDITURES

As a matter of budget policy, any open-ended expenditure is poorly designed. An open-ended expenditure, as defined here, is one in which the private sector largely determines the amount to be spent by the government. Analysts often apply the term *open-ended* to financial guarantees and subsidies, where beneficiaries of government assistance largely determine the amount and size of taxpayer subsidies. For example, private individuals rather than the government might determine the amount of financial guarantee by the amount of loans they make. In the case of Medicare, the open-ended nature of the system derives from the absence of effective limits either on total payments that will be made or on what demands will be met. Even the definition of what qualifies as health is an expansive one over time, as new products and procedures come to qualify for government payment. Note that an open-ended program may still be highly regulated—the government may limit the size of each guaranteed loan or the maximum price of a particular medical service— but where these limits are inadequate to set a cap on total costs, the program remains open-ended. In this regard, by the way, Social Security *cash* benefits are not open-ended. Some may believe that they are growing too fast, but the determination of how much is to be spent is known and determined by a fixed formula.[1]

Why do open-ended programs almost inevitably violate the principles laid out early in this book? As real expenditures on the open-ended program increase, they inevitably must crowd out something else—often other public expenditures, sometimes private expenditures. Since the increase in open-ended public expenditures is determined outside the budget—Congress establishes no formal budgetary limit—the most important needs of society are very unlikely to be met with the additional expenditures. Thus, even if Medicare is progressive in an overall sense, its open-ended features may fail to meet the strict principle of progressivity, which requires greatest attention to the *greatest* needs.

In much the same manner, additional Medicare expenditures are unlikely to be allocated efficiently so long as they are made without allowing individuals to choose alternative opportunities in the market or policymakers to choose different uses of funds. As one example, the open-ended nature of the Medicare subsidy creates an incentive for providers to adopt cost-increasing procedures and technology, rather than those that might be cost-saving (and thus reduce government subsidies).[2]

In Medicare, there is also no relationship between previous tax contributions and the size of the expenditure, much less its growth in value. Notions of individual equity, therefore, are ignored. Even horizontal equity can be violated more easily in an open-ended system, since individual demand or the entrepreneurship of providers, rather than individual need or ability, sometimes determines who gets the most benefits.

There are those who would claim that abolishing the open-ended nature of the system cannot be attempted without some major reform of the entire medical marketplace. For instance, some believe that cost controls in Medicare cannot be made effective absent cost controls for health care in general. They argue that attempts to control Medicare prices have sometimes resulted in cost-shifting, as providers compensated by charging those with private insurance more. Another worry is that if non-Medicare recipients have access, say, to surgeons whose incomes are $300,000 to $400,000 a year, then Medicare cannot provide equal access if it pays surgeons at a rate equivalent to $200,000 a year. Perhaps some surgeons won't be willing to serve the elderly at the lower rate. Similarly, it may be argued that if knee operations become common for non-Medicare recipients, then they should become common for Medicare recipients. These are certainly legitimate concerns that may or may not be addressed in broader health care reform. Regardless of what happens with national health reform, however, societal needs still ought to be weighed against each other in a budget process that is not inherently biased toward open-ended programs. Why should Medicare spending be expanded in an automatic fashion that does not force the hard choices to be made among society's needs? On what basis are these increased expenditures deemed automatically superior to helping flood victims, deterring nuclear threats, or meeting the needs—including health needs—of children?

To "close off" Medicare's open-ended features inevitably creates some losers; therein lies the difficulty. If spending were no longer to rise automatically to meet new costs, then either the price or quantity of health care consumed would have to be reduced from the levels they would otherwise attain. To be blunt, someone is going to get fewer health benefits or fewer dollars are going to be paid out to providers of medical goods and services.

To control the health budget also requires tough choices among administrative devices that are not without their own sets of worries. One alternative might be to provide equal-size credits or vouchers for the purchase of health insurance to everyone, along with market reforms guaranteeing that insurance policies were available to all elderly persons, regardless of medical condition. Since Congress would set the amount of the credit each year, the current system's open-ended features would be eliminated. Another option, closer to current law, would simply require that, notwithstanding other attempts to set prices and quantities of care, Medicare would adjust prices downward on a regular monthly basis to stay within a fixed budget constraint.

Unfortunately, either of these ways of exerting budget control would involve new, different, and difficult types of problems. For example, a credit-based approach might increase search costs for picking an insurance company; constraining prices to a budget might make it more difficult for hospitals and doctors to project how much they would be compensated for care given. Of course, this simply returns us to one of the dilemmas of government: it must regulate the use of its own subsidies.[3] To subsidize, but not limit the size and use of the subsidy, inevitably results in an open-ended system that is unsustainable.

Policymakers do attempt to apply some cost controls to Medicare; the job has simply been inadequate because the system has been left open-ended—squeezing one part of the balloon has sometimes merely shifted air to another part. In a budget agreement made in 1990, for instance, Congress enacted changes that were supposed to save $43 billion over the succeeding five years. By 1993, however, actual and projected Medicare expenditures during this period were almost exactly the same as predicted before the budget agreement.[4]

In sum, the problem of Medicare costs cannot be dodged on the grounds that there are no national cost controls on the entire health market. Whether or not broader controls are adopted in some national health reform effort, such as that proposed by President Clinton in September, 1993, the bottom line is the same. Budgets eventually cannot withstand the onslaught of open-ended expenditure programs. The open-ended nature of Medicare must be eliminated in almost any system—the one of today, tomorrow's "reformed" system, and the system that is likely to be newly "reformed" two or three decades from now.

COMBINING HEALTH CARE SYSTEMS FOR THE ELDERLY

A great source of confusion for the elderly, for children of the elderly put in charge of their parents' affairs, and for the public in general is the multiplicity of governmental health care programs for the elderly. As described earlier, Medicare has two parts, with different sources of financing and different calculations of financial solvency and balance. Hospital Insurance (HI) is covered out of payroll taxes, and Supplemental Medical Insurance (SMI) out of general revenues and premiums paid by the elderly. Medicaid, although not part of Social Security per se, increasingly pays for a large share of nursing home care for the elderly. Its costs are borne not only out of federal general revenues but also state taxes.

The current division of responsibilities makes little sense from a budgetary standpoint. When HI cost controls are put into place, the effect on SMI expenditures for out-patient care needs to be taken into account. When SMI provides in-home assistance for individuals, it has an impact on Medicaid. When the federal government relies on Medicaid to cover costs, the taxpayer is no better off simply because, unlike Medicare, some costs have been shifted to the states. Nor is the taxpayer better off when states figure out ways to shift Medicaid costs back to Medicare.

This does not mean that health care for the elderly should or should not be divided operationally into parts, based upon administrative efficiency and similar considerations. It does mean that as a budget matter, choices of expenditures among HI, SMI, and Medicaid—or any set of medical programs for the elderly under our new national health plan—should be made simultaneously. In effect, they should be treated together under a single budget line item. Under current law, with all three having certain open-ended features, the allocation of benefits, as well as taxes to support those costs, is sometimes determined separately and arbitrarily.

One of the reasons for the initial separation was the political desire to imply that Medicare was an earned right paid for out of payroll taxes. Medicare, Part B, was put into a separate pot partly because it relied upon general revenue financing, while Medicaid was separated still further because means testing went against the notion that Social Security was an earned right. The difficulty, of course, is that none of these programs establishes a relationship between taxes paid and benefits in the first place. For the future, some policymakers clearly want to charge a higher, income-related, premium for Medicare, Part B. Indeed, Congress enacted, then rescinded, an income-related premium under Catastrophic Care for the Elderly in 1988 and 1989.

We are not arguing that all health benefits should be means tested. There are legitimate reasons, such as the ability of the elderly to give away assets, that argue for providing some benefits that are not means-tested, although in 1993 even the Clinton Administration has proposed higher charges for the very high-income elderly in conjunction with other health reforms. But the issue again needs to be considered more comprehensively—on traditional grounds of progressivity, individual equity, efficiency (including administrative ease), and horizontal equity—and not by some arbitrary division that separates decision-making among programs and budget categories. Ditto for sources of financing. Whatever the allocation of funds between payroll taxes and federal general revenues, for instance, the choice should be made explicit and not on the basis of automatic growth rates in the different programs. Ditto again for deciding just what programs are most worthy of increased support. Of course, this last issue cannot be solved without also addressing the open-ended features of all three programs.

CASH VERSUS IN-KIND BENEFITS

Partly because of the open-ended nature of Medicare, programs for the aged have become increasingly health-dominated. Until the mid-1960s, all Social Security payments were in the form of cash. Even after the adoption of Medicare, cash payments were dominant; they comprised about 82 percent of total Social Security expenditures as late as 1970. Today, however, cash payments have fallen to about 68 percent of total Social Security expenditures, and they are expected to fall to about half of total expenditures by 2010.[5]

The shift from cash to in-kind benefits dramatically changes the character of Social Security and potentially threatens to distance it from its original purposes. Initially thought of as a means of providing the elderly with annuities that would give them freedom to choose how to live their last years with dignity, Social Security is being converted to a system in which a much greater portion of the benefits received are not under the control of recipients. With in-kind benefits, the government increasingly is directing what the elderly spend, how they spend it, at what price the spending can occur, and how producers must supply the goods and services they receive.

Before proceeding further we should emphasize that the cash/in-kind debate is itself enormously complex and also deserving of book-length treatment. Among the issues we do not cover here are the implications of a number of distortions in the U.S. health care market, limitations on information available to health care consumers, and the difficulties of ensuring that health care protection is obtainable by high-risk individuals.

Our intent is not to argue against a health care program for the elderly or for the population as a whole. Our purpose is to call into question the potential losses in well-being among the elderly due to the *continuing* trend within the total Social Security package away from cash to medical benefits, to urge that further tradeoffs between the two be made explicit, and to lay out dimensions that should guide those tradeoffs.

Inefficiency of In-Kind Benefits

Economic theory suggests that in-kind programs generally are less efficient than cash payments. Why? The former restrict choice of consumers and regulate producers; the latter do not. In-kind subsidies often force people to change their consumption patterns from what they would otherwise be, resulting in a lower level of consumer satisfaction than if the subsidies had been provided in cash. To understand this point, one must put aside for the moment the question of the income redistribution, which is a separate issue. Suppose in the simplest case that a government program provides the same level of total benefits to each person, no matter how divided between cash and health benefits. Would recipients in that world be better off with cash or with a required pattern of insurance consumption determined by the government?

In the case of public housing, another in-kind program, economic studies of the consumption patterns of low-income persons have suggested that they would typically prefer 80 cents in cash to $1 of public housing benefits (Smeeding 1982:65). Although valuing health benefits is more difficult, Timothy Smeeding has estimated that in 1979 recipients of Medicare and Medicaid would only have been willing to spend on average about half as much on their own health insurance as the government actually spent (Smeeding 1984:165).[6]

Results of consumer-expenditure studies on the value of in-kind benefits, of course, should be interpreted with caution. The estimates are, of necessity, based on a number of ad hoc assumptions. Figuring out how much the elderly would choose to spend on health care in the absence of Medicare is particularly difficult because almost all elderly are already covered by Medicare. One must also remember that the elderly would often have to pay as much or more than Medicare pays to receive the same level of insurance protection in an unreformed private market.[7] Economist Henry Aaron, moreover, argues that a consumer's preferences regarding health insurance protection will change greatly once he or she becomes seriously ill; therefore, a consumer's welfare may be improved over the long run by receiving more insurance protection than he or she would purchase independently.[8] While these caveats are not without merit, even they require further examination. For instance, some administrative saving in Medicare is due to limits on the number of plans that can be offered and the acceptance of all persons without testing as to prior conditions. Although these savings might not be available in an unregulated private market, they might be achievable in a regulated system other than Medicare as currently designed. Aaron's point is difficult to prove or disprove, but it does not tell us where limits should be set on in-kind benefits. Regardless of the benefits of Medicare as a whole, and we grant that they are many, the program cannot help but bear the inevitable costs of interfering in consumer and producer markets. Relative to cash benefits, in-kind benefits do restrict certain freedoms and choices. Such costs should be minimized.

Health Cost Inflation

Relying heavily on in-kind benefits may also contribute to the current tremendous cost inflation in health care. With in-kind benefits, the individual becomes less involved in trying to help restrict the cost of what is being provided—and, therefore, starts paying a higher price for the same benefits. A related reason for the relative inefficiency of in-kind benefits is that an unnecessarily high portion of the payments often accrues to the providers of services—in the case of Medicare, to doctors and other health providers—rather than to the recipients. Thus, as the government puts more money into in-kind health benefits rather than cash benefits, health providers raise fees or maintain them at a higher level than they might otherwise.[9] This problem, of course, is not confined to Medicare in the United States. Employer health insurance, which is also provided in-kind and in ways that remove individuals from cost considerations, suffers from similar high cost inflation.

Comparisons with other countries suggest that there is some room for reducing the prices we pay for Medicare, as well as for private health care. A recent study, for instance, found that Medicare pays around two-thirds more for particular health treatments than those same treatments would cost in Canada, although Canada operates with greater health price constraints in general (Welch, Katz, and Zuckerman 1993).[10] This, of course, is not to say that getting American health care costs under control will be easy, only that improvement is possible.

Cost Awareness

Increasing the degree to which elderly persons are directly involved in the purchase of their health insurance is one means of trying to restrain costs, as well as improving choices in the budgetary process. If costs were made more explicit, the elderly would be more likely to put pressure on insurance costs, which in turn would place pressure on the prices charged by health providers. If medical costs rise by $100 per person, for instance, it might be better to give the elderly $100 additional cash income to buy supplementary insurance than simply to increase continually the amount of government insurance provided. Limits may still need to be placed on this insurance; for instance, it may need to be priced or "rated" so that individuals cannot be charged different amounts solely on the basis of existing medical conditions.

Even if benefits change neither in character nor amount, it would still be worthwhile to let the elderly know the prices that are being paid for their health insurance. Suppose, for instance, that one Social Security system gave each elderly person $10,000 in cash and $5,000 in health insurance benefits. A better system would be one that gave each person $15,000 in cash and required payment of $5,000 for the health insurance that was provided, perhaps under identical rules.[11] Even though the two systems are essentially the same except for the method of accounting, at least the elderly (as well as policymakers) would be forced to confront explicitly the trade-offs that were being made in Social Security.

Under current procedures, the portion of Medicare costs seen— and, in all likelihood, understood—by elderly recipients has been steadily declining. Despite having risen in real value over time, Supplementary Medical Insurance premiums have declined from 50 percent of program costs at the inception of the program to around 25 percent today. This misleads the public as to the true cost of that insurance. It not only prevents the elderly from seeing how much of a subsidy they are receiving, but it also protects government policymakers when they fail to come up with ways of controlling those health expenditures. A better system would again provide the elderly sufficient cash to pay for the other 75 percent of the insurance's true cost, and then charge mandatory premiums equal to 100 percent of cost.[12] This would also force Congress to make trade-offs between cash and health benefits more explicitly. When the government did save on medical costs, it could share some of that gain with the elderly by allowing higher net cash benefits to be paid out.

Deductible amounts in the SMI portion of Medicare—the amounts that a beneficiary must pay for care outside of hospitals before insurance helps out—have also failed to keep pace with the cost of benefits. In 1995, the deductible of $100 will represent about 4.4 percent of the average SMI insurance benefit per enrollee. In 1970, by contrast, the $50 deductible was equal to about 44.3 percent of the average outlay per SMI beneficiary. Only Hospital Insurance deductibles have kept pace with costs. The HI deductible for the first 60 days of hospital stay is estimated at $776 in 1995. This represents about 27.0 percent of the average HI outlay per enrollee, an increase from 20.1 percent in 1970.[13] A strong case can be made for increasing deductibles, particularly in SMI, and keeping them tied to the growth in Medicare insurance costs. This would clearly introduce more cost-awareness into the system. It would also free up resources that could be better used to meet other needs, such as the large health costs that are borne by the older-elderly and by those with heavy out-of-pocket expenses due to catastrophic illness or chronic needs. To offset any negative impacts on the needy portion of the elderly population, compensating changes could again be made in Social Security benefit or tax formulas.

In health care, a few hundred dollars in payments is often treated as beyond the capability of the ordinary individual. Such costs, however, must be compared to the *average* annual amount of all health expenditures per household in the United States—over $8,000 in 1992.[14] Most households have little or no idea of the health cost burdens that they bear, because almost three-quarters of costs are paid indirectly through the lower wages that finance work-related insurance or through the higher taxes that support government programs. Both rich and poor elderly households today bear a smaller-than-average share of the burden since they are less likely than nonelderly households to pay in the form of either taxes or lower cash wages.[15] Since many elderly households are at least as well-off as the average nonelderly household, it is misleading to imply that annual expenses over a few hundred dollars are catastrophic for the elderly, but that younger people in similar or weaker financial circumstances can afford to pay many times as much.

Future Choices between Cash and In-kind Benefits

Congress will inevitably have to make tough choices between cash and in-kind benefits in the future. It must come to grips more directly with how these choices are going to affect the fundamental character of Social Security and the way that society treats the elderly. In no small part because of growth in health care costs, spending on the elderly constitutes a very large and growing share of total government expenditures. These pressures, in turn, have now made it almost impossible to exclude the elderly from deficit reduction efforts or other efforts to change priorities in the budget.[16] In 1993, as only one example, the elderly ended up paying a significant share of the deficit reduction effort—both through further attempts at cost controls in Medicare and through taxation of Social Security benefits.

Technically, there has been no Social Security enactment in which cash benefits were lowered in an *explicit* exchange for rising health costs, although there are many proposals to cut cash benefits in response to intensifying budgetary pressures. A common proposal mentioned earlier is to limit cost-of-living adjustments in many tax and expenditure programs, including Social Security. Rising health costs can lower cash benefits indirectly, as well. As both HI taxes and health insurance premiums for workers rise, for instance, the OASDI tax base is reduced—which, in turn, cuts back the finances available to support benefit levels.

Congress needs to consider explicitly the effect of these choices on the distribution of income. Health benefits tend to be distributed in fairly equal amounts among the elderly, whereas cash benefits in Social Security are larger for those with higher incomes. When resources are constrained, cash benefits at first may be a more appealing target for cutbacks, since growth in cash benefits can easily be reduced in a way that does not harm the needy portion of the elderly population. This does not mean, however, that restraining growth in cash benefits must necessarily be more progressive than restraining growth in Medicare. The same degree of progressivity could be achieved either way through the use of compensating adjustments in taxes or benefit formulas. If Medicare premiums or deductibles are to be increased, moreover, they could be adjusted according to one's income level in a progressive fashion. Finally, in a dynamic sense some of Medicare growth shows up in the incomes of providers, not in greater health care for the elderly.

MEDICARE ELIGIBILITY AGE

Choosing between cash and in-kind benefits requires coordination between what is done in OASDI and what is done in Medicare.

Chapter 7 discussed how increases in the retirement age would be preferable to many other benefit reductions when trying to bring Social Security back into financial balance. Old-Age and Survivors Insurance is already scheduled for a modest reduction through an increase in the normal retirement age from 65 to 67—although many people are likely to respond by accepting actuarially reduced benefits rather than delaying retirement. Such an increase in the Normal Retirement Age, however, has not yet been enacted for Medicare. Increasing the age of eligibility for Medicare at the same time as the Normal Retirement Age is raised would be one means of financing other changes in Social Security or of improving the financial health of the Medicare program. At the very least, those who want Medicare coverage, but are between 65 and the Normal Retirement Age, could be required to pay a larger share of the costs of their insurance.

Based on our analysis of well-being among the near-elderly, younger-elderly, and older-elderly, it is clear that resources and capacity to work are by far the greatest among the near- and younger-elderly. Most of those in their mid-sixties are as capable of buying health insurance as those who are several years younger and ineligible for Medicare. Those health reform proposals that would subsidize heavily the health insurance costs of very early retirees younger than 65 or 62 would, of course, move in the opposite direction. Even if a national health insurance system of some sort were adopted, many of those in their sixties, much less their fifties, could afford some of the associated fees, premiums, taxes, or other charges as well as the nonelderly. At the same time, the higher cost of health insurance for the older-elderly may still place limits on what is a reasonable share of costs.

Within Medicare itself, trade-offs can also be made that would move health expenditures more toward those with the most pressing unmet needs—catastrophic expenses that are truly catastrophic, assistance with chronic impairment or incapacitation, and so forth. Given a choice of where to spend health dollars, it is difficult to make a case that increases in expenditures should be concentrated automatically on those who, relative to expected lifespans, are younger and younger each year.

HEALTH EARNINGS TEST

Most citizens know that OASI benefits may be subject to an earnings test that reduces gains from work, although some offset is provided through the delayed retirement credit. Less well understood is that in recent years Congress has enacted an earnings test for health benefits that already may have become more onerous than the better-known test applied to cash benefits. This health earnings test acts as a significant barrier to the employment of the elderly in certain firms.

Here is how the test works: Medicare now has rules requiring that it be made a "secondary payor" relative to health insurance provided by employers of 20 or more workers. If an employer provides health insurance to employees and their spouses in general, it must also cover any elderly employee and spouse. The Medicare system will pay for health services only to the extent they are not already covered under the employer plan. The employee, but not the employer, can opt out of the employer coverage. Since older persons have higher health expenses, of course, the mandate requires that the amount spent on the health benefits of elderly workers be greater than the amount spent on other workers.

To see how this health earnings test operates, suppose that an elderly couple is eligible to receive $6,000 worth of Medicare, if retired. The husband, however, works full-time for $15,000 in cash wages and a health insurance policy that also costs $6,000. In effect, the $21,000 in total compensation earned by the individual is offset immediately by a loss of up to $6,000 in Medicare benefits.

Economic theory holds that workers will be paid compensation commensurate to the value of the product they make for their employers.[17] The elderly individual in our example produces $21,000 of goods and services for the economy and earns $21,000 in total compensation, yet receives cash wages of only $15,000. Since he already had Medicare, the additional $6,000 paid out to buy a duplicate insurance policy operates like an additional earnings test or tax. The employer might have been willing to hire him for a higher cash wage if Medicare had remained the primary payor.

The test probably operates in more indirect ways, such as encouraging retirement in firms with generous health plans. Take a worker who produces a marginal product of $20,000. The firm would eventually note that paying a cash wage of $15,000 and paying health insurance that costs $6,000 makes it unprofitable to retain this worker. It is likely to encourage the worker to retire. (If the business doesn't retire these people directly, of course, it may go bankrupt and retire them anyway.) Note also that some firms would be extremely reluctant to advertise to individuals over age 65 for fear that too many may come in the door and raise the cost of doing business.

A productive worker over age 65, in turn, may simply figure that taking a job is not worthwhile. Again, take a worker who would be glad to take a job for $20,000, but finds that no one with health insurance will pay more than $14,000. This disincentive comes on top of the disincentives to work created by the OASI system (discussed in chapter 9). In the end, the net gains from work may be quite small. We do not want to imply that eliminating the health earnings test would greatly expand labor supply, any more than eliminating the OASI earnings test would do so.[18] When a variety of institutional factors, including multiple government policies, both economically and symbolically encourage retirement a couple of decades before expected death, changing any one of those factors may have only minimal impact on work effort. Nonetheless, a strong case can be made for addressing these institutional biases even if only one at a time.

We have shown already how equity and efficiency considerations make it difficult to justify the normal earnings test that reduces the value of the cash benefits provided through Old-Age and Survivors Insurance. Similar considerations argue against the health earnings test. With the rise in the cost of health insurance and the implementation of the delayed retirement credit, the health earnings test in many cases has become the more powerful of the two work disincentives. The arguments against both, however, are similar: eligibility for old-age cash or health assistance should not be based upon employment status.

So long as the health earnings test exists, people with equal earnings are not taxed equally nor given equal Social Security benefits. The health earnings test also encourages inefficient labor market reorganization. That is, one way to get around this test is for the person over age 65 to work for an employer who provides no health insurance at all. Senior citizens, therefore, may migrate to one type of employer, while other workers needing insurance migrate to another type. If the senior citizen is able to find a job paying only cash wages, then some of the work disincentives of the health earnings test are mitigated, but only by causing this inefficient market segmentation. For many workers, young and old, this segmentation may simply increase the search costs of finding a job that makes best use of their skills. Once retired from a job paying health benefits, for instance, it may be difficult for a person to find a firm that requires the same types of skills.

Note, by the way, that the adoption of a national health insurance scheme that required all employers to provide health insurance to elderly workers could strengthen greatly the impact of the health earnings test by eliminating the option among the elderly of finding jobs paying only cash wages.

CONCLUSION

This chapter suggests that there are a variety of trade-offs in the health-care area that could improve the efficiency, fairness, and overall progressivity of the Social Security system. Cash benefits are often preferable to health benefits and can be distributed in a way that maintains the overall progressivity of the system under a variety of different health benefit schemes. Indeed, cutting back on some of the more generous health care benefits provided to even the highest-income recipients could be used to raise benefit levels for lower-income individuals, to finance a greater portion of costs of catastrophic or long-term care, and to increase progressivity.

Gradually raising the age of eligibility for Medicare, similarly, would orient the system back toward those with greater needs. By the same token, the health earnings test operates in a perverse fashion: it encourages many able-bodied individuals to retire, discourages employers from retaining older workers, and causes other labor market distortions.

Bringing into Medicare greater consciousness of the costs of insurance, in turn, might provide some help in efforts to bring health costs under control. An increase in deductible amounts, offset perhaps by higher minimum benefits, also seems quite justified on these grounds, as well as those of progressivity. Let us be clear, however: we do not claim that cost consciousness, higher charges for Medicare, or higher deductible amounts are sufficient to bring Medicare back into actuarial balance. Other reform efforts, not touched on in this chapter, will also be required.

Meanwhile, there are legitimate health care concerns of the elderly that are not being addressed, including catastrophic coverage and assistance in meeting more of the needs of long-term care. Whatever plan of health reform is ultimately adopted, it is hoped that it will include changes to reorient elderly programs back toward the original goal of Social Security, that is, to help the elderly meet their most important needs. That means concentrating on the very old.

Regardless of what changes are made in overall health care benefits for the elderly, reform also should require an appropriate budget process. Health care cannot continue to be provided through an open-ended system where choices and priorities are determined automatically without regard to changing needs and opportunities in society. Nor should elderly health care expenditures, taxes, and premiums continue to be determined arbitrarily because of conflicting, and sometimes confusing, separation into different Medicare Part A, Medicare Part B, Medicaid, and other program piles.

Notes

1. Note that *open-ended* has a different meaning than an entitlement. Both entitlements and other expenditures may be open-ended or not. Typically, an entitlement implies some obligation of the government to make payments even into the future. It, too, denotes some lack of budgetary control, at least on an annual basis—not because total expenditures are unlimited but because no annual appropriation is required.

2. In Medicare, a prospective payment system tries to relieve these pressures, with respect to particular medical problems. Even in this system, however, more money is made available by the government for diagnosis of more difficult problems, effectively encouraging research firms to devote greater shares of resources to those types of problems where government payments will grow over time.

3. Note that there is a large difference between controlling the prices the government will pay and controlling the prices that private individuals are allowed to pay in an open market.

4. See note 34, chapter 3.

5. In calendar year 1970, total disbursements in OASDI were $33.1 billion, compared to $5.3 billion for HI and $2.2 billion for SMI. In calendar year 1993, OASDI disbursements are estimated at $307.2 billion, compared to $85.2 billion for HI and $61.7 billion for SMI. Projections shown in table 3.5 suggest that OASDI spending would fall to about one-half of total Social Security and Medicare spending by 2010. (Board of Trustees, OASDI, HI, and SMI 1993, and authors' calculations).

6. The average government cost per recipient of Medicare and Medicaid in 1979 was estimated at $1,760. The "recipient value" (what recipients would spend on health care in the absence of those benefits) was estimated at $832, or 47 percent of the government cost.

7. Smeeding (1984) also estimated the "market value" of Medicare and Medicaid per recipient in 1979 at $2,258, compared to a "government cost" of $1,760 per recipient. This means that if recipients had to purchase the same insurance themselves with their own cash, it would likely cost them considerably more than it costs the government. Among the reasons for higher private costs are administrative costs and profits of the insurance companies, weaker bargaining position of individuals relative to the government, and inferior risk pooling. There is a difficulty, however, in carrying this argument too far. Any monopoly or monopsony—a single seller or purchaser of a good or service—may operate more cheaply in the short run because the variety offered by competitive markets usually entails some costs. This is probably truer, for instance, of cosmetics than of health care. Over the long run, however, monopsonies and monopolies are usually quite inefficient at responding to changing conditions of demand and supply.

8. See, for example, Aaron (1991:17).

9. Note that this is true regardless of whether Medicare pays prices that, on average, are less than prices paid by private insurance.

10. Canadian physicians apparently are able to offset some of this price differential with higher volume, although costs are still approximately one-third higher in the United States.

11. To prevent adverse selection—a system where the healthy opt out of the insurance, thus driving up costs for the unhealthy—initially it may be necessary to make such insurance mandatory. The current Medicare system essentially achieves this result by making HI mandatory and by subsidizing SMI to such an extent that almost no one will opt out of it. See Myers (1985:488–91).

12. SMI would have to be made mandatory to keep the two programs the same in their effect; otherwise, a number of adverse selection problems would arise. The suggestion here would not be significantly different from current practice, since practically all elderly currently participate in SMI anyway.

13. In 1970, the average outlay per enrollee was $113 for SMI and $259 for HI. The SMI deductible was $50, and the HI deductible for the first 60 days of hospital stay was $52. By 1995, outlays per enrollee are expected to rise to $2,298 for SMI and $2,867 for HI. The SMI deductible is expected to be $100 and the HI deductible $776. Note that there are additional HI deductibles for longer hospital stays, which have generally increased at the same rate as the deductible for the first 60 days (Board of Trustees, HI and SMI 1992, U.S. Congress, House Committee on Ways and Means 1992:142, and enrollee projections furnished by U.S. Health Care Financing Administration).

14. See Steuerle (1993). The $8,000 figure comes from dividing total U.S. health care expenditures in fiscal year 1992 by the total number of households in the United States. The average household size is approximately 2.63 persons.

15. In the future, of course, higher-income households will eventually pay high enough HI taxes during their lifetimes that they effectively could be said to have borne the burden of their health insurance cost (see Appendix table A.10).

16. See, for example, Penner (1991).

17. There are exceptions that apply over time, especially when there are transitions from one system to another. In general, however, it becomes impossible for employers consistently to pay workers either more or less compensation than the net value of the output they produce for the firm.

18. Anderson, Kennel, and Sheils (1987) have performed estimates of the impact of Medicare's secondary-payor provisions on the employment and earnings of the elderly using the Macroeconomic-Demographic Model of the firm, ICF. They estimated that in 1983 the provision raised employment costs for about 434,000 workers aged 65 through 69, and that the average increase in costs was substantial for these workers. However, they also estimated that the actual impacts on the employment levels and earnings of workers aged 65 through 69 was small. Of course, as the costs of Medicare and private health insurance rise over time (indeed, they have already risen dramatically since 1983), the impact could be expected to grow. If more people in their sixties decide to remain in the labor market, moreover, the impact will be even greater.

Chapter Eleven

CONCLUSION: TOWARD COMMON GROUND

Not uncommonly, discussions of Social Security begin with one of two striking, but contrasting, conclusions: that either the system is in extraordinary crisis or that all of its promises are sacrosanct and can easily be met with only a bit of legislative tinkering. Neither is true. Reforms can be made in a way that is evolutionary rather than revolutionary, and the required benefit or tax changes can be kept moderate. Even if benefit cuts are implemented, they can easily be designed so that real benefits are not reduced over time, but only cut back relative to current promises of future growth. At the same time, an imbalanced system with inconsistent promises cannot help but be reformed. Even if significant future deficits in the system were viable as a matter of social policy, they cannot be tolerated from a fiscal policy standpoint.

Reform is made inevitable not simply by the imbalance between long-run benefits and revenues. Other reforms—such as adjusting benefits to take better account of secondary workers, eliminating the earnings tests that apply both to cash earnings and to Medicare, and better meeting the long-term care needs of the older-elderly—are likely to be forced by changing demographics and societal needs, as well as simple notions of fairness and efficiency. With lifetime Social Security and Medicare benefits approaching $500,000 for an average-income couple retiring today, and $1 million for a high-income couple retiring in a few decades, society must also continue to reexamine whether allowing benefit amounts to increase represents the best use of its dollars or whether there are more pressing needs elsewhere.

Principles of Social Security do not allow one to state unequivocally whether future adjustments should be in the form of tax increases, benefit reductions, or both. Such decisions require judgment in a variety of areas—in particular, in how much redistribution or progressivity society wants at a particular point in time, including how much redistribution it considers appropriate across different generations and how it ranks different needs among its citizens. Principles, however, do allow one to sort through options in ways that allow some ranking of both benefit and tax options. Some benefit reductions are found to be inferior (or no better) than others by almost any criterion. Some proposals for tax increases can be ranked similarly.

We are not so naive as to believe that all readers will come to conclusions identical to our own. Some will claim that what we consider to be a useful guideline, such as the wage replacement rate, should be elevated to the level of a first principle. More commonly, many will give each principle a different weight—for instance, by exhibiting greater or less willingness to abandon the progressive, need-based, nature of the system. These types of differences are unavoidable, but they need not repress the search for common ground and the need to prepare together for inevitable future changes.

One means of achieving common ground is to agree that options for changing the tax or benefit sides of Social Security can and should follow logically from a basic set of principles. Those willing to commit themselves to starting with a set of principles are likely to arrive at many similar conclusions no matter how divergent their political views.

One great advantage of this approach is that it provides a means of narrowing the choice of options to be considered. Some options cannot be justified easily by appeal to any principle—that is, they can be discarded as "wrong" ways to proceed. Perhaps most importantly, cutting back on benefits by delaying or reducing cost-of-living adjustments (COLAs) tends to have its harshest impact on those for whom the system was built in the first place: those who are truly old and in need of income. If lower levels of benefits are sought, it would be better to cut back on benefits initially granted than upon the benefits received by the oldest and poorest part of the elderly population.

We also conclude that there is little basis for abandoning the way that past earnings are indexed in determining the lifetime earnings based upon which individual benefits are calculated. Previous years' income should be compared to this year's income by applying an interest rate or "wage index," as is done currently. The existing rule simply establishes a means of treating equally those who contribute roughly equal amounts to Social Security over their lifetimes. As used in the Social Security benefit calculation, indexing an individual's wages over time does nothing more than establish a reasonable means of comparing the value of contributions made in different years.

Although improving the financial health of both OASDI and Medicare are valuable goals, another mistake would be to cut back on

OASDI as a means of paying for larger and larger amounts of in-kind health benefits. Reducing the share of benefits paid in cash restricts the flexibility, adaptability, and freedom of retirees. This trade-off has already begun through the paring of cash benefit growth even while medical care expenditures are expanding rapidly.

To the extent that taxes must be increased or benefits reduced—inevitably one, the other, or both must happen—we believe that the principles underlying Social Security highlight several options that should be considered among the "right ways" to reform the system. Foremost among these changes are increases in the retirement age for both OASI and Medicare. If benefits must be paid to the near-elderly, then they ought at least to be phased in at a lower level than will apply in later years. Individuals with close to two decades of expected life remaining still have much to contribute to the economy; their well-being, income, assets, and ability to work are all much higher than those of the old-elderly and of many young families. With children now the poorest group in society, it is highly questionable whether there should be increased transfers from moderate-income young families with children to high-income individuals among the near-elderly and young-elderly.

Horizontal equity, as well as efficiency considerations, also argue strongly for the inclusion of all contributions to the Social Security system—including years not now counted, the contributions of partially retired workers, and all contributions of spouses—in the calculation of benefits to be received. In a progressive system, of course, not all taxes will receive the same rate of return. Nonetheless, there is no reason to provide a partial rate of return to the earnings of high-income individuals and a zero return to moderate-income spouses and persons who work for many extra years. This last change can be achieved while maintaining the overall progressivity of the existing system.

Expansion of the tax base toward including all forms of compensation is also appropriate. Failure to do so creates problems of both equity and efficiency by maintaining unequal treatment of similarly situated workers, while encouraging excessive consumption of health care and other employer-provided benefits. To prevent such a change from increasing benefit outlays substantially in the long run, some offset in the benefit formula may be required as well. This proposal is nothing more than basic tax reform applied to Social Security.

If the net benefits of current and near-future retirees are to be reduced, increasing the amount of benefits subject to income taxation is far preferable to cutting back on COLAs. Recent reforms not only yield savings but help recapture from current high-income retirees some of the subsidies that exceed the fair annuity value of their contributions. Currently, most high-income individuals over 65 already receive very large net transfers from the system, larger even than low-income retirees, leaving a system that is regressive within cohorts. A few decades from now, the equity of taxing OASI benefits does not follow as neatly from the principles laid down here. Lifetime redistributive patterns created by the Social Security benefit formula will at last become progressive within cohorts. Given the much higher level of overall benefits that are scheduled for future retirees, however, taxation—including some adjustment for nontaxed Medicare benefits—remains one way of modifying the net cost of the system and helping to bring it into overall balance. Straightforward adjustment of the benefit formula, of course, could achieve much of the same end. Taxation adjusts according to current income and need, while the Social Security benefit formula adjusts according to lifetime earnings. Neither is perfect, so that a mixture of the two may be a reasonable compromise.

In addition, we find no justification for the current-law practice of giving nonworking spouses of high-income workers greater benefits than are given to spouses of low-income workers and to most working spouses. A strong case can be made that spousal benefits should not consistently favor high-income spouses, much less provide net transfers to them. Any funds raised by gradually adjusting spousal benefits so that all spouses are treated more equally could be spent to help finance a conversion as just suggested: providing some marginal return or benefit for the contributions of all working spouses. Society may also wish to convert the spousal benefit into one that accounts for the needs of those who raise children. The current spousal benefit by no means meets this goal, since it goes to many who do not raise children, does not go at all to many single parents who do raise children, and implicitly rewards higher-income individuals for their child-raising more than it does lower-income individuals.

Within Medicare itself, the tendency to keep premiums and deductible amounts low is a much weaker policy than one that would spend this money to help the older and needier elderly—either in cash, say, through higher minimum cash benefits, or in other health benefits such as further in-home assistance for chronic impairment problems. Similarly, we conclude that the built-in growth and open-ended nature of Medicare violates most principles of Social Security by predetermining where expenditures would be increased without regard to need. As a matter of budget policy, open-ended expenditures are almost never sustainable.

At a slightly more controversial level, we conclude that the OASI earnings test makes little sense on horizontal equity or efficiency grounds. A similar objection can be raised to what we have labeled the "health earnings test": the requirement that employers be made primary payors for the health insurance of elderly workers. With mandated health benefits for all employees under national health plans, this policy could be extended significantly to those elderly employees now working solely for cash wages. Those who are worried about maintaining the additional progressivity brought about by the basic earnings test can make slight adjustments in the benefit formula or in the income taxation of benefits and come to a much more equitable and efficiently designed system.

If the normal earnings test is maintained, then implementation of increases in the delayed retirement credit should be accelerated and the credit adjusted so that it does not discriminate by age. Once those changes are implemented, the principal advantage of abandoning the earnings test is simply that its extremely complicated and confusing rules act to deter work efforts by some elderly persons. In our view, any signal by society that it does not want the elderly to work should be abandoned. Those features of the existing system that subsidize early retirement should also be abandoned. Individuals who retire early often *increase* their lifetime net transfer from Social Security, largely because they pay far fewer OASI payroll taxes, but don't have their lifetime benefits reduced significantly. Why should workers be subsidized for retiring before an already generous Normal Retirement Age? Reforming these features may not be sufficient to produce a large change in work behavior among the near-elderly, but it may be necessary.

In fact, given the tendency of the older-elderly to require assistance for long-term care and other needs, Social Security benefits ought to be restricted for those individuals who, by retiring early, increase their probability of falling back on the public sector for more support. The current system gives the misleading signal that adequate income at age 62 will be sufficient at age 82 or beyond; often it is not. For a given amount of lifetime payments to any individual, another option might be to exchange a reduced level of benefit in the early years of retirement for a higher benefit level later. In sum, the early retirement age of 62 should be increased or, at least, the requirements for its use should be made more restrictive. Thus, the gap between Normal Retirement Age and the early retirement age should not be allowed to expand, as scheduled after the turn of the century under current law. Note that with current provisions in place, even greater shares of benefits continue to go to those who, year after year, have more and more years until death and less and less need relative to other recipients of old-age insurance.

Some options are more neutral as to whether they fall in the category of "right" or "wrong" ways to reform the system. In most instances, the validity of these options depends upon how much weight one places on the progressivity of the system versus an insurance principle that requires equal returns on all contributions. For instance, a case could be made for price, rather than wage, indexing of the benefit formula itself—so that real benefit levels stay constant over time, while the replacement rate falls with rising real wages. Given a choice between this type of change and increasing the retirement age, we believe the latter to be far superior because of its ability to maintain retirement income for the very old who have lower incomes than both the younger-elderly and the nonelderly. We are also concerned that any permanent movement against wage indexing might make retirement incomes insufficient to meet certain needs, such as long-term care.

Among tax options, raising the tax rate and the limit on earnings subject to taxation might be justified by those who desire to maintain a larger Social Security system. Both, however, are less-efficient revenue-raising options than expanding the tax base to include untaxed compensation. Among very high-income individuals, raising the limit on taxable earnings also tends to increase benefit levels far beyond where they need to be and creates equity and efficiency problems as some individuals avoid Social Security taxes through incorporation or conversion of earnings into capital income.

In conclusion, there are some right and wrong ways or, at least, better and worse ways to reform Social Security. By getting back to basics and examining the underlying rationale for a Social Security system, it is possible to establish guidelines for how future reform should proceed. Universal agreement, of course, is almost impossible with respect to every proposal. Common ground, however, will be found by those willing to base their choices on a consistent application of fundamental principles to the inevitable reform of one of America's most successful social programs.

APPENDIX

Table A.1 OASI BENEFIT IN FIRST YEAR OF RETIREMENT (IN CONSTANT 1993 DOLLARS)

Year cohort turns 65	Single Worker			One-earner Couple			Two-earner Couple		
	Low wage	Avg. wage	High wage	Low wage	Avg. wage	High wage	Low & Low	Avg. & Low	High & Avg.
1940	2,128	3,097	5,108	3,191	4,646	7,662	4,255	5,225	8,205
1945	2,095	2,745	4,166	3,142	4,118	6,249	4,189	4,840	6,911
1950	1,736	2,362	3,256	2,604	3,544	4,883	3,472	4,098	5,618
1955	4,029	5,894	6,380	6,043	8,841	9,570	8,057	9,923	12,274
1960	4,146	6,263	6,967	6,219	9,394	10,450	8,292	10,409	13,230
1965	4,307	6,609	7,234	6,461	9,914	10,851	8,615	10,917	13,843
1970	4,739	7,425	8,377	7,109	11,138	12,565	9,478	12,164	15,802
1975	5,807	9,111	10,889	8,711	13,667	16,334	11,615	14,919	20,000
1980	6,120	10,167	12,909	9,179	15,251	19,363	12,239	16,287	23,076
1985	5,344	8,852	11,571	8,017	13,277	17,357	10,689	14,196	20,423
1990	5,797	9,570	12,954	8,696	14,355	19,431	11,594	15,367	22,524
1995	5,904	9,744	13,599	8,856	14,615	20,398	11,808	15,648	23,342
2000	6,130	10,160	14,650	9,194	15,241	21,975	12,259	16,290	24,811
2005	6,460	10,767	15,937	9,690	16,150	23,906	12,920	17,227	26,704
2010	6,832	11,397	17,402	10,247	17,096	26,103	13,663	18,229	28,799
2015	7,176	11,957	18,588	10,763	17,935	27,881	14,351	19,132	30,544
2020	7,531	12,530	19,605	11,296	18,796	29,407	15,061	20,061	32,135
2025	7,944	13,221	20,768	11,916	19,832	31,152	15,888	21,165	33,989
2030	8,337	13,855	21,853	12,505	20,783	32,779	16,674	22,192	35,708
2035	8,749	14,519	22,933	13,124	21,779	34,400	17,499	23,269	37,452
2040	9,192	15,236	24,053	13,788	22,854	36,080	18,383	24,428	39,289
2045	9,680	16,041	25,311	14,520	24,062	37,967	19,360	25,722	41,352
2050	10,203	16,908	26,683	15,305	25,362	40,025	20,406	27,111	43,591

Notes: Table's projections based on intermediate assumptions in 1993 OASDI Board of Trustees report. Assumes retirement at Normal Retirement Age. Couples are assumed to be the same age.

Table A.2 OASI REPLACEMENT RATES

Year cohort turns 65	Single Worker			One-earner Couple			Two-earner Couple		
	Low wage	Avg. wage	High wage	Low wage	Avg. wage	High wage	Low & Low	Avg. & Low	High & Avg.
1940	39.8	26.1	16.4	59.7	39.1	24.5	39.8	30.3	19.0
1945	29.3	17.3	16.9	43.9	25.9	25.3	29.3	21.0	17.0
1950	25.6	15.7	17.9	38.3	23.5	26.8	25.6	18.7	16.9
1955	52.8	34.7	33.0	79.1	52.1	49.4	52.8	40.3	33.8
1960	48.1	32.7	29.2	72.1	49.0	43.8	48.1	37.5	30.7
1965	44.8	31.0	32.3	67.2	46.4	48.4	44.8	35.3	31.6
1970	45.3	32.0	27.2	68.0	47.9	40.9	45.3	36.1	29.3
1975	54.8	38.7	28.1	82.2	58.0	42.2	54.8	43.7	32.1
1980	59.5	44.5	28.3	89.2	66.7	42.4	59.5	49.1	33.7
1985	52.9	39.4	22.0	79.3	59.1	33.0	52.9	43.6	27.2
1990	54.9	40.8	23.1	82.4	61.2	34.7	54.9	45.2	28.4
1995	55.4	41.1	23.5	83.1	61.7	35.3	55.4	45.6	28.6
2000	55.4	41.3	24.7	83.1	62.0	37.1	55.4	45.7	29.6
2005	55.1	41.3	25.7	82.7	62.0	38.6	55.1	45.6	30.3
2010	55.0	41.3	26.5	82.5	62.0	39.8	55.0	45.6	30.9
2015	54.8	41.1	26.9	82.2	61.7	40.4	54.8	45.4	31.1
2020	54.5	40.8	26.9	81.7	61.2	40.3	54.5	45.1	31.0
2025	54.1	40.5	26.7	81.1	60.7	40.1	54.1	44.7	30.8
2030	53.8	40.3	26.6	80.8	60.4	40.0	53.8	44.5	30.7
2035	53.6	40.0	26.5	80.4	60.0	39.8	53.6	44.2	30.5
2040	53.4	39.9	26.4	80.1	59.8	39.6	53.4	44.1	30.4
2045	53.4	39.8	26.3	80.1	59.7	39.5	53.4	44.0	30.3
2050	53.4	39.8	26.3	80.1	59.7	39.5	53.4	44.0	30.3

Notes: Replacement rate measured as OASI benefit in first 12 months of retirement as percentage of earned income in preceding 12 months, after adjusting for inflation. Assumes retirement at OASI Normal Retirement Age. Couples are assumed to be the same age. Projections based on intermediate assumptions in 1993 OASDI Board of Trustees report.

Table A.3 ACTUARIAL PRESENT VALUE AT AGE 65 OF LIFETIME OASI BENEFITS AND TAXES

1875 BIRTH COHORT (65 IN 1940)	Single Male			Single Female			One-earner Couple			Two-earner couple		
	Low	Average	High	Low	Average	High	Low	Average	High	Low/Low	Avg/Low	High/Avg
Assuming survival to age 65												
(A) Worker's benefit	17,459	24,712	38,554	20,378	28,736	44,394	17,459	24,712	38,554	37,837	45,090	67,290
(B) Spousal and survivors benefits	0	0	0	0	0	0	13,029	18,281	27,869	0	499	1,347
(C) Total OASI benefits (A + B)	17,459	24,712	38,554	20,378	28,736	44,394	30,488	42,993	66,423	37,837	45,589	68,637
(D) OASI taxes	319	710	1,917	319	710	1,917	319	710	1,917	639	1,029	2,626
(E) Net transfer (C - D)	17,140	24,002	36,637	20,059	28,026	42,477	30,169	42,283	64,506	37,199	44,560	66,011
Adjusting for the chance of death in all years after age 21												
(F) Worker's benefit	9,414	13,325	20,789	12,347	17,411	26,898	9,414	13,325	20,789	21,761	25,672	38,200
(G) Spousal and survivors benefits												
Type 1	0	0	0	0	0	0	6,182	8,630	12,978	0	303	816
Type 2	0	0	0	0	0	0	179	254	392	(0)	15	55
Type 3	0	0	0	0	0	0	0	0	0	0	0	0
(H) Total OASI benefits (F + G)	9,414	13,325	20,789	12,347	17,411	26,898	15,776	22,209	34,160	21,761	25,989	39,071
(I) OASI taxes	184	410	1,107	204	452	1,222	184	410	1,107	388	613	1,559
(J) Net Transfer (H - I)	9,230	12,915	19,683	12,143	16,958	25,676	15,592	21,800	33,053	21,373	25,376	37,512
(K) Benefit-to-tax ratio (H/I)	51.06	32.52	18.78	60.66	38.49	22.01	85.56	54.20	30.86	56.09	42.38	25.06
(L) Net transfer as a % of lifetime earnings	4.19	2.64	1.52	5.38	3.38	1.94	7.08	4.45	2.56	4.79	3.55	2.09
(M) Real internal rate of return	145.41	114.49	84.42	147.66	123.05	86.17	169.24	135.06	101.66	146.60	126.68	95.14

Table A.3 ACTUARIAL PRESENT VALUE AT AGE 65 OF LIFETIME OASI BENEFITS AND TAXES

1880 BIRTH COHORT (65 IN 1945)	Single Male			Single Female			One-earner Couple			Two-earner couple		
	Low	Average	High	Low	Average	High	Low	Average	High	Low/Low	Avg/Low	High/Avg
Assuming survival to age 65												
(A) Worker's benefit	27,273	35,242	48,674	32,653	42,140	57,712	27,273	35,242	48,674	59,926	67,895	90,815
(B) Spousal and survivors benefits	0	0	0	0	0	0	21,286	27,427	37,169	0	513	932
(C) Total OASI benefits (A + B)	27,273	35,242	48,674	32,653	42,140	57,712	48,558	62,669	85,843	59,926	68,408	91,747
(D) OASI taxes	1,001	2,225	5,030	1,001	2,225	5,030	1,001	2,225	5,030	2,002	3,226	7,254
(E) Net transfer (C - D)	26,272	33,017	43,645	31,652	39,916	52,682	47,557	60,444	80,814	57,923	65,182	84,492
Adjusting for the chance of death in all years after age 21												
(F) Worker's benefit	15,175	19,610	27,084	20,718	26,738	36,617	15,175	19,610	27,084	35,893	40,328	53,822
(G) Spousal and survivors benefits							12,260	15,889	21,533		341	736
Type 1	0	0	0	0	0	0	10,761	13,846	18,579	0	325	591
Type 2	0	0	0	0	0	0	1,499	2,043	2,954	0	15	145
Type 3	0	0	0	0	0	0	0	0	0	0	0	0
(H) Total OASI benefits (F + G)	15,175	19,610	27,084	20,718	26,738	36,617	27,436	35,498	48,617	35,893	40,668	54,558
(I) OASI taxes	635	1,411	3,228	695	1,544	3,520	635	1,411	3,228	1,330	2,106	4,773
(J) Net Transfer (H - I)	14,540	18,198	23,856	20,023	25,193	33,098	26,801	34,087	45,388	34,563	38,562	49,785
(K) Benefit-to-tax ratio (H / I)	23.89	13.89	8.39	29.81	17.31	10.40	43.20	25.15	15.06	26.99	19.31	11.43
(L) Net transfer as a % of lifetime earnings	5.96	3.36	1.70	8.00	4.53	2.30	10.99	6.29	3.23	6.99	4.87	2.54
(M) Real internal rate of return	39.85	31.28	23.87	41.29	33.92	25.25	46.36	37.42	29.52	40.62	35.18	27.15

continued

Table A.3 ACTUARIAL PRESENT VALUE AT AGE 65 OF LIFETIME OASI BENEFITS AND TAXES (continued)

1885 BIRTH COHORT (65 IN 1950)	Single Male			Single Female			One-earner Couple			Two-earner couple		
	Low	Average	High	Low	Average	High	Low	Average	High	Low/Low	Avg/Low	High/Avg
Assuming survival to age 65												
(A) Worker's benefit	36,246	46,820	56,986	44,423	57,313	69,559	36,246	46,820	56,986	80,669	91,243	114,299
(B) Spousal and survivors benefits	0	0	0	0	0	0	29,469	37,967	45,933	0	1,494	886
(C) Total OASI benefits (A + B)	36,246	46,820	56,986	44,423	57,313	69,559	65,715	84,787	102,920	80,669	92,737	115,185
(D) OASI taxes	1,809	4,021	7,727	1,809	4,021	7,727	1,809	4,021	7,727	3,619	5,830	11,748
(E) Net transfer (C - D)	34,437	42,799	49,259	42,614	53,292	61,832	63,906	80,766	95,193	77,050	86,907	103,437
Adjusting for the chance of death in all years after age 21												
(F) Worker's benefit	20,358	26,297	32,007	29,109	37,556	45,580	20,358	26,297	32,007	49,467	55,407	69,563
(G) Spousal and survivors benefits												
Type 1	0	0	0	0	0	0	18,995	24,546	30,158	0	1,055	677
Type 2	0	0	0	0	0	0	15,416	19,837	23,932	0	979	580
Type 3	0	0	0	0	0	0	3,579	4,709	6,227	0	76	97
(H) Total OASI benefits (F + G)	20,358	26,297	32,007	29,109	37,556	45,580	39,353	50,843	62,166	49,467	56,461	70,240
(I) OASI taxes	1,226	2,724	5,353	1,334	2,964	5,780	1,226	2,724	5,353	2,559	4,057	8,317
(J) Net Transfer (H - I)	19,132	23,574	26,654	27,776	34,592	39,800	38,127	48,120	56,812	46,908	52,404	61,923
(K) Benefit-to-tax ratio (H / I)	16.61	9.66	5.98	21.83	12.67	7.89	32.11	18.67	11.61	19.33	13.92	8.45
(L) Net transfer as a % of lifetime earnings	7.21	4.00	1.82	10.15	5.69	2.65	14.37	8.16	3.88	8.70	6.07	2.99
(M) Real internal rate of return	23.98	19.24	14.43	25.43	21.28	15.87	28.28	23.48	18.46	24.76	21.75	16.94

Table A.3 ACTUARIAL PRESENT VALUE AT AGE 65 OF LIFETIME OASI BENEFITS AND TAXES

1890 BIRTH COHORT (65 IN 1955)	Single Male			Single Female			One-earner Couple			Two-earner couple		
	Low	Average	High	Low	Average	High	Low	Average	High	Low/Low	Avg/Low	High/Avg
Assuming survival to age 65												
(A) Worker's benefit	45,806	67,004	72,504	56,751	83,017	89,830	45,806	67,004	72,504	102,557	123,755	155,521
(B) Spousal and survivors benefits	0	0	0	0	0	0	38,437	56,230	60,844	0	6,533	1,111
(C) Total OASI benefits (A + B)	45,806	67,004	72,504	56,751	83,017	89,830	84,243	123,234	133,348	102,557	130,288	156,633
(D) OASI taxes	3,236	7,191	11,802	3,236	7,191	11,802	3,236	7,191	11,802	6,472	10,427	18,993
(E) Net transfer (C - D)	42,570	59,814	60,702	53,515	75,826	78,028	81,007	116,043	121,546	96,085	119,861	137,640
Adjusting for the chance of death in all years after age 21												
(F) Worker's benefit	26,500	38,764	41,946	38,671	56,569	61,212	26,500	38,764	41,946	65,171	77,435	98,515
(G) Spousal and survivors benefits	0	0	0	0	0	0	27,493	39,233	43,723	0	4,825	781
Type 1	0	0	0	0	0	0	21,072	30,826	33,355	0	4,452	757
Type 2	0	0	0	0	0	0	6,422	8,407	10,368	0	373	24
Type 3	0	0	0	0	0	0	0	0	0	0	0	0
(H) Total OASI benefits (F + G)	26,500	38,764	41,946	38,671	56,569	61,212	53,993	77,997	85,669	65,171	82,259	99,296
(I) OASI taxes	2,301	5,113	8,659	2,488	5,528	9,252	2,301	5,113	8,659	4,788	7,601	14,187
(J) Net Transfer (H - I)	24,199	33,651	33,287	36,183	51,041	51,959	51,692	72,884	77,010	60,382	74,659	85,109
(K) Benefit-to-tax ratio (H/I)	11.52	7.58	4.84	15.55	10.23	6.62	23.47	15.25	9.89	13.61	10.82	7.00
(L) Net transfer as a % of lifetime earnings	8.29	5.19	2.20	12.04	7.64	3.35	17.71	11.24	5.08	10.19	7.87	3.90
(M) Real internal rate of return	18.17	15.24	11.20	19.52	16.98	12.58	21.80	18.80	14.64	18.90	17.05	13.51

continued

Table A.3 ACTUARIAL PRESENT VALUE AT AGE 65 OF LIFETIME OASI BENEFITS AND TAXES (continued)

1895 BIRTH COHORT (65 IN 1960)	Single Male			Single Female			One-earner Couple			Two-earner couple		
	Low	Average	High	Low	Average	High	Low	Average	High	Low/Low	Avg/Low	High/Avg
Assuming survival to age 65												
(A) Worker's benefit	50,108	75,633	84,154	64,102	96,741	107,636	50,108	75,633	84,154	114,210	139,734	180,895
(B) Spousal and survivors benefits	0	0	0	0	0	0	45,137	68,109	75,775	0	10,646	2,933
(C) Total OASI benefits (A + B)	50,108	75,633	84,154	64,102	96,741	107,636	95,245	143,741	159,929	114,210	150,380	183,828
(D) OASI taxes	5,391	11,980	17,887	5,391	11,980	17,887	5,391	11,980	17,887	10,782	17,371	29,867
(E) Net transfer (C - D)	44,717	63,653	66,267	58,711	84,761	89,750	89,854	131,761	142,043	103,428	133,009	153,961
Adjusting for the chance of death in all years after age 21												
(F) Worker's benefit	30,126	45,473	50,596	45,702	68,972	76,740	30,126	45,473	50,596	75,828	91,174	119,568
(G) Spousal and survivors benefits							36,222	53,390	60,413	923	10,810	2,527
Type 1	0	0	0	0	0	0	26,603	40,138	44,655	0	7,590	2,091
Type 2	0	0	0	0	0	0	9,423	12,968	15,292	0	1,539	154
Type 3	0	0	0	0	0	0	195	283	466	923	1,681	283
(H) Total OASI benefits (F + G)	30,126	45,473	50,596	45,702	68,972	76,740	66,348	98,862	111,009	76,751	101,984	122,095
(I) OASI taxes	4,035	8,967	13,771	4,329	9,621	14,608	4,035	8,967	13,771	8,365	13,297	23,392
(J) Net Transfer (H - I)	26,091	36,505	36,825	41,372	59,351	62,132	62,313	89,895	97,238	68,386	88,687	98,703
(K) Benefit-to-tax ratio (H/I)	7.47	5.07	3.67	10.56	7.17	5.25	16.44	11.02	8.06	9.18	7.67	5.22
(L) Net transfer as a % of lifetime earnings	8.04	5.06	2.35	12.40	8.01	3.90	19.21	12.47	6.21	10.39	8.41	4.28
(M) Real internal rate of return	13.14	10.97	8.45	14.52	12.63	9.86	17.02	14.64	11.87	14.25	13.00	10.32

Table A.3 ACTUARIAL PRESENT VALUE AT AGE 65 OF LIFETIME OASI BENEFITS AND TAXES

1900 BIRTH COHORT (65 IN 1965)	Single Male			Single Female			One-earner Couple			Two-earner couple		
	Low	Average	High	Low	Average	High	Low	Average	High	Low/Low	Avg/Low	High/Avg
Assuming survival to age 65												
(A) Worker's benefit	55,329	84,668	92,705	71,574	109,513	119,924	55,329	84,668	92,705	126,903	156,241	202,218
(B) Spousal and survivors benefits	0	0	0	0	0	0	51,229	78,373	85,837	0	13,864	3,619
(C) Total OASI benefits (A + B)	55,329	84,668	92,705	71,574	109,513	119,924	106,559	163,041	178,542	126,903	170,106	205,837
(D) OASI taxes	8,900	19,777	27,094	8,900	19,777	27,094	8,900	19,777	27,094	17,799	28,677	46,871
(E) Net transfer (C - D)	46,430	64,890	65,612	62,674	89,735	92,831	97,659	143,264	151,448	109,103	141,429	158,966
Adjusting for the chance of death in all years after age 21												
(F) Worker's benefit	34,392	52,628	57,624	52,953	81,022	88,725	34,392	52,628	57,624	87,345	105,582	138,647
(G) Spousal and survivors benefits	0	0	0	0	0	0	45,393	68,056	76,140	1,081	15,067	4,360
Type 1	0	0	0	0	0	0	31,756	48,577	53,207	0	10,258	2,678
Type 2	0	0	0	0	0	0	12,835	18,347	21,109	0	3,385	444
Type 3	0	0	0	0	0	0	803	1,132	1,823	1,081	1,424	1,239
(H) Total OASI benefits (F + G)	34,392	52,628	57,624	52,953	81,022	88,725	79,785	120,685	133,764	88,427	120,649	143,007
(I) OASI taxes	6,933	15,406	21,664	7,417	16,483	22,933	6,933	15,406	21,664	14,350	22,824	38,147
(J) Net Transfer (H - I)	27,459	37,222	35,960	45,536	64,539	65,792	72,852	105,278	112,100	74,076	97,825	104,860
(K) Benefit-to-tax ratio (H / I)	4.96	3.42	2.66	7.14	4.92	3.87	11.51	7.83	6.17	6.16	5.29	3.75
(L) Net transfer as a % of lifetime earnings	7.52	4.59	2.23	12.12	7.73	4.00	19.96	12.98	6.94	10.00	8.24	4.28
(M) Real internal rate of return	9.95	8.13	6.38	11.32	9.76	7.78	14.28	12.05	9.98	11.23	10.16	8.13

continued

Table A.3 ACTUARIAL PRESENT VALUE AT AGE 65 OF LIFETIME OASI BENEFITS AND TAXES (continued)

1905 BIRTH COHORT (65 IN 1970)	Single Male			Single Female			One-earner Couple			Two-earner couple		
	Low	Average	High	Low	Average	High	Low	Average	High	Low/Low	Avg/Low	High/Avg
Assuming survival to age 65												
(A) Worker's benefit	68,145	98,245	110,816	87,976	126,077	142,200	68,145	98,245	110,816	156,121	186,221	236,893
(B) Spousal and survivors benefits	0	0	0	0	0	0	62,937	89,624	101,077	0	13,289	5,873
(C) Total OASI benefits (A + B)	68,145	98,245	110,816	87,976	126,077	142,200	131,082	187,869	211,893	156,121	199,510	242,766
(D) OASI taxes	13,576	30,169	40,522	13,576	30,169	40,522	13,576	30,169	40,522	27,152	43,745	70,691
(E) Net transfer (C - D)	54,569	68,076	70,294	74,400	95,908	101,678	117,506	157,700	171,371	128,969	155,764	172,076
Adjusting for the chance of death in all years after age 21												
(F) Worker's benefit	43,389	62,554	70,559	67,634	96,925	109,320	43,389	62,554	70,559	111,023	130,188	167,484
(G) Spousal and survivors benefits	0	0	0	0	0	0	59,418	84,718	98,508	3,132	18,003	9,801
Type 1	0	0	0	0	0	0	40,701	57,758	65,137	0	10,216	4,515
Type 2	0	0	0	0	0	0	16,912	24,483	29,588	(0)	4,363	2,329
Type 3	0	0	0	0	0	0	1,805	2,476	3,783	3,132	3,424	2,957
(H) Total OASI benefits (F + G)	43,389	62,554	70,559	67,634	96,925	109,320	102,807	147,272	169,066	114,155	148,191	177,284
(I) OASI taxes	10,964	24,365	33,233	11,729	26,064	35,325	10,964	24,365	33,233	22,693	36,094	59,297
(J) Net Transfer (H - I)	32,425	38,189	37,326	55,905	70,861	73,995	91,843	122,907	135,834	91,462	112,097	117,987
(K) Benefit-to-tax ratio (H / I)	3.96	2.57	2.12	5.77	3.72	3.09	9.38	6.04	5.09	5.03	4.11	2.99
(L) Net transfer as a % of lifetime earnings	7.97	4.22	2.27	13.29	7.58	4.40	22.57	13.59	8.27	11.05	8.46	4.58
(M) Real internal rate of return	8.25	6.37	5.19	9.58	7.96	6.55	12.62	10.29	8.83	9.77	8.55	6.84

Table A.3 ACTUARIAL PRESENT VALUE AT AGE 65 OF LIFETIME OASI BENEFITS AND TAXES

1910 BIRTH COHORT (65 IN 1975)	Single Male			Single Female			One-earner Couple			Two-earner couple		
	Low	Average	High	Low	Average	High	Low	Average	High	Low/Low	Avg/Low	High/Avg
Assuming survival to age 65												
(A) Worker's benefit	71,893	112,118	133,991	91,265	141,835	169,505	71,893	112,118	133,991	163,158	203,383	275,826
(B) Spousal and survivors benefits	0	0	0	0	0	0	64,453	99,788	119,255	0	17,475	9,788
(C) Total OASI benefits (A + B)	71,893	112,118	133,991	91,265	141,835	169,505	136,346	211,906	253,246	163,158	220,858	285,615
(D) OASI taxes	19,637	43,637	58,807	19,637	43,637	58,807	19,637	43,637	58,807	39,273	63,274	102,444
(E) Net transfer (C - D)	52,257	68,481	75,184	71,628	98,198	110,698	116,710	168,269	194,439	123,885	157,584	183,170
Adjusting for the chance of death in all years after age 21												
(F) Worker's benefit	47,043	73,363	87,676	72,063	111,993	133,842	47,043	73,363	87,676	119,106	145,426	199,669
(G) Spousal and survivors benefits	0	0	0	0	0	0	66,627	100,500	120,701	6,556	27,840	15,929
Type 1	0	0	0	0	0	0	42,900	66,284	79,215	0	13,798	7,729
Type 2	0	0	0	0	0	0	19,819	28,857	34,216	6,556	6,659	2,162
Type 3							3,908	5,359	7,271	0	7,383	6,038
(H) Total OASI benefits (F + G)	47,043	73,363	87,676	72,063	111,993	133,842	113,670	173,864	208,377	125,662	173,266	215,598
(I) OASI taxes	16,392	36,427	49,420	17,464	38,808	52,522	16,392	36,427	49,420	33,856	53,890	88,228
(J) Net Transfer (H -I)	30,651	36,937	38,255	54,599	73,185	81,320	97,278	137,437	158,956	91,806	119,376	127,370
(K) Benefit-to-tax ratio (H / I)	2.87	2.01	1.77	4.13	2.89	2.55	6.93	4.77	4.22	3.71	3.22	2.44
(L) Net transfer as a % of lifetime earnings	6.78	3.67	2.31	11.65	7.03	4.77	21.51	13.67	9.59	9.97	8.10	4.72
(M) Real internal rate of return	6.44	5.00	4.30	7.68	6.48	5.56	10.86	8.85	7.81	8.13	7.16	5.76

continued

Table A.3 ACTUARIAL PRESENT VALUE AT AGE 65 OF LIFETIME OASI BENEFITS AND TAXES (continued)

1915 BIRTH COHORT (65 IN 1980)	Single Male			Single Female			One-earner Couple			Two-earner couple		
	Low	Average	High	Low	Average	High	Low	Average	High	Low/Low	Avg/Low	High/Avg
Assuming survival to age 65												
(A) Worker's benefit	80,123	133,164	169,092	99,936	166,095	210,912	80,123	133,164	169,092	180,059	233,100	335,187
(B) Spousal and survivors benefits	0	0	0	0	0	0	69,821	116,047	147,362	0	22,851	15,483
(C) Total OASI benefits (A + B)	80,123	133,164	169,092	99,936	166,095	210,912	149,945	249,211	316,454	180,059	255,951	350,670
(D) OASI taxes	26,511	58,913	83,455	26,511	58,913	83,455	26,511	58,913	83,455	53,022	85,424	142,368
(E) Net transfer (C - D)	53,612	74,251	85,637	73,425	107,182	127,457	123,434	190,298	232,999	127,037	170,527	208,302
Adjusting for the chance of death in all years after age 21												
(F) Worker's benefit	54,299	90,244	114,592	80,811	134,310	170,549	54,299	90,244	114,592	135,110	171,055	248,901
(G) Spousal and survivors benefits	0	0	0	0	0	0	75,034	119,615	149,721	11,778	37,391	24,323
Type 1	0	0	0	0	0	0	47,934	79,669	101,169	0	18,478	12,520
Type 2	0	0	0	0	0	0	21,180	31,448	37,754		7,109	1,842
Type 3										11,778	11,804	9,960
(H) Total OASI benefits (F + G)	54,299	90,244	114,592	80,811	134,310	170,549	129,333	209,859	264,312	146,888	208,446	273,224
(I) OASI taxes	22,929	50,954	71,863	24,233	53,850	76,141	22,929	50,954	71,863	47,162	75,186	125,713
(J) Net Transfer (H - I)	31,370	39,290	42,729	56,578	80,459	94,408	106,403	158,906	192,449	99,726	133,260	147,511
(K) Benefit-to-tax ratio (H/I)	2.37	1.77	1.59	3.33	2.49	2.24	5.64	4.12	3.68	3.11	2.77	2.17
(L) Net transfer as a % of lifetime earnings	6.25	3.52	2.52	10.88	6.96	5.38	21.19	14.24	11.33	9.76	8.15	5.17
(M) Real internal rate of return	5.33	4.24	3.78	6.43	5.54	4.91	9.18	7.66	6.94	6.95	6.16	5.05

Table A.3 ACTUARIAL PRESENT VALUE AT AGE 65 OF LIFETIME OASI BENEFITS AND TAXES

1920 BIRTH COHORT (65 IN 1985)	Single Male			Single Female			One-earner Couple			Two-earner couple		
	Low	Average	High	Low	Average	High	Low	Average	High	Low/Low	Avg/Low	High/Avg
Assuming survival to age 65												
(A) Worker's benefit	68,198	112,950	147,656	84,237	139,513	182,381	68,198	112,950	147,656	152,435	197,187	287,169
(B) Spousal and survivors benefits	0	0	0	0	0	0	58,497	96,882	126,651	0	18,686	14,492
(C) Total OASI benefits (A + B)	68,198	112,950	147,656	84,237	139,513	182,381	126,695	209,832	274,307	152,435	215,873	301,661
(D) OASI taxes	33,225	73,832	110,753	33,225	73,832	110,753	33,225	73,832	110,753	66,449	107,057	184,585
(E) Net transfer (C - D)	34,974	39,117	36,903	51,012	65,681	71,629	93,470	136,000	163,555	85,986	108,816	117,076
Adjusting for the chance of death in all years after age 21												
(F) Worker's benefit	48,011	79,517	103,950	69,550	115,189	150,583	48,011	79,517	103,950	117,561	149,067	219,139
(G) Spousal and survivors benefits	0	0	0	0	0	0	67,927	111,484	141,188	15,447	42,757	32,097
Type 1	0	0	0	0	0	0	41,484	68,706	89,817	0	15,428	11,965
Type 2	0	0	0	0	0	0	19,271	31,187	37,734	0	11,516	5,725
Type 3	0	0	0	0	0	0	7,172	11,592	13,637	15,447	15,813	14,407
(H) Total OASI benefits (F + G)	48,011	79,517	103,950	69,550	115,189	150,583	115,939	191,001	245,138	133,009	191,823	251,236
(I) OASI taxes	29,441	65,425	96,358	30,956	68,792	102,176	29,441	65,425	96,358	60,398	96,381	165,150
(J) Net Transfer (H - I)	18,570	14,092	7,592	38,594	46,397	48,407	86,498	125,576	148,780	72,611	95,442	86,086
(K) Benefit-to-tax ratio (H / I)	1.63	1.22	1.08	2.25	1.67	1.47	3.94	2.92	2.54	2.20	1.99	1.52
(L) Net transfer as a % of lifetime earnings	3.38	1.15	0.43	6.78	3.67	2.65	15.72	10.27	8.48	6.48	5.33	2.85
(M) Real internal rate of return	3.82	2.73	2.30	4.87	3.99	3.46	7.51	6.20	5.76	5.37	4.76	3.69

continued

Table A.3 ACTUARIAL PRESENT VALUE AT AGE 65 OF LIFETIME OASI BENEFITS AND TAXES (continued)

1925 BIRTH COHORT (65 IN 1990)	Single Male			Single Female			One-earner Couple			Two-earner couple		
	Low	Average	High	Low	Average	High	Low	Average	High	Low/Low	Avg/Low	High/Avg
Assuming survival to age 65												
(A) Worker's benefit	76,703	126,625	171,399	94,127	155,391	210,336	76,703	126,625	171,399	170,830	220,753	326,790
(B) Spousal and survivors benefits	0	0	0	0	0	0	65,123	107,509	145,524	0	20,447	18,338
(C) Total OASI benefits (A + B)	76,703	126,625	171,399	94,127	155,391	210,336	141,826	234,135	316,924	170,830	241,199	345,128
(D) OASI taxes	40,951	91,002	146,827	40,951	91,002	146,827	40,951	91,002	146,827	81,902	131,953	237,828
(E) Net transfer (C - D)	35,752	35,624	24,573	53,176	64,389	63,509	100,875	143,133	170,097	88,928	109,247	107,300
Adjusting for the chance of death in all years after age 21												
(F) Worker's benefit	55,446	91,533	123,898	78,708	129,935	175,880	55,446	91,533	123,898	134,153	170,240	253,834
(G) Spousal and survivors benefits	0	0	0	0	0	0	76,142	126,043	164,035	16,635	49,369	41,559
Type 1	0	0	0	0	0	0	47,189	77,902	105,447	0	17,097	15,334
Type 2	0	0	0	0	0	0	20,817	34,168	42,412	0	13,090	7,860
Type 3	0	0	0	0	0	0	8,137	13,974	16,175	16,635	19,182	18,365
(H) Total OASI benefits (F + G)	55,446	91,533	123,898	78,708	129,935	175,880	131,588	217,576	287,933	150,788	219,609	295,392
(I) OASI taxes	36,950	82,110	129,475	38,601	85,780	136,669	36,950	82,110	129,475	75,550	120,711	215,255
(J) Net Transfer (H - I)	18,496	9,423	(5,577)	40,107	44,156	39,210	94,638	135,466	158,458	75,238	98,898	80,138
(K) Benefit-to-tax ratio (H / I)	1.50	1.11	0.96	2.04	1.51	1.29	3.56	2.65	2.22	2.00	1.82	1.37
(L) Net transfer as a % of lifetime earnings	3.14	0.72	-0.29	6.59	3.27	1.98	16.06	10.34	8.31	6.28	5.16	2.46
(M) Real internal rate of return	3.45	2.39	1.82	4.42	3.55	2.95	6.83	5.66	5.24	4.78	4.30	3.26

Table A.3 ACTUARIAL PRESENT VALUE AT AGE 65 OF LIFETIME OASI BENEFITS AND TAXES

1930 BIRTH COHORT (65 IN 1995)	Single Male			Single Female			One-earner Couple			Two-earner couple		
	Low	Average	High	Low	Average	High	Low	Average	High	Low/Low	Avg/Low	High/Avg
Assuming survival to age 65												
(A) Worker's benefit	78,057	128,821	179,792	95,140	157,013	219,140	78,057	128,821	179,792	173,198	223,961	336,805
(B) Spousal and survivors benefits	0	0	0	0	0	0	65,583	108,234	151,060	0	20,388	20,472
(C) Total OASI benefits (A + B)	78,057	128,821	179,792	95,140	157,013	219,140	143,641	237,055	330,853	173,198	244,349	357,278
(D) OASI taxes	49,520	110,045	190,154	49,520	110,045	190,154	49,520	110,045	190,154	99,040	159,565	300,198
(E) Net transfer (C - D)	28,537	18,776	(10,361)	45,620	46,969	28,987	94,120	127,010	140,699	74,157	84,784	57,079
Adjusting for the chance of death in all years after age 21												
(F) Worker's benefit	57,984	95,693	133,557	80,552	132,937	185,538	57,984	95,693	133,557	138,536	176,245	266,495
(G) Spousal and survivors benefits	0	0	0	0	0	0	76,892	127,661	171,821	16,650	50,359	46,070
Type 1	0	0	0	0	0	0	48,583	80,178	111,902	(0)	17,262	17,333
Type 2	0	0	0	0	0	0	19,941	32,844	42,111	16,650	12,795	9,023
Type 3	0	0	0	0	0	0	8,368	14,639	17,807	16,650	20,302	19,714
(H) Total OASI benefits (F + G)	57,984	95,693	133,557	80,552	132,937	185,538	134,876	223,354	305,378	155,186	226,604	312,565
(I) OASI taxes	45,379	100,842	170,672	47,171	104,824	179,038	45,379	100,842	170,672	92,550	148,013	275,496
(J) Net Transfer (H - I)	12,605	(5,149)	(37,115)	33,381	28,113	6,500	89,497	122,512	134,706	62,636	78,592	37,069
(K) Benefit-to-tax ratio (H / I)	1.28	0.95	0.78	1.71	1.27	1.04	2.97	2.21	1.79	1.68	1.53	1.13
(L) Net transfer as a % of lifetime earnings	2.00	-0.37	-1.71	5.14	1.95	0.29	14.20	8.74	6.19	4.89	3.83	1.02
(M) Real internal rate of return	2.83	1.82	1.05	3.73	2.89	2.13	5.85	4.79	4.26	3.92	3.54	2.48

continued

Table A.3 ACTUARIAL PRESENT VALUE AT AGE 65 OF LIFETIME OASI BENEFITS AND TAXES (continued)

1935 BIRTH COHORT (65 IN 2000)	Single Male			Single Female			One-earner Couple			Two-earner couple		
	Low	Average	High	Low	Average	High	Low	Average	High	Low/Low	Avg/Low	High/Avg
Assuming survival to age 65												
(A) Worker's benefit	83,054	137,670	198,506	100,632	166,807	240,519	83,054	137,670	198,506	183,687	238,302	365,313
(B) Spousal and survivors benefits	0	0	0	0	0	0	69,158	114,635	165,292	0	21,581	24,039
(C) Total OASI benefits (A + B)	83,054	137,670	198,506	100,632	166,807	240,519	152,212	252,304	363,798	183,687	259,883	389,352
(D) OASI taxes	57,600	128,000	234,411	57,600	128,000	234,411	57,600	128,000	234,411	115,200	185,600	362,411
(E) Net transfer (C - D)	25,454	9,669	(35,905)	43,032	38,807	6,108	94,612	124,304	129,387	68,487	74,283	26,941
Adjusting for the chance of death in all years after age 21												
(F) Worker's benefit	63,128	104,639	150,880	86,082	142,687	205,741	63,128	104,639	150,880	149,209	190,721	293,567
(G) Spousal and survivors benefits	0	0	0	0	0	0	79,556	133,519	185,566	15,152	50,624	50,203
Type 1	0	0	0	0	0	0	52,199	86,525	124,760	0	18,461	20,563
Type 2	0	0	0	0	0	0	19,881	32,894	43,756	0	12,912	10,634
Type 3	0	0	0	0	0	0	7,475	14,101	17,050	15,152	19,251	19,005
(H) Total OASI benefits (F + G)	63,128	104,639	150,880	86,082	142,687	205,741	142,683	238,159	336,446	164,362	241,345	343,770
(I) OASI taxes	53,433	118,741	213,889	55,285	122,856	222,905	53,433	118,741	213,889	108,718	174,026	336,745
(J) Net Transfer (H - I)	9,694	(14,101)	(63,009)	30,796	19,831	(17,163)	89,250	119,418	122,556	55,643	67,319	7,025
(K) Benefit-to-tax ratio (H / I)	1.18	0.88	0.71	1.56	1.16	0.92	2.67	2.01	1.57	1.51	1.39	1.02
(L) Net transfer as a % of lifetime earnings	1.46	-0.95	-2.55	4.50	1.31	-0.67	13.42	8.08	4.95	4.13	3.11	0.18
(M) Real internal rate of return	2.54	1.59	0.72	3.37	2.56	1.72	5.25	4.31	3.65	3.43	3.11	2.07

Table A.3 ACTUARIAL PRESENT VALUE AT AGE 65 OF LIFETIME OASI BENEFITS AND TAXES

1940 BIRTH COHORT (65 IN 2005)	Single Male			Single Female			One-earner Couple			Two-earner couple		
	Low	Average	High	Low	Average	High	Low	Average	High	Low/Low	Avg/Low	High/Avg
Assuming survival to age 65												
(A) Worker's benefit	85,450	142,410	210,805	103,773	172,946	256,006	85,450	142,410	210,805	189,223	246,183	383,751
(B) Spousal and survivors benefits	0	0	0	0	0	0	71,712	119,515	176,914	65	23,087	27,681
(C) Total OASI benefits (A + B)	85,450	142,410	210,805	103,773	172,946	256,006	157,163	261,925	387,719	189,287	269,270	411,432
(D) OASI taxes	65,920	146,488	283,764	65,920	146,488	283,764	65,920	146,488	283,764	131,839	212,408	430,252
(E) Net transfer (C - D)	19,531	(4,078)	(72,958)	37,853	26,458	(27,758)	91,243	115,437	103,955	57,448	56,862	(18,820)
Adjusting for the chance of death in all years after age 21												
(F) Worker's benefit	66,175	110,286	163,253	89,693	149,481	221,271	66,175	110,286	163,253	155,868	199,979	312,734
(G) Spousal and survivors benefits												
Type 1	0	0	0	0	0	0	82,370	139,471	198,308	15,713	51,959	54,504
Type 2	0	0	0	0	0	0	55,236	92,056	136,267	53	19,954	23,925
Type 3	0	0	0	0	0	0	19,489	32,433	44,917	481	12,851	12,045
(H) Total OASI benefits (F + G)	66,175	110,286	163,253	89,693	149,481	221,271	148,545	249,757	361,561	171,580	251,938	367,237
(I) OASI taxes	61,606	136,903	261,877	63,616	141,368	271,970	61,606	136,903	261,877	125,222	200,519	403,245
(J) Net Transfer (H - I)	4,568	(26,617)	(98,624)	26,077	8,112	(50,699)	86,938	112,854	99,684	46,358	51,419	(36,008)
(K) Benefit-to-tax ratio (H/I)	1.07	0.81	0.62	1.41	1.06	0.81	2.41	1.82	1.38	1.37	1.26	0.91
(L) Net transfer as a % of lifetime earnings	0.66	-1.72	-3.51	3.64	0.51	-1.74	12.48	7.29	3.55	3.28	2.27	-0.82
(M) Real internal rate of return	2.22	1.32	0.35	3.02	2.26	1.32	4.77	3.91	3.11	3.04	2.74	1.68

continued

Table A.3 ACTUARIAL PRESENT VALUE AT AGE 65 OF LIFETIME OASI BENEFITS AND TAXES (continued)

1945 BIRTH COHORT (65 IN 2010)	Single Male			Single Female			One-earner Couple			Two-earner couple		
	Low	Average	High	Low	Average	High	Low	Average	High	Low/Low	Avg/Low	High/Avg
Assuming survival to age 65												
(A) Worker's benefit	88,050	146,893	224,293	107,389	179,157	273,558	88,050	146,893	224,293	195,439	254,282	403,450
(B) Spousal and survivors benefits	0	0	0	0	0	0	74,879	124,916	190,724	129	24,718	33,680
(C) Total OASI benefits (A + B)	88,050	146,893	224,293	107,389	179,157	273,558	162,929	271,809	415,017	195,569	279,000	437,130
(D) OASI taxes	72,744	161,653	334,520	72,744	161,653	334,520	72,744	161,653	334,520	145,488	234,397	496,173
(E) Net transfer (C - D)	15,306	(14,760)	(110,227)	34,645	17,504	(60,963)	90,185	110,156	80,497	50,081	44,603	(59,044)
Adjusting for the chance of death in all years after age 21												
(F) Worker's benefit	69,045	115,188	175,883	93,568	156,099	238,351	69,045	115,188	175,883	162,614	208,756	331,982
(G) Spousal and survivors benefits	0	0	0	0	0	0	85,583	143,586	212,697	16,275	52,987	62,201
Type 1	0	0	0	0	0	0	58,589	97,741	149,232	108	21,537	29,345
Type 2	0	0	0	0	0	0	19,247	32,026	46,615	958	13,385	14,463
Type 3	0	0	0	0	0	0	7,746	13,818	16,851	15,209	18,065	18,392
(H) Total OASI benefits (F + G)	69,045	115,188	175,883	93,568	156,099	238,351	154,629	258,774	388,580	178,889	261,743	394,182
(I) OASI taxes	68,168	151,485	310,845	70,418	156,484	322,401	68,168	151,485	310,845	138,586	221,903	467,329
(J) Net Transfer (H - I)	877	(36,297)	(134,962)	23,151	(384)	(84,051)	86,460	107,288	77,735	40,303	39,840	(73,146)
(K) Benefit-to-tax ratio (H/I)	1.01	0.76	0.57	1.33	1.00	0.74	2.27	1.71	1.25	1.29	1.18	0.84
(L) Net transfer as a % of lifetime earnings	0.12	-2.26	-4.23	3.11	-0.02	-2.54	11.96	6.68	2.43	2.75	1.69	-1.51
(M) Real internal rate of return	2.04	1.16	0.11	2.82	2.09	1.05	4.50	3.64	2.72	2.82	2.52	1.45

Table A.3 ACTUARIAL PRESENT VALUE AT AGE 65 OF LIFETIME OASI BENEFITS AND TAXES

1950 BIRTH COHORT (65 IN 2015)	Single Male			Single Female			One-earner Couple			Two-earner couple		
	Low	Average	High	Low	Average	High	Low	Average	High	Low/Low	Avg/Low	High/Avg
Assuming survival to age 65												
(A) Worker's benefit	93,603	155,969	242,468	113,927	189,834	295,114	93,603	155,969	242,468	207,531	269,896	432,302
(B) Spousal and survivors benefits	0	0	0	0	0	0	79,256	132,058	205,298	133	25,957	37,283
(C) Total OASI benefits (A + B)	93,603	155,969	242,468	113,927	189,834	295,114	172,859	288,027	447,766	207,664	295,853	469,585
(D) OASI taxes	78,175	173,722	379,758	78,175	173,722	379,758	78,175	173,722	379,758	156,350	251,897	553,480
(E) Net transfer (C - D)	15,429	(17,753)	(137,290)	35,752	16,112	(84,644)	94,684	114,305	68,008	51,314	43,956	(83,895)
Adjusting for the chance of death in all years after age 21												
(F) Worker's benefit	73,956	123,232	191,575	99,903	166,465	258,785	73,956	123,232	191,575	173,859	223,134	358,040
(G) Spousal and survivors benefits	0	0	0	0	0	0	90,153	151,222	231,305	15,112	54,520	69,712
Type 1	0	0	0	0	0	0	62,566	104,249	162,067	112	22,762	32,693
Type 2	0	0	0	0	0	0	19,964	33,194	50,388	963	13,872	17,109
Type 3	0	0	0	0	0	0	7,622	13,779	18,851	14,037	17,887	19,910
(H) Total OASI benefits (F + G)	73,956	123,232	191,575	99,903	166,465	258,785	164,109	274,454	422,880	188,972	277,655	427,753
(I) OASI taxes	73,398	163,106	354,681	75,881	168,625	367,686	73,398	163,106	354,681	149,279	238,987	523,306
(J) Net Transfer (H - I)	559	(39,874)	(163,106)	24,022	(2,160)	(108,901)	90,712	111,348	68,199	39,693	38,667	(95,554)
(K) Benefit-to-tax ratio (H/I)	1.01	0.76	0.54	1.32	0.99	0.70	2.24	1.68	1.19	1.27	1.16	0.82
(L) Net transfer as a % of lifetime earnings	0.08	-2.43	-4.65	3.15	-0.13	-3.00	12.29	6.79	1.94	2.65	1.61	-1.84
(M) Real internal rate of return	2.02	1.16	0.03	2.78	2.06	0.94	4.41	3.56	2.55	2.74	2.46	1.37

continued

Table A.3 ACTUARIAL PRESENT VALUE AT AGE 65 OF LIFETIME OASI BENEFITS AND TAXES (continued)

1955 BIRTH COHORT (65 IN 2020)	Single Male			Single Female			One-earner Couple			Two-earner couple		
	Low	Average	High	Low	Average	High	Low	Average	High	Low/Low	Avg/Low	High/Avg
Assuming survival to age 65												
(A) Worker's benefit	98,178	163,360	255,591	119,516	198,864	311,139	98,178	163,360	255,591	217,694	282,876	454,455
(B) Spousal and survivors benefits	0	0	0	0	0	0	83,184	138,407	216,557	183	27,217	39,763
(C) Total OASI benefits (A + B)	98,178	163,360	255,591	119,516	198,864	311,139	181,363	301,767	472,148	217,877	310,093	494,218
(D) OASI taxes	82,462	183,248	423,095	82,485	183,300	423,218	82,462	183,248	423,095	164,946	265,733	606,394
(E) Net transfer (C - D)	15,717	(19,888)	(167,504)	37,031	15,564	(112,078)	98,901	118,520	49,053	52,931	44,361	(112,177)
Adjusting for the chance of death in all years after age 21												
(F) Worker's benefit	77,892	129,605	202,777	105,321	175,245	274,186	77,892	129,605	202,777	183,213	234,926	378,023
(G) Spousal and survivors benefits	0	0	0	0	0	0	94,960	159,129	247,919	14,849	56,996	76,984
Type 1	0	0	0	0	0	0	66,119	110,013	172,131	154	23,985	35,041
Type 2	0	0	0	0	0	0	20,808	34,560	54,004	1,136	14,347	19,077
Type 3	0	0	0	0	0	0	8,032	14,555	21,783	13,558	18,665	22,866
(H) Total OASI benefits (F + G)	77,892	129,605	202,777	105,321	175,245	274,186	172,851	288,733	450,696	198,062	291,922	455,006
(I) OASI taxes	77,404	172,010	396,346	80,179	178,175	411,023	77,404	172,010	396,346	157,583	252,189	574,522
(J) Net Transfer (H - I)	487	(42,405)	(193,569)	25,142	(2,930)	(136,837)	95,447	116,724	54,350	40,479	39,734	(119,515)
(K) Benefit-to-tax ratio (H / I)	1.01	0.75	0.51	1.31	0.98	0.67	2.23	1.68	1.14	1.26	1.16	0.79
(L) Net transfer as a % of lifetime earnings	0.06	-2.53	-5.05	3.23	-0.17	-3.45	12.67	6.97	1.42	2.64	1.62	-2.15
(M) Real internal rate of return	2.02	1.15	-0.07	2.77	2.05	0.81	4.39	3.54	2.39	2.71	2.45	1.29

Table A.3 ACTUARIAL PRESENT VALUE AT AGE 65 OF LIFETIME OASI BENEFITS AND TAXES

1960 BIRTH COHORT (65 IN 2025)	Single Male			Single Female			One-earner Couple			Two-earner couple		
	Low	Average	High	Low	Average	High	Low	Average	High	Low/Low	Avg/Low	High/Avg
Assuming survival to age 65												
(A) Worker's benefit	98,389	163,746	257,217	120,874	201,168	316,000	98,389	163,746	257,217	219,263	284,621	458,385
(B) Spousal and survivors benefits	0	0	0	0	0	0	85,370	142,065	223,186	411	29,044	44,187
(C) Total OASI benefits (A + B)	98,389	163,746	257,217	120,874	201,168	316,000	183,759	305,812	480,402	219,675	313,665	502,573
(D) OASI taxes	88,412	196,471	467,734	88,557	196,793	468,499	88,412	196,471	467,734	176,969	285,028	664,526
(E) Net transfer (C - D)	9,977	(32,725)	(210,517)	32,318	4,376	(152,499)	95,347	109,341	12,669	42,706	28,637	(161,954)
Adjusting for the chance of death in all years after age 21												
(F) Worker's benefit	78,547	130,724	205,344	106,950	177,995	279,599	78,547	130,724	205,344	185,497	237,674	383,339
(G) Spousal and survivors benefits	0	0	0	0	0	0	98,018	164,392	257,838	17,004	60,667	84,365
Type 1	0	0	0	0	0	0	68,572	114,110	179,270	349	25,698	39,097
Type 2	0	0	0	0	0	0	20,615	34,196	53,975	1,965	14,829	19,501
Type 3	0	0	0	0	0	0	8,831	16,086	24,593	14,690	20,140	25,767
(H) Total OASI benefits (F + G)	78,547	130,724	205,344	106,950	177,995	279,599	176,565	295,116	463,182	202,501	298,341	467,704
(I) OASI taxes	83,182	184,850	440,036	86,223	191,606	456,144	83,182	184,850	440,036	169,405	271,072	631,641
(J) Net Transfer (H - I)	(4,635)	(54,126)	(234,692)	20,728	(13,611)	(176,545)	93,383	110,266	23,146	33,096	27,269	(163,938)
(K) Benefit-to-tax ratio (H/I)	0.94	0.71	0.47	1.24	0.93	0.61	2.12	1.60	1.05	1.20	1.10	0.74
(L) Net transfer as a % of lifetime earnings	-0.59	-3.10	-5.64	2.54	-0.75	-4.10	11.87	6.31	0.56	2.07	1.06	-2.75
(M) Real internal rate of return	1.83	0.97	-0.30	2.60	1.89	0.60	4.21	3.38	2.15	2.55	2.29	1.10

continued

Table A.3 ACTUARIAL PRESENT VALUE AT AGE 65 OF LIFETIME OASI BENEFITS AND TAXES (continued)

1965 BIRTH COHORT (65 IN 2030)	Single Male			Single Female			One-earner Couple			Two-earner couple		
	Low	Average	High	Low	Average	High	Low	Average	High	Low/Low	Avg/Low	High/Avg
Assuming survival to age 65												
(A) Worker's benefit	104,476	173,629	273,854	128,093	212,880	335,761	104,476	173,629	273,854	232,569	301,722	486,734
(B) Spousal and survivors benefits	0	0	0	0	0	0	90,266	149,999	236,611	422	30,454	46,909
(C) Total OASI benefits (A + B)	104,476	173,629	273,854	128,093	212,880	335,761	194,742	323,628	510,465	232,991	332,177	533,643
(D) OASI taxes	93,506	207,791	497,288	93,653	208,119	498,070	93,506	207,791	497,288	187,159	301,444	705,407
(E) Net transfer (C - D)	10,970	(34,161)	(223,434)	34,440	4,761	(162,309)	101,236	115,837	13,177	45,832	30,733	(171,764)
Adjusting for the chance of death in all years after age 21												
(F) Worker's benefit	84,026	139,643	220,250	113,736	189,020	298,129	84,026	139,643	220,250	197,762	253,379	409,270
(G) Spousal and survivors benefits	0	0	0	0	0	0	103,368	173,133	272,728	18,134	63,122	88,790
Type 1	0	0	0	0	0	0	72,933	121,195	191,178	360	27,041	41,652
Type 2	0	0	0	0	0	0	21,232	35,161	55,804	2,020	15,188	20,317
Type 3	0	0	0	0	0	0	9,202	16,776	25,746	15,754	20,894	26,821
(H) Total OASI benefits (F + G)	84,026	139,643	220,250	113,736	189,020	298,129	187,394	312,776	492,978	215,896	316,502	498,060
(I) OASI taxes	88,118	195,818	468,762	91,261	202,801	485,405	88,118	195,818	468,762	179,378	287,078	671,564
(J) Net Transfer (H - I)	(4,092)	(56,174)	(248,512)	22,476	(13,781)	(187,276)	99,276	116,958	24,216	36,517	29,424	(173,504)
(K) Benefit-to-tax ratio (H/I)	0.95	0.71	0.47	1.25	0.93	0.61	2.13	1.60	1.05	1.20	1.10	0.74
(L) Net transfer as a % of lifetime earnings	-0.50	-3.07	-5.67	2.64	-0.73	-4.13	12.06	6.39	0.55	2.18	1.10	-2.77
(M) Real internal rate of return	1.86	1.00	-0.25	2.61	1.90	0.62	4.20	3.37	2.15	2.57	2.29	1.11

Table A.3 ACTUARIAL PRESENT VALUE AT AGE 65 OF LIFETIME OASI BENEFITS AND TAXES

1970 BIRTH COHORT (65 IN 2035)	Single Male			Single Female			One-earner Couple			Two-earner couple		
	Low	Average	High	Low	Average	High	Low	Average	High	Low/Low	Avg/Low	High/Avg
Assuming survival to age 65												
(A) Worker's benefit	110,905	184,041	290,697	135,711	225,206	355,718	110,905	184,041	290,697	246,616	319,752	515,902
(B) Spousal and survivors benefits	0	0	0	0	0	0	95,432	158,348	250,143	434	31,930	49,441
(C) Total OASI benefits (A + B)	110,905	184,041	290,697	135,711	225,206	355,718	206,337	342,388	540,840	247,051	351,682	565,344
(D) OASI taxes	97,541	216,759	518,643	97,691	217,090	519,433	97,541	216,759	518,643	195,232	314,449	735,733
(E) Net transfer (C - D)	13,363	(32,718)	(227,947)	38,021	8,115	(163,715)	108,796	125,630	22,197	51,819	37,233	(170,390)
Adjusting for the chance of death in all years after age 21												
(F) Worker's benefit	89,987	149,328	235,867	120,963	200,732	317,060	89,987	149,328	235,867	210,950	270,291	436,598
(G) Spousal and survivors benefits	0	0	0	0	0	0	108,436	181,229	285,957	18,786	64,429	91,024
Type 1	0	0	0	0	0	0	77,639	128,823	203,505	372	28,460	44,068
Type 2	0	0	0	0	0	0	21,726	35,900	57,131	2,058	15,401	20,779
Type 3	0	0	0	0	0	0	9,071	16,506	25,321	16,356	20,568	26,177
(H) Total OASI benefits (F + G)	89,987	149,328	235,867	120,963	200,732	317,060	198,423	330,557	521,824	229,736	334,720	527,623
(I) OASI taxes	92,146	204,768	490,088	95,277	211,727	506,659	92,146	204,768	490,088	187,423	300,045	701,815
(J) Net Transfer (H - I)	(2,159)	(55,441)	(254,222)	25,686	(10,995)	(189,599)	106,277	125,789	31,736	42,313	34,675	(174,192)
(K) Benefit-to-tax ratio (H / I)	0.98	0.73	0.48	1.27	0.95	0.63	2.15	1.61	1.06	1.23	1.12	0.75
(L) Net transfer as a % of lifetime earnings	-0.25	-2.89	-5.54	2.88	-0.55	-4.00	12.32	6.56	0.69	2.41	1.23	-2.65
(M) Real internal rate of return	1.93	1.07	-0.19	2.67	1.94	0.67	4.24	3.40	2.18	2.62	2.33	1.15

continued

Table A.3 ACTUARIAL PRESENT VALUE AT AGE 65 OF LIFETIME OASI BENEFITS AND TAXES (continued)

1975 BIRTH COHORT (65 IN 2040)	Single Male			Single Female			One-earner Couple			Two-earner couple		
	Low	Average	High	Low	Average	High	Low	Average	High	Low/Low	Avg/Low	High/Avg
Assuming survival to age 65												
(A) Worker's benefit	117,808	195,278	308,284	143,891	238,514	376,539	117,808	195,278	308,284	261,700	339,170	546,797
(B) Spousal and survivors benefits	0	0	0	0	0	0	100,974	167,357	264,235	448	33,538	51,897
(C) Total OASI benefits (A + B)	117,808	195,278	308,284	143,891	238,514	376,539	218,782	362,635	572,519	262,147	372,708	598,694
(D) OASI taxes	102,284	227,298	542,022	102,435	227,633	542,822	102,284	227,298	542,022	204,719	329,733	769,655
(E) Net transfer (C - D)	15,524	(32,020)	(233,738)	41,456	10,880	(166,283)	116,498	135,338	30,497	57,428	42,975	(170,961)
Adjusting for the chance of death in all years after age 21												
(F) Worker's benefit	96,367	159,738	252,176	128,714	213,356	336,823	96,367	159,738	252,176	225,082	288,452	465,533
(G) Spousal and survivors benefits	0	0	0	0	0	0	113,701	189,671	299,004	18,741	65,599	92,552
Type 1	0	0	0	0	0	0	82,676	137,028	216,351	129,100	158,715	259,779
Type 2	0	0	0	0	0	0	22,262	36,702	58,362	(126,626)	(113,103)	(192,341)
Type 3	0	0	0	0	0	0	8,763	15,941	24,291	16,268	19,987	25,114
(H) Total OASI benefits (F + G)	96,367	159,738	252,176	128,714	213,356	336,823	210,068	349,409	551,180	243,823	354,051	558,085
(I) OASI taxes	96,916	215,369	513,612	100,004	222,231	529,953	96,916	215,369	513,612	196,920	315,373	735,843
(J) Net Transfer (H - I)	(549)	(55,631)	(261,436)	28,710	(8,875)	(193,130)	113,152	134,040	37,568	46,903	38,678	(177,758)
(K) Benefit-to-tax ratio (H / I)	0.99	0.74	0.49	1.29	0.96	0.64	2.17	1.62	1.07	1.24	1.12	0.76
(L) Net transfer as a % of lifetime earnings	-0.06	-2.75	-5.42	3.06	-0.43	-3.88	12.43	6.63	0.78	2.54	1.31	-2.57
(M) Real internal rate of return	1.98	1.12	-0.13	2.70	1.97	0.71	4.25	3.41	2.20	2.65	2.34	1.18

Table A.3 ACTUARIAL PRESENT VALUE AT AGE 65 OF LIFETIME OASI BENEFITS AND TAXES

1980 BIRTH COHORT (65 IN 2045)	Single Male			Single Female			One-earner Couple			Two-earner couple		
	Low	Average	High	Low	Average	High	Low	Average	High	Low/Low	Avg/Low	High/Avg
Assuming survival to age 65												
(A) Worker's benefit	125,413	207,826	327,918	152,904	253,381	399,798	125,413	207,826	327,918	278,317	360,729	581,299
(B) Spousal and survivors benefits	0	0	0	0	0	0	107,076	177,421	279,975	463	35,381	54,646
(C) Total OASI benefits (A + B)	125,413	207,826	327,918	152,904	253,381	399,798	232,489	385,246	607,893	278,779	396,110	635,946
(D) OASI taxes	107,749	239,442	569,995	107,902	239,783	570,808	107,749	239,442	569,995	215,652	347,345	809,778
(E) Net transfer (C - D)	17,664	(31,617)	(242,076)	45,001	13,598	(171,010)	124,740	145,804	37,899	63,128	48,765	(173,832)
Adjusting for the chance of death in all years after age 21												
(F) Worker's benefit	103,294	171,172	270,084	137,199	227,356	358,734	103,294	171,172	270,084	240,493	308,371	497,440
(G) Spousal and survivors benefits	0	0	0	0	0	0	119,851	199,809	314,653	18,524	67,803	95,548
Type 1							88,151	146,061	230,491	401	31,747	49,034
Type 2							23,015	37,917	60,203	2,134	16,071	21,551
Type 3							8,685	15,831	23,959	15,989	19,985	24,963
(H) Total OASI benefits (F + G)	103,294	171,172	270,084	137,199	227,356	358,734	223,146	370,981	584,738	259,017	376,173	592,988
(I) OASI taxes	102,359	227,465	541,455	105,433	234,295	557,728	102,359	227,465	541,455	207,792	332,898	775,750
(J) Net Transfer (H - I)	935	(56,293)	(271,370)	31,766	(6,940)	(198,994)	120,786	143,516	43,283	51,224	43,275	(182,762)
(K) Benefit-to-tax ratio (H / I)	1.01	0.75	0.50	1.30	0.97	0.64	2.18	1.63	1.08	1.25	1.13	0.76
(L) Net transfer as a % of lifetime earnings	0.10	-2.64	-5.34	3.21	-0.32	-3.80	12.57	6.72	0.85	2.63	1.38	-2.51
(M) Real internal rate of return	2.03	1.16	-0.08	2.73	2.00	0.75	4.25	3.42	2.22	2.67	2.36	1.21

continued

Table A.3 ACTUARIAL PRESENT VALUE AT AGE 65 OF LIFETIME OASI BENEFITS AND TAXES (continued)

1985 BIRTH COHORT (65 IN 2050)	Single Male			Single Female			One-earner Couple			Two-earner couple		
	Low	Average	High	Low	Average	High	Low	Average	High	Low/Low	Avg/Low	High/Avg
Assuming survival to age 65												
(A) Worker's benefit	133,575	221,353	349,324	162,574	269,409	425,161	133,575	221,353	349,324	296,149	383,927	618,733
(B) Spousal and survivors benefits	0	0	0	0	0	0	113,610	188,251	297,116	479	37,374	57,706
(C) Total OASI benefits (A+B)	133,575	221,353	349,324	162,574	269,409	425,161	247,185	409,604	646,440	296,628	421,302	676,439
(D) OASI taxes	113,581	252,403	600,957	113,739	252,754	601,795	113,581	252,403	600,957	227,320	366,142	853,711
(E) Net transfer (C-D)	19,994	(31,049)	(251,633)	48,835	16,655	(176,633)	133,604	157,201	45,483	69,308	55,160	(177,271)
Adjusting for the chance of death in all years after age 21												
(F) Worker's benefit	110,561	183,216	289,138	146,260	242,374	382,497	110,561	183,216	289,138	256,821	329,476	531,512
(G) Spousal and survivors benefits	0	0	0	0	0	0	126,892	211,525	333,145	18,688	71,020	100,188
Type 1	0	0	0	0	0	0	93,927	155,634	245,639	417	33,624	51,916
Type 2	0	0	0	0	0	0	24,000	39,540	62,780	2,196	16,745	22,472
Type 3	0	0	0	0	0	0	8,965	16,351	24,727	16,076	20,651	25,800
(H) Total OASI benefits (F+G)	110,561	183,216	289,138	146,260	242,374	382,497	237,454	394,741	622,284	275,509	400,496	631,700
(I) OASI taxes	108,045	240,101	571,625	111,203	247,118	588,355	108,045	240,101	571,625	219,249	351,304	818,744
(J) Net Transfer (H-I)	2,516	(56,885)	(282,487)	35,056	(4,745)	(205,858)	129,408	154,640	50,658	56,260	49,191	(187,044)
(K) Benefit-to-tax ratio (H/I)	1.02	0.76	0.51	1.32	0.98	0.65	2.20	1.64	1.09	1.26	1.14	0.77
(L) Net transfer as a % of lifetime earnings	0.25	-2.52	-5.26	3.36	-0.20	-3.73	12.76	6.86	0.94	2.73	1.49	-2.43
(M) Real internal rate of return	2.07	1.21	-0.03	2.76	2.03	0.78	4.27	3.43	2.24	2.69	2.39	1.24

Notes: All amounts are expressed in constant 1993 dollars and are discounted to present value at age 65 using 2 percent real interest rate. Type 1 includes spousal and survivors' benefits paid on the record of a worker who survives to age 65 or beyond. Type 2 includes benefits for survivors aged 65 or over whose working spouse dies before age 65. Type 3 includes benefits for survivors younger than 65. Couples are assumed to be the same age and to have two children, born when parents are aged 25 and 30. Assumes retirement at Normal Retirement Age. Does not include effects of income taxation of benefits. Parentheses indicate negative values.

Table A.4 ACTUARIAL PRESENT VALUE AT AGE 65 OF LIFETIME OASI BENEFITS

Year cohort turns 65	Single Male			Single Female			One-earner Couple			Two-earner couple		
	Low	Average	High	Low	Average	High	Low	Average	High	Low/Low	Avg/Low	High/Avg
1940	9,414	13,325	20,789	12,347	17,411	26,898	15,776	22,209	34,160	21,761	25,989	39,071
1945	15,175	19,610	27,084	20,718	26,738	36,617	27,436	35,498	48,617	35,893	40,668	54,558
1950	20,358	26,297	32,007	29,109	37,556	45,580	39,353	50,843	62,166	49,467	56,461	70,240
1955	26,500	38,764	41,946	38,671	56,569	61,212	53,993	77,997	85,669	65,171	82,259	99,296
1960	30,126	45,473	50,596	45,702	68,972	76,740	66,348	98,862	111,009	76,751	101,984	122,095
1965	34,392	52,628	57,624	52,953	81,022	88,725	79,785	120,685	133,764	88,427	120,649	143,007
1970	43,389	62,554	70,559	67,634	96,925	109,320	102,807	147,272	169,066	114,155	148,191	177,284
1975	47,043	73,363	87,676	72,063	111,993	133,842	113,670	173,864	208,377	125,662	173,266	215,598
1980	54,299	90,244	114,592	80,811	134,310	170,549	129,333	209,859	264,312	146,888	208,446	273,224
1985	48,011	79,517	103,950	69,550	115,189	150,583	115,939	191,001	245,138	133,009	191,823	251,236
1990	55,446	91,533	123,898	78,708	129,935	175,880	131,588	217,576	287,933	150,788	219,609	295,392
1995	57,984	95,693	133,557	80,552	132,937	185,538	134,876	223,354	305,378	155,186	226,604	312,565
2000	63,128	104,639	150,880	86,082	142,687	205,741	142,683	238,159	336,446	164,362	241,345	343,770
2005	66,175	110,286	163,253	89,693	149,481	221,271	148,545	249,757	361,561	171,580	251,938	367,237
2010	69,045	115,188	175,883	93,568	156,099	238,351	154,629	258,774	388,580	178,889	261,743	394,182
2015	73,956	123,232	191,575	99,903	166,465	258,785	164,109	274,454	422,880	188,972	277,655	427,753
2020	77,892	129,605	202,777	105,321	175,245	274,186	172,851	288,733	450,696	198,062	291,922	455,006
2025	78,547	130,724	205,344	106,950	177,995	279,599	176,565	295,116	463,182	202,501	298,341	467,704
2030	84,026	139,643	220,250	113,736	189,020	298,129	187,394	312,776	492,978	215,896	316,502	498,060
2035	89,987	149,328	235,867	120,963	200,732	317,060	198,423	330,557	521,824	229,736	334,720	527,623
2040	96,367	159,738	252,176	128,714	213,356	336,823	210,068	349,409	551,180	243,823	354,051	558,085
2045	103,294	171,172	270,084	137,199	227,356	358,734	223,146	370,981	584,738	259,017	376,173	592,988
2050	110,561	183,216	289,138	146,260	242,374	382,497	237,454	394,741	622,284	275,509	400,496	631,700

Notes: All amounts are in constant 1993 dollars, adjusted to present value at age 65 using 2 percent real interest rate. Adjusts for chance of death in all years after age 21.

Table A.5 ACTUARIAL PRESENT VALUE AT AGE 65 OF LIFETIME OASI TAXES

Year cohort turns 65	Single Male			Single Female			One-earner Couple			Two-earner couple		
	Low	Average	High	Low	Average	High	Low	Average	High	Low/Low	Avg/Low	High/Avg
1940	184	410	1,107	204	452	1,222	184	410	1,107	388	613	1,559
1945	635	1,411	3,228	695	1,544	3,520	635	1,411	3,228	1,330	2,106	4,773
1950	1,226	2,724	5,353	1,334	2,964	5,780	1,226	2,724	5,353	2,559	4,057	8,317
1955	2,301	5,113	8,659	2,488	5,528	9,252	2,301	5,113	8,659	4,788	7,601	14,187
1960	4,035	8,967	13,771	4,329	9,621	14,608	4,035	8,967	13,771	8,365	13,297	23,392
1965	6,933	15,406	21,664	7,417	16,483	22,933	6,933	15,406	21,664	14,350	22,824	38,147
1970	10,964	24,365	33,233	11,729	26,064	35,325	10,964	24,365	33,233	22,693	36,094	59,297
1975	16,392	36,427	49,420	17,464	38,808	52,522	16,392	36,427	49,420	33,856	53,890	88,228
1980	22,929	50,954	71,863	24,233	53,850	76,141	22,929	50,954	71,863	47,162	75,186	125,713
1985	29,441	65,425	96,358	30,956	68,792	102,176	29,441	65,425	96,358	60,398	96,381	165,150
1990	36,950	82,110	129,475	38,601	85,780	136,669	36,950	82,110	129,475	75,550	120,711	215,255
1995	45,379	100,842	170,672	47,171	104,824	179,038	45,379	100,842	170,672	92,550	148,013	275,496
2000	53,433	118,741	213,889	55,285	122,856	222,905	53,433	118,741	213,889	108,718	174,026	336,745
2005	61,606	136,903	261,877	63,616	141,368	271,970	61,606	136,903	261,877	125,222	200,519	403,245
2010	68,168	151,485	310,845	70,418	156,484	322,401	68,168	151,485	310,845	138,586	221,903	467,329
2015	73,398	163,106	354,681	75,881	168,625	367,686	73,398	163,106	354,681	149,279	238,987	523,306
2020	77,404	172,010	396,346	80,179	178,175	411,023	77,404	172,010	396,346	157,583	252,189	574,522
2025	83,182	184,850	440,036	86,223	191,606	456,144	83,182	184,850	440,036	169,405	271,072	631,641
2030	88,118	195,818	468,762	91,261	202,801	485,405	88,118	195,818	468,762	179,378	287,078	671,564
2035	92,146	204,768	490,088	95,277	211,727	506,659	92,146	204,768	490,088	187,423	300,045	701,815
2040	96,916	215,369	513,612	100,004	222,231	529,953	96,916	215,369	513,612	196,920	315,373	735,843
2045	102,359	227,465	541,455	105,433	234,295	557,728	102,359	227,465	541,455	207,792	332,898	775,750
2050	108,045	240,101	571,625	111,203	247,118	588,355	108,045	240,101	571,625	219,249	351,304	818,744

Notes: All amounts are in constant 1993 dollars, adjusted to present value at age 65 using 2 percent real interest rate. Adjusts for chance of death in all years after age 21.

Table A.6 NET LIFETIME OASI TRANSFER (BENEFITS MINUS TAXES)

Year cohort turns 65	Single Male			Single Female			One-earner Couple			Two-earner couple		
	Low	Average	High	Low	Average	High	Low	Average	High	Low/Low	Avg/Low	High/Avg
1940	9,230	12,915	19,683	12,143	16,958	25,676	15,592	21,800	33,053	21,373	25,376	37,512
1945	14,540	18,198	23,856	20,023	25,193	33,098	26,801	34,087	45,388	34,563	38,562	49,785
1950	19,132	23,574	26,654	27,776	34,592	39,800	38,127	48,120	56,812	46,908	52,404	61,923
1955	24,199	33,651	33,287	36,183	51,041	51,959	51,692	72,884	77,010	60,382	74,659	85,109
1960	26,091	36,505	36,825	41,372	59,351	62,132	62,313	89,895	97,238	68,386	88,687	98,703
1965	27,459	37,222	35,960	45,536	64,539	65,792	72,852	105,278	112,100	74,076	97,825	104,860
1970	32,425	38,189	37,326	55,905	70,861	73,995	91,843	122,907	135,834	91,462	112,097	117,987
1975	30,651	36,937	38,255	54,599	73,185	81,320	97,278	137,437	158,956	91,806	119,376	127,370
1980	31,370	39,290	42,729	56,578	80,459	94,408	106,403	158,906	192,449	99,726	133,260	147,511
1985	18,570	14,092	7,592	38,594	46,397	48,407	86,498	125,576	148,780	72,611	95,442	86,086
1990	18,496	9,423	(5,577)	40,107	44,156	39,210	94,638	135,466	158,458	75,238	98,898	80,138
1995	12,605	(5,149)	(37,115)	33,381	28,113	6,500	89,497	122,512	134,706	62,636	78,592	37,069
2000	9,694	(14,101)	(63,009)	30,796	19,831	(17,163)	89,250	119,418	122,556	55,643	67,319	7,025
2005	4,568	(26,617)	(98,624)	26,077	8,112	(50,699)	86,938	112,854	99,684	46,358	51,419	(36,008)
2010	877	(36,297)	(134,962)	23,151	(384)	(84,051)	86,460	107,288	77,735	40,303	39,840	(73,146)
2015	559	(39,874)	(163,106)	24,022	(2,160)	(108,901)	90,712	111,348	68,199	39,693	38,667	(95,554)
2020	487	(42,405)	(193,569)	25,142	(2,930)	(136,837)	95,447	116,724	54,350	40,479	39,734	(119,515)
2025	(4,635)	(54,126)	(234,692)	20,728	(13,611)	(176,545)	93,383	110,266	23,146	33,096	27,269	(163,938)
2030	(4,092)	(56,174)	(248,512)	22,476	(13,781)	(187,276)	99,276	116,958	24,216	36,517	29,424	(173,504)
2035	(2,159)	(55,441)	(254,222)	25,686	(10,995)	(189,599)	106,277	125,789	31,736	42,313	34,675	(174,192)
2040	(549)	(55,631)	(261,436)	28,710	(8,875)	(193,130)	113,152	134,040	37,568	46,903	38,678	(177,758)
2045	935	(56,293)	(271,370)	31,766	(6,940)	(198,994)	120,786	143,516	43,283	51,224	43,275	(182,762)
2050	2,516	(56,885)	(282,487)	35,056	(4,745)	(205,858)	129,408	154,640	50,658	56,260	49,191	(187,044)

Notes: All amounts are in constant 1993 dollars, adjusted to present value at age 65 using 2 percent real interest rate. Adjusts for chance of death in all years after age 21.

Table A.7 NET OASI TRANSFER AS PERCENTAGE OF LIFETIME EARNED INCOME

Year cohort turns 65	Single Male			Single Female			One-earner Couple			Two-earner couple		
	Low	Average	High	Low	Average	High	Low	Average	High	Low/Low	Avg/Low	High/Avg
1940	4.19	2.64	1.52	5.38	3.38	1.94	7.08	4.45	2.56	4.79	3.55	2.09
1945	5.96	3.36	1.70	8.00	4.53	2.30	10.99	6.29	3.23	6.99	4.87	2.54
1950	7.21	4.00	1.82	10.15	5.69	2.65	14.37	8.16	3.88	8.70	6.07	2.99
1955	8.29	5.19	2.20	12.04	7.64	3.35	17.71	11.24	5.08	10.19	7.87	3.90
1960	8.04	5.06	2.35	12.40	8.01	3.90	19.21	12.47	6.21	10.39	8.41	4.28
1965	7.52	4.59	2.23	12.12	7.73	4.00	19.96	12.98	6.94	10.00	8.24	4.28
1970	7.97	4.22	2.27	13.29	7.58	4.40	22.57	13.59	8.27	11.05	8.46	4.58
1975	6.78	3.67	2.31	11.65	7.03	4.77	21.51	13.67	9.59	9.97	8.10	4.72
1980	6.25	3.52	2.52	10.88	6.96	5.38	21.19	14.24	11.33	9.76	8.15	5.17
1985	3.38	1.15	0.43	6.78	3.67	2.65	15.72	10.27	8.48	6.48	5.33	2.85
1990	3.14	0.72	-0.29	6.59	3.27	1.98	16.06	10.34	8.31	6.28	5.16	2.46
1995	2.00	-0.37	-1.71	5.14	1.95	0.29	14.20	8.74	6.19	4.89	3.83	1.02
2000	1.46	-0.95	-2.55	4.50	1.31	-0.67	13.42	8.08	4.95	4.13	3.11	0.18
2005	0.66	-1.72	-3.51	3.64	0.51	-1.74	12.48	7.29	3.55	3.28	2.27	-0.82
2010	0.12	-2.26	-4.23	3.11	-0.02	-2.54	11.96	6.68	2.43	2.75	1.69	-1.51
2015	0.08	-2.43	-4.65	3.15	-0.13	-3.00	12.29	6.79	1.94	2.65	1.61	-1.84
2020	0.06	-2.53	-5.05	3.23	-0.17	-3.45	12.67	6.97	1.42	2.64	1.62	-2.15
2025	-0.59	-3.10	-5.64	2.54	-0.75	-4.10	11.87	6.31	0.56	2.07	1.06	-2.75
2030	-0.50	-3.07	-5.67	2.64	-0.73	-4.13	12.06	6.39	0.55	2.18	1.10	-2.77
2035	-0.25	-2.89	-5.54	2.88	-0.55	-4.00	12.32	6.56	0.69	2.41	1.23	-2.65
2040	-0.06	-2.75	-5.42	3.06	-0.43	-3.88	12.43	6.63	0.78	2.54	1.31	-2.57
2045	0.10	-2.64	-5.34	3.21	-0.32	-3.80	12.57	6.72	0.85	2.63	1.38	-2.51
2050	0.25	-2.52	-5.26	3.36	-0.20	-3.73	12.76	6.86	0.94	2.73	1.49	-2.43

Notes: All amounts are adjusted for inflation and interest at 2 percent real interest rate. Adjusts for chance of death in all years after age 21.

Table A.8 OASI LIFETIME BENEFIT-TO-TAX RATIO

Year cohort turns 65	Single Male			Single Female			One-earner Couple			Two-earner couple		
	Low	Average	High	Low	Average	High	Low	Average	High	Low/Low	Avg/Low	High/Avg
1940	51.06	32.52	18.78	60.66	38.49	22.01	85.56	54.20	30.86	56.09	42.38	25.06
1945	23.89	13.89	8.39	29.81	17.31	10.40	43.20	25.15	15.06	26.99	19.31	11.43
1950	16.61	9.66	5.98	21.83	12.67	7.89	32.11	18.67	11.61	19.33	13.92	8.45
1955	11.52	7.58	4.84	15.55	10.23	6.62	23.47	15.25	9.89	13.61	10.82	7.00
1960	7.47	5.07	3.67	10.56	7.17	5.25	16.44	11.02	8.06	9.18	7.67	5.22
1965	4.96	3.42	2.66	7.14	4.92	3.87	11.51	7.83	6.17	6.16	5.29	3.75
1970	3.96	2.57	2.12	5.77	3.72	3.09	9.38	6.04	5.09	5.03	4.11	2.99
1975	2.87	2.01	1.77	4.13	2.89	2.55	6.93	4.77	4.22	3.71	3.22	2.44
1980	2.37	1.77	1.59	3.33	2.49	2.24	5.64	4.12	3.68	3.11	2.77	2.17
1985	1.63	1.22	1.08	2.25	1.67	1.47	3.94	2.92	2.54	2.20	1.99	1.52
1990	1.50	1.11	0.96	2.04	1.51	1.29	3.56	2.65	2.22	2.00	1.82	1.37
1995	1.28	0.95	0.78	1.71	1.27	1.04	2.97	2.21	1.79	1.68	1.53	1.13
2000	1.18	0.88	0.71	1.56	1.16	0.92	2.67	2.01	1.57	1.51	1.39	1.02
2005	1.07	0.81	0.62	1.41	1.06	0.81	2.41	1.82	1.38	1.37	1.26	0.91
2010	1.01	0.76	0.57	1.33	1.00	0.74	2.27	1.71	1.25	1.29	1.18	0.84
2015	1.01	0.76	0.54	1.32	0.99	0.70	2.24	1.68	1.19	1.27	1.16	0.82
2020	1.01	0.75	0.51	1.31	0.98	0.67	2.23	1.68	1.14	1.26	1.16	0.79
2025	0.94	0.71	0.47	1.24	0.93	0.61	2.12	1.60	1.05	1.20	1.10	0.74
2030	0.95	0.71	0.47	1.25	0.93	0.61	2.13	1.60	1.05	1.20	1.10	0.74
2035	0.98	0.73	0.48	1.27	0.95	0.63	2.15	1.61	1.06	1.23	1.12	0.75
2040	0.99	0.74	0.49	1.29	0.96	0.64	2.17	1.62	1.07	1.24	1.12	0.76
2045	1.01	0.75	0.50	1.30	0.97	0.64	2.18	1.63	1.08	1.25	1.13	0.76
2050	1.02	0.76	0.51	1.32	0.98	0.65	2.20	1.64	1.09	1.26	1.14	0.77

Notes: All amounts are adjusted for inflation and interest at 2 percent real interest rate. Adjusts for chance of death in all years after age 21.

Table A.9 REAL LIFETIME INTERNAL RATE OF RETURN FROM OASI PROGRAM

Year cohort turns 65	Single Male			Single Female			One-earner Couple			Two-earner couple		
	Low	Average	High	Low	Average	High	Low	Average	High	Low/Low	Avg/Low	High/Avg
1940	145.41	114.49	84.42	147.66	123.05	86.17	169.24	135.06	101.66	146.60	126.68	95.14
1945	39.85	31.28	23.87	41.29	33.92	25.25	46.36	37.42	29.52	40.62	35.18	27.15
1950	23.98	19.24	14.43	25.43	21.28	15.87	28.28	23.48	18.46	24.76	21.75	16.94
1955	18.17	15.24	11.20	19.52	16.98	12.58	21.80	18.80	14.64	18.90	17.05	13.51
1960	13.14	10.97	8.45	14.52	12.63	9.86	17.02	14.64	11.87	14.25	13.00	10.32
1965	9.95	8.13	6.38	11.32	9.76	7.78	14.28	12.05	9.98	11.23	10.16	8.13
1970	8.25	6.37	5.19	9.58	7.96	6.55	12.62	10.29	8.83	9.77	8.55	6.84
1975	6.44	5.00	4.30	7.68	6.48	5.56	10.86	8.85	7.81	8.13	7.16	5.76
1980	5.33	4.24	3.78	6.43	5.54	4.91	9.18	7.66	6.94	6.95	6.16	5.05
1985	3.82	2.73	2.30	4.87	3.99	3.46	7.51	6.20	5.76	5.37	4.76	3.69
1990	3.45	2.39	1.82	4.42	3.55	2.95	6.83	5.66	5.24	4.78	4.30	3.26
1995	2.83	1.82	1.05	3.73	2.89	2.13	5.85	4.79	4.26	3.92	3.54	2.48
2000	2.54	1.59	0.72	3.37	2.56	1.72	5.25	4.31	3.65	3.43	3.11	2.07
2005	2.22	1.32	0.35	3.02	2.26	1.32	4.77	3.91	3.11	3.04	2.74	1.68
2010	2.04	1.16	0.11	2.82	2.09	1.05	4.50	3.64	2.72	2.82	2.52	1.45
2015	2.02	1.16	0.03	2.78	2.06	0.94	4.41	3.56	2.55	2.74	2.46	1.37
2020	2.02	1.15	-0.07	2.77	2.05	0.81	4.39	3.54	2.39	2.71	2.45	1.29
2025	1.83	0.97	-0.30	2.60	1.89	0.60	4.21	3.38	2.15	2.55	2.29	1.10
2030	1.86	1.00	-0.25	2.61	1.90	0.62	4.20	3.37	2.15	2.57	2.29	1.11
2035	1.93	1.07	-0.19	2.67	1.94	0.67	4.24	3.40	2.18	2.62	2.33	1.15
2040	1.98	1.12	-0.13	2.70	1.97	0.71	4.25	3.41	2.20	2.65	2.34	1.18
2045	2.03	1.16	-0.08	2.73	2.00	0.75	4.25	3.42	2.22	2.67	2.36	1.21
2050	2.07	1.21	-0.03	2.76	2.03	0.78	4.27	3.43	2.24	2.69	2.39	1.24

Notes: Table adjusts for inflation and chance of death in all years after age 21.

Table A.10 LIFETIME MEDICARE BENEFITS, TAXES, AND PREMIUMS (IN THOUSANDS OF CONSTANT 1993 DOLLARS)

Year cohort turns 65	Single Male			Single Female			One-earner Couple			Two-earner couple		
	Low wage	Avg. wage	High wage	Low wage	Avg. wage	High wage	Low wage	Avg. wage	High wage	Low & low	Avg. & low	High & avg.
1980												
HI payroll tax	2.0	4.4	6.6	2.2	4.9	7.4	2.0	4.4	6.6	4.2	6.6	11.5
SMI premiums	5.5	5.5	5.5	10.6	10.6	10.6	16.1	16.1	16.1	16.1	16.1	16.1
Income tax for SMI	0.1	0.6	1.1	0.1	0.6	1.2	0.1	0.5	1.1	0.4	0.8	1.9
Total taxes & premiums	7.6	10.5	13.2	13.0	16.1	19.2	18.2	21.1	23.8	20.7	23.5	29.5
Total Medicare benefits	32.7	32.7	32.7	53.8	53.8	53.8	86.5	86.5	86.5	86.5	86.5	86.5
1995												
HI payroll tax	7.4	16.4	32.7	7.8	17.4	34.8	7.4	16.4	32.7	15.2	24.3	50.1
SMI premiums	15.1	15.1	15.1	24.8	24.8	24.8	39.9	39.9	39.9	39.9	39.9	39.9
Income tax for SMI	0.8	3.2	9.8	0.9	3.4	10.6	0.2	2.6	9.0	1.9	4.3	14.6
Total taxes & premiums	23.3	34.7	57.6	33.5	45.6	70.2	47.5	59.0	81.7	57.1	68.5	104.6
Total Medicare benefits	75.0	75.0	75.0	110.7	110.7	110.7	185.7	185.7	185.7	185.7	185.7	185.7
2010												
HI payroll tax	18.5	41.1	89.1	19.3	42.8	93.1	18.5	41.1	89.1	37.8	60.4	131.9
SMI premiums	25.6	25.6	25.6	38.4	38.4	38.4	64.0	64.0	64.0	64.0	64.0	64.0
Income tax for SMI	3.2	11.4	40.1	3.4	12.0	42.4	0.5	8.7	34.6	6.7	15.0	56.2
Total taxes & premiums	47.3	78.1	154.7	61.0	93.3	173.8	83.0	113.8	187.6	108.4	139.4	252.1
Total Medicare benefits	124.7	124.7	124.7	171.4	171.4	171.4	296.1	296.1	296.1	296.1	296.1	296.1
2030												
HI payroll tax	40.2	89.3	213.2	42.0	93.4	223.1	40.2	89.3	213.2	87.5	140.9	329.2
SMI premiums	35.8	35.8	35.8	52.8	52.8	52.8	88.6	88.6	88.6	88.6	88.6	88.6
Income tax for SMI	11.2	35.7	134.0	11.8	37.5	140.7	2.6	26.8	113.0	21.0	46.8	182.1
Total taxes & premiums	87.2	160.8	383.0	106.6	183.7	416.6	131.4	204.6	414.8	197.0	276.2	599.8
Total Medicare benefits	179.8	179.8	179.8	242.9	242.9	242.9	422.7	422.7	422.7	422.7	422.7	422.7

Notes: All amounts are converted to present value at age 65 using 2 percent real interest rate. Adjusts for chance of death in all years after age 21. Projections based on HCFA 1993 intermediate assumptions, adjusted by authors for estimated impact of 1993 enactments. Assumes HI payroll taxes are set at rates necessary to keep system solvent on a pay-as-you-go basis after 1995. Assumes SMI premiums remain tied to 25 percent of program costs after 1995. Assumes all SMI costs not covered by premiums are paid for through the income tax.

Table A.11.A EFFECT OF VARIOUS RETIREMENT DECISIONS ON VALUE OF OASI FOR COHORT TURNING 65 IN 1995: AVERAGE-WAGE MALE (IN THOUSANDS OF CONSTANT 1993 DOLLARS)

	BASELINE	Early Retirement		ALTERNATIVE RETIREMENT OPTIONS							
	Normal Retirement			Delayed Retirement Under Current Law (4.5% Annual DRC)				Delayed Retirement If the DRC Were Increased to 8%			
Stops Working at Age:	65	62	65	67	67	70	70	67	67	70	70
Registers to Begin Collecting Benefits at Age:	65	62	62	65	67	65	70	65	67	65	70
(A) Baseline: Total expected benefit, normal retirement (age 65)	109.5										
(B) Gain or loss that would result from change in the number of years of benefits. (Before the impact of any of the effects listed below).	0.0	27.7	27.7	0.0	-16.6	0.0	-38.7	0.0	-16.6	0.0	-38.7
(C) Effect of retirement test	0.0	0.0	-22.0	-7.6	0.0	-18.0	0.0	-7.6	0.0	-18.0	0.0
(D) Effect of AIME recalculation	0.0	-1.0	-0.2	0.9	0.9	2.7	2.3	0.9	0.9	2.7	2.3
(E) Effect of early retirement penalty (-) or delayed retirement credit (+)	0.0	-27.3	-5.5	4.3	8.4	9.6	16.5	7.6	15.0	16.6	29.3
(F) Effect of income tax on OASI benefits	0.0			-0.5	0.0	-1.7	0.0	-0.7	0.0	-1.9	0.0
(G) Total expected benefits (A+B+C+D+E+F)	109.5	109.0	109.5	106.7	102.3	102.1	89.7	109.8	108.9	109.0	102.5
(H) Change in benefits caused by deviation from normal retirement age	0.0	-0.5	0.0	-2.8	-7.3	-7.4	-19.9	0.2	-0.7	-0.5	-7.1
(I) Lifetime OASI tax contributions	103.4	96.2	103.4	107.8	107.8	113.6	113.6	107.8	107.8	113.6	113.6
(J) Change in contributions caused by deviation from normal retirement age	0.0	-7.2	0.0	4.3	4.3	10.2	10.2	4.3	4.3	10.2	10.2
(K) Net lifetime transfer from the OASI system (G-I)	6.1	12.8	6.1	-1.0	-5.5	-11.5	-24.0	2.0	1.1	-4.6	-11.2
(L) Change in net lifetime OASI transfer caused by Deviation from normal retirement age (K-K1)	0.0	6.7	0.0	-7.2	-11.6	-17.6	-30.1	-4.1	-5.0	-10.7	-17.3
(M) OASI taxes paid and benefits lost due to working past age 65, as a % of expected work earnings	-	-	-	17.6%	28.5%	18.4%	31.4%	10.1%	12.3%	11.2%	18.0%

Notes: All amounts discounted to present value at age 62 assuming 2 percent real interest rate. Includes both employer and employee portions of OASI payroll tax.

DRC = delayed retirement credit.

Table A.11.B EFFECT OF VARIOUS RETIREMENT DECISIONS ON VALUE OF OASI FOR COHORT TURNING 65 IN 1995: HIGH-WAGE MALE (IN THOUSANDS OF CONSTANT 1993 DOLLARS)

	BASELINE	Early Retirement		ALTERNATIVE RETIREMENT OPTIONS							
	Normal Retirement			Delayed Retirement Under Current Law (4.5% Annual DRC)				Delayed Retirement If the DRC Were Increased to 8%			
Stops Working at Age:	65	62	65	67	67	70	70	67	67	70	70
Registers to Begin Collecting Benefits at Age:	65	62	62	65	67	65	70	65	67	65	70
(A) Baseline: Total expected benefit, normal retirement (age 65)	152.9										
(B) Gain or loss that would result from change in the number of years of benefits. (Before the impact of any of the effects listed below).	0.0	38.7	38.7	0.0	-23.2	0.0	-54.0	0.0	-23.2	0.0	-54.0
(C) Effect of retirement test	0.0	0.0	-30.0	-24.9	0.0	-61.1	0.0	-26.0	0.0	-62.5	0.0
(D) Effect of AIME recalculation	0.0	-6.2	-1.2	3.3	3.2	8.0	6.7	3.3	3.2	8.0	6.7
(E) Effect of early retirement penalty (-) or delayed retirement credit (+)	0.0	-37.1	-7.5	13.5	12.0	30.8	23.8	24.0	21.3	53.0	42.2
(F) Effect of income tax on OASI benefits				0.0	0.0	-0.2	0.0	0.0	0.0	-0.7	0.0
(G) Total expected benefits (A+B+C+D+E+F)	152.9	148.3	152.9	144.9	144.9	130.4	129.4	154.2	154.2	150.7	147.9
(H) Change in benefits caused by deviation from normal retirement age	0.0	-4.6	0.0	-8.0	-8.0	-22.5	-23.5	1.3	1.3	-2.2	-5.0
(I) Lifetime OASI tax contributions	178.5	160.8	178.5	189.0	189.0	203.2	203.2	189.0	189.0	203.2	203.2
(J) Change in contributions caused by deviation from normal retirement age	0.0	-17.7	0.0	10.5	10.5	24.7	24.7	10.5	10.5	24.7	24.7
(K) Net lifetime transfer from the OASI system (G-I)	-25.6	-12.5	-25.6	-44.2	-44.2	-72.8	-73.8	-34.8	-34.8	-52.5	-55.4
(L) Change in net lifetime OASI transfer caused by Deviation from normal retirement age (K-K1)	0.0	13.1	0.0	-18.5	-18.5	-47.2	-48.2	-9.2	-9.2	-26.9	-29.7
(M) OASI taxes paid and benefits lost due to working past age 65, as a % of expected work earnings	-	-	-	18.8%	18.8%	20.3%	20.8%	9.3%	9.4%	11.6%	12.8%

Notes: All amounts discounted to present value at age 62 assuming 2 percent real interest rate. Includes both employer and employee portions of OASI payroll tax.
DRC = delayed retirement credit.

Table A.11.C EFFECT OF VARIOUS RETIREMENT DECISIONS ON VALUE OF OASI FOR COHORT TURNING 65 IN 1995: LOW-WAGE MALE (IN THOUSANDS OF CONSTANT 1993 DOLLARS)

	BASELINE	Early Retirement		ALTERNATIVE RETIREMENT OPTIONS							
	Normal Retirement			Delayed Retirement Under Current Law (4.5% Annual DRC)				Delayed Retirement If the DRC Were Increased to 8%			
Stops Working at Age:	65	62	65	67	67	70	70	67	67	70	70
Registers to Begin Collecting Benefits at Age:	65	62	62	65	67	65	70	65	67	65	70
(A) Baseline: Total expected benefit, normal retirement (age 65)	66.4										
(B) Gain or loss that would result from change in the number of years of benefits. (Before the impact of any of the effects listed below).	0.0	16.8	16.8	0.0	-10.1	0.0	-23.4	0.0	-10.1	0.0	-23.4
(C) Effect of retirement test	0.0	0.0	-4.1	-0.1	0.0	-0.4	0.0	-0.1	0.0	-0.4	0.0
(D) Effect of AIME recalculation	0.0	-0.4	-0.1	0.4	0.4	1.2	1.0	0.4	0.4	1.2	1.0
(E) Effect of early retirement penalty (-) or delayed retirement credit (+)	0.0	-16.5	-12.6	0.1	5.1	0.2	9.9	0.1	9.1	0.4	17.6
(F) Effect of income tax on OASI benefits				0.0	0.0	0.0	0.0	0.0	0.0	0.0	0.0
(G) Total expected benefits (A+B+C+D+E+F)	66.4	66.2	66.5	66.7	61.8	67.4	53.9	66.8	65.8	67.6	61.6
(H) Change in benefits caused by deviation from normal retirement age	0.0	-0.2	0.1	0.4	-4.6	1.0	-12.5	0.4	-0.6	1.2	-4.8
(I) Lifetime OASI tax contributions	46.5	43.3	46.5	48.5	48.5	51.1	51.1	48.5	48.5	51.1	51.1
(J) Change in contributions caused by deviation from normal retirement age	0.0	-3.2	0.0	2.0	2.0	4.6	4.6	2.0	2.0	4.6	4.6
(K) Net lifetime transfer from the OASI system (G-I)	19.8	22.9	19.9	18.3	13.3	16.3	2.8	18.3	17.3	16.5	10.5
(L) Change in net lifetime OASI transfer caused by Deviation from normal retirement age (K-K1)	0.0	3.1	0.1	-1.6	-6.5	-3.6	-17.1	-1.5	-2.5	-3.4	-9.4
(M) OASI taxes paid and benefits lost due to working past age 65, as a % of expected work earnings				8.7%	35.5%	8.3%	39.6%	8.3%	13.8%	7.8%	21.8%

Notes: All amounts discounted to present value at age 62 assuming 2 percent real interest rate. Includes both employer and employee portions of OASI payroll tax.

DRC = delayed retirement credit.

Table A.11.D EFFECT OF VARIOUS RETIREMENT DECISIONS ON VALUE OF OASI FOR COHORT TURNING 65 IN 1995: AVERAGE-WAGE FEMALE (IN THOUSANDS OF CONSTANT 1993 DOLLARS)

	BASELINE Normal Retirement	Early Retirement		ALTERNATIVE RETIREMENT OPTIONS Delayed Retirement Under Current Law (4.5% Annual DRC)				Delayed Retirement If the DRC Were Increased to 8%			
Stops Working at Age:	65	62	65	67	67	70	70	67	67	70	70
Registers to Begin Collecting Benefits at Age:	65	62	62	65	67	65	70	65	67	65	70
(A) Baseline: Total expected benefit, normal retirement (age 65)	138.9										
(B) Gain or loss that would result from change in the number of years of benefits. (Before the impact of any of the effects listed below).	0.0	28.2	28.2	0.0	-17.3	0.0	-40.9	0.0	-17.3	0.0	-40.9
(C) Effect of retirement test	0.0	0.0	-22.4	-7.9	0.0	-19.1	0.0	-7.9	0.0	-19.1	0.0
(D) Effect of AIME recalculation	0.0	-1.2	-0.2	1.2	1.2	3.6	3.2	1.2	1.2	3.6	3.2
(E) Effect of early retirement penalty (-) or delayed retirement credit (+)	0.0	-33.2	-5.6	5.5	11.1	12.5	22.8	9.8	19.7	21.7	40.5
(F) Effect of income tax on OASI benefits				-0.5	0.0	-1.8	0.0	-0.8	0.0	-2.0	0.0
(G) Total expected benefits (A+B+C+D+E+F)	138.9	132.7	138.9	137.3	133.9	134.2	124.0	141.2	142.5	143.3	141.7
(H) Change in benefits caused by deviation from normal retirement age	0.0	-6.2	0.0	-1.7	-5.0	-4.7	-14.9	2.3	3.6	4.4	2.8
(I) Lifetime OASI tax contributions	103.5	96.2	103.5	108.0	108.0	114.3	114.3	108.0	108.0	114.3	114.3
(J) Change in contributions caused by deviation from normal retirement age	0.0	-7.3	0.0	4.5	4.5	10.8	10.8	4.5	4.5	10.8	10.8
(K) Net lifetime transfer from the OASI system (G-I)	35.4	36.5	35.4	29.2	25.8	19.9	9.7	33.2	34.4	28.9	27.4
(L) Change in net lifetime OASI transfer caused by Deviation from normal retirement age (K-K1)	0.0	1.1	0.0	-6.2	-9.6	-15.5	-25.7	-2.2	-1.0	-6.4	-8.0
(M) OASI taxes paid and benefits lost due to working past age 65, as a % of expected work earnings	-	-	-	14.6%	22.5%	15.3%	25.4%	5.2%	2.3%	6.4%	7.9%

Notes: All amounts discounted to present value at age 62 assuming 2 percent real interest rate. Includes both employer and employee portions of OASI payroll tax.

DRC = delayed retirement credit.

Table A.11.E EFFECT OF VARIOUS RETIREMENT DECISIONS ON VALUE OF OASI FOR COHORT TURNING 65 IN 1995: HIGH-WAGE FEMALE (IN THOUSANDS OF CONSTANT 1993 DOLLARS)

	BASELINE	Early Retirement		ALTERNATIVE RETIREMENT OPTIONS							
	Normal Retirement			Delayed Retirement Under Current Law (4.5% Annual DRC)				Delayed Retirement If the DRC Were Increased to 8%			
Stops Working at Age:	65	62	65	67	67	70	70	67	67	70	70
Registers to Begin Collecting Benefits at Age:	65	62	62	65	67	65	70	65	67	65	70
(A) Baseline: Total expected benefit, normal retirement (age 65)	193.9										
(B) Gain or loss that would result from change in the number of years of benefits. (Before the impact of any of the effects listed below).	0.0	39.3	39.3	0.0	-24.1	0.0	-57.1	0.0	-24.1	0.0	-57.1
(C) Effect of retirement test	0.0	0.0	-30.4	-25.9	0.0	-64.7	0.0	-27.1	0.0	-66.1	0.0
(D) Effect of AIME recalculation	0.0	-7.5	-1.3	4.3	4.2	10.7	9.3	4.3	4.2	10.7	9.3
(E) Effect of early retirement penalty (-) or delayed retirement credit (+)	0.0	-45.1	-7.6	17.3	15.7	40.3	32.9	30.7	27.8	69.3	58.4
(F) Effect of income tax on OASI benefits				0.0	0.0	-0.2	0.0	0.0	0.0	-0.8	0.0
(G) Total expected benefits (A+B+C+D+E+F)	193.9	180.5	193.9	189.6	189.6	180.0	178.9	201.8	201.8	206.9	204.5
(H) Change in benefits caused by deviation from normal retirement age	0.0	-13.3	0.0	-4.3	-4.3	-13.9	-15.0	8.0	7.9	13.0	10.6
(I) Lifetime OASI tax contributions	178.8	160.8	178.8	189.7	189.7	204.9	204.9	189.7	189.7	204.9	204.9
(J) Change in contributions caused by deviation from normal retirement age	0.0	-17.9	0.0	10.9	10.9	26.1	26.1	10.9	10.9	26.1	26.1
(K) Net lifetime transfer from the OASI system (G-I)	15.1	19.7	15.1	-0.1	-0.1	-24.9	-26.0	12.1	12.0	2.0	-0.5
(L) Change in net lifetime OASI transfer caused by Deviation from normal retirement age (K-K1)	0.0	4.6	0.0	-15.2	-15.2	-40.0	-41.1	-3.0	-3.0	-13.1	-15.5
(M) OASI taxes paid and benefits lost due to working past age 65, as a % of expected work earnings	-	-	-	14.8%	14.8%	16.3%	16.7%	2.9%	3.0%	5.3%	6.3%

Notes: All amounts discounted to present value at age 62 assuming 2 percent real interest rate. Includes both employer and employee portions of OASI payroll tax.
DRC = delayed retirement credit.

Table A.11.F EFFECT OF VARIOUS RETIREMENT DECISIONS ON VALUE OF OASI FOR COHORT TURNING 65 IN 1995: LOW-WAGE FEMALE (IN THOUSANDS OF CONSTANT 1993 DOLLARS)

	BASELINE	ALTERNATIVE RETIREMENT OPTIONS										
	Normal Retirement	Early Retirement		Delayed Retirement Under Current Law (4.5% Annual DRC)				Delayed Retirement If the DRC Were Increased to 8%			
Stops Working at Age:	65	62	65	67	67	70	70	67	67	70	70
Registers to Begin Collecting Benefits at Age:	65	62	62	65	67	65	70	65	67	65	70
(A) Baseline: Total expected benefit, normal retirement (age 65)	84.2										
(B) Gain or loss that would result from change in the number of years of benefits. (Before the impact of any of the effects listed below).	0.0	17.1	17.1	0.0	-10.5	0.0	-24.8	0.0	-10.5	0.0	-24.8
(C) Effect of retirement test	0.0	0.0	-4.2	-0.1	0.0	-0.5	0.0	-0.1	0.0	-0.5	0.0
(D) Effect of AIME recalculation	0.0	-0.5	-0.1	0.5	0.5	1.6	1.5	0.5	0.5	1.6	1.5
(E) Effect of early retirement penalty (-) or delayed retirement credit (+)	0.0	-20.1	-15.1	0.1	6.7	0.3	13.7	0.2	11.9	0.6	24.3
(F) Effect of income tax on OASI benefits	0.0	0.0	0.0	0.0	0.0	0.0	0.0	0.0	0.0	0.0	0.0
(G) Total expected benefits (A+B+C+D+E+F)	84.2	80.6	81.9	84.7	80.9	85.7	74.5	84.8	86.1	85.9	85.2
(H) Change in benefits caused by deviation from normal retirement age	0.0	-3.6	-2.3	0.5	-3.3	1.5	-9.7	0.6	1.9	1.7	1.0
(I) Lifetime OASI tax contributions	46.6	43.3	46.6	48.6	48.6	51.4	51.4	48.6	48.6	51.4	51.4
(J) Change in contributions caused by deviation from normal retirement age	0.0	-3.3	0.0	2.0	2.0	4.9	4.9	2.0	2.0	4.9	4.9
(K) Net lifetime transfer from the OASI system (G-I)	37.6	37.3	35.3	36.1	32.3	34.2	23.1	36.1	37.5	34.5	33.7
(L) Change in net lifetime OASI transfer caused by Deviation from normal retirement age (K-K1)	0.0	-0.3	-2.3	-1.5	-5.3	-3.4	-14.5	-1.4	-0.1	-3.1	-3.9
(M) OASI taxes paid and benefits lost due to working past age 65, as a % of expected work earnings		-	-	8.0%	27.7%	7.4%	31.8%	7.6%	0.5%	6.9%	8.5%

Notes: All amounts discounted to present value at age 62 assuming 2 percent real interest rate. Includes both employer and employee portions of OASI payroll tax.

DRC = delayed retirement credit.

Table A.12 LIFETIME OASI BENEFITS, TAXES, AND TRANSFERS UNDER 1992 TAX LAW (IN THOUSANDS OF CONSTANT 1993 DOLLARS)

Year cohort turns 65		Single Male			Single Female			One-earner Couple			Two-earner Couple		
		Low wage	Avg. wage	High wage	Low wage	Avg. wage	High wage	Low wage	Avg. wage	High wage	Low & Low	Avg. & Low	High & Avg
1960	Benefits	30.1	45.5	50.6	45.7	69.0	76.7	66.3	98.9	111.0	76.8	102.0	122.1
	Taxes	4.0	9.0	13.8	4.3	9.6	14.6	4.0	9.0	13.8	8.4	13.3	23.4
	Net Transfer	26.1	36.5	36.8	41.4	59.4	62.1	62.3	89.9	97.2	68.4	88.7	98.7
1980	Benefits	54.3	90.2	114.6	80.8	134.3	170.5	129.3	209.9	264.3	146.9	208.4	273.2
	Taxes	22.9	51.0	71.9	24.2	53.9	76.1	22.9	51.0	71.9	47.2	75.2	125.7
	Net Transfer	31.4	39.3	42.7	56.6	80.5	94.4	106.4	158.9	192.4	99.7	133.3	147.5
1995	Benefits	58.0	95.7	133.6	80.6	132.9	185.5	134.9	223.4	305.4	155.2	226.6	312.6
	Taxes	45.5	101.0	171.2	47.3	105.1	179.6	45.5	101.0	171.2	92.7	148.3	276.2
	Net Transfer	12.5	-5.4	-37.6	33.3	27.9	5.9	89.4	122.3	134.2	62.4	78.3	36.3
2010	Benefits	69.0	115.2	175.9	93.6	156.1	238.4	154.6	258.8	388.6	178.9	261.7	394.2
	Taxes	69.0	153.4	315.5	71.3	158.5	327.4	69.0	153.4	315.5	140.4	224.8	474.1
	Net Transfer	0.0	-38.2	-139.6	22.2	-2.5	-89.0	85.6	105.3	73.1	38.5	37.0	-79.9
2030	Benefits	84.0	139.6	220.3	113.7	189.0	298.1	187.4	312.8	493.0	215.9	316.5	498.1
	Taxes	90.6	201.3	481.8	93.8	208.5	499.0	90.6	201.3	481.8	184.4	295.1	690.3
	Net Transfer	-6.5	-61.6	-261.6	19.9	-19.4	-200.8	96.8	111.5	11.2	31.5	21.4	-192.2

Notes: All amounts are discounted to present value at age 65 using 2 percent real interest rate. Adjusts for chance of death in all years after age 21. Data reflect 1992 OASI tax law. Includes actuarial value of all OASI worker's, spousal, and survivors' benefits payable over a lifetime. Includes both employer and employee portions of OASI payroll tax. Couples are assumed to be the same age and to have two children born when parents are aged 25 and 30. Assumes retirement at OASI Normal Retirement Age. Projections based on intermediate assumptions in 1993 OASDI Board of Trustees report.

Table A.13 BASIC FEATURES OF OLD-AGE AND SURVIVORS' INSURANCE IN
SELECTED INDUSTRIALIZED NATIONS: JANUARY 1, 1991
(ALL AMOUNTS CONVERTED TO U.S. DOLLARS IN JANUARY 1991)

Australia

Old-age pension: All benefits are means-tested except for those paid
to the permanently blind. Benefit of up to $5,830 annually for singles
and $9,728 annually for couples. Survivor pension is the same as
the old-age pension. Rental assistance of up to $1,600 per year is
available. A $5,830 pension is also available for someone whose
primary responsibility is to take care of an elderly person ($4,860 if
it is the elderly person's spouse).

Normal retirement age: Age 65 for men and 60 for women.

Financing: All old-age, survivors', and disability benefits are financed
out of general revenues.

Canada

Old Age Security (OAS): A universal, flat-rate grant paid to all retirees
of about $3,650 per year.

Guaranteed Income Supplement (GIS): An income-tested supplement to the OAS. Raises the OAS benefit to about $7,990 for a single
person and $12,950 for a couple. Reduced by 50 cents for every dollar
of other income (except OAS) received by the elderly individual or
couple.

Canada and Quebec Pension Plan (C/QPP): An earnings-related pension that provides 25 percent of average wage-indexed earnings
between ages 18 and 64, disregarding 15 percent of years in which
earnings are lowest. Maximum benefit ceiling set equal to about the
average industrial wage. Allows years in which a person had a child
under age 7 to be dropped from the computation. Maximum pension
of about $6,220 per year.

Credit splitting for divorcées: A divorced couple can evenly split
credits earned by either spouse during the years they were married.

Voluntary pension splitting: A married couple may elect to split the
total of their C/QPP pensions equally while both are alive. This would
not change the total value of pension benefits going to the couple; it
merely rearranges the amounts written on the checks to each spouse.

Provisions for survivors: Survivor receives universal OAS and means-tested GIS in own right, regardless of when spouse dies. Earnings-related C/QPP provides survivor with a benefit of about 60 percent of insured person's pension, up to a maximum of about $3,730.

Normal retirement age: Age 65. Reduced benefits available for retirement between 60 and 64; credit available for those who delay retirement, up to age 70.

Financing: OAS and GIS are financed out of general revenues. C/QPP is financed by a payroll tax on earnings up to $26,140 of 4.6 percent split evenly between employee and employer. Earnings equal to 10 percent of ceiling are exempt from tax.

France

Earnings-related pension: Fifty percent of average wage-indexed earnings in 10 highest earning years after 1947. Minimum benefit is about $6,860, maximum is about $13,610.

Means-tested spousal supplement: Income-tested benefit for spouses of those eligible for the earnings-related pension. Maximum benefit equal to about $3,050 per year.

Old-age allowance ("Solidarity"): Income-tested benefit for low-income pensioners of approximately $4,110 for a single person and $6,740 for a couple.

Means-tested allowance: Benefit of about $3,050 per year for retired low-income workers who are ineligible for a pension.

Voluntary contribution for entitlement: Homemakers may make voluntary contributions to the earnings-related pension plan.

Special provisions for women: Earnings-related pension is increased by 10 percent if the insured person raised at least three children. An insured woman receives one-fourth of a year of insurance credit for each birth, and can receive two years of credit for each child raised during at least nine years. Single mothers and women who care for disabled family members also receive credits.

Provisions for survivors: Provides a benefit to a surviving spouse equal to 52 percent of the insured person's earnings-related pension, with a minimum of about $3,050.

Normal retirement age: Age 60 for those with 150 quarters of coverage; age 65 with reduction at ages 60–64 for those with less than 150 quarters of coverage. Recipient must have stopped work at preretirement firm, and earnings from other work are subject to a special tax.

Financing: All old-age, disability, and death benefits are financed through a payroll tax of 7.6 percent of pensionable earnings plus 0.1 percent of total earnings of employees, 8.2 percent of employer payroll, and 1.1 percent of total income form all sources (effective Feb. 2, 1991).

Germany (West)

Old-age pension: Provides an earnings-related benefit equal to 1.5 percent of average wage-indexed annual earnings times the number of years in which contributions were made (plus years of unemployment and schooling after age 16). For example, someone earning an average of $25,000 a year with 45 years of coverage would receive about $15,000 per year in pension benefits. The maximum benefit is about $22,400. Low-income workers with at least 25 years of coverage are treated as though their annual earnings were 75 percent of the average national wage for purposes of benefit calculation (effectively a minimum pension).

Credit splitting for divorcées: A divorced couple can evenly split credits earned by either spouse during the years they were married.

Special provisions for women: Maternity leave may be counted in the contributory pension period.

Voluntary contributions for homemakers: Homemakers may make voluntary contributions to the earnings-related pension plan.

Normal retirement age: Age 63 for those with 35 years of coverage, 65 for those with at least 5 years. Reduced to age 60 for those with 15 years of coverage who are unemployed 12 out of the last 18 months and who worked in covered employment for 8 out of the last 10 years. Age 60 for women with 15 years of coverage including 10 of the last 20.

Financing: All old-age, disability, and death benefits are financed by a payroll tax of 17.7 percent on earnings up to about $52,700 annually, split equally between employer and employee, plus a subsidy from general revenues.

Japan

National Pension Program: Provides a flat-rate benefit of about $5,400 per year to fully insured retired workers (40 years of contributions).

Employees' Pension Insurance: Earnings-related pension program, providing 0.75% of indexed monthly wages times the number of months of coverage (up to 420). For example, someone who earns $25,000 a year for 35 or more years gets about $6,500 per year in earnings-related pension benefits.

Spousal supplement: Flat-rate benefit of about $1,560 a year for a dependent spouse.

Provisions for survivors: Widow receives flat-rate benefit of about $5,400 per year. Earnings-related pension provides a lump sum of between $770 and $1,540, plus an annual benefit equal to 75 percent of pension payable to insured worker.

Normal retirement age: Age 65. Benefits are reduced for retirement at ages 60 to 64, and are increased for age 66 or over.

Financing: Old-age, disability, and death benefits financed mainly by a tax on earnings up to $48,900 annually, split evenly between employer and employee, of 14.5 percent for men and 14.15 percent for women. Earnings below $8,490 annually are exempt. Rates differ for some professions. General revenue subsidy pays for one-third of benefits plus administrative costs.

Sweden

Universal old-age pension: Provides a flat-rate benefit of about $5,570 a year to single retirees and $9,110 for a couple. Supplement of about $3,130 per year for those ineligible for the earnings-related pension.

Earnings-related old-age pension: Provides a benefit equal to 60 percent of the difference between average annual covered earnings and a base amount of about $5,800.

Partial pension: Sixty-five percent of income loss connected with changeover to part-time work.

Special provision for child-rearing: Male or female workers may have up to 3 years of child-rearing credited to the earnings-related pension.

Provisions for survivors: Elderly widows and widowers receive universal old-age pension of about $5,570, plus a supplement of $3,130 a year if ineligible for earnings-related pension. A means-tested housing supplement is also available. For those widowed in 1990 or later, a 1-year "adjustment pension" of 40 percent of the earnings-related pension of the deceased is available. After that, a special survivor pension will be paid only if illness or unemployment prevent self-support. Transition rules provide a minimum benefit of 50 percent of deceased's and own earnings-related pensions to women aged 60 and above and to women currently aged 45–49 becoming widows before reaching age 65.

Normal retirement age: Age 65. Reduced for retirement at ages 60 to 64 unless "unable to cope with job" or unemployed with no prospect of job. Partial pension available for reduced work schedule at ages 60–64.

Financing: Universal pension financed by employer contribution of 7.45 percent of payroll, plus a 25 percent subsidy from general revenues. Earnings-related pension financed by employer contribution of 13.0 percent of payroll, and partial pensions by employer contribution of 0.5 percent of payroll.

United Kingdom

Old-age pension, basic component: Universal flat-rate benefit of about $4,780 a year.

Old-age pension, earnings-related component: Annual benefit of 1.25 percent of average annual earnings per year since 1978, payable to those retiring since 1979. For example, someone retiring in 1990 who earned an average of $25,000 a year would get an earnings-related benefit of $3,750 (15 percent times $25,000).

Old persons' pension: Flat-rate benefit of about $2,880 per year, reduced by the amount of any private pensions.

Spousal supplement: Flat-rate benefit of about $2,880 per year.

Age addition: Supplement of about $25 a year if over age 80.

Invalid care allowance: Flat-rate benefit of about $2,880 a year.

Special provisions for child-rearing and invalid care: Male or female worker can take credits towards the earnings-related pension for child-rearing and caring for severely disabled adults.

Provisions for survivors: For widows 55 or older, a flat-rate survivor's benefit equal to basic component of the old-age pension (about $4,780 a year). Supplementary income-tested allowance.

Normal retirement age: Age 65 for men and 60 for women. Credit for delayed retirement.

Financing: Pensions are financed through a progressive tax schedule. Employee pays approximately 2 percent of wages up to $4,690, plus 9 percent of wages between $4,690 and $35,690. Employer pays at a graduated rate of between 5 percent and 10.45 percent, depending on employee's wage level. Government contributes about 5 percent of program costs plus full cost of income-tested allowances.

Sources: Adapted by authors from SSA (1992), with additional information from Reinhard (1988), Tracy (1988), and Wolfson (1988).

REFERENCES

Aaron, Henry J. 1991. *Serious and Unstable Condition: Financing America's Health Care.* Washington, D.C.: Brookings Institution.

————. 1982. *Economic Effects of Social Security.* Washington, D.C.: Brookings Institution.

————. 1977. "Demographic Effects on the Equity of Social Security Benefits." In *The Economics of Public Services,* edited by M. S. Feldstein and R. P. Inman. New York: Macmillan Co.

Aaron, Henry J., Barry P. Bosworth, and Gary Burtless. 1989. *Can America Afford to Grow Old? Paying for Social Security.* Washington, D.C.: Brookings Institution.

Achenbaum, W. Andrew. 1986. *Social Security: Visions and Revisions.* New York: Cambridge University Press.

————. 1978. *Old Age in the New Land: The American Experience since 1790.* Baltimore: Johns Hopkins University Press.

Acs, Gregory, and Eugene Steuerle. Forthcoming. "Trends in the Distribution of Nonwage Benefits and Total Compensation." Draft paper, Urban Institute, Washington, D.C., August, 1993.

Advisory Council on Social Security. 1991. *Social Security and the Future Financial Security of Women.* Washington, D.C.: U.S. Government Printing Office.

————. 1964. *The Status of the Social Security Program and Recommendations for Its Improvement.* Washington, D.C.: U.S. Government Printing Office.

————. 1949. *Final Report.* U.S. Senate Document 208, 80th Congress. Washington, D.C.: U.S. Government Printing Office.

————. 1939. *Final Report.* U.S. Senate Document 4, 76th Congress, Washington, D.C.: U.S. Government Printing Office.

Altmeyer, Arthur J. 1966. *Formative Years of Social Security.* Madison, Wis.: University of Wisconsin Press.

Anderson, Joseph M., David L. Kennell, and John F. Sheils. 1987. "Health Plan Costs, Medicare, and Employment of Older Workers." In *The Problem Isn't Age: Work and Older Americans*, edited by Steven H. Sandell. New York: Praeger Publishers.

Applebaum, Joseph A., and Orlo R. Nichols. 1983. *Some Comparisons of Workers' Social Security Taxes and Benefits*. U.S. Social Security Administration, Office of the Actuary. Photocopy.

Auerbach, Alan J., Jagadeesh Gokhale, and Laurence J. Kotlikoff. 1991a. "Generational Accounts: A Meaningful Alternative to Deficit Accounting." In *Tax Policy and the Economy*, vol. 5, edited by David Bradford (55–110). Cambridge, Mass.: National Bureau of Economic Research.

————. 1991b. "Social Security and Medicare Policy from the Perspective of Generational Accounting." *National Bureau of Economic Research Working Paper Series*, no. 3915. Cambridge, Mass.: National Bureau of Economic Research, November.

Auerbach, Alan J., and Laurence J. Kotlikoff. 1987. "Life Insurance of the Elderly: Adequacy and Determinants." In *Work, Health, and Income among the Elderly*, edited by Gary Burtless. Washington, D.C.: Brookings Institution.

Baily, Martin Neil. 1987. "Aging and the Ability to Work: Policy Issues and Recent Trends." In *Work, Health, and Income among the Elderly*, edited by Gary Burtless. Washington, D.C.: Brookings Institution.

Bakija, Jon, and Eugene Steuerle. 1993. *Social Security Disability Insurance: Fiscal Imbalance and Lifetime Value*. Urban Institute Project Report. Washington, D.C.: Urban Institute, April.

————. 1991. "Individual Income Taxation since 1948." *National Tax Journal* 44(4, Part 2, December): 451–75.

Ball, Robert. 1985. "The 1939 Amendments to the Social Security Act and What Followed." *Report of the Committee on Economic Security of 1935 and Other Basic Documents Relating to the Development of the Social Security Act—50th Anniversary Edition*. Washington, D.C.: National Conference on Social Welfare.

————. 1978. *Social Security Today and Tomorrow*. New York: Columbia University Press.

Baumol, William J., Sue Ann Batey Blackman, and Edward N. Wolff. 1989. *Productivity and American Leadership: The Long View*. Cambridge, Mass.: MIT Press.

Behrman, J., R. Sickles, P. Taubman, and A. Yazbeck. 1991. "Black-White Mortality Inequalities." *Journal of Econometrics* 50: 183–203.

Bernheim, B. Douglas. 1988. "Social Security Benefits: An Empirical Study of Expectations and Realizations." In *Issues in Contemporary Retirement*, edited by Rita Ricardo-Campbell and Edward P. Lazear (312–50). Stanford, Calif.: Hoover Institution Press.

Blinder, Alan S. 1988. "Why Is the Government in the Pension Business?" In *Social Security and Private Pensions: Providing Retirement in the Twenty-first Century*, edited by Susan M. Wachter (17–34). Lexington, Mass.: D.C. Heath & Co.

Blinder, Alan S., Roger H. Gordon, and Donald E. Wise. 1980. "Reconsidering the Work Disincentive Effects of Social Security." *National Tax Journal* 33(4, December): 431–42.

Board of Trustees, HI. *See* U.S. Board of Trustees of the Federal Hospital Insurance Trust Fund.

Board of Trustees, OASDI. *See* U.S. Board of Trustees of the Federal Old-Age and Survivors Insurance and Disability Insurance Trust Funds.

Board of Trustees, SMI. *See* U.S. Board of Trustees of the Federal Supplemental Medical Insurance Trust Fund.

Boaz, Rachel F. 1987. "Labor Market Behavior of Older Workers Approaching Retirement: A Summary of the Evidence from the 1970s." In *Social Security: A Critique of Radical Reform Proposals*, edited by Charles W. Meyer (103–26). Lexington, Mass.: D.C. Heath & Co.

Boskin, Michael J. 1986. *Too Many Promises: The Uncertain Future of Social Security*. Homewood, Ill.: Dow Jones Irwin.

Boskin, Michael J., Marcy Arvin, and Kenneth Cone. 1983. "Modeling Alternative Solutions to the Long-Run Social Security Funding Problem." In *Behavioral Simulation Methods in Tax Policy Analysis*, edited by Martin Feldstein. Chicago: University of Chicago Press.

Boskin, Michael J., and Michael Hurd. 1985. "Indexing Social Security: A Separate Price Index for the Elderly?" *Public Finance Quarterly* 13(4, October): 436–49.

Boskin, Michael J., Laurence J. Kotlikoff, Douglas J. Puffert, and John B. Shoven. 1987. "Social Security: A Financial Appraisal across and within Generations." *National Tax Journal* 40(1, March): 19–34.

Brocas, Anne-Marie, Anne-Marie Cailloux, and Virginie Oget. 1990. *Women and Social Security: Progress towards Equality of Treatment.* Geneva: International Labour Office.

Burkhauser, Richard V. 1980. "The Early Acceptance of Social Security: An Asset Maximization Approach." *Industrial and Labor Relations Review* 33(4): 484–92.

Burkhauser, Richard V., and Jennifer L. Warlick. 1981. "Disentangling the Annuity from the Redistributive Aspects of Social Security in the United States." *Review of Income and Wealth,* no. 27: 401–21.

Burtless, Gary. 1987. "Occupational Effects on the Health and Work Capacity of Older Men." In *Work, Health, and Income among the Elderly,* edited by Gary Burtless. Washington, D.C.: Brookings Institution.

———. 1986. "Social Security, Unanticipated Benefit Increases, and Timing of Retirement." *Review of Economic Studies,* no. 53 (November): 781–805.

Burtless, Gary, and Robert A. Moffitt. 1985. "The Joint Choice of Retirement Age and Postretirement Hours of Work." *Journal of Labor Economics,* 3(2): 209–36.

———. 1984. "The Effect of Social Security Benefits on the Labor Supply of the Aged." In *Retirement and Economic Behavior,* edited by Henry J. Aaron and Gary Burtless (135–74). Washington, D.C.: Brookings Institution.

CBO. *See* Congressional Budget Office.

Congressional Budget Office. 1993. *Reducing the Deficit: Spending and Revenue Options.* Washington, D.C.: U.S. Government Printing Office.

———. 1990. *The Economic Effects of Uncompensated Changes in the Funding of Social Security.* Washington, D.C.: U.S. Government Printing Office.

———. 1986. *Earnings Sharing Options for the Social Security System.* Washington, D.C.: U.S. Government Printing Office.

Center for Women Policy Studies. 1988. *Earnings Sharing in Social Security: A Model for Reform,* edited by Edith U. Fierst and Nancy Duff Campbell. Washington, D.C.: Center for Women Policy Studies.

Chambers, Letitia. 1993. "Taxation of Social Security Benefits." Statement before the U.S. Senate Committee on Finance, 103rd Congress, First Session, May 4.

Chernick, Howard, and Andrew Reschovsky. 1985. "The Taxation of Social Security." *National Tax Journal* 38(2, June): 141–52.

Cohen, Wilbur J. 1983. "The Development of the Social Security Act of 1935: Reflections Some Fifty Years Later." *Minnesota Law Review* 68: 379–408.

Cohen, Wilbur J., and Milton Friedman. 1972. *Social Security: Universal or Selective?* Washington, D.C.: American Enterprise Institute.

Cohen, Lee, and Alisa Male. "Social Security Micro-Model Presentation to the Economic Team/Public Policy Institute." Washington, D.C.: American Association of Retired Persons.

Crawford, Vincent P., and David Lilien. 1981. "Social Security and the Retirement Decision." *Quarterly Journal of Economics* 96(3): 505–29.

Crystal, Stephen. 1982. *America's Old Age Crisis*. New York: Basic Books.

Derthick, Martha. 1979. *Policymaking for Social Security*. Washington, D.C.: Brookings Institution.

Dewar, Helen. 1990. "Senate Shelves Cuts in Social Security Tax; Moynihan Bill Scuttled by GOP Maneuver." *Washington Post*, Oct. 11: A-16.

Diamond, Peter A., and Jerry A. Hausman. 1984. "Individual Retirement and Savings Behavior." *Journal of Public Economics* 23(1/2): 81–114.

Duggan, James E. 1991. "Social Security and the Public Debt." *Public Finance* 46(3): 382–404.

Duggan, James E., Robert Gillingham, and John S. Greenlees. 1993a. "Progressive Returns to Social Security? An Answer from Social Security Records." Paper presented at the meeting of the Econometric Society in Anaheim, Calif., January 5.

———. 1993b. "The Returns Paid to Early Social Security Cohorts." *U.S. Treasury Research Paper Series*. Washington, D.C.: U.S. Treasury Department, Office of the Assistant Secretary for Economic Policy.

Duleep, Harriet Orcutt. 1989. "Measuring Socioeconomic Mortality Differentials over Time." *Demography* 26(2, May): 345–51.

Economic Report of the President. 1993. Washington, D.C.: U.S. Government Printing Office.

Elster, Jon. 1979. *Ulysses and the Sirens: Studies in Rationality and Irrationality*. New York: Cambridge University Press.

Elving, Ronald D. "Lawmakers' Agenda for Year Begins and Ends With Cuts." 1990. *Congressional Quarterly* 48(4):221–26.

Feldstein, Martin, and Anthony Pellechio. 1979. "Social Security and Household Wealth Accumulation: New Microeconomic

Evidence." *Review of Economics and Statistics* 61(3, August): 361–68.

Feldstein, Martin, and Andrew Samwick. 1992. "Social Security Rules and Marginal Tax Rates." *National Tax Journal* 45(1, Spring): 1–22.

Fischer, David Hackett. 1977. *Growing Old In America*. New York: Oxford University Press.

Forman, Jonathan Barry. 1993a. "Does Bill Clinton Really Mean to Subject Elderly Workers to Confiscatory Tax Rates?" *Tax Notes* 59(1, Apr. 5): 5–6. Expanded in letter to the editor, 59(2, Apr. 12): 291–2.

————. 1993b. "Taxation of Social Security Benefits." Statement before the U.S. Senate Committee on Finance, 103rd Congress, First Session, May 4.

Friedman, Milton. 1962. *Capitalism and Freedom*. Chicago: University of Chicago Press.

Fries, James F. 1980. "Aging, Natural Death, and the Compression of Morbidity." *New England Journal of Medicine* 303(July 17): 130–35.

Fries, James F., and Lawrence M. Crapo. 1981. *Vitality and Aging: Implications of the Rectangular Curve*. San Francisco: W. H. Freeman & Co.

Fuchs, Victor R. 1984. "'Though Much Is Taken': Reflections on Aging, Health, and Medical Care." *Milbank Memorial Fund Quarterly* 62(1, Spring): 143–66.

Fullerton, Howard N. 1991. "Labor Force Projections: The Baby Boom Moves On." *Monthly Labor Review* 114(11, November): 31–44.

GAO. *See* U.S. General Accounting Office.

Goodin, Robert E. 1990. "Stabilizing Expectations: The Role of Earnings-Related Benefits in Social Welfare Policy." *Ethics* 100(April): 530–53.

Gordon, Margaret S. 1988. *Social Security Policies in Industrial Countries: A Comparative Analysis*. New York: Cambridge University Press.

Gordon, Roger, and Alan Blinder. 1980. "Market Wages, Reservation Wages, and Retirement Decisions." *Journal of Public Economics* 14(2): 277–308.

Goss, Stephen C. 1993. "Comments on Two Recent Articles on Taxation of Social Security Benefits in *Tax Notes—Information*." Memorandum, photocopy.

Goss, Stephen C., and Orlo R. Nichols. 1993. "OASDI Money's Worth Analysis for Hypothetical Cohorts." Memorandum, Social Security Administration Office of the Actuary, Washington, D.C., Mar. 1. Photocopy.

Grad, Susan. 1992. *Income of the Population 55 and Older, 1990.* Social Security Administration Office of Research and Statistics, Pub. No. 13-11871. Washington, D.C.: Superintendent of Documents.

Graebner, William. 1980. *A History of Retirement: The Meaning and Function of an American Institution, 1885–1978.* New Haven, Conn.: Yale University Press.

Gustman, Alan L., and Thomas L. Steinmeier. 1989. "Changing the Social Security Rules for Workers over 65: Proposed Policies and Their Effects." *National Bureau of Economic Research Working Paper Series,* no. 3087. Cambridge, Mass.: National Bureau of Economic Research, August.

Hadley, Jack. 1982. *More Medical Care, Better Health.* Washington, D.C.: Urban Institute Press.

Hadley, Jack, and Anthony Osei. 1982. "Does Income Affect Mortality? An Analysis of the Effects of Different Types of Income on Age/Sex/Race-Specific Mortality Rates in the United States." *Medical Care* 20(9, Sepember): 901–14.

Hanoch, Giora, and Marjorie Honig. 1983. "Retirement, Wages, and Labor Supply of the Elderly." *Journal of Labor Economics* 1(2): 131–51.

Hausman, Jerry A., and David A. Wise. 1985. "Social Security, Health Status, and Retirement." In *Pensions, Labor, and Individual Choice,* edited by D. A. Wise. Chicago: University of Chicago Press.

Head, John G. 1992. "Tax Fairness Principles: A Conceptual, Historical and Practical Review." *Australian Tax Forum* 9(1): 65–125.

Honig, Marjorie, and Cordelia Reimers. 1989. "Is It Worth Eliminating the Retirement Test?" *American Economic Review* 79(2, May): 103–7.

Hurd, Michael D. 1990. "Research on the Elderly: Economic Status, Retirement, and Consumption and Saving." *Journal of Economic Literature* (June): 565–637.

Hurd, Michael D., and John B. Shoven. 1985. "The Distributional Impact of Social Security." In *Pensions, Labor, and Individual Choice,* edited by David Wise. Chicago: University of Chicago Press.

Ippolito, Richard A. 1990. "Toward Explaining Earlier Retirement after 1970." *Industrial and Labor Relations Review* 43(5, July): 556–69.

Johnston, William B., and Arnold H. Packer. 1987. *Workforce 2000: Work and Workers for the 21st Century.* Indianapolis: Hudson Institute.

Kahn, James A. 1988. "Social Security Liquidity and Early Retirement." *Journal of Public Economics* 35(1): 97–117.

Kennickell, Arthur, and Janice Shack-Marquez. 1991. "Changes in Family Finances from 1983 to 1989: Evidence from the Survey of Consumer Finances." *Federal Reserve Bulletin* 78(1, January): 1–18.

Kitagawa, E., and P. Hauser. 1973. *Differential Mortality in the United States.* Cambridge, Mass.: Harvard University Press.

Kolata, Gina. 1992. "New Views on Life Spans Alter Forecasts on Elderly." *New York Times,* Nov. 16: A-1.

Kollman, Geoffrey. 1992. "How Long Does It Take New Retirees to Recover the Value of Their Social Security Taxes?" Washington, D.C.: Congressional Research Service.

Kopits, George. 1992. "Toward a Cost-Effective Social Security System." Paper presented at the 24th General Assembly of the International Social Security Association, Acapulco, Nov. 26.

Kopits, George, and Padma Gotur. 1980. "The Influence of Social Security on Household Savings: A Cross-Country Investigation." *International Monetary Fund Staff Papers* 27(1, March): 161–90.

Kotlikoff, Laurence J. 1992. *Generational Accounting: Knowing Who Pays, and When, for What We Spend.* New York: Free Press.

Kutscher, Ronald E. 1991. "New BLS Projections: Findings and Implications." *Monthly Labor Review* 114(11, November): 3–12.

Lee, Ronald D., and Lawrence R. Carter. 1992. "Modeling and Forecasting U.S. Mortality." *Journal of the American Statistical Association* 87(419, September): 659–75.

Le Grand, Julian. 1990. "Equity versus Efficiency: The Elusive Trade-off." *Ethics* 100(April): 554–68.

Leimer, Dean R., and Peter A. Petri. 1981. "Cohort-Specific Effects of Social Security Policy." *National Tax Journal* 34(1, March): 9–28.

Leonesio, Michael V. 1991. "Social Security and Older Workers." *ORS Working Paper Series,* no. 53. Washington, D.C.: U.S. Social Security Administration, Office of Research and Statistics, December.

_____. 1990a. "Economic Retirement Studies: An Annotated Bibliography." *ORS Working Paper Series*, no. 45. Washington, D.C.: U.S. Social Security Administration, Office of Research and Statistics.

_____. 1990b. "The Effects of the Social Security Earnings Test on the Labor-Market Activity of Older Americans: A Review of the Evidence." *Social Security Bulletin* 53(5): 2–21.

Lesnoy, Selig D., and Dean R. Leimer. 1987. "Social Security and Private Saving: Theory and Historical Evidence." In *Social Security: A Critique of Radical Reform Proposals*, edited by Charles W. Meyer (69–101). Lexington, Mass.: D.C. Heath & Co.

Levit, Katharine R., Helen C. Lazenby, Cathy A. Cowan, and Suzanne W. Letsch. 1991. "National Health Expenditures, 1990." *Health Care Financing Review* 13(1, Fall): 29–54.

Manton, Kenneth G. 1993. "Trends for the Elderly—Implications for Support, Health, and Provisions for Long Term Care." Paper presented at Conference on Future Income and Health Care Needs and Resources for the Aged. Washington, D.C.: Department of Health and Human Services.

_____. 1982. "Changing Concepts of Morbidity and Mortality in the Elderly Population." *Milbank Memorial Fund Quarterly* 60 (Spring): 192.

Marmot, M. G., Shipley, M. J., and Rose, G. 1984. "Inequalities in Death: Specific Explanation of a General Pattern?" *Lancet* 1(8384): 1003–6.

McCarty, Therese A. 1990. "The Effect of Social Security on Married Women's Labor Force Participation." *National Tax Journal* 43(1): 95–110.

McGill, Dan M. 1975. *Fundamentals of Private Pensions*. Homewood, Ill.: Richard D. Irwin.

Menchik, Paul L. Forthcoming. "Economic Status as a Determinant of Mortality among Nonwhite and White Older Males: Does Poverty Kill?" *Population Studies*.

Meyer, Charles W. 1987. "The Economic and Political Implications of a Phase-Out: A Summing Up." In *Social Security: A Critique of Radical Reform Proposals*, edited by Charles W. Meyer (127–48). Lexington, Mass.: D.C. Heath & Co.

Meyer, Charles W., and Nancy L. Wolff. 1987. "Intercohort and Intracohort Redistribution under Social Security." In *Social Security: A Critique of Radical Reform Proposals*, edited by Charles W. Meyer (49–68). Lexington, Mass.: D.C. Heath & Co.

Moffitt, Robert A. 1987. "Life Cycle Labor Supply and Social Security: A Time Series Analysis." In *Work, Health, and Income among the Elderly*, edited by Gary Burtless. Washington, D.C.: Brookings Institution.

Munnell, Alicia H. 1977. *The Future of Social Security*. Washington, D.C.: Brookings Institution.

Musgrave, Richard A. 1990. "Horizontal Equity, Once More." *National Tax Journal* 43(2, June): 113–22.

———. 1986. *Public Finance in a Democratic Society*. New York: New York University Press.

———. 1959. *The Theory of Public Finance: A Study in Public Economy*. New York: McGraw-Hill.

Musgrave, Richard A., and Peggy B. Musgrave. 1984. *Public Finance in Theory and Practice*. New York: McGraw-Hill.

Myers, Robert J. 1993a. "Is the 85-Percent Factor for Taxing Social Security Benefits Perpetually Correct?" *Tax Notes*, Mar. 15: 1545–46.

———. 1993b & 1985. *Social Security*. Philadelphia: University of Pennsylvania Press.

———. 1992. "Which CPI Should Be Used to Adjust Benefits?" *Pension Section News* (13, June): 9–10.

———. 1989. "Social Security's Funding Basis: Fiction and Fact." In *Proceedings of the Conference of Actuaries in Public Practice* Vol. 39(272–76). Conference of Actuaries in Public Practice: Schaumberg, Ill.

———. 1986. "The Social Security Double-Indexing Myth." *Benefits Quarterly* 2(3): 21–25.

Myers, Robert J., and Bruce D. Schobel. 1993. "An Updated Money's-Worth Analysis of Social Security Retirement Benefits." *Transactions* (Society of Actuaries), 44: 247–75.

———. 1983. "A Money's-Worth Analysis of Social Security Retirement Benefits." *Transactions* (Society of Actuaries), 35: 533–45.

National Academy of Social Insurance. 1988. *The Social Security Benefit Notch: A Study*. Washington, D.C.: Author.

Newhouse, Joseph P. 1992. "Medical Care Costs: How Much Welfare Loss?" *Journal of Economic Perspectives* 6(3, Summer): 3–21.

Nichols, Orlo R., and Richard G. Schreitmueller. 1978. "Some Comparisons of the Value of a Worker's Social Security Taxes and Benefits." Actuarial Note no. 95. Baltimore: U.S. Social Security Administration Office of the Actuary.

O'Higgins, Michael. 1988. "The Allocation of Public Resources to Children and the Elderly in OECD Countries." In *The Vulnerable,* edited by John L. Palmer, Timothy Smeeding, and Barbara Boyle Torrey (201–28). Washington, D.C.: Urban Institute Press.

Okun, Arthur M. 1975. *Equality and Efficiency: The Big Tradeoff.* Washington, D.C.: Brookings Institution.

OMB. *See* Office of Management and Budget.

Office of Management and Budget. 1993a. *Budget Baselines, Historical Data, and Alternatives for the Future.* Washington, D.C.: U.S. Government Printing Office, January.

————. 1993b. *Budget of the United States Government, Fiscal Year 1994.* Washington, D.C.: U.S. Government Printing Office, April.

————. 1993c. *A Vision of Change for America.* Washington, D.C.: U.S. Government Printing Office, February.

————. 1990. *Midsession Review of the Budget.* Washington, D.C.: U.S. Government Printing Office, July.

————. 1988. *Budget of the United States Government, Fiscal Year 1989.* Washington, D.C.: U.S. Government Printing Office.

Packard, Michael D. 1990a. "The Earnings Test and the Short-Run Work Response to its Elimination." *Social Security Bulletin* 53(9): 2–16.

————. 1990b. "The Effects of Removing 70- and 71-Year-Olds from Coverage under the Social Security Earnings Test." *ORS Working Paper Series,* no. 44. Washington, D.C.: Social Security Administration, Office of Research and Statistics.

Pechman, Joseph A. 1983. *Federal Tax Policy.* Washington, D.C.: Brookings Institution.

Pechman, Joseph A., Henry J. Aaron, and Michael K. Taussig. 1968. *Social Security: Perspectives for Reform.* Washington, D.C.: Brookings Institution.

Pellechio, Anthony J. 1978. "The Social Security Earnings Test, Labor Supply Distortions, and Foregone Payroll Tax Revenue." *NBER Working Paper 272.* Cambridge, Mass.: National Bureau of Economic Research.

Pellechio, Anthony, and Gordon Goodfellow. 1983. "Individual Gains and Losses from Social Security before and after the 1983 Amendments." *Cato Journal* 3(2, Fall): 417–42.

Penner, Rudolph G. 1993. *Entitlements for the Elderly: Planning Ahead.* Washington, D.C.: Urban Institute Press.

————. 1991. "Federal Government Growth: Leviathan or Protector of the Elderly?" *National Tax Journal* 44(4, Part 2, December): 437–50.

Peterson, Peter G., and Neil Howe. 1988. *On Borrowed Time: How the Growth in Entitlement Spending Threatens America's Future.* San Francisco: Institute for Contemporary Studies.

Poterba, James M., and Lawrence H. Summers. 1987. "Public Policy Implications of Declining Old-Age Mortality. In *Work, Health, and Income among the Elderly,* edited by Gary Burtless. Washington, D.C.: Brookings Institution.

Pozzebon, Silvana, and Olivia S. Mitchell. "Married Women's Retirement Behavior." *NBER Working Paper* 2104. Cambridge, Mass.: National Bureau of Economic Research.

Quinn, Joseph F. 1978. "Job Characteristics and Early Retirement." *Industrial Relations* 17(3): 315–23.

————. 1977. "Microeconomic Determinants of Early Retirement: A Cross-Sectional View of White Married Men." *Journal of Human Resources* 12(3): 329–46.

Radner, Daniel B. 1993. "An Assessment of the Economic Status of the Aged." *Studies in Income Distribution,* no. 16. U.S. Social Security Administration, Office of Research and Statistics. Washington, D.C.: U.S. Government Printing Office, May.

————. 1992. "The Economic Status of the Aged." *Social Security Bulletin* 55(3, Fall): 3–23.

————. 1991. "Changes in the Incomes of Age Groups, 1984–1989." *Social Security Bulletin* 54(12, December): 2–18.

————. 1987. "Money Incomes of Aged and Nonaged Family Units, 1967–84." *Social Security Bulletin* 50(8, August): 9–28.

Random House College Dictionary. 1973. New York: Random House.

Rawls, John. 1971. *A Theory of Justice.* Cambridge, Mass.: Harvard University Press.

Reinhard, Hans-Joachim. 1988. "The Splitting of Pension Credits in the Federal Republic of Germany and Canada—An Appropriate Way to Achieve Equality in Social Security Treatment for Men and Women?" In *Equal Treatment in Social Security.* Geneva: International Social Security Association.

Reno, Virginia P. 1993. "The Role of Pensions in Retirement Income." In *Pensions in a Changing Economy,* edited by Richard Burkhauser and Dallas Salisbury. Washington, D.C.: Employee Benefit Research Institute.

Report of the Committee on Economic Security of 1935 and Other Basic Documents Relating to the Development of the Social

Security Act—50th Anniversary Edition. 1985. Washington, D.C.: National Conference on Social Welfare.

Robertson, A. Haeworth. 1992. *Social Security: What Every Taxpayer Should Know.* Washington, D.C.: Retirement Policy Institute.

————. 1981. *The Coming Revolution in Social Security.* McLean, Va.: Security Press.

Rogers, R. G. 1992. "Living and Dying in the U.S.A.: Sociodemographic Determinants of Death among Blacks and Whites." *Demography* 29(2, May): 287–303.

Rogot, Eugene, Paul D. Sorlie, and Norman J. Johnson. 1992. "Life Expectancy by Employment Status, Income, and Education in the National Longitudinal Mortality Study." *Public Health Reports* 107(4, July–August): 457–61.

Rosen, S., and P. Taubman. 1979. "Changes in the Impact of Education and Income on Mortality in the U.S." In *Statistics of Income and Related Administrative Record Research.* Washington, D.C.: U.S. Department of the Treasury.

Rosenbaum, David. 1991. "Washington Talk: A Question of Fairness in Social Security." *New York Times,* Mar. 22: A-14.

Ross, Jane A., and Melinda M. Upp. 1988. "The Treatment of Women in the United States Social Security System, 1970–1988." In *Equal Treatment in Social Security.* Geneva: International Social Security Association.

Ruggles, Patricia. 1990. *Drawing the Line: Alternative Poverty Measures and Their Implications for Public Policy.* Washington, D.C.: Urban Institute Press.

Sammartino, Frank, and Robertson Williams. 1991. "Trends in Income and Federal Taxes of the Elderly." Paper presented at the thirteenth annual research conference of the Association for Public Policy Analysis and Management, Bethesda, Md., Oct. 24–26.

Sandell, Steven H. Forthcoming. "Are Retirement Benefits Too High and Will They Be Too Low? An Examination of Wage Indexation in Social Security." Research Paper. Washington, D.C.: Urban Institute.

Sandell, Steven H., ed. 1987. *The Problem Isn't Age: Work and Older Americans.* New York: Praeger Publishers.

Sander, Kenneth G. "The Retirement Test: Its Effect on Older Workers' Earnings." *Social Security Bulletin* 31(6): 3–6.

Schlesinger, Arthur M., Jr. 1958. *The Coming of the New Deal.* Boston: Houghton Mifflin Co.

Sherman, Sally R. 1989. "Public Attitudes toward Social Security."
    Social Security Bulletin 52(12, December): 2–16.
————. 1985. "Reported Reasons Why Workers Left Their Last Job:
    Findings from the New Beneficiary Survey." *Social Security
    Bulletin* 48(3): 22–30.
Silverman, Celia, and Paul Yakoboski. 1993. "Public and Private
    Pensions Today: An Overview of the System." Paper pre-
    sented at "Pension Funding and Taxation: Achieving Benefit
    Security" Employee Benefit Research Institute Policy Forum,
    Washington, D.C., May 5.
Smeeding, Timothy M. 1989. "Full Income Estimates of the Relative
    Well-Being of the Elderly and the Nonelderly." In *Research
    on Economic Inequality*, vol. 1, edited by Daniel J. Slottje.
    Greenwich, Conn.: JAI Press.
————. 1984. "Approaches to Measuring and Valuing In-Kind Sub-
    sidies and the Distribution of Their Benefits." In *Economic
    Transfers in the United States*, edited by Marilyn Moon. Vol.
    49 of *National Bureau of Economic Research, Studies in
    Income and Wealth*. Chicago: University of Chicago Press.
————. 1982. *Alternative Methods for Valuing In-Kind Transfer
    Benefits and Measuring Their Impact on Poverty*. Technical
    Report 50, U.S. Bureau of the Census. Washington, D.C.: U.S.
    Government Printing Office.
Social Security Technical Panel. 1990. "Report to the 1991 Advisory
    Council on Social Security." *Social Security Bulletion* 53(11,
    November): 2–34.
Sonnenfeld, Sally T., Daniel P. Waldo, Jeffrey A. Lemieux, and David
    R. McKusick. 1991. "Projections of National Health Expendi-
    tures through the Year 2000." *Health Care Financing Review*
    13(1, Fall): 1–27.
Sorlie, P., E. Rogot, R. Anderson, N. Johnson, and E. Blacklund. 1992.
    "Black-White Mortality Differences by Family Income." *Lan-
    cet* 340(Aug. 8): 346–50.
SSA. *See* U.S. Social Security Administration.
Stein, Bruno. 1987. "Phasing Out Social Security: A Critique of Fer-
    rara's Proposal." In *Social Security: A Critique of Radical
    Reform Proposals*, edited by Charles W. Meyer (35–48). Lex-
    ington, Mass.: D.C. Heath & Co.
Steuerle, C. Eugene. 1993a. "Finance-Based Reform: The Search for
    an Adaptable Health Policy." In *American Health Policy:
    Critical Issues for Reform*, edited by Robert B. Helms. Wash-
    ington, D.C.: American Enterprise Institute.

————. 1993b. "Taxation of Social Security Benefits." Statement before the Committee in Finance, U.S. Senate, 103rd Congress, First Session, May 4.

————. 1992. *The Tax Decade: How Taxes Came to Dominate the Public Agenda.* Washington, D.C.: Urban Institute Press.

————. 1990. "Social Security Taxation." Statement before the Committee on Finance, U.S. Senate, 101st Congress, Second Session, Feb. 8.

Straka, John W. 1992. "The Demand for Older Workers: The Neglected Side of the Labor Market." *Studies in Income Distribution,* no. 15. Washington, D.C.: U.S. Social Security Administration, Office of Research and Statistics, June.

Taubman, P., and S. Rosen. 1982. "Healthiness, Education, and Marital Status." In *Economic Aspects of Health,* edited by Victor Fuchs (121–40). New York: National Bureau for Economic Research.

Townshend, Peter, and Nick Davidson, eds. 1988. "The Black Report." In *Inequalities in Health.* London: Penguin Books.

Tracy, Martin B. 1988. "Equal Treatment and Pension Systems: A Comparative Study." In *Equal Treatment in Social Security.* Geneva: International Social Security Association.

Tullock, Gordon. 1983. *Economics of Income Distribution.* Boston: Kluwer Nijhoff Publishing.

U.S. Board of Trustees of the Federal Hospital Insurance Trust Fund. Various years. *Annual Report.* Washington, D.C.: U.S. Government Printing Office.

U.S. Board of Trustees of the Federal Old-Age and Survivors Insurance and Disability Insurance Trust Funds. Various years. *Annual Report.* Washington, D.C.: U.S. Government Printing Office.

U.S. Board of Trustees of the Federal Supplementary Medical Insurance Trust Fund. 1992. *Annual Report.* Washington, D.C.: U.S. Government Printing Office.

U.S. Bureau of the Census. 1992a. *Population Projections of the U.S., By Age, Sex, Race, and Hispanic Origin, 1992–2050. Current Population Reports,* ser. P25, no. 192. Washington, D.C.: U.S. Government Printing Office.

————. 1992b. *Poverty in the United States: 1991. Current Population Reports,* ser. P-60, no. 181. Washington, D.C.: U.S. Government Printing Office.

————. 1991. *Statistical Abstracts of the United States.* Washington, D.C.: U.S. Government Printing Office.

_____. 1990. *Household, Wealth, and Asset Ownership: 1988. Current Population Reports,* ser. P-60, no. 22. Washington, D.C.: U.S. Government Printing Office.

_____. 1975. *Historical Statistics of the United States, Colonial Times to 1970, Bicentennial Edition.* Washington, D.C.: U.S. Government Printing Office.

U.S. Bureau of Economic Analysis. 1992a. *National Income and Product Accounts of the U.S., Volume One, 1929–58.* Washington, D.C.: U.S. Government Printing Office.

_____. 1992b. *National Income and Product Accounts of the U.S., Volume Two, 1959–88.* Washington, D.C.: U.S. Government Printing Office.

_____. Various years. *Survey of Current Business.* Washington, D.C.: U.S. Government Printing Office.

U.S. Bureau of Labor Statistics. 1993. *Employment and Earnings.* Washington, D.C.: U.S. Government Printing Office. January.

_____. 1991. *Employment and Earnings.* Washington, D.C.: U.S. Government Printing Office, January.

_____. 1989. *Handbook of Labor Statistics.* Washington, D.C.: U.S. Government Printing Office.

U.S. Congress, House Committee on Ways and Means. 1992. *Green Book: Overview of Entitlement Programs.* Washington, D.C.: U.S. Government Printing Office.

U.S. Congress, House of Representatives. 1950. *Social Security Act Amendments of 1950: Conference Report, no. 2771.* 81st Congress, Second Session. Washington, D.C.: U.S. Government Printing Office.

U.S. Congress, Joint Committee on Taxation. 1993. "Summary of the Revenue Provisions of the Omnibus Budget Reconciliation Act of 1993." 103rd Congress, First Session. Washington, D.C.: U.S. Government Printing Office.

U.S. Department of the Treasury. 1990. *Financing Health and Long-Term Care: Report to the President and Congress.* Washington, D.C.: U.S. Government Printing Office.

U.S. General Accounting Office. 1992. *Budget Policy: Prompt Action Necessary to Avert Long-Term Damage to the Economy.* Washington, D.C.: Superintendent of Documents.

_____. 1988. *Social Security: The Notch Issue.* Washington, D.C.: Superintendent of Documents.

U.S. Social Security Administration. 1993. *Social Security Bulletion Annual Statistical Supplement, 1992.* Washington, D.C.: U.S. Government Printing Office.

_____. 1992. *Social Security Programs throughout the World.* Washington, D.C.: U.S. Government Printing Office.

_____. 1992a. *Life Tables for the United States Social Security Area, 1900–2080.* Actuarial Study No. 107. Baltimore, Md.: Author.

_____. 1992b. *Social Security Area Population Projections: 1991.* Baltimore, Md.: Author.

_____. 1990. *History of the Provisions of Old-Age, Survivors, Disability, and Health Insurance, 1935–1989.* Washington, D.C.: Superintendent of Documents.

U.S. Social Security Administration, Office of Legislative and Regulatory Policy. 1985. "A Study of the Implementation of Earnings Sharing in the United States' Social Security System." *International Social Security Review,* 38(April): 367–77.

Van der Gaag, Jacques, and Eugene Smolensky. 1982. "True Household Equivalence Scales and Characteristics of the Poor in the United States." *Review of Income and Wealth* 28(1, March): 17–28.

Varian, Hal R. 1980. "Redistributive Taxation as Social Insurance." *Journal of Public Economics* 14(11, November): 49–68.

Verbrugge, Lois M. 1984. "Longer Life but Worsening Health? Trends in Health and Mortality of Middle Aged and Older Persons." *Milbank Memorial Fund Quarterly* 62(3, Fall): 475–519.

Vroman, Wayne. 1985. "Some Economic Effects of the Social Security Retirement Test." In *Research in Labor Economics,* vol. 7, edited by Ronald G. Ehrenberg (31–89). Greenwich, Conn.: JAI Press.

Weaver, Carolyn L. 1983. "On the Lack of a Political Market for Compulsory Old-Age Insurance Prior to the Great Depression: Insights from Economic Theories of Government." *Explorations in Economic History,* no. 20: 294–328.

Weaver, Carolyn L., ed. 1990. *Social Security's Looming Surpluses: Prospects and Implications.* American Enterprise Institute Study, no. 511. Washington, D.C.: American Enterprise Institute Press.

Welch, W. Pete, Steven J. Katz, and Stephen Zuckerman. 1993. "Physician Fee Levels: Medicare versus Canada. Assessing Cost Containment in the U.S. and Canada." Urban Institute. Working Paper 6185-02. Washington, D.C.: Urban Institute, September.

Whitehead, Margaret. 1988. "The Health Divide." In *Inequalities in Health.* London: Penguin Books.

Wilkinson, R. 1986. *Class and Health*. London: Tavistock.

Witte, Edwin E. 1963. *The Development of the Social Security Act*. Madison, Wis.: University of Wisconsin Press.

Wolfson, Michael C. 1988. "Homemaker Pensions and Lifetime Redistribution." *Review of Income and Wealth*, ser. 34(3, September): 221–50.

Yankelovich, Skelly, and White, Inc. 1985. *A Fifty-Year Report Card on the Social Security System: The Attitudes of the American Public*. New York: Author.

Zedlewski, Sheila R. 1984. *The Distributional Consequences of an Earnings Sharing Proposal*. Washington, D.C.: Urban Institute.

Zedlewski, Sheila R., and Jack A. Meyer. 1989. *Toward Ending Poverty among the Elderly and Disabled through SSI Reform*. Urban Institute Report 89-1. Washington, D.C.: Urban Institute Press.

Zedlewski, Sheila R., Roberta O. Barnes, Martha R. Burt, Timothy D. McBride, and Jack A. Meyer. 1990. *The Needs of the Elderly in the 21st Century*. Washington, D.C.: Urban Institute Press.

C. Eugene Steuerle is a senior fellow at the Urban Institute, president of the National Economists Club Educational Foundation, and author of a column "Economic Perspective" for *Tax Notes* magazine. He has worked under four different U.S. presidents on a wide variety of social security, health, tax, and other major reforms, including service both as Deputy Assistant Secretary of the Treasury and as the original organizer and Economic Coordinator of the Treasury's 1984-86 tax reform effort. He testifies frequently before Congress and has authored over one hundred books, articles, reports, and testimonies. His previous book, *The Tax Decade: How Taxes Came to Dominate the Public Agenda*, is cited by one historian as "required reading for all who study the development of public policy in the twentieth century."

Jon M. Bakija was a research associate at the Urban Institute specializing in social security issues and public finance. He is currently pursuing a Ph.D. degree in economics at the University of Michigan.